The World Year Book of Education 1969
Examinations

The World Year Book of Education 1969

Examinations

Joint Editors:

Joseph A. Lauwerys, D.Sc., D.Lit., F.R.I.C.
Professor of Comparative Education in the University of London

David G. Scanlon, Ed.D.
Professor of International Education, Columbia University

Published in the United States of America by

Harcourt, Brace & World, Inc.
New York   Chicago   San Francisco   Atlanta

First American edition 1969

Printed in 11/12 Bembo (270) in Great Britain by
Hazell Watson and Viney Ltd, Aylesbury, Bucks

The World Year Book of Education 1969

Contents

Editors' Introduction

Almost everywhere policies designed to broaden access to education and to promote equality of opportunity are now pursued. In consequence the importance of examinations grows, since success in them determines entry to higher education and thus to professional posts. They are therefore a major instrument of social mobility and promotion which affects social structure by applying criteria of selection nearly always accepted unconsciously and uncritically. Furthermore, these criteria are often irrelevant to the purposes envisaged. Children and young people are deeply affected by all this. They are often made very unhappy by the pressure to 'get through' examinations. Some believe that failure is a tragedy, their whole lives ruined by it. Others feel that they have let down and disappointed their parents by not 'doing as well' as had been hoped. Many teachers narrow their vision, myopically and anxiously concentrating on 'covering the syllabus'. In fact, the whole situation is very confused. Everyone agrees that things could be and should be improved but no one is quite sure of what should be done.

Our aim, in selecting Examinations as the theme of the 1969 WORLD YEAR BOOK, was to present a comparative analysis of the way in which examinations are devised, administered and assessed, to find out *why* we are examining, and to look at the ways in which we examine to see if these are efficient, relevant and reliable. We also hoped to give a world view of the effects of examination systems on society and on education itself, in the sense that there is a danger that examinations are becoming ends-in-themselves, almost independent of the educational process. Lastly, we wished to discover whether there was any movement towards modification, reform, or even elimination of the examination system.

The different sections of the present volume are arranged as follows: Section I puts the whole subject of examinations into perspective, tracing their evolution and development in the light of changing educational and philosophical climates. In Section II our contributors discuss the aims, explicit and implicit, of present-day examinations, and the associated theories and techniques. Section III evaluates the efficiency and reliability of types of examination in current use, and expresses some disquieting thoughts on the difficulties of ensuring dispassionate judgement and 'fair' assessment of candidates. Sections IV and V contain national studies; the first group is mainly concerned with organization and administration of examinations in various countries, and the second with examinations as selection tools, barring or opening the way to higher education. Section VI discusses the socio-economic role played by examinations in a number of highly industrialized and developing countries and Section VII describes some of the effects of the examination system on education and the curriculum, on children, teachers and parents. The final section outlines current trends and possible future developments, and brings us inescapably to the conclusion that despite the growing unease among educationists and students alike, examinations are here to stay. Improvements and modifications have been suggested and are being tried out, and we hope that a study of the contributions to this YEAR BOOK will be of help to those concerned with the future planning and organization of examinations.

We hope, too, that we have succeeded to some degree in satisfying a hope expressed by Dr. Frank Bowles. He told us that we should try to help 'the teacher to understand the use of examinations as an instructional tool and the pupil to understand that the examinations that he gets in the course of his studies at whatever level are only a tiny fraction of the examinations to which he is being subjected at every stage in his life – that these examinations will, in fact, become more rigorous after he leaves formal examination rooms than they ever are while he is in school or university'.

As always, we are conscious of gaps and omissions – some intentional and some inadvertent. We have not, for example, concerned ourselves with 'tests' specifically designed to measure or assess personality, intelligence, reading ability, aptitude, etc., nor have we attempted to cover vocational guidance tests which were, however, discussed in the 1955 YEAR BOOK, nor professional and technical examinations. We have concentrated on the secondary and tertiary levels of education, because, it is here that the stresses and pressures of competitive examinations are greatest.

Finally, we must disclaim responsibility for the contents of each author's contribution, although full responsibility for the organization of the articles and choice of contributors rests with us.

J. A. Lauwerys
University of London

David G. Scanlon
Columbia University

1 *Education and Examinations*

Brian Holmes
Reader in Comparative Education in the University of London

J. A. Lauwerys
Professor of Comparative Education in the University of London

In all human societies, the young are prepared for their future roles through processes which may be institutionalized or not. Then, at some stage, comes initiation into adulthood. This may be highly formalized, with much ritual and ceremony, or it may be informal, a mere matter of registering for voting or of handing over a front-door key.

The place of schools in all this varies within wide limits. One thing, however, is clear: schools are always transitional institutions. They prepare pupils for a next stage – for another kind of school or for occupation or for political activities or for family life and so on. They are institutions which pupils join with the idea of leaving them soon.

Thus, we have on the one hand the educational institutions and on the other the social, economic, political institutions in which, as adults, the pupils will be expected to participate. There are linking mechanisms between the two sets of institutions which assess the extent to which the young are ready to perform assigned roles. One of these mechanisms is the examination system.

The structure of each society determines the pattern of duties and rights for each individual as he plays his roles – a pattern which changes with time. During the twentieth century, for example, there has been a movement towards an acceptance of the notion that all individuals – whatever their sex or race – should enjoy the same human rights to work, to freedom of speech, and to education. By the same token the trend has been towards the view that all individuals are or should be capable of exercising their civic duties responsibly and, some would say, rationally. These egalitarian movements have found expression in the charters of world organizations and in the institutions and legislation of many sovereign states. Here is one feature of the modern world which is part of the backcloth against which the roles will be played or, to put it in other terms, here is one of the factors to be taken into account in any discussion of the functions of examinations seen as agencies of initiation.

Evidently in a period when both institutions and social myths are changing rapidly and drastically, those agencies are subjected to scrutiny and hostile criticism. Some argue that they are futile and useless as links with future employment and occupation, that different means of assessment would be better. Others deplore their influence on the methods and content of teaching, saying that only bad methods and out-of-date content lead to success. The possibility of devising new arrangements adapted to new conditions, replacing the familiar examination systems we have, is the theme of the 1969 Year Book. The historical, sociological and administrative aspects of present systems have been explored in the belief that it will become easier to find solutions and to suggest improvements if the complex problems involved are first analysed. We are not concerned with the internal tests set by teachers at regular intervals and evaluated by them. These play an important part in the teaching process and in the inner organization of the school. What we have tried to deal with is the public or external examination, in which the opinion of the teachers and of the school may be used in the final assessment, without, however, being the determining factor.

The Functions of Examinations

Things become clearer if one considers first two main sociological functions performed by examinations and tests in relation to (a) various aspects of life and (b) changes taking place in climates of opinion as well as in socio-economic and political institutions. Viewed sociologically examinations and tests may be said to perform the following tasks. First, they are used to assess the extent to which an individual has benefited from the education he has received. What does he know? Has he learned what he has been taught? This function – the measurement of *attainment* or *achievement* – has always received explicit recognition. Tests and examinations designed to this end may take place frequently throughout education, or they may terminate a particular stage or level of education. A combination of continuous assessment of one kind or another and terminal tests constitutes, in many countries, a system of examinations. The second function is *selection*. This process implies that the examinee or testee is being selected for something – either for further education or for some task or role in society. It implies that not all young people are expected to reach the same levels of achievement and that societal roles are differentiated and specialized. That is to say, even if a society is egalitarian and based upon the concept of equal human rights, its functioning depends upon the fact that not all individuals are expected to perform the same duties and to accept identical responsibilities.

Examinations, of course, fulfil other functions than those of measurement of achievement and of selection – for instance, they are incentives which may persuade indolent youth to strenuous effort. In the past, too, they tended to be used for selection rather than for evaluation. But now, with new ideas of social organization, the extent to which traditional examinations do in fact act as incentives and, in addition, predict future competence is being brought into question. The difficulty of devising new instruments to perform these tasks is at the heart of the problem of educational reform.

The circumstances under which all these functions have to be performed will, of course, influence the characteristics and magnitude of the problems which arise. Consider for example the role of education in preparing young people for and initiating them into political life. Claims that a society should be democratic are of fairly recent origin in the history of mankind. Effective claims that monarchical forms of democracy should be replaced by democratic republics are even more recent. The widespread rejection of imperialism is another symptom of change. Elitism in politics is being replaced at the conceptual level by mass participation. How different from the concept of Athenian democracy in which a distinction was drawn between the few citizens with full political rights and the rest or, indeed, from the view that individuals should be selected for positions of political power on the basis of birth. A monarch and an aristocracy based on inheritance finds practical expression even now in a number of African, Asian and European countries.

To be sure, effective power has in most cases been taken away from the monarch and his court. The move to replace kings by presidents has succeeded in the Americas and the trend everywhere is strongly in this direction. The classic view expressed by Condorcet in France and Jefferson in the U.S.A. that an aristocracy of talent should replace an aristocracy based on birth or wealth finds growing favour. It implies new criteria of selection based on educational tests. These may, as in some African societies, include physical prowess, though now never to the extent of victory over competitors by inflicting defeat in mortal combat!

Even such criteria of selection for political power have become a little dated. Certainly Walter Lippman's anxiety that the public at large might come to control political action in democracies through a power of veto has now been largely dissipated by events. In short – there is a reluctance today to accept any theory of elitism in politics although in practical terms leaders have to be selected, and educational background, including examination success may play an important part in the processes of selection. A careful comparative study of the academic records of political leaders would reveal the extent to which this is the case. No doubt in France the proportion of *aggregés* in positions of political power is high. In the U.S.A. less importance in politics is given to the Ph.D. Several British prime ministers have distinguished themselves at the university.

Certain 'public' schools – for example Eton and Winchester – are noted for the number of cabinet members who attended them. The adequacy of methods of selection involving such factors may be questioned. Another issue relates to the soundness of the political education of the masses, i.e. those who are not chosen for positions of leadership.

The Origins of Examination Systems

Political power in a society is shared by politicians, however chosen, and officials. It was in order to select the latter that the Imperial Chinese examinations were established. By common consent the first system of its kind – it developed a little before the beginning of the Christian era and remained in force until its abolition round the turn of the twentieth century – it was based on the Confucian dictum that positions in the bureaucracy should go to men of proven merit and ability. In a society where family obligation – and hence nepotism – was strong the intention was partly to broaden the social basis of recruitment. Although at one time some 40 per cent of successful doctoral candidates came from civil service 'families' a clear majority were candidates without this background. Men from all parts of the empire were drawn in although the central government reserved to itself the power to appoint. Social control and nepotism were thereby weakened.

The system was, of course, highly competitive. At each stage only a small proportion of the large number of candidates was successful, the rest were eliminated. Promotion up to a certain level depended on examination success. Indeed a brilliant young scholar could gain very rapid promotion. It also made it possible to bring into the civil service from outside able men who had not been through the full sequence of examinations. Much therefore depended on success, and great care was taken to ensure that the examinations were justly administered. At one stage the names of candidates were obliterated and an identifying number substituted. At another period copyists wrote out the answers of candidates so that their handwriting would not be recognized. Each paper was read independently by two examiners; a third examiner received their sealed grades, opened them and reconciled them if necessary. These attempts to bring impartiality and honesty into the selection of bureaucrats made achievement an important criterion of success. In contrast the early European bureaucracies were built up on the basis of sponsorship. Custom and the personal judgement of superiors were the basis of selection in the Roman Empire. The royal bureaucrats of medieval Europe were nominated by a few officers, or by the king or one of his ministers. The adoption of written examinations in Europe after 1700, civil service examinations in France in 1791, in Germany about 1800, in India in 1855 and in England about 1870 gives some indication of the movement away from sponsorship to competition and achievement as the basis of selection for positions conferring a certain amount of political authority.

It should be noted that one social consequence of the introduction of examinations was the greater equality of opportunity which they provided. Against this should be weighed some educational consequences. The subject matter in which the Imperial Chinese examinations were set was varied and included letters, law, history, rituals and the classics. The chief emphasis, however, was on the study of the older writings as a guide to present conduct. In order to admit a wide range of potential candidates a standard body of literature had to be used. Such restrictions tended to promote an intellectual conservatism. The methods of examining had a similar effect. Candidates had to commit test passages to heart and then comment on them in writing. Originality in reasoning and expression was looked for but was not strongly encouraged because it would call for more subjective judgements on the part of examiners. Traditional compositions could be marked mechanically according to set rules.

Similar examinations in modern guise are severely criticized today. It is said that they encourage rote learning, stifle creativity and are difficult to assess objectively. They are, however, used very extensively both for the purpose of measuring what has been learned and for that of selecting from a large number of candidates a small number of the 'best'. In some countries one set of examinations serves both functions – selection and assessment of achievement. The tendency in England, for example, is for the competitive scholarship examination to disappear in name if not in practice. In France, on the other hand, a distinction is still drawn between the *concours* – a competitive examination serving a specific selective function – and certificates and diplomas awarded at the close of one stage or level of education. The German examination system was designed to meet the needs of growing bureaucracy. Examination success was closely correlated with a position in the civil service hierarchy and this served as an instrument of selection. Only in the U.S.A. has the selection function of tests been called seriously into question in practice, but in that country selection played little part at school or undergraduate levels. It is noteworthy that the American contributions in this *Year Book* are concerned chiefly with the tertiary rather than secondary level of education. Today, under more competitive conditions, tests are again being used for the purposes of selection in establishments of high prestige. As usual, a broad distinction can be made between the pattern of examinations in the U.S.A. and those of Europe and, to some extent, of those countries where education has been influenced by European models.

In general terms it may be said that in Europe examinations (external or public) are usually held at the end of the primary level of education when pupils are between 10 and 12 years old; at the end of the middle school or of compulsory education when they are between 14 and 16 years of age and at the end of the complete second stage at about 18 or 19. In most countries the examinations serve both functions. The tests at the end of the primary stage are used to select pupils for different kinds of secondary school. At the end of compulsory education the examinations indicate which of the pupils should go on to further study. The school leaving examinations at the end of the English grammar school, the French *lycée*, and the German, Dutch and Scandinavian *gymnasium* is the link between school and university. Success in the German *abitur* or the French *baccalauréat* traditionally gave right of entry to the university. It was the sole criterion of selection. In England, university departments select those they wish to admit from among candidates with the minimum number of general certificate of education successes.

Effects of Recent Changes in Educational Systems

In Europe movements to abolish structural differentiation by school type at the middle or second stage of education have resulted in a change of emphasis in the use of examinations. Where the trend toward a common or comprehensive second stage system is strong, the need for selection tests for second stage schools is reduced. The selection function of tests at this point of transition no longer applies in the U.S.A. where 'common' elementary schools are followed by comprehensive junior and senior high schools.

In spite of such tendencies examinations have come to dominate most educational systems. They are used vicariously as agencies of political and social selection and to assess the competence of young people to enter adult life. They select those pupils at one level of education who will be allowed to move on to the next level. They also assess the extent to which pupils have the necessary basis of knowledge to profit from this promotion. There is, however, no guarantee that any one examination can perform all these functions. On the contrary it seems likely that different types of examinations or tests are needed for different functions, particularly under modern socio-economic conditions.

At the moment, apart from the essay-type examinations which demand rather general answers to somewhat vague questions, there are practical, oral and objective tests. The essay tests are still perhaps most widely used and it is these that are subject to the most criticism. Are the attacks, however, fair, in so far as they operate within the educational sphere? The answer to this question depends to a considerable extent on the number of candidates and the stated objective of the examination. One difficulty in assessing the effectiveness of essay-type tests is that there is often no consensus of opinion about what they should do or evaluate.

Those concerned frequently think of them as performing functions very different from the officially stated intentions of the examiners. Parents and pupils see them as opening the way to more education and/or better jobs. Employers may see them as giving them some indication of whom to employ and what such persons will know. Examiners, on the other hand, may see them as testing knowledge, understanding, power to reason well, originality and so on. Teachers may feel they offer powerful incentives for learning. In short, there are many different opinions about what examinations and tests ought to do. Is it possible on the basis of comparative analysis to reach any reliable conclusions?

Psychometrists have paid great attention to the validity and reliability of psychological tests. Since a valid test measures what it is intended to measure, that is achieves stated objectives, it is evident that the latter have to be made very explicit and then accepted. Confusion and disagreement concerning objectives makes it difficult to reach consensus; consequently it is difficult to evaluate validity. When considered in comparative perspective it should be clear that to state unequivocally and in precise terms any universal objectives for examinations and tests is even more difficult. The objectives are, in short, culture-bound, at least in terms of specific purposes. This would appear to hold whether the tests are intended for selection or for measuring what has been learned. Reliable tests are those that, when repeated, would give the same result. More precisely, the rank order of candidates would be the same and the scores of each more or less the same.

Arguments in favour of psychological tests stress the greater possibilities of making them both more valid and more reliable than essay-type examinations or oral tests. The assumptions behind these claims need, perhaps, to be examined. They depend, for example, on the belief that a normal distribution of intelligence and ability will be found amongst most groups of individuals. They also assume that objective assessment of answers is possible, thereby increasing reliability. Certainly as the numbers of candidates increase the difficulties of achieving both validity and reliability with essay-type examinations increase greatly.

Continuous Assessment

Students almost everywhere manifest increasing dislike and suspicion of the tests to which they are subjected. 'Reform the Examinations' is a slogan paraded during demonstrations and it is a demand usually included in the programmes of the militants. There is much justice in the complaints and there is certainly need for change. In England, for instance, three years of University study lead to a marathon-like climax. The candidates sit for a week or more writing essay answers for three hours at a stretch, twice a day. The scripts are evaluated, usually by two or three examiners and ultimately a compounded mark emerges. Not many fail – probably fewer than 10 per cent or 15 per cent – which is a tragedy for the unfortunates. As for the rest, their future careers depend, or at least are thought to depend upon the actual marks awarded. The 5 per cent or so who are awarded 'Firsts' rejoice and are a source of pride to their families. The 25 per cent or 30 per cent who get only 'Thirds' are humbled and ashamed. All this is harsh, or at least severe. To be forced to write so much in so short a time, under such conditions, is exhausting physically and mentally. And the elements of arbitrariness and sheer luck play too large a part: the questions may or may not suit, they may not be clearly worded, they may contain hidden traps. The examiners may not be absolutely objective, they may be irritated by tricks of style, they may overlook shades of meaning in the answers. In brief, the reliability of the whole thing is bound to be low and its validity questionable.

Many educationists, particularly in colleges of education, accept these arguments and favour replacing end-of-course anonymous examinations by 'continuous assessment' of the type which has long been common in the U.S.A. The students would be awarded marks during their years of study, by each professor for each course, on the strength of essays written, tests answered, demonstration lessons given, contributions made to discussion and so on. Finally, without the once-for-all final comprehensive examination, a grade would be awarded.

There are more and stronger arguments against such a method than those who are not very familiar with it realize. In the first place – and this is a fundamental objection – it alters radically the relation between teacher and taught. The student is continuously on trial, constantly being examined. The teacher is always evaluating and weighing: a task difficult to reconcile with helping and guiding. Too much power is placed in his hands. Secondly, teachers – being kind and generous – are rather easily pressured, often without knowing it, into awarding better marks than they should to weak students who have tried hard. Thirdly, the anonymous examination may well provide a defence for the gifted students who lacks social grace and who antagonizes his teachers by his manner and personality. Fourthly, it is almost impossible to equate continuous assessment grades awarded in one institution with those of another: each is bound to have its own internal currency and there is no agreed rate of exchange. Fifthly, no examination fulfils its purpose unless some candidates 'fail' – and it is precisely failure which is objected to by some reformers.

The method of continuous assessment can be well used – it may indeed then be preferable – only if three conditions exist: the percentage of failures is exceedingly small; the skills to be evaluated are largely practical; the grades awarded are not important for a selection process – for example, to decide admissions and rejections to postgraduate courses. But, of course, a combination of marks awarded by continuous assessment and of marks awarded by the traditional (anonymous, external) method may well prove to be the most acceptable way of awarding final grades – at least, at the present time.

Meeting the Difficulties

It is by no means impossible that, in the course of time, the pressures caused by difficulties such as those listed may force the examination industry to turn towards policies such as those long ago adopted by the Chinese, namely restricted material and strictly laid down rules for assessing essays. If, however, the examinations are to be used for the purpose of rigorous selection, the issue of reliability may be less serious. Whether or not the English interview technique, or the French *concours* make selections that are valid must be debateable. What seems certain, however, is that, given a selective educational system, traditional forms of examinations may be both reliable and valid provided that only a few out of many candidates are to be selected for *further education.*

Problems arise (*a*) when the criterion of judgement is what candidates have learned (particularly when large numbers are involved) and (*b*) when the results are used to predict success outside the sphere of education.

These conditions apply strongly in many countries today and are becoming more and more apparent everywhere. Merit, measured in educational terms, has become the acceptable criterion of selection for virtually any sphere of life. The view that education is a human right has made the expansion and extension of provisions necessary at all three levels – primary, secondary and tertiary.

Under these conditions what lines of action seem possible? One solution is to reduce educational selection to a minimum. The situation in the United States until recently at least, was a reflection of this kind of policy. Pupils expected to progress annually from one grade to the next – from the primary school to the same kind of junior high or middle secondary school and then on to the same kind of senior high or complete secondary school. Selection for college from among high school graduates was reduced to a minimum. In short, at one point the tendency was to solve the problem of educational selection by doing away with competition within the schools. Associated with these trends was the tendency to rely more and more heavily on objective-type standardized tests which made it possible to place individuals in rank order without establishing cut-off points of acceptability. The validity of any kind of test, however, has been questioned by some teachers who follow the argument to its logical conclusion. Of course, this policy did not quite prevail and a movement back towards selective admission to colleges and universities can be discerned, at least in the highly respected and most popular ones. With this reversal there is also a tendency to reintroduce and pay more attention to essay-type examinations at the tertiary level. The pressure, it should be noted, which has brought about this reversal was largely the work of professors in the liberal arts colleges who generalized their needs by saying that what was a good test for them was good for all. Some of the consequences of these fluctuations in policy will be examined later.

In the U.S.S.R., selection on the basis of innate ability is, of course, rejected but competition within the school system remains high. Written examinations in mathematics and Russian are usual. As in most continental European countries, heavy reliance is still placed on oral testing. Parenthetically the possibility of objective assessment of oral tests is correlated to the prevailing ideology, psychology and epistemology. In the same way the validity and reliability of objective tests used widely in the United States depend to a considerable extent on a set of psychological theories and assumptions. Both systems are, it is claimed, egalitarian and lead to a society based on achievement rather than sponsorship. It should be noted that in the U.S.S.R. social status and economic position are clearly relative to educational background. In the United States, over the whole range of social, economic and political life this is rather less so.

Elitism is dead or dying but the schools have still to prepare young people for life and one of the most important areas of life is work. To the argument that individuals should be trained to make a living has been added the claim that the schools should meet social needs by training young people for industry and commerce. Traditionally this training was through an apprenticeship system where the tests were largely practical. As the craftsman gave way to the quicker and more efficient specialist worker, the tests of competence were changed. Those applied in the schools to judge the competence of individuals to continue their education were carried over to a considerable extent into industry and commerce. The essay-type test became in effect a test of practical competence. Failure rates in English Ordinary and Higher National Certificate and Diploma examinations are extremely high. So high in fact that one is led to one of two conclusions: either such examinations do not adequately test the ability of a student to perform a range of technical tasks nor to apply principles in practice, or, secondly, that the English are incapable of running a highly complex industrial society. The first of these hypotheses seems likely to be nearer the mark than the second! In short, the validity of many technical examinations is brought into question.

Another point needs to be mentioned. It is that the results of examinations used to predict future success in education are often also taken as predictors of success in a wide range of industrial or commercial activities. It may be that those results are clearly correlated with a level of general intelligence which is in turn correlated with ability to perform technical tasks. Yet attention has been drawn to the importance of 'spatial ability' in predicting vocational success and the argument here could be extended. Do all school examinations act effectively as a link between education and industry? The increasing complexity of modern industry raises even graver doubts. School examinations and tests may fail to measure either what needs to be known by a growing person entering economic life or to predict his future success. They may offer little incentive to students who find that without examination success they can, at least initially, obtain adequate, well paid and satisfying jobs. Examination success should, therefore, be closely and immediately linked with economic success, as in the U.S.S.R., if it is to operate as an incentive. What worked well when bureaucrats only were picked out by school examinations does not necessarily work at all well when virtually one kind of examination is used for multiple purposes and across many spheres of activity.

Examinations and Prestige

A glaring example of the inadequacy of examinations is found in countries such as India where the economy is such that an educated man is always at some advantage over one with less education, but which is not well enough developed to provide sustained effort throughout life. Against parental pressure to make use of the young boy or girl on the farm, the school, which may bestow long-term but unrecognized benefits loses its appeal. Children drop out before completion of a minimal course. Wastage rates are extremely high. The tests of educational success within the schools deny promotion from one grade to the next to a large proportion of children. They stagnate in the lower classes. On the other hand, success does not always bring its economic reward. If the economy cannot absorb them at an acceptable level, highly educated personnel may feel frustrated and because the value system makes certain kinds of work unacceptable, they join the pool of educated unemployed. The examination system of course, may be blamed but some analysis of the aspirations developed by examination success should be made. The successful engineer in India is no more likely to take a job as a labourer than is the successful arts graduate. Modification of the examination system would have some beneficial results but to lay all the ills of the Indian economy and her school system at its feet would be dangerously short-sighted.

   In industrial societies, nevertheless, the relationship between economic position and social class status becomes increasingly close. Certainly the tests used to place individuals in a particular social class are many and varied. Accent, style of dress, manner of walk, style of life, and personal associations are all, to some degree, criteria of class. The tests are informal and subtle. Those who fail them may not even be aware that they have been applied and resent the consequences of failure. Success in formal school examinations may not bring looked-for social class mobility and status. The known, and to a large extent openly accepted criteria of social class may, in fact, be less important than those which it would be right to apply. The achievement or contest society often slips back into the sponsored or ascription society. Against this observation which applies still in those countries where educational success has not yet been fully accepted as a criterion of social position, it should be noted that where the climate of opinion is different examination success counts. In India a university degree is an asset as far as marriage is concerned. In Japan the educated man and teacher still enjoy considerable social prestige not consistent with their relatively low economic position. In France and Germany social status is closely linked with examination successes. In Germany the links with political and industrial power are much less close than in France. The latter is *par excellence* the nation of intellectuals sustained in large measure by an examination system which, at the professional level, is overtly and highly competitive and at other manpower levels is closely linked to vocational training for a very large number of particular trades and occupations.

Linking Education to Life

In general, the position has been reached where in some countries one pattern of examining forms the link between education and further education and between the schools and a great many other aspects of socio-economic and political life. These examinations may or may not be valid, that is to say they may or may not perform the task for which they are intended. The likelihood is that they will function more effectively as links between school levels – primary/secondary, secondary/tertiary – and between the schools and the traditional professions than as a link with politics, commerce or industry. It is questionable whether the traditional (Chinese type) examinations any longer pick out the best public officials or bureaucrats or whether they ensure that they are as well prepared as they could be to perform their tasks.

The greater complexity of society suggests that the links should be more varied, each being designed to perform rather specific linking functions. Moreover, an analysis of function needs to be made and the possibilities of designing tests to serve one function effectively considered. The assumption that one type of test – be it essay-type, oral, practical or objective – can measure what has been learned, select candidates for a wide range of occupations and activities, predict future success and provide learning incentives for the majority of pupils, is no longer tenable.

The complexity of a society should, if this point be taken, determine the examination system. Evidently in North America, Europe, the

British Commonwealth and Japan a battery of tests of all kinds needs to be developed so that profiles of performance and possibly future success may be drawn up. This is particularly necessary in situations where the notion of selection or rejection has been abandoned in favour of the principle of guidance and counselling. The new view reduces the competitive element and sustains the argument that each individual should be encouraged fully to develop his own potential and personality. These child-centred views have entered quite deeply into several educational systems, particularly in the United States. The realities of the adult world continue to make selection on the basis of competition a necessary evil. When the competitive element in schools is reduced, adult society may become more competitive and criteria other than educational success may become very important. In the modern world the clash between the school educated leaders and those who have been educated in and promoted by the armed services is all too apparent.

One criterion of success is perhaps dangerous in its political implications. The egalitarianism of modern educational thinking may replace one form of sponsorship and nepotism by another. One plea of the egalitarians is that competitive tests should be abolished and continuous assessment of pupils by teachers substituted. The success of such a policy will depend on a reduction of competition in education and society at large. If selection and competition remain a fact of life then the tests on which they are based must not only be as objective as possible, but must clearly be seen to be. The wisdom of the Chinese system here becomes apparent. The external examination system in England, the system of independent marking by two examiners and checking by a third goes some way towards ensuring that justice is not only done but is seen to be done. The achievement of objectivity exacts a price. The content of education becomes fixed and is determined on the basis of what is examinable: the effects of this on the schools of France and India have often been discussed. The possibilities of abandoning the assessments of oral examinations are, of course, greater in countries where the climate of philosophical opinion suggests that sure and certain knowledge over a wide range of subjects can be acquired than in those countries where the truth is regarded as necessarily relative. Interviewers may allow for otherwise unexceptionable qualities of personality and character to reveal themselves. Practical tests may well be disguised to measure technical competence. In short, the effectiveness of examinations should be judged on the basis of function. Clear statements of objectives are needed before any assessment of efficiency can be made. As a predictor of suitability for an occupational objective assessment and aptitude tests may be desirable. Specific occupations may require specific tests as indications of competence. Different tests may be needed to predict success in this same operation. The value of examinations as incentives to learning will depend on many factors within the school system and society. Attitudes towards learning and the educated man, i.e. his status, will be important. The financial rewards following educational success will arise when the attitudes within education towards selection and competition are markedly different from corresponding attitudes in society generally. Tests and examinations will provide an unsatisfactory link. They will also suffer if they have remained unchanged, in spite of educational and social changes.

This analysis leads us to accord to examinations and tests a central role. Introduced to increase social mobility in Imperial China, they may in the name of objectivity inhibit creativity and confer upon a favoured few – those who can afford education – privileges which in fact were inherited. Then, when conditions change, the effects of examinations change too. As the basis of knowledge alters, the effectiveness of a given examination may change. Scholarships in the classical languages doubtless picked out the most able men in England during the nineteenth century – for the bureaucracy, professional and political life. The knowledge they possessed was adequate to the tasks they were called upon to perform. Today, in a technological age, classical scholarship may be an adequate basis for selecting clever men. Their knowledge, however, would not enable them to deal effectively with a wide range of problems, the solutions to which require a knowledge of science and technology. Or again, victory as an Oxbridge debater may lead to success as a parliamentarian in England but neither the quick repartee of the Union debate nor verbal victories in Parliament are useful tests in the modern world.

The International Dimension

One problem, not discussed in this YEAR BOOK, promises to grow in importance: the international equivalence of degrees and diplomas. More and more students go abroad for postgraduate study and research: where do they stand? What is the value of the U.S.A. or Germany of a certificate awarded in Lima, Cairo or Shanghai? And when they return, what will their foreign degrees be worth? Not only this: various associations of states, such as those of the European Common Market, favour the free movement of capital and of workers, presumably including professionals. Should a medical degree awarded in Rio de Janeiro be accepted in Amsterdam? Or a Pontifical University award be recognized by Al Azhar?

This question of equivalences, a subtle and complex one, was already being studied in League of Nations days and it has been the concern of Unesco since its earliest days – not to mention many other international bodies. There are two aspects to it. First, the professional: a degree, say in medicine or pharmacy, may award a legal right to practice. Secondly, the academic: a degree may be the qualification entitling the holder to proceed to further courses of study and to enter examinations leading to higher degrees.

There is no room here to discuss all this: we must content ourselves by noting that progress will be made only when those two aspects are clearly distinguished and studied separately. We may perhaps add our own conviction that it will prove futile to study in close detail the programmes and curricula which, in various countries, lead to, say, a degree in chemistry. There are too many differences, even within one country. More formal and general criteria, such as years and hours of study, will have to suffice. And the liberal use of 'qualifying examinations' will help to simplify the situation.

Of course, at the level of university entrance, the whole business is much simpler. There it may well prove possible to obtain world acceptance of an 'International Baccalaureate' or 'International University Admission Examination' like that now being developed in Geneva under the patronage of a group of distinguished educationists from many countries. This examination has already been widely accepted in principle. Many universities in the U.S.A., most of the universities of Britain and Canada, the Swedish, Swiss and German, the Bulgarian, Indian, Australian and New Zealand universities have already accepted this examination as satisfying general matriculation requirements.

The educational systems of the world are becoming more and more alike and at the tertiary level increasingly interdependent. Already there is talk of agreed concentration on certain fields and of a sharing of responsibilities. It is becoming clear that in some branches of specialization a whole continent may have to co-operate. South America, for instance, can in reality afford only one first-class department of astrophysics, and only one first-class School of Meteorology – nor is there a need for more. One of the necessary conditions for closer integration and improved planning is mutual recognition of awards and it is fervently to be hoped that the problem of equivalences will be tackled with the seriousness and sense of urgency which it deserves.

Conclusion

In spite of all criticisms and attacks, the importance of success in examinations, particularly those set up by an external authority, grows continually in all countries. Two chief reasons for this can be readily identified.

First, success is usually rewarded by the granting of a certificate or university degree. These are labels which are easily recognized by employers and, indeed, by the public. They come, like university hoods and gowns, in different colours and sizes. Some have very high prestige indeed, as trademarks of famous and respected enterprises. In England, for instance, all degrees are still associated to some extent in people's minds with attendance at Oxford and Cambridge: and thus they are vastly more reputable than any kind of certificate or diploma. They have high snob-appeal.

Labels fulfil a very useful purpose in modern commerce, particularly if they describe correctly the content of the package – or even if they only give some rough indication of it. So employers and appointing committees are fond of labels and, like everyone else, are impressed by colour, size, design and so on. Candidates, on the other hand, not only recognize this tendency but are well aware of the fact that the atmosphere of modern professional and commercial life becomes ever more like that of a giant supermarket, its shelves laden with unfamiliar products, beautifully packaged. Hence *la chasse aux diplomes*.

Secondly, suppose that there are more applicants for a place in a college or for a particular post than there are vacancies. How is one to decide who shall be selected? Only four methods seem possible. The first would be chance: the drawing of lots, the throw of dice. The second would involve nepotism of some kind: paying attention to family and birth, to recommendations from influential patrons and so on. The third would be to charge high tuition fees, commissions etc. As regards admission to higher education, none of these tests is now acceptable. The first would reduce the whole process to frivolity. The other two clearly run counter to the whole notion of equality of educational opportunity, itself a powerful moving myth of modern society, which states that access to education must be independent of race, class, sex, or money.

What then is left? Only some sort of examination procedure. It therefore seems that, ineluctably, the progress of democracy involves the strengthening of the power and influence of examinations – at least at all points where selection is essential. And this has happened.

Yet to note all this does not involve losing hope that things might be better. It is certainly not beyond the wit of man to devise procedures of assessment and examination which, while respecting social and democratic ideals, will also serve to reinforce sound educational practices; which will do justice both to the individual and to society; which will be accepted as both just and wise.

As technical and professional competence becomes ever more important and as the range of professional activities grows, the need for tests of it becomes more urgent. What is evident from this *Year Book* is that profound scepticism of traditional examination systems has not yet been matched by the collective creativity needed to devise tests which are not only valid and reliable, nationally, but are capable of assessing competence in an international setting.

2

The Evolution of Examinations

A. V. Judges
Emeritus Professor of History of Education in the University of London

The business of examining, since the record began, has been almost entirely taken up with the assessment of human ability *in esse* or *in posse*. *Almost* entirely, inasmuch as it is not unknown for examiners to wield their powers in such a way as to penalize deviants and to disallow minority opinions. The abilities under test may of course extend no farther than the use of a sort of competence to recall knowledge furnished by others. The operation itself may have no other end than the testing of the effectiveness of a particular group or groups of teachers, as was the case when English elementary schools received grant aid from the state according to 'results'. Thus the principal purpose may be completely indifferent to the fortunes of the individual contestants, and be satisfied by the provision of data towards the building of a common *standard*. In yet another setting one brisk stroke of rigorous selection among a number of competing candidates may exhaust the examiner's function. Examinations can be put to almost any use.

A theory of examinations can hardly be said to exist; but if one takes current discussion and looks for its characteristic feature, it shows itself, I believe, in a heightened concern with the degree to which objectives can be explicitly stated and also realized, indeed even made clear to the examinee himself. This is an important development brought about partly by the universal spread of examining techniques; partly too by the popularization of programmes of standardized tests involving objective measurement, tests capable moreover of operating with a high degree of precision and constancy, as compared (so it is claimed) with the traditional type of miniature prose-essay test in which the ingredient of subjective judgement exercised by both performer and marker has been bigger than requirements warrant.

We are concerned in this chapter to look for some of the elements of continuity in the history of examinations. It is a commonplace, for instance, that one assumes that the examinee is displaying the best of what he has to offer. Often enough his fortunes and life chances may depend on the showing forth of what he has in him. There is a further assumption, less regularly put to the proof, that the examiner has a clear notion of what he is about and is aware of the degree of credibility his methods will command. This may extend to an appreciation of the proven value of his procedure in the setting of the whole environment, as, for example, when papers in science are made a compulsory part of the school-leaving examination, because the community believes that this requirement will assist a developing technology. The examiner may well be aware that he is using what is now being called 'a tool of social engineering'.

The Recruitment of the Mandarin Class

The first example of a clearly institutionalized technique known to us was the scheme of competitive examinations for admission to public office which was passed on from one Chinese dynasty to another over a period two millenia until its ultimate and unlamented abandonment in 1905, when the need to change over to western styles of education forced both the candidate's form of preparation, based on the Confucian canonical writings, and the style of the test he submitted to, into sudden obsolescence.

Early sinologues in Europe conceived the idea that the public examinations, nominally open to the vast majority of male citizens, irrespective of means, were the gateway through which a classless society recruited its bureaucrats under the mandate of heaven, without fear or favour. Educational success, it appeared, was a powerful adjunct of social mobility. That the competition was, within limits, searching and just is not in question; nor is it disputed that imperial administration at all levels was the concern of a class of gentry (chin-shên) enjoying the highest esteem, which embraced the literati and constantly refreshed its quality through scholarly channels. Government was accustomed to carry on its business without an hereditary élite; and the elaborately tiered and (to the outsider's view) extremely complicated and protracted apparatus of literary examinations provided the men of power. They constituted the mandarin hierarchy of a humanely inspired autocracy founded on a self-operating principle of shared surveillance. Under the final Ch'ing dynasty we find, to be sure, the elements of family influence which must inevitably go with restricted educational opportunity and a strong suggestion of a closed shop in the enrolment of the bureaucracy. For not only was there an impressive front entrance, guarded by conditions of the fiercest competition, but there were also unobtrusive side entrances which admitted through purchase. It cannot be doubted, even so, that educational prowess was canalized and put to effective use in selecting an intelligent officialdom in a manner unknown elsewhere in the world until an apparatus of enrolment by examination in the humanities, possessing striking similarities, was set up for the civil service of the United Kingdom in mid-Victorian times.

Confucianism, which provided the moral philosophy and the political outlook of the Manchu dominion, pervaded the syllabus; and it ensured that the living bureaucracy was indoctrinated by a deep and proud tradition. It might be said that the tenacity which upheld the old empire for so long and the final collapse of the system are in neither case explicable without an understanding of the social functioning of the examination system with all its bizarre features. In modern terms it can be seen to be effective in the working of a *screening service*, in the provision of *professional incentives* and an *esprit de corps*. It acted as a *stabilizer* of the membership of the power hierarchy, if not of the ethos of the whole political system. It *maintained a tradition of scholarship* by allowing it to discriminate among talents. In short the system's characteristics hint at some of the elements we must expect to find in the growth of examining practice elsewhere, e.g., the power of a developed and accepted system to maintain culture and tradition, its steadiness as a social control, its power to rationalize human functions and norms of competence, its virtues as a neutral discriminator of talent, finally its potential as a means of dividing a population in a plausible way into status groupings.

Competitive Grading in the Ancient World

When we turn to the ancient world of the West, there is nothing to be found to match these institutions of the celestial empire. It is undeniable, of course, that competitiveness was the life and soul of the Greek city state. Most of all it displayed itself in athletic contests which themselves were part of the public ritual: here expertise could be *measured*. Such clues as there are suggest that in the non-physical divisions of schooling the spirit of emulation entered into the learning process. But the examination, as we know it, seems nowhere to have played its part. Certainly, exercises in the art of public address were esteemed as an essential part of the training of young men of the governing class in the schools of antiquity. The desire to outshine others in persuasiveness and elegance of style seems to have been present. As Isocrates argued, *logos*, the art of discourse, taught men not only how to write, but also how to think connectedly and to live becomingly. And this theory of education was transferred to imperial Rome. There the practice of the rhetorical art helped to govern admission to the administrative cadre. Of the establishment of pass lists and grading methods there is, however, no sign.

With the barbarian invasions the intellectual landscape lost its points of reference. Centuries pass between the decline of academic sophistication in the days of Augustine of Hippo and its revival – be it noted on the same groundwork of classical texts, now somewhat eroded – in the cathedral schools, dominated by free-lance lecturers, of Chartres, Orleans and Rheims. Looking at the technique of exposition followed by the new humanists of the twelfth century, we are once more, to our surprise, under the guidance of Quintilian, one of the most enduringly influential of all guides to formal instruction, and, moreover, a teacher sometimes credited, (though falsely, I believe), with a kind of fixation upon the importance of emulation in the schoolroom. Not that the schoolmasters of the Middle Ages, with their admitted fondness for disputation as a test of competence and as an educational method, were much exercised by theories of motivation. But the atmosphere of debate and competition was real enough; and methods of employing contrived rivalries to stimulate effort in the classroom certainly preceded the Jesuits, who as we shall see, turned competition into a fine art.

In the meantime the Byzantine East long held its own, indeed more than its own, in the dissemination of culture, both in monastic schools and in secular strongholds like the University of Constantinople. Further (before the great invasions) the classical values were kept alive in the great schools of Alexandria, Nicaea and Thessalonika. That there is so little information concerning what we should call the structure of education is partly the result of what has aptly been called 'the disconcerting looseness in the Byzantine use of educational terms' (Buckler). Plenty of evidence exists that higher education was regularly financed from imperial and municipal treasuries. This, and our knowledge that future administrators and judges were deliberately trained in law and rhetoric at public expense, hint, but no more, at the existence of techniques for sifting and discovering talent.

Early University Practice

In the West, with the reception of Arabic science and a return of the professional grammarians' interest in persuasiveness and elegance of style, a concentration of teaching power at certain nodal points was accompanied by the revival of the *trivium* and *quadrivium* (the seven liberal sciences) and the appearance of something which has a hint of a resemblance to modern examination conditions. We find the early universities of the twelfth century behaving as academic societies with a permanent function and structure; we see them engaging purposefully in scholarly and professional exercises of discrimination among their students. As for the devices employed in early medieval times for proving and establishing degrees of competence – in Bologna, in Paris; only a little later in Oxford – a most interesting store of miscellaneous evidence has been made available. This has been ingeniously interpreted, and in all there seems to be no difficulty in discerning a meaningful degree structure with a commonsense setting in the requirements of life at this period.

In the medieval university 'the word examination ... included any process of inquiry into the candidate's fitness as well as a direct testing of his scholastic attainments' (Rashdall). The way of attaining fitness naturally affected the means of proving it. The route was followed by attending closely on the words of the teacher and by the systematic use of prescribed texts, digests and collections of excerpts; and here we see parallels with Confucian culture. After the preliminary stages of study, much was to depend on intellectual agility in disputation with fellow-students and teachers, using the logical forms and the textual ammunition acquired in the study of the *trivium*, followed in due course by the subjects of the *quadrivium*. The latter provided experience in handling the skills and interests of the former; and together they completed the groundwork of culture, in other words the liberal education, which was the province of the faculty of arts. From this foundation, further and more applied studies, leading perhaps to a doctorate, could be pursued and accredited. Within this world of learning, which can best be regarded as a network of virtually autonomous academic societies, all with very similar conventions, we see something like a professional brotherhood or a trading guild, making itself responsible for the serious business of testing candidates for promotion in the hierarchy, and for the picturesque pageantry associated with the conferment of titles and degrees.

Often enough, it would seem, the actual testing of competence was carried out by informal methods, having little regard to paper work, within the young man's faculty. The solemn formalities of acceptance into the university's degree of bachelorship (cf. journeyman worker, novice in knighthood or of a fraternity of regular clergy) and subsequently into the mastership, made only a mockery of testing for competence; a fact which has encouraged the belief that until our latter-day adoption of written papers and published syllabuses the university seniors pursued no rigour when they vouched for their products.

Thus the master and his bachelor assistant were partners in the teaching process. Each had himself only been adopted into the society by the chancellor and regent-masters after a course of severe discipline, finalized in a series of tests. Whether laxly or strictly administered – and over the centuries standards sometimes wavered, sometimes stood firm – the degree-giving function in its dominant purpose was to certify or to accredit trained personnel within the teaching profession, whether as internal participants in their own university or as claimants to the status as masters elsewhere, exercising the *jus ubique docendi*. It was by no means certain that this claim to be able to come in and teach would everywhere be admitted; Paris, for long the unchallenged centre and model of European light and learning, was notoriously sticky in such matters. Yet the degree of master of arts had universal meaning as the mark of acquired maturity in the profession of scholar. And thus the *determination* (preceded by *responsions*) of B.A. degrees and the faculty's *inception* of masters, which finally accompanied the grant by the chancellor of the teacher's licence, were parts of a grading and sifting process carried through on stylized patterns in a hierarchy of professional academics. Bits of these patterns, their origins forgotten, remain with us today in many peculiar forms.

The *scolae* set up by the doctors and masters advanced the techniques of learning; they became workshops of opinion. The large university became an intellectual power-house in the world at large, a producer of theologians, physicians and lawyers, a taking-off point for ambitious secular clergy who were destined to be royal administrators, church dignitaries and business managers in the households of magnates and great landowners; but, in the sight of the cultural historian, its abiding function was as the teacher of grammar and literary skills to the young who themselves would teach the young. Many of the external contributions made by these institutions, whether as reserve pools of ability or as selective agencies, were certainly not within their original field of vision. A by no means negligible part of the history of examinations is taken up with the adoption of unexpected functions within a machinery once designed for quite different purposes.

The Decline of Trial by Disputation

A lapse of interest in trial by examination as an educational tool was part of the Northern renaissance. The inventive impulse declined. Forms and methods still alive and full of meaning in the fourteenth century lost their original significance. It is true that the schoolmaster, now wide open to the disciplines of humanism, was now bringing more competitive elements into teaching method. But meanwhile the universities of Europe were losing their old initiative in the opening up of knowledge; so that the defence of a thesis as a testing device now signified little more than the survival of an old-fashioned attitude to the scholastic curriculum. In his *Oxford and Cambridge in Transition, 1558–1642* (1959) Mark Curtis speaks of 'disputations which measured nothing so much as a young man's ability to learn well-worn arguments by rote' and of 'collusion in viva voce examinations'.

Where should the transition line between school and university be drawn? The successful candidate for the *maitrise-ès-arts* in the University of Paris in the later sixteenth century 'would be no older than most of the boys who leave the sixth form in the modern public school' (H. C. Barnard). The prime responsibility for pioneering new methods passed to (i) the schools formed under the influence of the Counter-Reformation, (ii) the new academies. Some of the latter were of royal foundation; some were bent toward administrative and professional interests, or toward military specialism (e.g., the Ritter-Akademien); some were concerned with science and commerce. Pioneers in curriculum experiment, they had little use for the practices which clung to the mystique of the liberal arts; and thus it was not these vocational studies, but the ancient forms of scholastic learning, not excluding the sciences of the *quadrivium*, which, paradoxically enough, nourished the germ of modern testing procedures.

The Standardization of Excellence

This line of evolution was evident in England first when Cambridge University adopted the mathematical tripos in the mid-eighteenth century, a decision which has been called 'almost a new discovery in the mechanics of education' (Sadler). The aims of the new examination were to *raise and standardize performance*, thus conceding the needs of serious-minded under-graduates who were willing to work methodically under supervision and have their scholarship submitted to a rigorous test. The same needs existed at Oxford, and there they were met within the structure created by the famous Examination Statute of 1800. Whilst putting to effective use the range of traditional subjects inherited from earlier times, the reform concentrated on special attainment in classics, mathematics and physics. Admittedly only a minority of degree claimants were expected to use the privilege, and it was thus possible to introduce standards and stringencies into the examination of an order hitherto unknown. In both universities an *Honours* system was gradually built up, steeply graded and highly competitive, admitting new disciplines and constellations of related sub-jects as reformers slowly got their way. Whilst in France the tradition of the polished oral presentation of an argument in a highly competitive atmosphere survives to this day, in Britain, paper work, mostly 'unseen', was deliberately introduced in place of rehearsed disputation. The ques-tion asked of honours examiners was not whether a candidate was com-petent to achieve graduation, but with what degree of excellence he was deemed to have performed. Gradually most of the survivals of earlier custom fell away from the structure. Enormous pains were taken to ensure that the honours degrees were sharply distinguished from the ordinary pass (or poll) degrees, that they were objectively assessed, and that they really tested techniques of exposition and intellectual quality, as well as factual material. Such moves, putting a premium on a high and perhaps excessive measure of specialism, helped to define the nature of a graded first degree. The pattern was adopted – in some cases actually extended – with considerable success in the externally taken degrees of the University of London (chartered 1836), followed closely by the newer universities of England and Wales as they achieved independence of London tutelage.

But not so the Scottish universities. For a long time they refrained from using their examinations to force a narrow subject-concentration, under the name of honours, upon their undergraduates. They took credit, in a manner difficult to attack, for their superior understanding of the nature of the problem, namely to define a true liberal education in terms of a range of general studies, including more than a bowing acquaintanceship with metaphysics and moral philosophy. Yet in Scotland, too, they moved some way towards specialization after 1889. The leading monograph, by G. E. Davie, on the struggle to maintain the broad spectrum in the first-degree examination is aptly named *The Democratic Intellect* (1961).

From School to University

The stress placed upon an undergraduate curriculum which was forced to become, under the examiners' rules, both narrow *and* deep, distinguishes Britain from most of the rest of the world. Still, university studies have their ultimate footing in the school. Whatever significance be given to the happenings just described, the important phases of development must be sought near the ever-fluctuating boundary line which separates the status of school child from that of the successful university entrant. The problem has been, in part, to define the threshold; in part, to supervise the passage over it of the candidates. In point of fact the tidiest and, on the whole, the most effective solution was found in Germany. It happened at a time when both the secondary-school course and university objectives were simultaneously undergoing substantial change, during the period of Frederick the Great and his two successors. The devices adopted under the reformed Prussian state system, and imitated elsewhere in Germany, enabled the work of the two institutions to be clearly separated. At the same time the curricula were got into phase; and a workable order of progression, imbued with the German sense of organic relationship, became possible. The invention of the *abitur*, the classical-school leaving examination, was an elegant and precocious piece of academic engineering. It enabled the new-model German university, – predicted at Göttingen and Halle, realized in Berlin and Bonn – to find its identity and become a pattern for the world in respect of scholarly prowess. In our own century, the *abiturientenexamen*, true to its function, has absorbed into itself, as the true termination of school studies, the old bachelor's degree of the universities (cf. the *baccalauréat* in France). But has it functioned to excess as an instrument of control? We note its double role in (i) providing exit visas for those terminating their regular education and (ii) as a boarding pass for those in transit to a higher stage. The chequered history of attempts to make senior school certificates and general certificates of education perform a similar dual function in Britain – where, indeed, analagous displacements of achievement levels have occurred – manifests the same obscurity and distortion as to purpose. Such doublings of function are unplanned; nevertheless they happen.

Even though the high standards of the *abitur* seem from the first to have been entrusted to those running the secondary schools, which themselves have habitually set the papers and assessed the results (under very close inspectorial moderation, it is true), still the national prestige of the examination had always stood high; partly no doubt because it served, without challenge from subordinate examinations, to give the only available profile of a young person's school career. Criticisms have reflected, not disillusionment, but changes of emphasis in regard to the spread of work under test, though in general the *abitur* has stood for a broad grounding, including compulsory mathematics, and, moreover, ability to handle ideas. So that not only has it been a certificate providing entry to any German university, but would-be employers, safe in the knowledge that only those expected by the school to pass the final part of the course would be admitted as candidates, have been persuaded of the high quality of all the participants. There has been much social significance in the fact that the proportion of the age-group reaching the examination has always been small. The distinction between this ratio and that which represents the number reaching 'commencement' at senior high schools in the United States prompts reflections upon how differently the purposes of examining institutions can be realized within cultures of the same order of economic development.

Much closer comparisons have been possible between the *abitur* and its French counterpart the *baccalauréat*, the second part of which has been taken by pupils in the top classes of the *lycées* and of the communal *collèges*. What has distinguished the '*bachot*' has been its capacity for rejection – this was notorious – and the extreme inflexibility of the machinery; the emphasis being placed on a series of essay topics and written questions set before candidates, under forms of rigorous control, within a close-knit national system. Reflecting some of the characteristics of such a uniform structure, it has served to bring into prominence the difficulties besetting (until recently) all those in pursuit of the most sought-after kinds of higher education; whilst at the same time compelling our admiration as perhaps the most brilliantly conceived test of the training of intellectual potential known in the history of examinations. On its own merits alone the *baccalauréat* has been coveted by members of the French white-collar classes; and here again the comparison with Germany, where the factor of wastage has been less conspicuous, is to be noted. The leaving examination owes, however, most of its national image in each case to its status as virtually the only pathway of admission to the university.

The Instruments of Formal Education: Jesuit Schooling

Almost everywhere in Europe, the strength of the humanities, tempered often enough by a discreet association with Aristotelian logic and some philosophy, comes out in the history of the leading types of secondary schools. In a measure the teachability of the subjects came to connote their examinability, first in disputation and oral testing, later on in paper exercises. Rigorous methods in the practice of formal education accompanied the revival of language study within the classical tradition. Assuming that the skills and shrewdness of outlook acquired within the limits of such curricula were in some way or other transferable to the wider requirements of life, then the grading of such abilities, however remote the medium of their acquisition, provided a prognostic index or set of measurements of what education had done for the complete man or woman.

Two things distinguish the pioneering of modern examination methods by the Jesuits. They are by no means unconnected with the determination to organize the education of an *élite* – at any rate an *élite* of intellectual merit – which was already present during the lifetime of the founder of the Society. First, the course, as enjoined by the Ratio Studiorum of 1586, was one of great length, even for the lay students, and those who pursued it to the end found themselves in due course in an elevated world of scholastic philosophy and theological learning well above the university level of the day. In this setting, secondary and higher education merged painlessly into one another.

Secondly, the idea of 'making the grade' was prominent in all stages of the teaching method, a method which insisted on the continuous rehearsal and memorization of work previously covered, and which was constantly taking stock of progress. Promotion up the school had always to be earned by performance. The technique of teaching emphasized the *measurement of attainment*; and the disputation and the formal exercises in class were put to competitive use. In these schools, the Jesuits, admired and feared as they were all over Europe, 'brought competition to a higher state of effectiveness than ever realized before – or perhaps since' (Brubacher). *Grading*, the essence of the method, became a fine art.

It is by no means easy to describe the ways in which the advanced techniques of the Jesuit fathers served as a general example. Far from admiring this method, some reformers – and one notes particularly the Jansenists with their 'little' (scil., modest and unpretentious) schools – felt as much revulsion from the highly strung teaching of the Jesuit schools as they felt admiration for the assurance and precocity of the pupils emerging from the course. The developments in question had success, though perhaps no great novelty, in combining secondary with what may be called tertiary studies. They are interesting, too, because they bridge the gap between the earlier forms of scholastic training and the formal exercises of the nineteenth-century *lycée*, *athénée* and *gymnasium*. The bridge is, even so, an invisible one, inasmuch as it was the banishment from the Catholic world of the Jesuit order, with its great network of schools, in the 1760s that called into being the demand for an alternative upper-class education with more secular, or at any rate fewer ultramontane, connexions. Before many years, the French Revolution pressed egalitarian doctrines into the arena. How were the new cadres of republican administration to be filled? The idea of the career open to talent called for ways in which talent could be identified, trained, measured and promoted, without the intrusion of influence or class prejudice. And on all this there was much debate. But meanwhile the institutional framework of education in France was badly damaged and suffered many years of decay. Thus in this new world of administrative change, it was left to Britain and British India to turn the possibilities of the competitive examination to use in reforming the public services. This was indeed the opening of a new chapter.

Broader Uses in Britain and Elsewhere

In some sense it was a development forced on by the very untidiness of the educational situation in Britain. The disorder was particularly noticeable at the level between secondary and higher education. Nothing like the *abitur* has ever existed in these islands. Recruitment into positions of leadership and responsibility occurred within a limited social field with access to education. The choice was not exactly haphazard; but no pattern was evident. To be sure, a complex system of scholarship awards had helped to enlarge the field of opportunity. It had operated since medieval times to feed ability into the classical schools and thence to the Oxford and Cambridge colleges. In the important collection called *Essays on Examinations* (1936), put together by Sir Michael Sadler, the editor's own contribution, occupying nearly half the volume, is given over to the rise of English endowed scholarships and the mutations they underwent. Here, Sadler felt, was a quite unique national institution which stretched across the centuries, from the days of the early foundations like Winchester College, offering free places to promising children from relatively needy families (*pauperes et indigentes*). A line of continuity could be discerned up to the adoption of the nationalized avenues of opportunity which were becoming etched on the educational map in the early years of the present century. 'The system [ultimately] developed', wrote R. H. Tawney, social historian and educational reformer, in 1922, 'has been the principal means of bridging the gulf between primary and secondary education'.

But important as a scholarship system may be in influencing the evolution of examiners' methods, historians have failed to agree about the extent to which grants and selective free places have actually stimulated social mobility, or how far one can make specific reference to competitive elements in the processes involved. There was, and is, inevitably a rivalry between objectives. On the one hand trustees controlling the means of assistance wanted to help forward zeal and promise without officiously seeking out special distinction; on the other there could be a definite pursuit of excellence through all the stringencies of competitive selection. The current view among specialists is that the reform of the universities in the nineteenth century, far from netting an extended range of talent, succeeded merely in removing most of the opportunities that remained for the poorer children. What is most surprising is the relative lateness of the realization of the defects of any kind of educational ladder, selectively employed, in the finding and exploiting of innate ability – supposing this to be capable of being earmarked with any precision.

Alfred Binet, with his exploration of the minds of mental defectives in the opening decades of the twentieth century, unwittingly opened the way to surprising extensions of the field of examining – the new techniques for assessing potential as against performance, the handling of novel material, the shift of attention to the earlier days of the school career, the broadening of the ability field brought under scrutiny. Environmental influence as stimulant and depressant, nowadays very much the centre of attention, was extraordinarily slow in disclosing itself under these novel conditions; and it was not perhaps until the 1950s that the weaknesses of testing methods in the lower age-ranges became apparent, or indeed that it could be admitted that the 'dual function of educational systems – to educate and to assign people to roles – is a *perennial* source of difficulty' (R.A.C. Oliver). It is something of a paradox that the selective functions, i.e., the use of examinations for the *ascription of status*, fall more deeply under suspicion as their processes achieve greater refinement and as they extend their popularity in use.

Social Uses and Joint Functions

The earliest endeavours to enlarge competitive testing and its scope beyond the fringes of education proper were untinged by the kind of doubts which now assail us about the *predictive value* of formal examining. Jeremy Bentham, in his campaign against inefficiency and obscurantism, had in 1827 worked out a detailed and, at the same time, absurdly impracticable programme for screening candidates for public employment, with oral questions to be selected by lottery. William Lovett, the radical Chartist, believed that the queen's ministers should be required to submit to written tests, presumably on matters of the public weal, before taking office. But it was not until the 1850s that heavy pressure from the Administrative Reform Association successfully urged the need for examinations as instruments of selection, in this way 'shutting', as they hoped, 'all the back doors which lead to public employment'. Nothing, it was felt, could be more fittingly devised for the surveillance of an individualist economic order than an administrative system staffed by people scrupulously chosen for their intellectual merit under conditions in which limited demand was satisfied by the best who would come forward.

There was already experience to go upon. Teachers for service in approved grant-aided schools were being successfully chosen from the pupil-teaching pool by a new battery of examinations held by government inspectors. The inspectors had already devised a nation-wide machinery for assessing results in order of merit. And now the general policy for a reformed public system – beginning rather experimentally with officers chosen for the Indian civil administration – was laid down in a famous report submitted in 1852 by Sir Stafford Northcote and Sir Charles Trevelyan. Examination by written papers was by degrees to become the means of recruitment and promotion in both of what the authors called 'the intellectual and mechanical branches' of the home civil service. Oddly enough, the new policy in its most influential aspect – i.e., touching the syllabus and expected range of performance – was contributed in an appended document by Benjamin Jowett, later to be Master of Balliol and hard-working patron of a generation of Oxford careerists. Following Jowett's advice, the new written examinations took on a decided flavour of pure scholarship. Certainly this was true of the papers set for admission to the upper division, though science was not excluded in its applied aspects. Moreover the papers bore more than a passing resemblance to those set in the honours schools of the older universities. The marking was done by Oxford and Cambridge men. As the result of what was recently described as 'one of the smartest confidence tricks in history' (Max Nicolson), the pattern was fixed whereby new entrants were admitted from among those who could claim a polished liberal education, without any specific knowledge of the business of administration which would have to be carried through. All that could be said was that *indirect tests* of suitability were provided, inasmuch as they sought to 'measure a candidate's capacity for one thing by testing him in something else' (Norman Morris). However sensible the practice of indirect testing, in a social sense the senior civil servants continued to come from the same top drawer, whilst meantime the standardization of their conditions and their expansion in numbers created a new and respectable profession.

All this was not done overnight. Nor can the application of improved examination processes, which were now seen to be adaptable to a variety of new subject requirements, be treated as signs of anything but a widening acceptance of objective ways of measuring personal qualities. Was there anything that an examination could not do? The older universities, conscious of a fresh public mission, led the way, pushing out into the field of adult education among the under-privileged. Examining became a universal industry, Britain leading the civilized world; so that everywhere sheer weight of numbers of entrants forced inspecting authorities to

abandon individual oral tests and take to the use of written papers –
'in self defence', as Norman Morris has remarked. The full effects of this
revolution – a precipitate flight to paper questioning and anonymity –
have never, as far as I know, been carefully explored.

In the United Kingdom the new methods were exemplified in the
elaborate examination schemes of the Science and Art Department.
Fortified by the stimulus of ingeniously calculated government subsidies –
payment by results – these tests were planned to attract new science teachers and to *systematize the curricula* of new applied science subjects and of
other novelties which might encourage juvenile craftsmen. This was the
thin end of national technological planning, a pale and distant reflection
of what was going on in Germany. In the meantime professional associations proceeded to develop the use of written examination tests of their
own, or to borrow those of other bodies, in order to provide the necessary
threshold qualifications for the admission of their own licentiates and fellows
to careers as physicians, pharmacists, solicitors, gas engineers, accountants
and the like.

At a lower age-level the newly discovered interest of the British
universities in the outside world asserted itself in a desire to improve the
work of the secondary schools and to introduce some rules of uniformity.
In the main it was the quality of their undergraduate admissions that
exercised them. And their new 'local examinations' (England, 1858;
Scotland, 1865), in which they authorized their own officers to set up
temporary outposts in provincial halls, and later in the schools themselves,
were designed to the end of improving mutual contacts. In this they were
creating 'something like a unified teaching corporation' (J. P. C. Roach).
Membership of the system bestowed a special status on the chosen
secondary schools, giving them a position not unlike that of American
'accredited high schools'.

This was the real beginning of the school-leaving examination which
wields such enormous influence over the lives of young people in England
today.   Changes in nomenclature notwithstanding, the academic surveillance exercised by the universities survived the assumption by the
state of responsibility for secondary education and finally responsibility
for the conduct of the universities themselves. The takeover by the government's own sponsored body, the Secondary Schools Examination Council
(1917), failed to remove the continuing confusion between university
entrance trials and school-leaving examination standards; and the business
of correlation of standards among all kinds of examination itself became a
minor industry, for much depended on parities and exemptions. The
remains of the old pioneering 'local' system have shown through in
various ways, for example in the concentration of power and initiative
in seven or eight examining boards, each attached to one or more university

centres. Further, there was the delimitation of subjects in more or less uniform groups which was traditional; so that it could be said of the pre-1951 arrangements that, with 'their clearly stated grades of pass, [they] constructed a fine complicated hierarchy of achievement and corresponding endeavour' (Frances Stevens).

Even so, the system was held to be too rigid. In order to introduce pliability and, above all, to provide the schools with more liberty in the curriculum, a radical overhaul was rather clumsily attempted by official-dom in 1951. Subsequent experiments and a vast amount of discussion have aimed once more at introducing organic relationships between subject elements, and at reducing the dangers of specialization to which the British are peculiarly prone; and, equally important, they have attempted to provide something in the way of a certificate worth taking away from school by a new and broader generation of potential examinees of somewhat lower intellectual calibre. The results have been more pro-liferation, not to say fragmentation; and they represent, too, a serious attempt to devolve responsibility out of the hands of remote bodies of examiners into those of the teachers themselves – responsibility, that is, for teaching programmes, for setting papers and for marking itself. At the moment of writing no important group of educators can claim to be satisfied.

BIBLIOGRAPHY

H. Rashdall, (Eds. Powicke and Emden). *The Universities of Europe in the Middle Ages* vols 1–,3 (1936).

F. M. Powicke *Ways of Medieval Life and Thought* (1949).

R. Schwickerath, *Jesuit Education* (2nd ed. 1905).

R. K. Kelsall, *Higher Civil Servants in Britain* (1935).

J. A. Petch, *Fifty Years of Examining: the Joint Matriculation Board* (1953).

M. Sadler, *Essays on Examinations* (1936).

H. C. Barnard, *The French Tradition in Education* (1922).

S. Wiseman, (Ed.) *Examinations and English Education*) 1961).

F. Paulsen, *German Education Past and Present* (1908).

Section II: Introduction

Examination Aims, Theories and Techniques

Brian Holmes
Reader in Comparative Education in the University of London

A number of purposes can be ascribed to examinations, a fact which gives rise to several problems. J. L. Brereton suggests three aims, all of which have been advocated by theorists for many years with differing emphasis. They test achievement, they provide goals or incentives for students, and they are competitive (p. 37). Examiners, of course, may regard one or more of these objectives as inadmissible. Examinees may see the purpose of an examination in quite a different light. Then there are the consumers of examination success, namely employers and educationists. A distinction, therefore, should be drawn between the stated aims of an examination or a test (and Brereton contrasts examinations with tests on p. 39) and the functions they very evidently serve. Sharply defined goals may not ensure effective examinations or tests, but at least they should direct attention to the danger of assuming that one kind of examination or test will meet effectively a multiplicity of purposes. From a functional viewpoint, the tests made by the consumers of success will be pragmatic.

Multiple purposes and functions imply a variety of techniques. The main categories are: written, oral and practical. Each category includes a number of different types, e.g. 'written' may be either essay or objective. The choice of a suitable type of examination or test depends on the task it is expected to perform. P. E. Vernon points out that the professional skills of a doctor or teacher are inadequately tested by written work alone (p. 43). Suitability also depends on the level of education (p. 47) and presumably the kind and age of candidates. Types of examination which are suitable at the level of university work are less appropriate at the primary school level even though the stated aim may be the same. Again, the acquisition of certain kinds of data can be assessed better by some types of test than others. What has the candidate learned? Knowledge of facts? The ability to interpret and extrapolate? How to apply principles? To see relationships? To draw together or synthesize points? Or, how to make value judgements? (p. 49).

Given that the purpose of an examination or test is known and accepted and that a choice of type has been made there remain technical problems related to its validity and reliability. Examinations or tests can discover only a proportion of what a candidate knows. The adequacy of sampling is of importance in relation to the objectives of the examination; thus Vernon writes that 'It is a reasonable claim by the advocates of the objective examination that, as it includes 50 or 100 or more short questions, it can sample a field much more comprehensively than an essay paper lasting the same time' (p. 43). Again, he reiterates the findings in the 1930s (p. 45) of Hartog, Rhodes and Burt, who highlighted the problems of subjectively marked examinations. Of course the number of candidates and the frames of reference of different examiners will influence the reliability of marking essay-type examinations. They may look for different things; but their idiosyncrasies tend to cancel each other out (p. 47). Vernon suggests marking procedures which may increase the validity and reliability of essay-type tests (p. 48).

The solution to these problems does not necessarily lie in the objective test. A. J. Stauffer outlines the assumptions on which objective tests are based and indicates how the conditions under which the tests are administered, the group to which they are given, and the cultural lines on which they are founded may seriously impair the level of 'objectivity' (pp. 53–5). He gives some of the major steps in test construction and points to the hazards involved when the classroom teacher makes up his or her own test (pp. 57–8). These reminders are salutary, as are his words of caution on the possibilities of classifying creativity in order to measure it (p. 58). Nevertheless he concludes that availability of computer services will accelerate the improvement in objective testing (p. 59).

In the last chapter in this section, Z. Sardi agrees that ' . . . psychometric tests and inventories are probably the most reliable tools of establishing objective data about a person' (p. 63). In the area of vocational guidance, one of the main difficulties is to construct tests which will predict success in a specific occupation (p. 64), when the skills associated with it may change even though, after a certain age, the interests of the worker may remain relatively stable (p. 64).

Tests of validity really depend upon whether the purposes and criteria of the examiner are acceptable. Certain methods of selection may be very reliable and efficient, but totally unacceptable. Nepotism, for example, finds little overt favour today. Interviews for a job or admission to a college are frowned upon. Other techniques of selection have had to be devised. One of the major social purposes of examination is to make certain processes of evaluation and selection *appear* fair. What is just depends on the norms of a society and not merely on whether the tests are reliable. Such norms should be taken into account in any comparative study.

3

Theories of Examinations

J. L. Brereton
Former General Secretary, Local Examinations Syndicate of Cambridge University

In this chapter we have to consider various claims that are made or have been made about the purposes served by examinations. We shall start by attempting to define an examination, i.e. to pinpoint its essential features. We shall then relate these to the alleged reasons for holding examinations.

An examination is (1) a certain kind of task . . . (2) to be performed as well as possible by the examinee . . . (3) at some determined future date. This definition disposes of the matter so far as the individual is concerned. However, most exams have another characteristic. They are taken not just by one person, but by a group of persons who are effectively placed in competition with each other by the exam. Let us consider these various characteristics separately.

(1) *a certain kind of task* – This might be to answer oral questions about certain matters, or to write an essay on certain kinds of topics, or to translate a passage from one language to another, or to fill up the blanks in a multiple-choice question, or to carry out a certain kind of project over a given period. It has to be made clear to the candidate what the kind of task is. Sometimes the conveying of this information is left entirely until the examination itself; more often guide-lines are laid down in advance in a syllabus or course of study or become known by tradition. Sometimes the guide-lines are defined by the authority responsible for devising the examination, sometimes by the authority responsible for the course of study on which the exam is based.

(2) *To be performed as well as possible* – In almost every kind of examination some reward is offered either directly or indirectly; it is this reward which encourages the candidate to perform his task 'as well as possible'. The reward may be a monetary or prestige prize or a place in a university or a certificate of competence. But what does 'as well as possible' mean? The criteria for deciding what is a good and what a bad performance may be directly defined or may be hallowed by tradition. It is essential that both candidates and examiners should know what these criteria are. The question also arises as to how the degree of success achieved by the candidate is to be expressed by the examiners. It is sometimes in terms of 'pass' or 'fail';

sometimes in terms of five or six letter-grades; sometimes in terms of percentage marks.

(3) *at some determined future date* – The fact that the students know, not only what kind of task they will be asked to perform and that they must do it as well as possible, but also when it will have to be done, determines one of the most important characteristics of all examinations, namely that the exam exerts an influence on the behaviour of the candidate in the interval between his deciding to take the examination and the event itself.[1] The character of the task to be performed and the known criteria for excellence lead the candidate, who is anxious to receive the reward offered, to practise so that he will be able to do well. The kind of practice is the educationally relevant feature of the examination.

Non-competitive Exams

Before considering the competitive aspect of exams it is worth while to pause and note that some have no obvious competitive aspect. One example is a project exam. I was interested to notice that, in the poly-technical high schools of East Germany, as part of the school-leaving exam, each student was assigned a project for which some six months were allowed. These students were not much aware of anything other than their own task. Similarly, many musicians have called attention to the fact that a concert performance has for them the character of an exam, exerting the same influence on the performer, who is preparing himself for the concert, as the exam exerts on a student preparing to take it. Yet there is no discernable competition involved. Similarly, an athlete often appears to be striving to achieve a standard rather than to do better than another individual. In all these cases, the student, the musician, or the athlete is striving for perfection. He is trying to do his best without necessarily considering what others do. He wants the reward even though, in order to achieve it, he does not – at least obviously – have to do better than anyone else.

Most examinations involve both comparison and competition. All examiners find it impossible when assessing one candidate to ignore the others. Comparison is one of the main aids to reliable assessment or grading. The competitive element affects the examinee rather than the examiner; it is something added to the simple attempt to achieve. In some exams its influence is obvious. Yet, even a great musician is aware of standards set by performers at other times and places, and reflected in the reaction of the audience. The effect of competition can be increased or reduced at will by those devising examinations – mainly by varying the

---

[1] One group of exam-like procedures lacks this characteristic. These, which are usually referred to as 'tests', are better considered quite separately. However, they are noticed briefly at the end of this chapter.

reward and the manner of classifying the successful candidates. In examinations, as in many other fields, standards are settled through competition and codified by comparison.

Assessing Results

This brings us to the different methods used in the process, variously known as marking, grading, or assessing. Some types of exam task can only be assessed by the examiners bringing their almost intuitive judgement to bear while comparing candidate with candidate. On the other hand some tasks can only be graded by the use of marks. The extreme example is provided by objective tests, in which the grade is decided by adding up a large number of independent units. In this case, it might be thought that there was no need to compare candidate with candidate in order to fix standards. Yet it has to be remembered that objective marking can only be graded by resort to statistical procedures which, in effect, also involve comparison – comparison between all the candidates. For example, it is well known that even the examiner who has prepared a paper in mathematics cannot tell whether it will be easy or difficult until it has been tackled by a number of the candidates for whom it is intended. He decides about his 'gradings' only when he has assigned arbitrary 'marks' to a large group of answers. When assessing the work, most examiners are prepared to use a combination of these apparently quite distinct methods. Some examiners, however, believe that absolute standards exist and that they use these when assessing standards. These examiners are not prepared to admit that it is the comparison – conscious or unconscious – which they are continually making between students that enables them to define these standards.

Having noted the main factors which influence the character of an examination we are in a position to consider the different ostensible reasons which have been given for holding examinations.

Ostensible Reasons for Instituting Exams

Perhaps the main reason why exams were held in the first place was that teachers wanted to find out how much their students had learned. In the teaching situation this is most inextricably bound up with a desire to get them to learn more. I am teaching a group to write. Obviously I have to get them to write something; otherwise, neither I nor they will know whether they are achieving what is wanted. A student writes: I criticize his writing: he tries again: I compare his work with that of his neighbours: he is encouraged to do better because his neighbour can. Thus even the simplest form of exam is inevitably (1) an attempt to find out what is known; (2) an attempt to provide an aid to learning; (3) a competition. In many ways finding out what is known turns out to be the least important of the three. Most teachers have a good idea of this without a formal examination. Not so the students; they need to be made to demonstrate to themselves how much or how little they have learned.

Thus, even in the very simplest forms of examination the main features quickly show themselves. For the student the attempt to demonstrate his knowledge or skill becomes a goal – an objective. At the same time he is interested in comparing what he can do with what others can do; he realizes that he is taking part in a competition. Out of these elements the reward – and there is always a reward – assumes importance. It might be merely that he cannot proceed to the next lesson until he has shown himself proficient in the present one. An observant teacher soon notices that competition is a great spur to effort, so he begins to take steps to intensify the competitive element. The first to finish or the best product will be singled out for special praise or for some more concrete reward.

No matter what reasons the theorists may assign for holding an examination, three basic characteristics remain – test of achievement, goal for the student, competition. Examinations, in the West at least, were first devised as an aid to teaching and learning. It seems possible that, in Ancient China – which was the birthplace of examinations – they were first thought of by the emperor as a means of selecting the best people for his civil service. But, very soon, their main function became to encourage good people to prepare themselves for government service. The element of competition was extreme in these imperial exams.

Large-scale Exams

Only when exams are used on a large scale for students with a variety of teachers must the question be asked. 'What is the purpose of this examination?' A good example is the Public Competition for the Senior Civil Service in Britain. When this exam was set up in the nineteenth century there was a long discussion in the House of Commons. It was intended to do away with nepotism and all kinds of favouritism and corruption connected with civil service appointments. The purpose of the new examination, frankly based on the ancient Chinese system, was to select a few hundred very able young men for public service in Britain and for service in India. The first question that had to be decided was, 'What task shall we ask them to perform?' It was decided that the exam should be based on academic studies available in universities. The question as to how to pinpoint for the candidates what kinds of question would be asked was mainly settled by reference to questions set in previous years. The reward was a very substantial one – a permanent post in the higher civil service, with access to all the top jobs, Besides specialized essay-type papers in the selected group of subjects – classics, history, mathematics, etc. – there was an interview. The maximum number of marks assigned for the interview in relation to those for the special subjects was known to the candidates. The marks in different subjects were statistically standardized and combined with those assigned at the interview. Finally, an order of merit was established. Those highest in the list could consider themselves well on the way to a good post.

This type of examination may be contrasted with a university matriculation exam in which the element of competition is supposed not to exist. The student either reaches the required standard in each of the required subjects or he fails to do so. There is generally a printed syllabus of work to be covered and the reward is admission to the university. Instead of an order of merit there is an alphabetical list of students who have passed. These two examinations are the same in all essentials. The main difference is that the civil service exam led the best students to work very hard to get a high placing, whereas, in the matriculation exam, the best students need do little special work because they know they will pass with ease. The weak students have to work very hard to secure a place.

Exams as Prognostic Agents

An interesting point that has to be settled about both these exams is whether or not they give a reliable indication to the authorities about the suitability of the candidates for the work they will be engaged upon after admission. This resolves itself into the question as to whether a person who has carried out a certain task well, will, therefore, be able to do some other job as well. No statistical work is required to see that the more the task resembles the job, the more likely it is that success in the first will be a guarantee of success in the second. It has to be remembered that the life of a university student is very different from that of a high school student; that the methods of teaching are different and the degree of distraction and discipline may be quite different. Still, it is found that success in matriculation correlates quite well with success in finals.

In the case of the civil service the problem is much more difficult. The fact that a student can study assiduously and then do meaningful translations from English into Greek or write interesting scholarly essays on classical philosophy is no guarantee that he will make a good civil servant. It seems more likely to guarantee only that higher civil servants will approach the problems of government in an academic fashion. The realization of this danger led to the institution of the 'interview' as an essential part of the open competition. The interviewing committee was expected to assign low marks to those who seemed impractical or lacking in social qualities of the kind judged to be necessary.

Why Exams are Seldom Discontinued

It can be laid down as a general principle that the main reason for continuing an examination, once established, is that it stimulates students to work well in a direction which will lead to their being more useful in some way. The main reason for discontinuing established examinations is that they have ceased to be necessary as a stimulus to good effort in the educational field. We can illustrate from the exams just mentioned. The Civil Service Examination was instituted to obviate nepotism and to draw a better type of young person into the service. It was discontinued when higher education in universities had become so well and widely established that a good supply of candidates, suitable for recruitment, was available. Matriculation exams in Britain ceased to be important when the school system, with its own leaving exams, was so far advanced that there was no longer need for universities to stimulate would-be university students to work hard. The ancient Chinese exams continued for several thousand years but disappeared when the country had a reasonable school system.

While established exams exist mainly as a goal and a stimulus for students, reasons for their establishment in the first place may have been many and various. One reason is to safeguard a powerful group from criticism or to avoid argument between groups. For instance, degree exams were established in Oxford and Cambridge because each of these universities consisted of separate, powerful, independent colleges. It had to be decided, on some basis that could be generally accepted, how to allocate the degrees among the colleges or, rather, among their students. Until the end of the eighteenth century this had been done by means of Disputations, an elaborate oral exam system carried out in Latin, which gave place to the modern written essay-type exam. According to this view, the main reason why universities have degree exams today is that, without them, students would do little work. Not a bad reason!

Tests Proper

At this point we should note the characteristic differences between examinations proper and tests.[2] Tests have been developed as measuring instruments, pure and simple. They are intended to have none of the effects that have just been mentioned on the work done by students. The person undergoing a test is a passive agent; he does not need to know in advance when he is to be tested; the result need be of no more concern to him than the result of having his weight or blood pressure measured. An 'exam', on the other hand, involves a striving to achieve. The examinee knows when he is to perform his task; he prepares for it; he tries to do well; he *minds* how well he does. Thus, the fact that he is to take the exam influences his educational behaviour. The motivation or tension produced by an examination, the influence on teaching, the relationship to a course

---

[2] This subject is discussed at length in my book, *Exams! Where Next?* P.N.H. Publications, P.O. Box 157, Victoria, B.C.

of study are, for the deviser of tests, non-existent. He is concerned with making sure that he knows what is to be measured; then he uses all his ingenuity to ensure that extraneous factors are weeded out.

It is essential that the student of the theory of examinations should be clear that he is not allowing his grasp of the purpose of the exams he is studying to be weakened by a kind of thinking that has been imported from the field of tests. He will then be able to bring his mind to bear on his main task – to understand how exams should be devised if they are to exert certain stated influences on the students who are to become involved in what could be described as an educational happening. In *Exams! Where Next?*, besides considering the relationship of exams to tests, I have discussed at some length their relationship to the much wider field of competitions, shows, and festivals, the object of which is to stimulate interest and involvement in such things as sports, craft skills, musical performance of individuals or groups, and various agricultural activities.

What Makes a Good Exam?

If an examination is to be successful in achieving the motivation which is its main characteristic, certain conditions must be fulfilled. Three of these conditions may be noted.

(1) The examination must not only be fairly conducted; it must be seen by the candidates to be fair. One of the reasons why exams are not being properly developed in the direction which will foster progressive education is that those responsible are obsessed by the supposed need for absolute objectivity in assessment. They want to safeguard themselves against any arguments about the examiners' verdicts. They therefore avoid any questions or tasks which can only be marked 'subjectively' – the very questions and tasks which we need for their educational value! Actually, these aspects of the matter do not worry students who, generally speaking, are prepared to trust the judgement of those assessing their work. Students know well enough that there is room for argument as to what constitutes a 'good' musical composition, the 'best' dancer or a 'good' essay; but that does not mean they want to forego the opportunity of raising their standards in these activities. All they ask is confidence that examiners are doing their honest best to assess the work fairly; that they are impartial and have not made clerical errors. The rule in Sweden is that examinees see and discuss their written exam work with the examiner after it has been assessed.

(2) The difficulty of the tasks set must be neither too great nor too small. It is no use asking students to solve mathematical problems which are, in the main, beyond them. Nor can one expect examinees to become involved in the exam as an educational happening if they know that the tasks to be performed will be child's play to them.

(3) Attention must be paid to many details that might, at first glance, seem unimportant. In Sweden, for example, students taking written essay type exams are allowed almost twice as long as is given for similar exams in Britain. The extra time is spent in making a fair copy of the work. This exercises a profound influence on the whole school system because students are aware that they must be able to present well set out work. In the German Democratic Republic, candidates taking oral exams are allowed to see the questions they will have to answer half an hour in advance. They sit with paper and pencil but no books, under supervision in another room, with the opportunity to assemble their thoughts. In some exams, e.g. the Cambridge A level G.C.E. Physics, and the College Entrance Board (New York) achievement tests in English, there is – or used to be – a tradition that led the candidates to expect an unknown type of exercise. Such features in themselves have an effect on how students tackle their work in the period before they sit an exam.

The Parting of the Ways

The message of this chapter can be summarized thus: the broad stream of examinations originated in ancient Chinese administrative machinery, in the schools of classical Rome, in medieval universities, and in sixteenth century Jesuit schools, and continued through the separate oral traditions of the *abitur* and the *baccalauréat*, the nineteenth-century British written exams, and the 'new-type' North American exams. This broad stream has now reached a parting of the ways; it is proceeding as two different streams moving in different directions.

One stream is developing into an elaborate system – almost an industry in itself – of objective testing of various kinds, designed to provide an accurate standardized measurement of certain abilities or skills without influencing teacher or student and without creating any tension in the student who, as a result of the test, is expected to fit passively into a framework of aptitudes, skills and abilities or to be placed on a scale of achievements.

The other stream – often now referred to as subjective examinations – is a dynamic part of the whole educational process, involved with motivation and with defining the character of the education in which the student is involved – a type of happening which incorporates many of the characteristics of human life itself – competition and rivalry, purposeful activity directed towards a goal, the planning of a course of work and maintenance of standards.

It is essential that we do not confuse these two quite separate streams, the one properly assigning a passive role to the student, the other frankly designed to activate students in useful directions.

4

Types of Examination

Philip E. Vernon
Professor of Psychology, University of London Institute of Education

While examinations can be used for a number of different purposes and couched in a variety of forms, much the same basic principles of mental measurement apply throughout. In essence they supply us with samples of the knowledge and skills of the pupils or students in a given area, on the basis of which we assess their over-all competence or achievement in that area on a quantitative scale. The samples may consist of written, oral or practical work; if written, the questions may be of the objective type where the student tries to select the right response, or they may require one word or a sentence or two, sometimes calculations or drawings or, most often, extended essays. However in all of these the important thing to consider is – are the tasks representative and trustworthy samples of the competence we wish to assess, or are they unreliable or biased? The final result, again, can be expressed in many ways ranging from imprecise terms like Good or Poor, through Pass-Fail, letter grades and percentage marks, to standard scores or percentiles. But all of these raise the same problem of mental measurement – what do the assessments or numbers mean; how good is a 'Good', or a 70 per cent or an Attainment Quotient of 105, and so on?

Adequacy of Sampling

Any kind of competence is complex; it is made up of many skills, knowledge of facts and their relations, insights and attitudes. Thus a student will vary in his performance according to the questions set. In arithmetic he may know the multiplication tables but be unable to tackle a simple reasoning problem. A budding teacher may be slipshod in preparing lessons, yet excellent in handling his pupils. Hence any one question or task will give only a partial picture, and a good examination should cover all aspects of a subject which are deemed important. If, as so often happens in European secondary schools and universities, the examination requires essay-type answers to a few (say 3 to 6) long questions, these cannot provide good coverage of the total field. Hence a great deal depends on the luck of the questions set, which happen to suit some and seem unduly difficult to others; and if a second paper is set with a different selection of questions on the same topic, there are likely to be considerable discrepances between the two sets of marks. If the results of several papers are combined, as in a university final examination, the resulting reliability will be much more satisfactory, since the errors due to poor sampling on different papers tend to cancel out. Nevertheless it is a reasonable claim by the advocates of the objective examination that, as it includes 50 or 100 or more short questions, it can sample a field much more comprehensively than an essay paper lasting the same time.

Representativeness of Sampling

Are the skills or abilities involved in the examination relevant to the general competence with which we are concerned? Clearly the most suitable type of examination will vary with the subject. In most instances scholastic achievement can be reasonably assessed by written papers, but competence in modern languages should surely include an oral test, while competence in the sciences and some other fields involves appropriate practical work. Obviously the professional skills of a doctor or teacher would be very inadequately sampled by written work only, and it is open to question whether undue stress is not laid on theory papers in the training of such persons.

The kind of use that is to be made of the results also affects the choice of examination. Thus an examination may be set to secondary school students which adequately samples the work done during the past year, but offers little scope for the display of qualities which are relevant, say, to university entrance. The questions may cover knowledge of the syllabus, but a different type of question might better elicit the students' interest, initiative, independent thinking and grasp of the applications of the subject.

Considerable caution is needed in judging what an examination measures from its apparent content. Psychologists have good grounds for being suspicious of the so-called 'face validity' of an examination or test. For example, an examiner may set essay questions which are intended to sample insight in, say, history or geography. But in fact he marks them very largely for: (*a*) accuracy of reproduction of detailed facts; (*b*) agreement of the examinee's views with the examiner's own pet theories; (*c*) length of answers, literary style and legibility. Every examination indeed involves a great many factors, or sources of error, of which the people concerned are only partially aware, but which nevertheless reduce the generality of the results. In the case of essay papers, the outstanding factor might be termed 'the gift of the gab', i.e. ability to write fluently and make a good impression on paper, regardless of subject matter. While this is a perfectly legitimate quality in English essay writing, it is obviously less relevant in a paper in the natural or social sciences. But there is no doubt that examinees who are good at it can often bluff their way through with very little real knowledge of the subject. In the objective or multiple-choice examination, verbal fluency is eliminated, but there are other sources of distortion; in particular, reading, comprehension and sophistication. Whatever the subject matter, the student who can quickly grasp the gist of the question and the provided alternatives is at an advantage. In addition, familiarity in taking such tests enables him to distribute the available time wisely, to make shrewd guesses based on unintended clues in the responses (e.g. the longest of the provided responses is very often the correct one), and to penetrate the tortuosities in which complex items are often wrapped up. Again it seems highly probable that, in the typical oral examination, good or poor marks depend as much on social confidence or 'nerves', and the interaction of the two personalities concerned, as on acquired language skills.

Other Influences

Many students, it is said, 'fail to do themselves justice' in an examination. They have an off day or suffer from examination strain. Such circumstances are apt to be exaggerated; variations in performance on different occasions are more likely to arise from variations in the questions (discussed above), or in the marking (see below) than from variations in mood or health. Admittedly, though, a serious illness or severe emotional trauma can affect the performance of the occasional examinee, and a few may develop neurotic phobias about important examinations. The major problem again is one of representativeness. Is the ability to revise and marshal all one's knowledge, and to commit it to paper in a limited time without recourse to notebooks, sufficiently typical of the competence we are trying to assess? It is probable that work done in class under normal conditions over a year or more, or the production of some form of dissertation in one's own time, provide better samples. However these raise more serious difficulties of assessment than when all examinees tackle the same limited set of questions under rather artificial, but nevertheless uniform, conditions.

A student's success must inevitably depend very largely on the efficiency of his teachers as examination coaches and question-spotters, as well as on his own abilities and industry; and unfortunately, efficient coaching is by no means synonymous with good education in its broadest sense. Many setters, either of essay-type or objective questions, are aware of this and try to set papers which defeat the 'crammer' and favour the well-educated. But the unusual question is apt to be more chancy; many students may misinterpret it, or be thrown into confusion since they have no experience of how to tackle it. Also, the views of different markers on what constitutes a good answer may vary even more than with a relatively conventional paper. Likewise, in an objective test, complex items designed to elicit higher educational qualities rather than knowledge and drills, are particularly liable to contain unsuspected flaws, and it is especially necessary to try them out before using them for examination purposes.

The possibility of guessing a proportion of correct answers introduces a certain amount of unreliability into all objective tests. With 5- or 6-choice items this element is small, but it becomes more serious the smaller the number of plausible alternatives, and is a considerable drawback to the True-False test. Although there has been much discussion and investigation of guessing corrections, and of the effects of differently worded instructions, there are no clear conclusions. In any case the correction only helps to even up the cautious student with the rash guesser and does nothing to reduce the chance error. The influence of other 'response sets' has been noted in such tests, e.g. undue preference for first alternatives; but no doubt many other irrelevant sets affect essay-writing or other types of examination.

Subjectively Marked Examinations: Differences in Distributions

Discrepancies between the marks awarded by different examiners to the same candidates have been pointed out since the 1890s, and were highlighted in the International Examinations Inquiry and the work of Hartog, Rhodes and Burt in the 1930s. Two sources of variation should be distinguished: first, differences in standards (i.e. means or standard deviations) as when one examiner is more generous all round or spreads out his marks more widely than another; and secondly, differences in rankordering or relative grading of the candidates. The former raises the whole question of the 'meaning' of mental measurements.

Having been brought up to accept the marks that teachers, examiners and testers award to us as sacrosanct, we find it difficult to realize that these numbers are not measurements in at all the same sense as physical measurements of, say, height and weight. We tend to assume that a B or Second Class represents some absolute standard of competence which everyone can recognize, or even that 50 per cent means halfway between complete incompetence and perfect competence. Yet innumerable investigations have shown that even experienced examiners differ widely in leniency, in pass and fail rates and in the shape of their distributions, unless their marks are moderated or scaled to uniform standards. Such grades or numbers are in fact merely labels which, in the light of our individual experience as exam-takers and exam-markers, we have learned to attach to subjective notions of various levels of work. The result is that neither the marks given by two examiners to the same papers, nor the marks awarded in different papers or subjects, are comparable. The meaning of a 50 per cent varies with who awards it. True, many examinations such as spelling tests or arithmetic sums, and all objective or new-type tests, yield true numbers in the form of total, or per cent, correct. Yet even these marks vary widely with the difficulty of the questions or items the examiner chooses to set, hence the numbers as such are uninterpretable. Almost any other type of examination – written, oral or practical – involves judgements of quality rather than adding up quantities, and the distributions are therefore highly subjective.

This is not the place to expound statistical theories and techniques, but some indications may be given of the psychometrist's approach to examining. In the absence of any real zero point for scores or marks (technically speaking the scores do not constitute a 'ratio scale'), the effective baseline is fixed in terms of the mean performance of a defined group of examinees, and a 'good' or 'poor' mark is determined by its position in the distribution above or below this mean. It is assumed also that the distribution should conform to the normal or Gaussian curve if the score units are to be accepted as equal throughout. These principles apply both to scores based on counting the number of correct items and to subjectively assessed percentages or grades. Each obtained distribution of 'raw' marks is converted to an arbitrary but uniform and convenient scale, either by adjusting the mean and standard deviation or through the percentile system (cf. McIntosh *et al.*). Thus in the case of an attainment test for, say, 11-year-olds the test is applied beforehand to a representative sample of the age group; the obtained mean score is labelled 100 and scores above and below converted to a scale ranging roughly from 145 to 55 (i.e. standard deviation 15). In a school or university examination involving several examiners of the same, or different, subjects, the same object is achieved if each one awards the same proportion of As or Es, or of 70 per cents, 60 per cents etc. to comparable batches of papers. The process becomes more complex if there is reason to believe that there are real variations in average or spread of ability between different batches, not just variations in setters' or markers' standards, though appropriate moderation or calibration of the marks can usually be effected provided all candidates have taken some other paper or test in common (cf. *Examinations Bulletin* No. 3). There will then be some guarantee that a 70 per cent in Physics is as good as one in French, in the sense that equal proportions of similar students are equally likely to achieve this mark.

Differences in Rank-Ordering

Even when marking scales are comparable, the marks awarded to the same paper by different examiners are liable to vary because different markers are looking for different things. An essay answer, or other extended piece of work, is so complex that no clear criteria for assessment can be laid down, though some improvement can be brought about if the examiners decide in common on what they are marking for (i.e. the correlations between examiners are raised). Even when the same examiner re-marks a set of scripts after an interval, he will be found to have altered his judgements considerably. Here again the reliability of marks can be much improved if the judgements of several examiners are combined, since their various idiosyncrasies tend to cancel out. Indeed, in English essay marking, Wiseman makes a good case for combining the quick-impression marks of four independent markers, rather than relying on more thorough analytic marking according to some marking scheme, by any single marker.

The same holds good of assessments of practical or oral work. Indeed the award of a practical teaching mark is even more difficult because each student who is being assessed is seen in a different situation. Similarly, no direct comparisons of individual projects or dissertations are possible since the topics differ. It is commonly alleged that the new-type examination, composed of multiple-choice or simple completion items, overcomes this subjectivity, since the marking process is objective; there is only one right answer to each item. But this is a misunderstanding: the examiner's subjective views enter at the setting stage instead of at the marking stage. Different examiners who set objective tests in the same subject analyse what good students should be able to do differently, and produce very different items. Hence the correlations between scores on their tests are about as low as the correlations between the results of essay-type papers set and marked by different people. Where they may be superior is where a group of examiners have agreed on a systematic scheme of objectives, and have scrutinized their items to see that these provide a good sampling of the scheme, and are as free as possible from ambiguities. (Similarly, we have seen, the objectivity or reliability of essay examinations is improved by consultation and combination). In addition the major part of the work is done beforehand at convenient times, whereas essay marking often has to be done under pressure in a restricted time. If the objective paper or test can be tried out beforehand, item analysis will reveal weaknesses that can be eliminated, whereas the setters of conventional examinations always have to guess how examinees will interpret their questions, how difficult they are, etc.

Types of Examination: Essay-type

Having surveyed the general problems and principles of examining, we have already mentioned most of the main types. But some additional points may be made about each of these. The essay-type is most widely applicable at secondary and tertiary levels, not only for assessing native language, but in any subject which does not clearly call for calculations, practical or other operations. In theory it offers most scope for the display of higher educational qualities such as reasoning, organization and originality, though in practice the assessment of these is considerably more subjective than that of straight factual knowledge. Its main weakness is that it is used too haphazardly by educationists who rely on the infallibility of their own judgements and standards. Far too few realize the need for clear formulation of agreed objectives, careful scrutiny of sampling in relation to these objectives, and attention to the statistical aspects of marking. Far too many questions are set where the candidates have to guess what the examiner wants (if indeed he knows); and there is experimental evidence that precise indications of what the answers should include improve the reliability. The common plan of allowing candidates a wide choice of questions is almost certainly mistaken, since it allows them to concentrate on a few aspects of the work which frequently turn up and to neglect the rest. Naturally the candidates themselves prefer this, but the only justification one can suggest is that it provides some insurance against several questions being badly set.

Marking should be carried out one question at a time, and the answers should be compared with a clear outline of desirable and undesirable features. Essentially, the marking of each question is a process of rank-ordering the scripts, rather than trying to evaluate their 'absolute' level. When the raw marks for all questions have been totalled, they can be redistributed according to an acceptable scale. Then any script falling near an important borderline (e.g. the possible failures or the B+s/A—s) can be reconsidered and evaluated as a whole. Second and even third markers should mark independently wherever possible, and their judgements averaged or discussed.

Short-answer Papers

In most subjects other than English composition and Philosophy, it is possible to cover most objectives by setting 20 or so rather specific questions, each of which can be answered in a sentence or two or a short paragraph. No choice of questions is allowed. These can be marked much more objectively than 3 to 6 full-length essay-questions, and will spread out the candidates' marks more widely. Thus the short-answer paper possesses several of the advantages of the objective test, but does require candidates to formulate their answers in their own words. While obviously most appropriate to the sampling of factual knowledge, arithmetical skills and the like, it can certainly bring in marshalling, organization and application of knowledge, though, less easily, original, independent thought.

Objective Examinations

The opposition between these and conventional examinations has been over-stressed. Both, as we have seen, have their subjective components, both are liable to distortions and inadequate sampling of competences. The amateur-constructed test, whose items have not been pre-tested, can be very bad indeed. Many items will be too easy or too difficult, or ambiguous and nondiscriminative, and it is likely to concentrate unduly on testing of factual details. American authorities point out, however, that 'higher' educational qualities can and should be sampled, and Bloom has formulated a taxonomy of various categories or levels of educational achievement, illustrating these with specimen items:

   (i) knowledge of facts, concepts, generalizations, methods, etc.;
   (ii) comprehension, interpretation and extrapolation;
   (iii) application of principles;
   (iv) analysis of material, recognizing relations and organization;
   (v) synthesis of parts to produce a new communication (this normally requires essay-type answers);
   (vi) evaluation or judgement.

However, the greater the emphasis on higher qualities, the more complex the items are likely to become, the more they depend on reading comprehension and sophistication, and the greater the need for expert authorship and pre-testing. On the whole, therefore, essay-type examinations are likely to continue to be the predominant instrument for advanced secondary and university examinations, whereas there is a stronger case for objective examinations at more elementary levels and with largely factual, e.g. scientific, subjects. Obviously, though, there is no reason why both should not be employed to test rather different aspects of achievement; in combination they are likely to provide distinctly better sampling. The economic aspects are important also. The larger the number of candidates the more marking time is saved by objective examining. With a small number it is more economic to have essay papers doubly or trebly marked than it is to call on the services of expert test constructors, who are in extremely short supply outside North America.

A further aspect of examining which must always be borne in mind is its 'backwash' effect on methods of instruction and study. Objective examinations provide no incentive to students to write well, and it has been found that they tend to read textbooks with an eye to likely questions. However in answer to this objection it has been pointed out that it is inappropriate to force students to learn English writing by setting essay papers in, say, Science; better to do so through requiring extended essays during ordinary school or homework periods.

Almost all objective examinations nowadays rely on multiple-choice questions with 4 or 5 alternatives, though sometimes the extended form of multiple-choice known as the matching item is useful. These are the most versatile and are particularly suitable for machine-scoring. True-False statements have many defects, and the simple recall or completion type is limited to very elementary knowledge. Nevertheless the National Foundation for Educational Research in England and Wales has produced a long series of English tests for 8- to 12-year-olds, where most items require the writing of words or short sentences. These avoid the backwash of multiple-choice, but can still be marked with almost complete objectivity.

School Records or Assessments of Class Work

These have the great merit of reflecting work done under normal conditions over a considerable period, and we know from follow-up studies of the British '11+' selection examinations that they can provide at least as good estimates of educational capacity over the next few years as any battery of aptitude or attainment tests, probably because the teacher pays considerable attention to qualities of motivation and persistence in making his judgements. This also means, however, that they are affected by 'halo': teachers will tend unwittingly to overrate students whom they like personally and underrate the less amenable or well-behaved student. Hence it is preferable to combine such estimates with the more impersonal evidence of formal examinations or tests. An even greater difficulty is that of variations of standards. Most teachers can rank-order a class of students very accurately, but have little basis for comparing their class with classes in other schools. Thus in university entrance, the selectors can seldom accept such school gradings at their face value, and have to interpret them in the light of their knowledge of each school's, or rater's, standards.

Oral Examinations

As indicated above, these are apt to be particularly unreliable. However, many of the skills involved in foreign language usage can be tested objectively, e.g. oral comprehension by answering multiple-choice questions about a passage heard from tape. The same principle applies as with written work, namely break down the complex totality of conversation, and sample the main components by means of tasks which can be given under standard conditions and scored objectively. The tape recorder is proving of value not only in presentation of tasks, but also for recording responses which can be marked carefully afterwards.

Practical Examinations

In the conventional examination in the natural sciences, very few practical problems can be tackled within a reasonable time, hence sampling is poor and question-spotting and coaching are rife. A better examination can be devised along the lines of the Short Answer paper, in which numerous short tasks are chosen to sample important skills (e.g. identification of biological specimens, completing partially set-up electrical circuits, or taking specified readings, testing chemical substances for particular elements, etc.). Quite large numbers of candidates can be examined simultaneously, moving around from one task to another.

Many competences, however, are too complex to be reduced to standardized elements – practical teaching for example. Even here, however, somewhat greater reliability and objectivity can be achieved if the supervisors or examiners check a standard list of rather specific behaviours. Ryans has shown, for example, that the items on such a list can be combined to yield scores for three major factors or dimensions of good teaching:

X. understanding, friendly, *v.* aloof, egocentric;
Y. responsible, business-like, systematic *v.* evading, unplanned, slipshod;
Z. stimulating, imaginative, enthusiastic *v.* dull, routine.

In addition it is obviously preferable to observe the student teacher in several normal classroom periods, with different classes, rather than basing the final assessment of competence on a single specially-prepared lesson.

Dissertations, Projects, Theses

Here each product is unique and to some extent original, hence assessment may be highly subjective. However, an experienced examiner will have read many other products on comparable topics previously, and will have built up a series of criteria or points to look for; and through co-operation with other examiners he should be familiar with recognized even if imprecise, standards of merit. Nevertheless the best guarantee of reliability is to combine the assessments of three or more such examiners. A candidate's success must obviously depend very greatly on lucky choice of a fruitful topic which interests him, on the quantity and quality of guidance he receives from his supervisor and many other factors outside his control. And yet the work he puts into it normally provides such a broad and varied sampling of his capacities, at every level from correct spelling to critical judgement and creative thought, that most academics, at least, are inclined to accept this as one of the best types of examination. Possibly our trust is misplaced, and scientific follow-up might well show that the quality of, say, a Ph.D. thesis gives rather poor predictions of later professional capacities.

BIBLIOGRAPHY

B. S. Bloom, *Taxonomy of Educational Objectives. Handbook I: Cognitive Domain.* (New York: Longmans Green, 1956.)

F. V. Edgeworth, 'The Statistics of Examinations.' *J. Royal Stat. Soc.*, 1888, **51**, 599–635.

P. Hartog, E. C. Rhodes and C. L. Burt, *The Marks of Examiners.* London: Macmillan, (1936.)

E. F. Lindquist, (ed.) *Educational Measurement.* Washington, D.C.: American Council on Education, (1951.)

D. A. McIntosh, D. A. Walker and D. Mackay, *The Scaling of Teachers' Marks and Estimates* (rev. edit.). Edinburgh: Oliver and Boyd, (1962.)

J. C. Nunnally, *Educational Measurement and Evaluation.* New York: McGraw-Hill, (1964.)

D. G. Ryans, *Characteristics of Teachers.* Washington, D.C.: American Council on Education, (1960.)

Secondary Schools Examination Council, 'The Certificate of Secondary Education: An Introduction to some Techniques of Examining'. *Examinations Bulletin*, No. 3. London: H.M.S.O., (1964).

P. E. Vernon, *The Measurement of Abilities.* London: University of London Press, (1956.)

P. E. Vernon, 'An Introduction to Objective-Type Examinations'. *Examinations Bulletin*, No. 4. London: H.M.S.O., (1964.)

S. Wiseman, 'The Marking of English Composition for Grammar School Selection'. *Brit. J. Educ. Psychol.*, 1949, **19**, 200–209.

Objective Testing

A. J. Stauffer
Associate Professor, College of Education, University of Georgia

The relative merits of objective and subjective tests have been discussed extensively in the educational literature and in school life. The purpose in this chapter is to review objective test premises, objections, biases, construction, and uses. In objective testing, techniques are suggested for improving the teacher-made test.

Premises, Objections, and Biases

In administering a group test to students the examiner assumes a number of premises (knowingly or unknowingly) regarding the individual's physiological and mental state. The physical condition of students varies during the day and from day to day. Anyone assigned the task of administering a test immediately after the students have had a heavy meal or an exhausting day knows that remaining awake is an effort for many testees. Two factors frequently overlooked by the examiner are the temperature of the room and lighting conditions. The adequacy of the testees' physiological system as to visual acuity and hand-eye co-ordination is normally assumed. The test administrator should ascertain that none of these premises is working against the student. This is important in all testing but especially important in objective testing, as the students are frequently compared with a normative group which took the same test in situations approaching ideal conditions.

A number of earlier experimenters have varied test conditions to alter the mental state of the students. For example, Hutt (15) and Standt (23) varied the conditions of test administration to alter the mental state of the student and obtained statistically significant results for the altered test conditions. The demonstrated significant differences caused by varying test conditions indicate the necessity for specifying and adhering to designated test administration procedures.

More recently, experimenters have measured test anxiety and correlated the results with achievement. For example, Sarason, Hill, and Zimbardo (20) are conducting a longitudinal study to determine the relationship of test anxiety to performance on intelligence and achievement tests. Test anxiety as measured by Sarason's *Test Anxiety Scale for Children* was found, in the early childhood years, to have an insignificant negative correlation with changes in achievement and intelligence scores. However, the correlations increased significantly in a negative direction over time through the fifth grade. Sarason plans to conduct follow-up studies of the children through the seventh grade. It will be interesting to observe if the statistically significant negative correlations between anxiety and change in achievement and between anxiety and change in intelligence continue to increase during the school years.

Among the statistical premises causing criticisms of objective tests are those that assume the test scores are normally distributed, that standard scores have equality of units, and that converting from one set of tests scores to another on the basis of mathematical equivalence is appropriate.

Periodically one finds test data presented in which the assumption of normality appears to be violated. Such a result can be obtained by administering achievement tests that are either too easy or too difficult for a given class, or by selecting test items having high internal consistency and a very broad range of difficulty. Skewed distributions are not necessarily bad – in fact they may serve specific purposes better than normal distributions. However, the test designer must know the conditions and the consequences. Fisher (13) presented relatively easy tests based on the K statistics which can be used to determine if the assumption of normality is tenable.

The requirements, underlying assumptions, and appropriate statistics for various categories of numbers were defined by Stevens (24). Whether the requirements and assumptions are satisfied for the statistics used in measurement has been asked by many psychometricians. Emphasis was given to this problem by writers such as Lorge (16) in his discussion of the fundamental nature of measurement. More recently there has been an effort to avoid the requirement for asking the question of equality of units rather than to answer it. Bereiter (3) suggests that today the practical demands for decision-making might be used as a guide for educational theorizing; however, measurement inquiry in the future might be reoriented towards what is logically possible.

Baker (1) suggests that faulty test construction is indicated by a lack of symmetry between intervals on the test score scale and the criterion being measured. Intelligence, aptitude, and achievement tests tend to be furnished with norms covering a number of years in age or grade. Baker recommends a short screening test to approximate the student position on the criterion and an intensive test for the student at that position. Baker would not use the conventional item analysis of difficulty and internal consistency but would use item characteristic plots. The item characteristics which are plotted are the criterion variable against the proportion of students selecting the desired response. This method is time-consuming and has not been utilized extensively in test construction. However, today, a complete computer programme is available for estimating the statistics.

Test publishers are frequently requested by the users to provide tables of equivalences among non-parallel tests. Before honouring this request, one should establish the premises of the same content or psychological function measured, and the equivalence of test populations and using situations. To the extent that these premises are not satisfied, the precision of the conversion tables is reduced. The reduction normally favours the less capable student and less reliable test.

Objection has been raised against the objective tests on the ground that they contain culture biases. The performance of an individual on a test is a combination of his ability and experiences as related to the content of the test. Certain groups are reasoned to have been deprived of many test-related experiences. Thus, attempts have been made to remove those biases. Cattell (4) has offered a culture 'fair' test, and Davis and Ells (8) have their culture 'free' test. Psychometricians are not agreed that either objective has been achieved or that either is desirable. More recently Coffman (5) investigated the evidence of culture factors. Coffman concluded that one should inquire into the significance of each test item, language usage and testing-time limits in the new culture.

Objective tests have been criticized repeatedly for determining the curriculum content. In this chapter several methods are suggested for test development to assure that the test conforms to an existing curriculum. In developing a course of instruction for a new area there is a current trend to follow an operations analysis approach such as that of the United States Air Force (29). In the operations analysis approach the tests are developed concurrently with the other training materials. Compatibility of tests with the total course of instruction is designed into the programme.

Objective tests have been criticized for the ways in which they are used. Standard practices for distributing tests and reporting results are being debated. It is to be noted that it is the practices relating to testing that are questioned, not the essential nature of objective tests.

Objective Test Construction and Uses

The objective test is defined as one consisting of questions in which the keyed answer is determined when the item is written and the total score is some selected combination of the student responses. The objective test does not, by definition, determine the objectives of the course nor the mental process utilized in obtaining the keyed response. The objective test can be teacher-made or standardized. The objective test is

TABLE I: EDUCATIONAL TESTS AND MEASUREMENT

Objectives of the Course The Student:	Supporting Content of Course	Process Used in Measurement					Number of Test Items
		Recall	Comprehension	Application	Analysis Synthesis	Evaluation	
1 Learns a brief historical background of educational measurement	Work of Wundt, Galton, Cattell, and Binet; Measurement in four periods since 1900	3					3
2 Acquires a brief over-view of measurement	Evaluation and measurement; Observation techniques; Functions measured; Individual differences	4					4
3 Develops an understanding of teacher-made tests	Objectives, Functions, Content, Item types, Scoring Characteristics	1	2	2			5
4 Writes test items	Multiple choice, Matching, True-False, Essay	1	1	1	1	1	5
5 Administers a test	Directions, Timing, Key, Reproduction of test, Scoring	1	1	1		2	5
6 Interprets test scores	Frequency Distribution, Mean, Mode, Median, Histogram, Standard Deviation, Correlation		1	1	2	1	5
7 Develops a working knowledge of normative data	Norms, Percentiles, Standard Scores, Profiles	1	1	1	2	1	6
8 Acquires an understanding of desired test characteristics	Validity, Reliability, Objectivity, Practicality, Criterion		1	1	2	2	6
9 Gains experience in finding test information	Indexes, Abstracts, Sources, Types of information, Evaluation	3	1	1			5

designed to measure such functions as ability, achievement, and aptitude.

Test construction methods and techniques are rather common to the various functional measures. The approach in test construction is first to define the test objectives and outline the content. Items are written sampling the content and employing the desired mental processes. The items are reviewed by a group of people normally including subject matter, test construction, and language specialists. The items are assembled in a try-out test form and administered. The data from the try-out test are analysed to obtain the internal consistency and difficulty of the items. The items are selected and revised according to the analysis. The revised test form is administered to obtain normative data, estimates of reliability, and error of measurement. However, when a pure factor test is developed a factor analytic is sometimes used as an alternate in determining the internal consistency measure.

In this chapter the test purpose, construction, and use are discussed with reference to the teacher-made achievement test. The choice is based upon the idea that greatest opportunity for immediate improvement lies in this area. The teacher-made test should be designed to measure the student's achievement in relation to the specific course objectives, content, mental processes employed, and topic emphasis. In addition to these specific course features the teacher should also be concerned with the common characteristics of tests such as item difficulty, internal consistency, and norms.

The practices used in constructing teacher-made tests have evolved through the years. Thorndike and Hagen (26) describe a test plan in which the course objectives are defined and the content for the teacher-made test is outlined. An outline for the test is prepared to assure that the content conforms with the objectives of the course. Bloom *et al.*, (2) in the *Taxonomy of Education Objectives*, presents a classification device for six major classes of educational objectives: 'Knowledge; Comprehension; Application; Analysis; Synthesis; Evaluation'.

The two concepts, test outline and taxonomy, can be combined as a guide in preparing teacher-made achievement tests. A guide used in preparing an Educational Test and Measurement achievement test is shown in Table I. The specific objectives, supporting content, mental processes, and topic emphasis (number of items) are depicted. The author finds this model helpful in providing guidance for item writing.

The reader might question the capability of a teacher correctly to categorize items by mental process. Indeed, the process might differ with the amount of knowledge possessed by the student. However, Stanley and Bolton (21) and Stoker and Kropp (25) found that raters demonstrated a high degree of agreement in categorizing items using the Bloom

Taxonomy, and McGuire (17) has employed the taxonomy in the construction of medical examinations.

After the test items are written, reviewed and tried out, an item analysis is performed. There are many methods of item analysis, and each method can be expected to yield a comparable solution; that is, approximately the same items will be selected for the revised test. The author has a habit of utilizing the method of item analysis described by Flanagan (10). If the table (Abac) contained in reference 10 is not available, the method described by Findley (12) is suggested. This method has simplicity and ease of computation to recommend it. In schools having computer service available, a complete item analysis utilizing conventional statistics is recommended.

An alternate approach to the test guide and item analysis has been developed by the Educational Testing Service (9). Booklet No. 4 provides a 'guide for teachers' in 'making the classroom test', and No. 5 gives 'short-cut statistics for teacher-made tests'. This alternate approach tends to be less exacting and more easily understood in its taxonomy and statistics.

A word of caution is given to the classroom teacher selecting items according to an item analysis. If any given category of the taxonomy is represented by a great number of items, those items tend to contribute more to the total score and to have higher internal consistency coefficients. Thus, items might be discarded because they belong to a small group. Cox (6) has demonstrated this tendency. The problem can be avoided by computing the item analysis for each mental process separately.

Dane (7), in his paper delivered to the International Conference on Educational Testing, cited surveys in which more than 90 per cent of achievement test items were found to be information questions. Dane developed a model for the construction of objective-based test items using processes other than recall. The bases are the instructional objective and content topic. In this procedure the nature and boundaries of the objective and content topic are internalized by the item writer to discover an appropriate testing situation. After the situation is discovered the item writer chooses form, language, expected answer, difficulty, and discrimination values for the test items. Either approach, that of Dane, Educational Testing Service, or the guide, should assist the classroom teacher in improving teacher-made tests.

The topic of creativity is somewhat difficult to classify. Some experimenter would place it after evaluation in Bloom's *Taxonomy*. Objective test questions for creativity tests have been written in the form of completion items and scored by summing the number of unique responses. Recent experimenters tend to write operational definitions for creativity, observe the creative process, develop tests, and recommend classroom conditions for developing creativity. Starkweather (22) noted problems encountered in testing pre-school children for creativity and observed that the children tend to suggest solutions. Merrifield (18) distinguished between facilitating and differentiating items in creativity tests. The facilitating items are common information to the testees and the differentiating items are the discriminating. Merrifield recommends that the differentiating items be used in determining the factors of creativity and in interpreting the results. Michaels (19) indicated that special tests for measuring creativity are required and suggested a committee consisting of a psychometrician, guidance counsellor, teacher, and students for developing those tests.

Torrance (27) has defined creativity operationally and proceeded to observe it in the behaviour of children. He has conducted numerous studies to test hypotheses about conditions in the classroom which promote creativity. Torrance cautions that the average teacher tends to require and reward conformity rather than creativity. Based upon these studies Torrance developed a series of learning experiences for teachers to improve their skill in nurturing creativity. In addition, Torrance (28) has recently published the Torrance *Test of Creative Thinking*, measuring the following aspects: fluency, flexibility, originality, and elaboration.

Modern technology is playing an increasing role in objective testing. Hopkins, Lefever, and Hopkins (14) conducted a study of 'TV vs. Teacher Administration of Standardized Tests: Comparability of Scores'. An analysis of variance indicated no significant difference in test means for the specific aspect of television and teacher administration. Problems, exercises, texts, and tests have been programmed on computer systems and the resulting materials have been found feasible for learning in an operational situation. Thus, television and computer assistance hold promise for accomplishing the massive and routine aspects of both objective testing and instruction.

Objective tests are currently being utilized in many major evaluative programmes, for example, Project Talent (11) and Educational Opportunities Survey (30). Included in Project Talent objectives were 'to survey the available talent, to identify predictors of creativity, and to study procedures for realizing individual potential' of selected high school students in the United States. The battery included measures of ability achievement, interest, biographical information, and student activities. Follow-up studies are planned for 1, 5, 10, and 20 years later. During the initial testing it was found that variance within groups is great compared to variance between groups for ability, learning rate, understanding, and subject matter knowledge. The test results have strong implications for practices in the school programmes. In the first year follow-up the lack of utilization of talent in the United States was apparent. Later follow-ups should show whether this trend increases and recommend procedures for better utilization.

In the Educational Opportunities Survey a test battery measuring mainly comprehension, ability, and general information was administered to students in public schools. In addition, questionnaires were completed by the students, teachers, principals, and superintendents of those schools. The purpose of the survey and questionnaires was to determine whether between-school variance in achievement was significant for various ethnic groups. As a result of the survey, not only was equal opportunity questioned but also the criterion for measuring it.

Thus, in two major evaluation programmes, objective tests were utilized in efforts as diverse as investigating talent utilization in a society and establishing a partial basis upon which to make decisions regarding educational opportunities.

Summary

Objective tests are a tool. The tool is being refined and improved. With the increased availability of computer service and knowledge of operations analysis techniques, improvement in objective testing is expected to accelerate. The value of tests is pragmatically suggested by their expanded applications. There remain the partially completed tasks of improving objective test characteristics and utilization.

BIBLIOGRAPHY

1 F. B. Baker, 'An Interaction of Test Score Interpretation and Item Analysis.' *Journal of Educational Measurement*, **1**, (1964,) pp. 23–28.

2 B. S. Bloom, Editor. *Taxonomy of Educational Objectives. Handbook I: Cognitive Domain*, (New York: David McKay Company, Inc., 1956).

3 Carl Breiter, 'How May Units of Measurement Be Safely Ignored?' *Journal of Educational Measurement*, **1** (1964), pp. 19–22.

4 R. B. Cattell and A. K. S. Cattell, *IPAT Culture Free Intelligence Test*, (Champaign, Ill.: 1963).

5 W. E. Coffman, 'Evidence of Cultural Factors in Response of African Students to Items in an American Test of Scholastic Aptitude,' *Twentieth Yearbook, National Council on Measurement in Education* (East Lansing, Michigan: 1963), pp. 27–37.

6 R. C. Cox, 'Item Selection Techniques and Evolution of Instructional Objectives', *Journal of Educational Measurement*, **2** (1965), pp. 181–85.

7 R. H. Dane, 'Objective-Based Testing in Subject Fields'. *International Conference on Education Testing*. (Berlin: Mimeographed, 1967), pp. 1–17.

8 A. Davis and K. Ells, *Davis-Ells Games: Davis Ells Test of General Intelligence or Problem Solving Ability*. (New York: World Book Co., 1953).

9 Educational Testing Service, 'Test and Measurement Kit'. (Princeton, New Jersey: *Evaluation and Advisory Service*), Booklets No. 4 and 5.

10 J. C. Flanagan, 'General Considerations in the Selection of Test Items and a Short Method of Estimating the Product – Moment Coefficient from data at the Tails of the Distribution'. *Journal of Educational Psychology*, **30**, (1939), pp. 674–680.

11 J. C. Flanagan, J. T. Dailey, *et al.*, Project Talent: 'The Identification, Development and Utilization of Human Talent'. *Final Report*, Project Talent Office, University of Pittsburgh (1964).

12 W. G. Findley, 'A Rationale for Evaluation of Items Discrimination Statistics', *Educational and Psychological Measurement*, **16**, (1956), pp. 175–180.

13 R. A. Fisher, 'Moments of Sampling Distribution', *Proceedings of the London Mathematical Society*, **30**, (1928), pp. 199–238.

14 K. K. Hopkins, D. W. Lefever and B. R. Hopkins. 'TV vs Teacher Administration of Standardized Tests: Comparability of Scores', *Journal of Educational Measurement*, **4** (1967), pp. 35–40.

15 M. L. Hutt, 'A Clinical Study of Consecutive and Adaptive Testing with the Revised Stanford-Binet', *Journal of Consultant Psychology II* (1947), pp. 93–103.

16 Irving Lorge, 'The Fundamental Nature of Measurement', *Educational Measurement, American Council on Education*, Chapter 14 (Washington, D.C.: 1951), pp. 553–50.

17 Christine McGuire, 'Research in the Process Approach to the Construction and Analysis of Medical Examination', *Twentieth Yearbook National Council on Measurement in Education* (East Lansing, Michigan: The Council, 1963), pp. 7–16.

18 P. R. Merrifield, 'Facilitating vs. Differentiating Components of Creativity', *Journal of Educational Measurement*, **1** (1964), pp. 103–107.

19 W. B. Michael, 'The Realization of Reliable and Valid Criterion Measures for Special Undergraduate Programs and Courses Aimed at the Development and Expression of Creative Behavior', *Journal of Educational Measurement*, **1** (1964), pp. 97–102.

20 Sarason, Hill, and Zimbardo, 'A Longitudinal Study of the Relation of Test Anxiety to Performance on Intelligence and Achievement Tests', *Monogram of the Society for Research in Child Development*, **27**, No. 7.

21 J. C. Stanley and D. Bolton, Book Review, *Educational and Psychological Measurements*, **17** (1957), pp. 631–634.

22 E. K. Starkweather, 'Problems in the Measurement of Creativity in Preschool Children', *Journal of Educational Measurements*, **1** (1964), pp. 109–113.

23 V. M. Standt, 'The Relationship of Test Conditions and Intellectual Level', *Journal of Psychology*, **26** (1948).

24 S. S. Stevens, 'On the Theory of Scales of Measurement', *Science*, **103** (1946), pp. 677–680.

25 H. W. Stoker and R. P. Kropp, 'Measurement of Cognitive Processes', *Journal of Educational Measurement*, **1** (1964), pp. 39–42.

26 R. L. Thorndike and E. Hagen, *Measurement and Evaluation in Psychology and Education*, (New York: John Wiley & Sons, Inc., 1961), pp. 27–50.

27 E. P. Torrance, *Rewarding Creative Behavior: Experiments in Classroom Creativity*, (Englewood Cliffs: Prentice Hall, Inc., 1965).

28 E. P. Torrance, *Torrance Tests of Creative Thinking*. (New Jersey: Personnel Press, Inc., 1966).

29 USAF System Command, *System Command Manual AFSCM* 300.1F. (Washington, D.C.: United States Air Force, 1966). Part Q.

30 U.S. Office of Education, 'Equality of Educational Opportunities'. (Washington, D.C.: U.S. Government Printing Office, 1966).

6

Guidance Testing

Zeev Sardi
Director, Hadassah Vocational Guidance Institute, Jerusalem

Guidance and counselling services are used more extensively today than ever before. This stems from the necessity for continuous adaptation to an ever more rapidly changing environment. Choice situations and dilemmas follow in quick succession, while alternatives are more numerous today than they were before. The resulting problems are, therefore, more complex and numerous.

Vocational adjustment seems to be particularly difficult. Here the dilemmas are more tangible: the choice made must be implemented and steps once taken are difficult to revoke. Above all, the occupational world is probably expanding and changing faster than most other environmental factors. While the scope of occupations and specializations and of present and future job opportunities is constantly expanding and training facilities are becoming more and more diversified, there is much lack of elementary knowledge in this field among youngsters about to make their vocational choice. Accordingly, they find themselves in a considerable state of confusion and anxiety. No wonder that the new profession of vocational guidance has been rapidly gaining ground.

Whether a person seeks the help of a vocational counsellor or not, he can choose wisely only on the basis of reliable information in two main areas: about occupations and how to prepare for them, and about himself and his development in relation to the world of careers. Test results may help him to achieve the necessary self-knowledge.

Testing in Vocational Guidance

Psychometric tests and inventories are probably the most reliable tools for establishing objective data about a person. Though developed mainly for selection purposes, they can also be effectively used in guidance and counselling. These tests and inventories, predicated on the existence of congenital and acquired individual differences, try to measure a person's special traits: his achievements and aptitudes, interests and values. Today only very few counsellors consider these to be independent characteristics. Interest may originate both from values and from past achievements.

Aptitude can be defined almost solely in terms of achievement, and can certainly not be measured otherwise. The measurement of these traits is no easy matter, especially since they also are not very stable. Research and experience show that people's needs change and with them their values and interests, whereas the use of test results, especially for prediction, presupposes a comparative stability of traits. The main difficulties seem to be how to construct tests capable of predicting success in specific occupations, and how to relate results of non-specific tests with occupational requirements. With some effort, occupations may be classified in terms of human traits, but the overlap between the tasks comprised within one occupation and another and of the traits required, often makes it difficult to apply test results to vocational choice.

Considering the difficulty of defining and measuring personality factors and the constant and rapid change in occupational requirements, it seems extraordinary that any progress at all has been achieved in vocational guidance testing. Nevertheless, progress has been remarkable. Achievement can now be objectively measured in most areas by the use of achievement tests and can to a great extent be predicted from the results of aptitude tests. After a certain age, interests have been proven to be comparatively stable and they can be related to factors conducive to vocational success. Value statements, though there is little agreement among psychologists on their definition and interrelation, can be used to forecast differential satisfaction in various study and work activities. Though the present measuring instruments may often seem rather crude they are a valuable source of information and generally provide better predictors than most other means, such as interviews, rating scales, etc. They are particularly useful in predicting success in studies, which is an important, though not the only, prerequisite for successful job performance. The better constructed and validated aptitude tests yield correlation coefficients of 0·50 to 0·60 with success in vocational training or work, and when several such tests are combined into batteries, the multiple correlation may even be higher. Personality tests and inventories measuring values and interests are still comparatively the least reliable and valid, partly because their development started later, and partly because these factors still escape exact definition in measurable terms.

Testing and Guidance in the Schools

One of the goals of school is to prepare its pupils for life. Since most of a person's waking life is spent at work, preparation for vocational life is an important part of this goal.

Though as a rule the vocational choice is made at a specific point of time, for instance at the end of formal schooling, it is usually preceded by a series of cognitive or emotional interim decisions. The choice of courses and streams of studies is the result of previous school experience and at the same time the basis for future vocational decisions. This means that vocational choice is a process continuing throughout the whole schooling period. The pupil's self-image is, of course, also affected by other factors, such as his home environment, but school experiences probably account for most of the self-image which is later translated into vocational terms. At any rate, school must be considered the crucial period for often irreversible, pre-vocational decisions. Therefore both vocational and general counselling are called for in school settings. Tests and inventories are useful tools for both these functions. They enable the teacher and the counsellor to present their pupils with objective data on which the latter may base their decisions.

Testing and Vocational Guidance in Israel

Vocational guidance – and tests – were first introduced in the Jewish community of what was then Palestine after its sudden population and economic growth during the early 1930s. Test results were used mainly in the last (eighth) grade of elementary school for purposes of guidance and selection. Even today, most testing is done in school, and is therefore mainly pre-vocational, but a few public and private institutes also offer more vocationally-oriented testing facilities.

The great cultural diversity of Israel's present population is a handicap to objective measurement. The use of test results of younger children for predicting future school success may be misleading owing to the un-avoidable cultural bias. For new immigrants and their children, tests may represent an unaccustomed task and the results may be greatly influenced by temporary adaptation difficulties. Tests are therefore more often used for establishing the present situation than as indicators of future achieve-ment and work satisfaction. Much stress is put on re-testing to determine the rate of change and of learning. Nevertheless fairly good results have been obtained with achievement-aptitude batteries designed to predict future success in studies and at work.

The tests are either constructed locally along generally accepted prin-ciples, or adapted from foreign – mainly American, French, or German – sources. Verbal tests are in Hebrew, though for new immigrants other languages are also used. Since only few tests are used on a country-wide basis, their standardization is sometimes rather poor. The usual criterion for validity studies is success in vocational or academic training. High correlation coefficients have been obtained: 0·55 for high school studies, 0·75 for training in dentistry, etc. The application of tests can therefore drastically cut down drop-out rates. The main weakness of the present testing programmes is the lack of well-constructed and validated interests and personality inventories, and efforts are now being made to fill this gap.

Pre-vocational and vocational guidance standardized group tests are used mainly at the following stages:

(1) In the eighth grade, for guidance on further studies. The aptitude-achievement test (the 'Seker') usually comprises about eighty questions, and every year a new edition is compiled by the Ministry of Education. It is administered by the class-teacher under an outside supervisor and is then centrally machine-scored. Results are used in conjunction with school grades. The total year-class of about 50,000 pupils is tested.

(2) In the seventh and eighth grade, for guidance on the type of post-elementary education (vocational, academic, agricultural, etc.). Test batteries consist mainly of aptitude tests, which are developed by various agencies and administered and evaluated by psychologists of the local educational-psychological services. Since there usually is no such service except in the towns, aptitude testing is available to only about 60 per cent of the year-class.

(3) Before entering the ninth grade, for admission to certain vocational or academic high schools (i.e. selection).

(4) In the ninth or tenth grade, for guidance on the field of specialization (humanities, science, etc.) in academic high schools, and different trades in vocational high schools.

For stages 3 and 4 the aptitude test batteries sometimes include performance tests. The batteries are custom-built on the basis of follow-up studies in each school – especially the vocational schools.

(5) Applicants to some university departments and other post-high-school courses have to pass aptitude tests.

In addition, individual testing – sometimes as an extension of group testing – is carried out by psychologists in the local guidance services and other public agencies at the request of the schools. Predominantly foreign tests are used (WISC, Stanford-Binet, Bender, etc.) which are adapted to and standardized in Israel.

Vocational guidance and counselling proper are still not considered the task of the schools but are left to public agencies or private psychologists. Selection by means of tests is widespread and is extensively applied by the Israel Army, the Civil Service, and various public institutes and industries.

The extent to which tests are used and the reliance placed on the results varies. For counselling or guidance the test results are generally integrated with data obtained from other methods of appraisal, but in selection or admission they constitute the major part. The weight attached to them is determined by the validity of the specific test for the purpose at hand and the philosophy of the institute or psychologist in charge.

Summing up

Only half a century ago considered a magic tool by some and a sham by others, tests have now found a permanent place in vocational guidance. In Israel, as in other countries, counsellors now use them as one of many means to obtain comparatively objective information on such aptitudes, interests and values as are known to influence future need-satisfaction at work. Especially in guidance however, test results are by no means considered infallible and are never used exclusively but only cautiously in conjunction with other information. They usually are given greater weight for selection purposes, in school as well as in other settings.

Considering that the main purpose of tests in guidance is to develop the client's self-knowledge so as to enable him to make a wise vocational choice at every new stage in his career, they certainly have an important role to play. Yet in view of the multitude and heterogeneity of the available tests it has become the general rule that each test should always be considered on its own merits.

It may be added as an afterthought that since a comparatively high level of accuracy has already been reached in the testing of personal traits it would seem that increasing attention should be devoted to the less developed tools of vocational guidance, such as occupational information facilities, group guidance techniques, decision-making procedures, and the development of vocational maturity. Real progress in vocational guidance can only be made by advancing on all fronts.

BIBLIOGRAPHY

Leo Goldman, *Using Tests in Counseling*. (New York: Appleton-Century-Crofts, 1961).

Hadassah, Vocational Guidance Institute, numerous unpublished follow-up studies. (Jerusalem, Israel).

International Bureau of Education and Unesco, *The Organization of Educational and Vocational Guidance*. Publication No. 254, 1963, pp. 80–82.

Maurice Reuchlin, 'Pupil Guidance' Council for Cultural Co-operation of the Council of Europe. Education in Europe, Section II, No. 3. (Strasbourg, 1964).

Z. Sardi, 'Vocational Guidance in Israel' in *Youth Employment*. Special Overseas Issue, County Youth Employment Office, Civil Service, St. Albans Heitz. Summer 1967, pp. 38–41.

Donald E. Super and John O. Crites, *Appraising Vocational Fitness by Means of Psychological Tests*. (New York: Harper, 1962).

Section III: Introduction

Efficiency of Examinations

Brian Holmes
Reader in Comparative Education in the University of London

In this section particular attention is paid to the technical efficiency of examinations and tests. The cultural norms which help to determine the purposes of examinations and what is 'fair' or just about the types used and the way they are administered, are not considered in any depth. The two major tests of efficiency, reliability and validity are discussed. Mr Cox takes the term reliability to mean 'the differences that occur when we repeat what is meant to be exactly the same measurement' (p. 71). He outlines the complexity of the factors which affect reliability and make it difficult to assess. A summary in historical perspective of the published evidence on reliability is given (p. 72) and the classic work of Hartog and Rhodes is again given prominence. Research into the reliability of English essays, mathematics honours papers, and history honours papers is very briefly reviewed along with notes on other researches and criticisms of examinations on these grounds (p. 73). The latter persist and are in many cases justified.

F. Bacher in Chapter 9 classifies some of the major criticisms of traditional methods of assessing knowledge. She refers to evidence from comparing average marks and to the dispersion of marks awarded by different examiners, to the correlation between marks obtained in different types of examination (oral/written) on the same subject, and to the errors introduced when assessments of a year's work are made (pp. 95–7). Mme Bacher then goes on to indicate how objectivity in marking may be improved by adjusting the marks of examiners to bring their averages and dispersions into alignment (p. 98). This assumes, of course, that the rank orders are more or less the same. But the achievement of this itself constitutes a major problem. It may be met, to some extent, by standardizing marking schemes 'indicating the number of points to be given to each question and the weight to be attached to each kind of mistake' (p. 98).

An account is given by Dr Weiss in Chapter 10 of procedures adopted in Austria to ensure some 'unity of marking' over the country as a whole (p. 101). Two criteria are involved. The external criterion attempts to rate performances required for the different grades by the Ministry of Education. It would suffice if different teachers evaluated the same performance of a pupil on the basis of approximately equal standards. But over the country as a whole, this is impossible; consequently, an internal criterion is used. Performance is measured against the average reached by the class. The reliability of these methods was tested by asking more than one hundred men and women teachers to evaluate performance in composition and arithmetic tests. Weiss concludes that the number marking system 1–5 for stated qualities (spelling, interest, style), was 'extremely unreliable in marking compositions and, to a smaller extent, also in marking arithmetic tests' (p. 107).

As for validity, Cox concludes that 'as long as examinations remain as unreliable as most still are, validity must, of course remain low' (p. 77). In order to assess whether an examination is valid the aims of education need to be stated and ways devised of assessing whether they have been achieved. Examinations are themselves frequently taken to be the most effective instrument of measuring educational aims. If these are stated in very broad terms, the achievement of them may be extremely difficult to measure. It is difficult to invent ways of measuring much more specific aims. One solution, of course, is to ignore the issue of validity or transform it by studying the extent to which examination marks have predictive value. S. Marklund discusses in detail the problem of regulating access to higher education in Sweden (p. 81). He acknowledges the fundamental role school marks play but maintains that selection for higher education 'cannot for long be based *only* on marks awarded in schools' (p. 81). He examines how successful prediction is to be defined, what predictors may be used, the correlations obtained between success in further studies, and the type of assessment used according to types of criteria and predictors (p. 86).

Of course, this analysis limits the scope of educational outcomes to success in further studies. The difficulties of predicting success in other spheres of life are enormous. But success in school examinations has been taken as an indication that a person will do well in business, politics and industry, as well as in education. The possibilities of using the criterion of successful prediction as a measure of reliability offer, in a subtle way, an alternative test of reliability. The difficulties are enormous if the manifold social and political overtones of education are included among those which are to be predicted by examination or test results. Some of these problems are dealt with in later chapters.

7

Reliability and Validity of Examinations

Roy Cox
Research Officer, University of Essex

It is now over thirty years since Hartog, Rhodes and Burt wrote *The Marks of Examiners* (1936). But although this book revealed the extreme difficulty of reliably marking long essays of the traditional type of exam, only in the United States of America has the practice of examining changed significantly, and even there the only widespread change has been the introduction of 'objective' exams for limited purposes. There are many reasons for this inertia (Cox, 1967), but now there are signs that the attitudes of both staff and students are changing and the problem is whether innovation and improvement can overtake the disillusion and rejection which is becoming only too apparent. The situation is critical since this growing criticism comes at a time when examination qualifications are becoming increasingly important – there is, in fact, an increase in the external rewards while the internal reward of recognition of competence which is meaningful to the students themselves, their peers and the staff diminishes. If this continues, there will be an increasing dissociation between assessments and educational aims – exams may be thought of entirely in instrumental terms and completely divorced from the opportunity for intellectual self-expression. There are signs that a defensive stereotype is developing which encourages exaggeration of the present deficiencies of this exam system and a contracting-out of the exam system as a source of personal esteem. But the importance of the system to the students' future means that something must take its place and this tends to be a cynical development of exam techniques.

From recent research at Essex University it does not seem that lack of reliability is the prime focus of student discontent, but this is partly due to the fact that it is only recently that the evidence which has been gathering dust for so many years, has begun to be discussed at all widely. The danger now is that the somewhat scandalous nature of the evidence as it becomes better known will be taken up by the more militant students in a destructive way which will either drive examiners into a defensive position or encourage premature reforms which will soon have to be retracted if educational practice is not to be seriously distorted. If this is to be avoided it is important that the evidence should no longer be ignored, and the main aim of this paper is to give an introduction to some of the research on reliability and mention some of the problems concerned with validity.

I. RELIABILITY

Unfortunately space does not allow a detailed inquiry into both the sources of different types of error in examining and the particular studies that have been made of different subjects, so only a brief mention will be made of the general problem of error.

The use of 'reliability' in this context is not quite the same as its common use. It is used here to refer to the differences that occur when we repeat what is meant to be exactly the same measurement. Even with this use, however, the term is still vague and there may be some point in dropping it and only thinking in terms of particular aspects of reliability like homogeneity, stability or marker variability. The factors involved are certainly very complex. In the process of marking, examiners themselves are likely to vary in alertness and attitude and different examiners have different approaches. Candidates may choose different questions and the papers vary from year to year. Instruction for different students even in the same year can be quite variable and, of course, the fitness of the students is likely to vary even more than that of the examiners. M. Dunstan (1966) has recently discussed a formidable list of sources of error covering observation conditions, readers' acuity, suitability of the instrument or scale, idiosyncracies of different instruments, inconsistencies of an instrument, inappropriate treatment of readings (including questionable assumptions about unidimensionality of marks), sampling fluctuations of the characteristics, and the medium of observation. Variations between examiners which result simply in different average marks for the same or similar students may not be serious, since the marks can easily be adjusted in a common mean. Differences in the range or dispersion of marks awarded by different examiners can again be adjusted – this time to a common standard deviation, but when this is not done examiners with a wide range will carry more weight in the final result than narrow-range markers. Most error, however, is probably more random than this and cannot be mechanically corrected although of course 'corrected' is in many ways an inappropriate word for this manipulation.

What, then, is the published evidence on reliability?

A classic in this field is the work of Hartog and Rhodes, but it should not be regarded as a lone piece of evidence on examination reliability; as early as 1888 an English statistician, Edgeworth, was reporting considerable divergences amongst examiners. In 1913 D. Starch reported wide divergences in English and mathematics essays. In 1930 W. C. Eells had sixty-one teachers re-mark two history and two geography essays at an interval of eleven weeks. The average correlation between the two markings was 0·365. (The correlation coefficient is an index of the relationships between variables. If it is 0·0 it is completely random, whereas 1·0 denotes a one to one relationship; less than 0·2 might be described as negligible, 0·2 to 0·4 as small). On individual essays it was 0·25, 0·51, 0·31 and 0·39. Three years later G. P. Williams reported that when almost a hundred teachers marked fifty mathematics essays, one of these received marks from 16 to 96 (out of 100) and another from 26 to 92.

There was thus quite a lot of rather tentative research available when the Carnegie Corporation of New York gave funds to support an International Conference on Examinations. At this conference, national commissions were set up to produce evidence for discussion at later conferences. The English Commission of eight members contained three very eminent psychologists, Cyril Burt, C. E. Spearman and Godfrey Thomson. The experiments carried out by this commission were extremely rigorous and every attempt was made to select only very experienced examiners and avoid any artificiality. The scripts used for marking were not specially written ones but were taken from actual examinations. The results are most fully set out in *The Marks of Examiners* by Hartog and Rhodes with Cyril Burt (1936). A briefer version of only 81 pages was published a year earlier under the title *An Examination of Examinations*. For an adequate account of the experiments the shorter version at least should be read but it may be worthwhile summarizing here some of the main results.

(a) *English Essays*—A college entrance three-hour paper was taken as an example. In this paper, four subjects were given and the candidates had to choose one of them to write on for the whole three hours. In the experiment there were fifty scripts covering all four subjects, some of them more popular than others, but none were chosen by less than eight candidates. The essays were marked out of a possible hundred by five examiners and the average marks awarded by each of these five were quite close. The average of the ranges of marks, that is the interval between the lowest and highest for each candidate, was however quite high, 19·6, the lowest being 7 and the highest 36. For the three most extreme cases the following marks were given:

Candidate	Examiners					Range
	a	b	c	d	e	
25	60	32	65	50	68	36
1	45	38	20	55	20	35
40	40	44	70	75	50	35

This experiment was with a particularly long essay where agreement is more difficult to reach but there have been many other studies with shorter essays which have had particularly low correlations between examiners, usually in the region of 0·5.

(b) *Mathematics University Honours Papers*—Here there were twenty-three candidates taking a paper consisting of twelve questions – four were differential equations and eight concerned with analytical geometry. Any number of questions might be answered on the three-hour paper, but full marks could be obtained on six. Again, the averages from the six markers were very close but the ranges were very big, the lowest being 17 out of a maximum mark of 300 and the highest 64 with an average of 34·7. Settling the marks on the verdicts of two examiners had little effect upon the averages but reduced the range to an average of 18·3 with extremes of 3 and 46. Nevertheless, the differences can still be quite considerable.

Candidate	Examiners		
	a,b	c,d	e,f
20	132	127	169
4	186	177	210

Using two examiners notably diminished the differences in the order in which the candidates were placed; nevertheless, for some individual candidates there still were considerable differences – No. 1 being placed tenth, fifth and sixth by the three pairs. We shall return to the question of improving the reliability of essay type exams later. The intercorrelations between examiners (0·89) reported by the French Carnegie Committee were quite encouraging. Nevertheless, the individual discrepancies in the English research should not encourage complacency. Moreover Dale (1959) suggests that examining in mathematics has other difficulties peculiar to itself. Not much actual research has been done on it but it seems that variation in student performance is more marked in mathematics than in other subjects. In contrast to the small differences in other subjects he gives the marks of four maths candidates who failed a June examination and were allowed to sit again in September.

Candidate	June per cent	September per cent
a	27	58
b	25	63
c	32	59
d	36	76

He shows the mark of one candidate swinging wildly from fail to first class standard over a series of exams. In more literary, essay-type examinations such fluctuation would be very unlikely. Research by Crawford and Burnham (1946) shows that correlations reflecting the stability of performance for students tested at school and in their first year at university were 0·82 for verbal comprehension but only 0·56 for mathematical ingenuity. Studies of the 11+ examination have shown that arithmetic has a lower re-test reliability than other subjects. Dale suggests a likely explanation; that it is much more difficult to set questions of equal difficulty in mathematics and that re-scaling after an examination is not so practicable. Moreover minor mistakes create a disproportionate amount of difficulty, especially if they occur at the beginning of a problem.

(c) *History Honours Papers*—The marking experiment with history was carried out with four university honours papers, three of which were marked by ten examiners and one by five with eighteen candidates. They were marked with 24 grades, using Greek letters and signs. The average marking ranged over seven grades on the first paper, eleven on the second, ten on the third and nine on the fourth. For a number of individuals there were extremely wide ranges.

Candidate	Paper	Range
13	1	17 grades
8	2	18 grades
9	3	18 grades
8	4	16 grades

In the later report of Hartog and Rhodes (1936) the inter-examiner correlations of these marks were given as ranging from –0·41 to +0·85 with an average of +0·44.

(d) *Other Inquiries*—In the French Carnegie inquiry correlations of other subjects were given, of which the worst was philosophy with a mean inter-examiner correlation of 0·438 ranging between 0·112 and 0·636. Other low correlations were for French composition, 0·58 ranging between 0·37 and 0·76, and English, 0·78 ranging between 0·601 and 0·916. Latin had quite a high correlation, 0·836 and physics was one of the highest, 0·843 ranging between 0·794 and 0·902.

In the field of medicine, recent work by Bull (1956) has shown that despite the very factual nature of a large number of medical examinations the reliability was not kept within acceptable limits. As with the Hartog and Rhodes work, average differences were not very great. One examiner marking thirty scripts out of a hundred, on re-marking after an interval of several weeks had an average difference of only 0·9 per cent with the sign taken into account and 6·2 per cent neglecting the difference. The correlation, however, between these two sets of marks was so low as to be not significantly different from a completely random allocation of marks, r = 0·28, P > 0·1. If we look at the marks in terms of passing or failing at a pass mark of 50 per cent we see that eight students out of the thirty change from pass to fail or fail to pass on re-marking.

It is not quite clear how typical this particular examiner was, but very few examiners were involved in this experiment and Bull quotes the correlation of another one as being very little better, r = 0·42. It is not easy to see quite why these correlations should be as low as any recorded in any subject and Bull does not go into the question. Perhaps where a very large amount of factual information is required by a question the subjective element arises in assessing just how much information can be expected and is adequate.

Pieron (1963) sums up the position as far as reliability of traditional exams is concerned:

'All the experimental data has shown that for a particular performance expressed in terms of an exam script, assessment by different examiners produces marks with considerable variability such that in the determination of these marks the part played by the examiner can be greater than that of the performance of the examinee'. [my translation].

(e) *Other Criticisms Concerned with Reliability*—Not very much work has been done on variations in standards from year to year and subject to subject. Since average marks by different examiners have tended to be very similar, not a great deal of variation might be expected. But in Australia, Hohne came to the conclusion that 'failure rates did not vary concomitantly with improved student quality – i.e. that university examiners preferred to pass and fail almost identical proportions of students year after year rather than ascertaining the true calibre of the students and adjusting their fail rates accordingly'. He felt there were 'fixed, deeply ingrained departmental pass policies' involved.

In Robbins (1963, appendix 2(a), annex k) we actually find a decline in the proportion of firsts in arts, science and technology between the years 1953 and 1959, although there was at the same time an increase in the proportion of firsts and seconds. In Robbins, too, we find evidence of quite marked discrepancies in the proportion of firsts awarded in different subjects – in general this seems to be directly related to mathematical content.

A particularly important criticism of traditional exams related to reliability is the poor sampling of the field of knowledge. In subjects like medicine, coverage is very important and it is no doubt because of this that other methods of examining have been more popular. Tyler (1961) suggests, without going into any detail, that the situation is quite clear: 'The typical examination with five, ten, or twenty questions did not give an adequate sample of the student's responses to serve as a basis for a dependable estimate of his attainments. When the student was given a second set of questions covering the same material, his mark was often widely at variance with that obtained from the first examination'.

As these criticisms of reliability began to be felt, various attempts were made to improve them but without much practical success. Increasing the number of markers seemed promising, but with long, complex university essays it is not often possible to find enough to make much difference. There might indeed be some disadvantage in this averaging-out of marks. The candidate who shows a particular type of brilliance to the detriment of some other quality might, under normal systems, either do very well or badly. In either case some interesting reaction might follow; but averaging the marks would make him just an average student, perhaps depriving him of any special attention which might be called for.

Marking by using a more analytic approach instead of a general impression of the whole answer is unlikely – from evidence of work at school – to lead directly to much improvement (although it may well do so indirectly).

The most successful way of increasing marker reliability is by increasing the number of questions set. G. M. Bull has shown a progressive increase in reliability of marking by increasing the number of questions from four in three hours (r = approximately 0·4) to thirty-two in three hours (r = approximately 0·7). But this creates a new set of problems which are discussed elsewhere in this volume.

II. VALIDITY

The problem of assessing the validity of examination systems is an extremely complex one and research in this field has barely touched on the very profound questions which are involved. More than thirty years ago Kandel (1936) saw that 'the problem of examinations strikes at the very roots of the whole meaning and significance of education in society . . . the essence of the problem is . . . the validity of education'. But thirty years later D. P. Hoyt (1965) made a review of the literature in this field which included business, teaching, engineering, medicine, scientific research, miscellaneous occupations and non-vocational accomplishment as well as a section on studies of eminence. He came to the conclusion that 'present evidence strongly suggests college grades bear little or no relationship to any measures of adult accomplishment'. In Britain, Hudson's (1966) research has shown similar results in more limited areas.

Practically all researchers in this field stress the need for a better understanding of aims in education and it seems clear that unless greater attention is given to this question and to the general problem of the meaning of the assessments which are made of students and indeed to the understanding of the great variety of skills and abilities necessary for adult accomplishment, little will be achieved.

III CONCLUSIONS

As long as examinations remain as unreliable as most still are, validity must, of course, remain low. However, while it is extremely important that efforts should be made to improve reliability it would be a mistake to suppose that because criticism may focus upon unreliability this should be the main target for reform. America was to some extent stampeded into 'objectivity' and while there were undoubted benefits there have also been serious difficulties as a result. But the introduction of some completely reliable 'objective' exams in some areas can allow more freedom to develop forms of assessment more suited to less factual aspects. If we want to avoid the difficulties of over-emphasizing reliability without appearing to be unduly hesitant in the eyes of students who are becoming increasingly involved in academic decision-making, we must raise the question of diversifying the system. But we need to do this without introducing a new kind of rigidity. It is certainly an advance to think in terms of devising different forms to assess different abilities but it is easy to slip into the mistake of assuming that what measures one type of ability with one group of students will do the same for all. The modern emphasis on training for flexibility must be paralleled by flexibility in the use of diverse forms of assessment.

BIBLIOGRAPHY

G. M. Bull, (1956) 'An Examination of the Final Examination in Medicine', *Lancet*, 25, August 1956.

R. J. Cox, (1967) 'Resistance to Change in Examining', *Universities Quarterly*, **21**, 3, June 1967.

R. R. Dale, (1959) 'University Standards', *University Quarterly*, **13**, 2, 1959.

M. Dunstan, (1966) 'Sources of Variation in Examination Marks', Dept. Higher Education, Lancaster University. Bulletin No. 1. (Reprinted from Educ. Res. Unit Univ. New South Wales (Australia) Bulletin No. 3.

W. C. Eells, (1930) 'Reliability of Reported Grading of Examinations' *J. of Educ. Psychol.* 1930, Vol. 21.

P. Hartog and E. C. Rhodes, (1935) *An Examination of Examinations*, London.

P. Hartog, E. C. Rhodes and C. Burt, (1936) *The Marks of Examiners*, London.

H. H. Hohne, (1955) 'Success and Failure', Scientific Faculties of the University of Melbourne. Australian Council for Educational Research, Melbourne.

D. P. Hoyt, (1965) *The Relationship between College Graduates and Adult Achievement*, ACT Research Report No. 7. Sept. 1965. Amer. Coll. Testing Prog., Iowa.

L. Hudson, (1966) 'Degree Class and Attainment in Scientific Research'. *Br. J. Psychol.* 15.

I. Kandel, (1936) *'Examinations and their Substitutes in the United States'*, Carnegie Foundation for the Advancement of Teaching, Bulletin 28, New York.

H. Pieron, (1963) *Examens et Docimologie*, Paris.

Report of the Committee on Higher Education (1963) (Robbins Report) London: H.M.S.O.

D. Starch, (1913) 'Reliability and Distribution of Grades', *Science* 1913, Vol. 38.

R. W. Tyler, (1961) 'Evaluative Aspects of Learning', in T. Harris and W. Schwahn, eds. *The Learning Process*, New York.

G. P. Williams, (1933) *The Northampton Study Composition Scale*, London.

8

The Predictive Value of School Marks and Tests for Higher Education in Sweden

Sixten Marklund

Director, Teacher Training Bureau, National Board of Education, Stockholm

Since 1965, a Government Committee has been working in Sweden on the problem of how access to higher studies can be arranged in a more clearly ordered system. The problem involves both practical aspects and questions of principle. Previously, higher education meant, almost exclusively, university studies. Such studies were, in principle, available to all who had passed through the higher secondary school (*gymnasium*); no entrance tests or examinations were required. University studies are no longer the only form of higher education. Parallel with the university, a number of post-secondary school educational institutions have arisen. Education at these institutions is sometimes – but not always – closely associated with university studies.

Another fundamental alteration is that school attendance up to this higher education has changed considerably in character. Fifteen years ago only 12 per cent of each year-group passed through the *gymnasium*. Now 30 per cent attend such schools, and, side by side with this school, new types of secondary education have been established, which have a larger proportion of each year-group. The school system is being designed so that most students will attend some kind of secondary school. It is estimated that by 1970, 85 per cent of the students in each year-group will attend school up to the age of eighteen years. Selection to higher education will, to an ever-increasing extent, take place *after* attendance at a secondary school, not, as previously, *before* secondary school.

It is in these circumstances that it has been found necessary to study and revise the present rules for access to higher studies. The Government Committee investigating this problem has begun a series of studies on the predictive value of school marks, examinations and tests for higher studies. These studies will be reported briefly in this chapter, but to enable the reader to understand the implications of the problem, it is necessary first to give an account of marking in Swedish schools.

Normalization of Marking in School

Up to 1949, selection of students for secondary school education was performed with the help of special entrance examinations arranged by the receiving school. This system was gradually considered to be far too unreliable and too subject to chance. As the lower school became more uniform and of equal standard throughout the country, it was decided to use the marks awarded by the lower school as the basis for selection. This has been done since 1949.

This procedure, of course, demands a reliable system of marking in school. As early as the 1930s, experiments were begun with tests for the normalization of marks in the elementary school. A pioneer in this field was Dr Fritz Wigforss, who was entrusted by the Swedish National Board of Education with the task of designing the first standardized achievement tests for the country as a whole. The first of these tests (in writing, reading and arithmetic in classes 2, 4, and 6) were available in 1944. In the testing and construction of these – as in all later standardized tests – a sample of students representative of the whole country was used.

The tests were successful and have been used widely. Primarily they refer to the class as a whole – not just the individual student. They give the teacher information about the mean and deviation in his class, i.e. what is called the 'standard' of the class. With the help of these tests and intelligence tests it has also been found that rural schools give as good results as schools in towns, and that single-grade, double-grade and multigrade classes (classes of one, two, or more age-groups) attain equally good results. Marking has become acceptably uniform, and since 1949, therefore, school marks have become the instrument of selection. The tests are being revised continuously. Now they are set in classes 3, 6, and 8. Plans are being made to move the test for the eighth class to the ninth. In addition to Swedish and mathematics, tests are set in English.

During recent years similar efforts have also been made to normalize marks in the secondary school. Centrally designed tests to normalize marks are now set in most classes of the secondary school. They are available in the subjects Swedish, English, German, French, mathematics and physics, in some branches of economics and in technical subjects. Marking is also checked by special state secondary school inspectors, a method that has been in force for a couple of years. Experience of normalization in the secondary school is still limited, for it was not started until 1966.

The central tests for both the compulsory and the higher secondary schools are now constructed, distributed and continually revised by a special test department at the National Board of Education.

The tests are not compulsory for the teachers, but are, nevertheless, used by almost every teacher. But it is always the individual teacher who is responsible for the marking of students' work. Thus, the centrally constructed tests are intended only as aids in this procedure, but as such they have proved to be of great value for the attainment of uniform marking for the whole country.

In this respect, the Swedish system is unique in the Western world. It must be regarded as a consequence of the postwar school reforms, which have given Sweden as a whole a new type of school which is, it is true, richly structured, but which has the same character wherever in the country a school may be situated.

The Problem of the Predictive Value of School Marks and Test Results

The central tests, therefore, are of the 'achievement test' type, but they are not used to measure the knowledge of individuals. They are aids of a 'monitorial character'. It is also considered to be of value for teachers to include in their marking, qualifications in their students that cannot be evaluated by tests.

The problem now facing us is how, in the future, access to higher education is to be regulated. The fundamental role of school marks cannot be denied. Experience in Sweden, where, after many years' work, a uniform system of marking has been attained, is very valuable. But a number of circumstances – in particular, the increasing demand for education – suggest that selection for higher studies cannot for long be based *only* on marks awarded in schools.

In the first place, selection for post-secondary school education is far more complicated than transfer from primary to secondary education, at which level we have most experience. The secondary school is differentiated, and higher education is still more differentiated.

In the second place, attempts should be made, as mentioned above, to take into consideration other predictive factors not measured by school marks. Measurement of intelligence and other measurements of suitability for study must be considered. This brings to the fore a number of personality traits in the domains of emotion and volition, of whose relation to later success in studies we are still rather uncertain.

In the third place it has been shown that the role of marks in selection for higher studies has a clearly retroactive effect on studies up to the point when marks are awarded. Work in school is influenced by the fact that future marks are of decisive importance for this work. Short-sighted striving for high marks may easily eclipse the more long-term work of development of personality in the school. This experience is by no means new, but its significance has been greatly underestimated. If, in addition to school marks, other instruments are used in selection, the derogatory effects will be reduced.

Other reasons may be given for such tests. To get a clearer conception of the situation and a safer foundation on which to base proposals for new instruments, the Government Committee investigating these problems decided to make an inventory of all investigations made hitherto of the predictive value of school marks for later success in studies and of the corresponding predictive value different tests may have.

Design of the Inventory

The first problem is to decide *what* is to be predicted, i.e. how is success to be defined? The later in life the criterion is considered, the greater its validity will be. Criteria of success in a profession may be characterized by rapid promotion, salary, rate of increase in salary, security of employment, number of subordinates, independence of decision, etc. Feeling of well-being at work, professional status, number of days of illness (negative criterion) and similar factors may be included. Occupational psychologists and industrial psychologists have long been working on the problem of how such variables are to be defined. They are not only technically unwieldy, but it is extremely difficult to agree on a definition of what success really is. Evaluations vary and opinions change.

The farther away from the prediction the criterion is, the more difficult it is to define it. In its deliberations the Committee came to the conclusion that a prediction must – at least the first time – refer to more immediate criteria of success; primarily, success in further studies. This means technical simplification. But in principle, of course, the question of the ultimate value of this success still remains. This problem will not be discussed here, however interesting and important it may be.

If, therefore, we restrict ourselves mainly to success in studies, our task will be simpler. Even so, it is enormously complicated. If we take university studies, what faculty, what subjects and what levels are we to consider? Are we concerned with general education or clearly goal-directed studies, such as training for posts in communications – post-office, railway – for example? Or are we concerned with the level of marks of those who complete their education, or with that proportion of those accepted who manage to complete their studies, regardless of marks, etc.?

All this, thought the Committee, was evidence that the first thing to be done was to make an inventory of all previous investigations in this realm made in Sweden. Not until this was done could the Committee begin investigating problems of prediction. This has now been done. The inventory, partly of foreign experience and partly of Swedish, has been drawn up. The latter will be reported here. The Committee has begun a more detailed study of the problems of prediction, as well as work on the construction of tests to measure suitability for study.

It was found later that work on the inventory was far greater than had been anticipated at first. The term 'inventory' is hardly adequate. The work was more an investigation of investigations, a study of prediction and success in studies, with a strategy of its own for the comparison and evaluation of experience and results.

The predictors in our problems of prediction are rather indefinite; they must include school marks and anything else that is available – in the first place, tests of various kinds. Although the *content* may be unclear, the *level* is definite. The terms of reference of the Committee restrict the level to the end of the secondary school studies, i.e. to matriculation and equivalent levels.

This limitation provided a starting point for the drawing up of the inventory. It was considered necessary to question the institutions providing post-secondary school education. It might have been easier to apply directly to the central authorities for these institutions, e.g. the Office of the Chancellor of the Swedish Universities and so on. However, when information is collected through these bodies, there is a great risk that the institutions, considering themselves confronted with demands for completeness and bureaucratic perfection, refrain from mentioning unfinished and otherwise incomplete studies.

In addition to educational institutions of academic and other post-secondary school character, other receiving agencies deemed to be able to provide valuable information were approached. The number of agencies applied to, which also sent written replies to questions, is shown in Table I. The questions asked were identical on relevant points.

Group A represents university studies in Sweden. Group B comprises most of the so-called non-academic lines of education. Group C comprises a group of institutions and bodies which are not responsible for such a large proportion of education, but are concerned with investigations, judgement of personality traits and selection of personnel, and includes the psychotechnical institutions in Stockholm and Gothenburg, the Swedish Council for Personnel Administration, the Swedish Institute of Military Psychology, an institute of applied psychology at Uppsala, a similar institute at Saltsjöbaden and the Scandinavian Test Publishing Company.

It was considered urgent to make a survey of the experience of study prediction and success in studies in the other Scandinavian countries. It was found that these countries had only few investigations to report; those available are included here in the total material.

Between half and one-third of the material delivered had not been processed at all. It consisted of raw data, which were scrutinized and processed in the secretariat of the Committee. This, in its turn, gave rise to re-checking and further contacts and collection of material.

The fact that the Committee was not only willing but anxious to receive

TABLE I

EDUCATIONAL INSTITUTIONS, etc., at POST-SECONDARY SCHOOL LEVEL, WHICH SENT
WRITTEN ANSWERS TO QUESTIONS

Institutions and equivalent	Number	
	Questioned	Written replies
A *University institutes and equivalent at*		
Gothenburg University	40	9
Lund University	50	32
Stockholm University	47	16
Umeå University	22	7
Uppsala University	56	15
Certain independent institutions	34	22
B *Certain post-secondary so-called non-academic institutions*	16	8
C *Occupational psychological institutes, etc.*	6	5
D *Institutions in other Scandinavian countries*	13	7
TOTAL	284	121

raw data and incomplete investigation reports was probably one important reason why the material collected was so comprehensive. This does not exclude the possibility that some investigations were overlooked, but contacts with institutions have been frequent and informal, and the number of investigations missed cannot be great.

The Criteria

As was feared, the criteria of success in higher studies were rather diffusely defined. Only in a few cases were they given unambiguously; for example, in time to be taken for a certain study result, or a quantitative expression of study performance during a definite time. If we start from the given criteria and ignore the fact that the definition is unclear, and that they thereby contain an element of unreliability, the criteria used in the investigation may be divided into the following seven main groups:

(1) *Mean marks.* This refers to the lines of continued study which include several subjects, and in which time and extent of courses are more or less restricted.

(2) *Distinction,* i.e. the frequency of positive quality marks in academic studies.

(3) *Time taken to pass examination.* Time is a good variable, but its reliability depends, naturally, on what is meant by 'examination', which is often diffuse.

(4) *Number of courses passed.* By this is meant the number of partial

study courses, or examinations, with time mainly fixed. The time varies, however, from one investigation to another.

(5) *Number of examinations to degree.* This variable is a variant of the time variable. It refers to the number of examinations to get a degree or the number of examinations failed.

(6) *Assessment of aptitude for studies.* This variable, which is found in only two investigations, refers to the assessment by the teachers in the course of the person's ability to *continue* the course, or continue his studies. Thus, the variable is a criterion, as well as a predictor for the future.

(7) *Mean.* This variable is only the sum or mean of the six criteria mentioned above, and is not, therefore, an independent assessment.

The six assessment criteria have been related to different predictions according to the following tabulation. The predictive variables were either marks or tests. The inventory was found to contain 127 and 180 relationships respectively, as shown below.

Criterion	Predictive instrument	
	Marks	*Test*
(1) Mean marks	68	120
(2) Distinction	7	—
(3) Time to examination	7	—
(4) Number of courses passed	33	39
(5) Number of examinations to degree	10	14
(6) Assessment of aptitude for studies	2	7
(7) Sum or mean of above	127	180

Predictors

As shown above, the predictors are of two types, marks (degrees) and tests. Here we ignore the so-called background factors. The predictors, too, may be divided into subgroups. The relationships in which the predictors comprised different assessments of marks and the following values:

Mean marks	71	
whereof weighted		15
whereof unweighted		56
Only marks for written subjects	41	
whereof languages		16
whereof mathematics-physics		25
Subjects other than written	10	
Practical subjects	5	
TOTAL	127	

Where predictors consisted of tests, the number of test relationships was distributed as follows:

Complete test batteries	37	
Individual tests	114	
whereof in technical comprehension		14
whereof in spatial aptitude		10
whereof in logical-inductive aptitude		21
whereof in verbal aptitude		17
whereof other tests		52
Assessment of aptitude for learning	6	
Other assessments	23	
TOTAL	180	

Relation between Predictors and Criteria

A survey of the results is given in Tables II and III below. The first of these refers to marks as a predictive instrument, the other to tests.

It must be pointed out that the tables are strongly generalizing, and that they are condensed as far as possible. The centre column gives the average coefficient of correlation. This average was calculated with each individual correlation as a statistical unit, regardless of the total number of individuals included in the calculating. The right-hand columns of the tables show how the individual correlations deviate above and below the average. Only the highest and lowest correlations are given, however. The total picture for both tables indicates that the mean correlations are positive but rather weak. The lowest are below 0, but nevertheless all but two may be regarded as null-correlations. The highest exceed 0·70 and, in one case 0·80.

In Tables II and III the results are reported according to type of criterion of success in studies. Corresponding surveys according to type of predictor are given in Tables IV and V. Table IV refers to marks, the other to tests. In all important points, the coefficients are of the same character as in the previous two tables.

Problems of Interpretation

An inventory of the type described above of the predictive value of school marks and test results involves many problems of interpretation. The total result is obviously dependent on the results of the individual studies. Since space does not permit an account of all these (a comprehensive report of the investigations is available in Swedish), an attempt must be made to arrive at a total assessment, an investigation of the investigations. This is of great importance from the aspect of educational policy.

The number of investigations is very large. For school marks, 127 correlations exist, and for test results and ratings no fewer than 180.

TABLE II

SURVEY OF CORRELATIONS BETWEEN SCHOOL MARKS AND LATER SUCCESS IN STUDIES ACCORDING TO TYPE OF CRITERION

Type of Criterion	Number of correlations	Mean value of correlations	Lowest correlations	Highest
Mean marks	68	+0·26	−0·31	+0·67
Distinction	7	+0·42	+0·27	+0·55
Time to examination	7	+0·29	+0·21	+0·47
Number of courses passed	33	+0·25	−0·41	+0·58
Number of examinations to degree	10	+0·24	+0·01	+0·60
Assessment of aptitude for studies	2	+0·23	+0·20	+0·26
TOTAL	127	+0·28	−0·41	+0·67

TABLE III

SURVEY OF CORRELATIONS BETWEEN TEST RESULTS AND SUCCESS IN FURTHER STUDIES ACCORDING TO TYPE OF CRITERION

Type of criterion	Number of correlations	Mean value to correlations	Lowest correlations	Highest
Mean marks	120	+0·26	−0·13	+0·69
Number of courses passed	39	+0·30	−0·04	+0·82
Number of examinations to degree*	14	+0·12	+0·07	+0·25
Assessment of aptitude for studies	7	+0·25	+0·02	+0·35
TOTAL	180	+0·26	−0·13	+0·82

* All correlations are derived from one study.

TABLE IV

SURVEY OF CORRELATIONS BETWEEN SCHOOL MARKS AND SUCCESS IN STUDIES ACCORDING TO TYPE OF PREDICTORS

Type of predictor	Number of correlations	Mean value of correlations	Lowest correlations	Highest
Mean marks	71	+0·29	−0·31	+0·67
weighted mean marks	15	+0·32	+0·03	+0·62
unweighted mean marks	56	+0·28	−0·31	+0·67
Written subjects	41	+0·27	−0·09	+0·60
foreign languages	8	+0·32	+0·13	+0·55
Swedish composition	18	+0·18	−0·01	+0·40
mathematics and physics	25	+0·30	−0·09	+0·60
Non-written subjects	10	+0·18	−0·41	+0·45
Practical subjects	5	+0·06	−0·09	+0·15
TOTAL	128	+0·27	−0·41	+0·67

TABLE V

SURVEY OF CORRELATIONS BETWEEN TEST RESULTS AND LATER SUCCESS IN STUDIES
ACCORDING TO TYPE OF PREDICTOR

Type of predictor	Number of correlations	Mean value of correlations	Lowest correlations	Highest correlations
Test batteries	37	+0·34	+0·04	+0·82
Individual tests	114	+0·24	−0·13	+0·65
technical comprehension	14	+0·24	+0·09	+0·47
spatial aptitude	10	+0·25	−0·04	+0·49
logical-inductive patitude	21	+0·25	+0·03	+0·60
verbal aptitude	17	+0·11	−0·13	+0·38
other tests reported	52	+0·26	−0·04	+0·65
Assessment of learning aptitude	6	+0·39	+0·19	+0·62
Other assessments reported	23	+0·26	−0·06	+0·52
TOTAL	180	+0·26	−0·13	+0·82

To these must be added a large number of determinations of a secondary nature of the significance for success in studies of various background factors such as sex, age, socio-economic status, practice, physical and mental health, and so on.

The number of individuals in these correlations is great, too. If certain double countings are eliminated, the individuals were still more than 30,000 in number. Nothing important will be gained by adding more sub-studies or more individuals. What might be done instead is to attempt to find possibilities of generalization and to make assessments of significance of 'higher potency'. Thus it would be valuable not only to find *that* marks and tests correlate with later success in studies but also *how often* this occurs; how consistently and 'persistently' the correlations appear. It is in the possibilities of making such interpretations that the greatest value of the inventory lies. For the first time a survey of the predictive possibilities has become available.

It is obvious that the correlations between predictors and criteria are often far more complicated than the tables above show. Some of the correlations refer to groups of up to 3,000 students, others to only a score or so. As a rule, numerically large investigations refer to less clearly defined variables, e.g. number of examinations in 'academic studies', and the correlations are usually low. The high correlations – but also some of the low ones – are found in more restricted investigations, with fewer students and with definitely goal-directed studies. This is shown in Tables VI and VII. Success in studies in the humanistic, social science or science faculty without any definite goal have generally lower correlation with school marks and test results than, for example, success in technical education. In the same way it seems easier to predict success in scientific studies than in the humanities. The reason for this is probably that criteria of success differ in reliability. In scientific studies, objective methods of assessment are used more often than in humanistic studies.

This brings us to a more general problem. Why are the correlations between predictors and criteria usually so weak? They are only about 0·30. One reason for this – perhaps the most important one – is that the criteria are extremely uncertain. The conception 'higher studies' has always implied something of freedom from order and rules in evaluation. It seems likely that it will *not* be as free in the future, and the correlations will therefore rise in consequence. One need do no more than compare the Swedish results with corresponding results for higher education in the United States. There the correlation between predictors and criteria is usually higher, about 0·50. This difference is probably because the criteria of success in higher studies are more reliable in the United States than in Sweden. Organizationally, studies in American colleges are more like studies in European higher secondary schools than those in a European university.

If certain obvious shortcomings in reliability are eliminated, the correlation rises markedly. To this must be added that some very general studies of prediction could be excluded from the Swedish survey. There are undoubtedly good reasons for doing so, and if this is done, the Swedish investigations show that success in studies can be predicted with a probability of about 0·50 with the help of the marks awarded by the lower school. And with about the same degree of probability it seems possible to predict success in study with the help of test results.

As regards the predictive value of school marks, it must be pointed out that all marks had been awarded before the measures to normalize marks, described above, were introduced two years ago. This alone makes the correlations obtained underestimations. Future investigations of this kind might therefore show that the predictive value of school marks is higher.

Table VI gives another survey of the correlation between school marks and results in higher studies. The correlations are mean values; none of them embrace fewer than four investigations. The lowest and highest correlations are given in parentheses. Support is found here for what has already been said, namely that success in studies of a more general nature (column 2) is more difficult to predict than in studies of a more specific type (columns 3, 4, 5).

If predictors are taken into consideration, in this case different kinds of marks in the matriculation examination, it is found that school marks in the so-called writing subjects have higher predictive value than marks for other subjects (marks in Swedish composition also have low predictive value). The weighting of school marks made at selection for higher

TABLE VI

MEAN CORRELATION BETWEEN MATRICULATION EXAMINATION MARKS (COLUMN 1) AND RESULTS OF DIFFERENT KINDS OF FURTHER EDUCATION (COLUMNS 2-5). ALL THE CORRELATIONS ARE POSITIVE. THE FIGURES IN PARENTHESES GIVE THE LOWEST AND HIGHEST CORRELATIONS.

Matriculation marks (1)	Studies at faculties of arts, social sciences and science (2)	University studies in languages (3)	University studies in science subjects (4)	Higher technical education (5)
Mean marks from school				
weighted	0·15 (0·09-0·23)	0·27 (0·09-0·43)	0·34 (0·08-0·58)	0·42 (0·21-0·67)
unweighted	0·15 (0·09-0·23)	0·27 (0·09-0·43)	0·34 (0·08-0·58)	0·38 (0·23-0·62)
School marks in writing subjects				
foreign languages		0·31 (0·13-0·55)	0·32 (0·01-0·60)	0·47 (0·21-0·67)
Swedish composition		0·31 (0·13-0·55)		0·27 (0·19-0·57)
				0·30 (0·16-0·44)
				0·19 (0·10-0·40)
mathematics and physics			0·32 (0·01-0·60)	0·32 (0·02-0·57)
School marks in other subjects*			0·19 (0·13-0·24)	0·33 (0·02-0·45)
TOTAL	0·15 (0·09-0·23)	0·29 (0·09-0·55)	0·31 (0·01-0·60)	0·33 (0·02-0·67)

* The other subjects are history, history of literature, social sciences (including civics), philosophy, geography, biology and chemistry.

TABLE VII

MEAN CORRELATION BETWEEN TEST RESULTS AND RATINGS (COLUMN 1) AND RESULTS IN DIFFERENT KINDS OF FURTHER EDUCATION (COLUMNS 2, 3, 4). THE FIGURES IN PARENTHESES GIVE LOWEST AND HIGHEST CORRELATIONS

Tests and ratings (1)	Studies at faculties of arts, social sciences and science (2)	Higher technical education (3)	Lower technical education (4)	Officer training (5)
Test batteries	0·28 (+0·04—+0·84)	0·14 (+0·12—+0·18)	0·47 (+0·20—+0·69)	0·28 (+0·15—+0·40)
Individual tests				
technical comprehension	0·31 (+0·17—+0·51)	0·24 (+0·16—+0·32)	0·09*	0·16 (+0·06—+0·29)
spatial aptitude	0·19 (+0·03—+0·36)		0·32 (—0·04—+0·49)	0·17 (+0·14—+0·24)
logical-inductive aptitude	0·08 (—0·13—+0·27)		0·35 (+0·20—+0·60)	0·22 (+0·09—+0·31)
verbal aptitude			0·38*	0·14 (+0·02—+0·22)
other tests			0·40 (+0·24—+0·49)	0·18 (0·00—+0·42)
Assessment of aptitude for studies	0·27 (—0·04—+0·62)	0·24 (+0·09—+0·46)	0·40 (—0·01—+0·62)	0·29 (+0·02—+0·52)
TOTAL	0·24 (—0·13—+0·84)	0·21 (+0·09—+0·46)	0·38 (—0·04—+0·69)	0·22 (+0·02—+0·52)

* Refers to one correlation investigation only.

technical education does not have the importance attributed to it; it gives lower rather than higher correlation with success in studies when marks are unweighted, i.e. ordinary average marks.

Table VI gives a total picture of the predictive value of school marks for success in further education. It comprises the 127 correlations between marks and success in studies mentioned earlier. In Table VII is given a corresponding survey of the 180 correlations referring to tests and ratings. The correlations are mean values, and the variation range is given in parentheses, too.

Tests and ratings seem to have a slightly higher mean predictive value than school marks for success in general education in the faculties of humanities, social science and science. Otherwise, tests and ratings seem to be of about the same predictive value as school marks. The predictive value seems to be disquietingly low for the training of officers. A more detailed analysis of the results shows, however, that the outcome is better than the average correlation suggests. It was found that the groups studied were greatly reduced because many who began training as officers did not complete, nor even intended to complete, the officer-training course.

The correlation for higher technical education is equally low. The possibilities of prediction are clearly greater in respect of lower technical education. Here, too, a detailed analysis of the correlations provides evidence that the difference is illusory. The tests have less discriminative ability in the higher technical education than in the lower. So-called restriction of range gives ceiling effects in the former groups, which reduces the correlations.

In the cases in which the test batteries were used, important testing could be performed. In none of these cases did the individual sub-test score as high as the test batteries. Thus the whole gives more than the parts. The advantage of batteries seems, therefore, to be in their giving measurements in many dimensions. Once again the thesis is confirmed that the 'pure' tests, the one-dimensional ones, are of smaller predictive value, however perfect they may be from the technical aspect. Assessments of aptitude for study (see Table VII) provide an example of this. They contain a large measure of subjectivity and are often technically faulty, but these shortcomings are compensated by a more varied rating than the 'pure' tests give.

Conclusions

Many details of the material collected may be analysed. One conclusion is that school marks really do have predictive value. In the general discussion during recent times, it has been maintained that students with low marks in school are as successful in higher education as students with high marks, and that selection might just as well be made by drawing lots as by marks. The results demonstrate clearly that school marks *are* of predictive value, although it is low. With the normalization of school marks now being carried out, there is reason to anticipate that the predictive value will be increased further. The calculated mean correlations do not give a correct picture. There is reason to pay the greatest attention to the higher correlations obtained, and these are often at the 0·50 or 0·60 level.

Tests and ratings give results as high as those of marks, but the possibilities of raising the correlations by perfecting the instruments are not so clear here. There are, therefore, reasons for a general assumption that the predictive value of marks is greater than that of tests.

Further, for both marks and tests, the predictive value does not give a correct impression, on account of the fact that the criteria to which the prediction refers are so diffuse and unreliable. The imminent reform of higher education, recently decided by the Swedish Parliament and now being tried out by the universities, with a switch-over to more stringent, time-determined studies gives rise to a certain degree of optimism of a further improvement in the possibilities of prediction.

The types of tests hitherto found best as predictors are the general tests of aptitude for study. Test batteries for the measurement of general skills and general intelligence should therefore be possible to combine advantageously with school marks. Without giving a detailed account of this, the results suggest that more specific tests, and tests to assess personality traits in the emotional and volitional life, on the other hand, still have little to give. The predictive value of such tests is therefore small, generally speaking. There are, of course, certain kinds of study for which such tests are useful, but they have not the same general predictive value as marks and tests of aptitude for study.

The conclusions that can be drawn – or, rather, the hypotheses that can be enunciated – on the basis of the investigations in the inventory are in brief:

(1) The best instrument for the prediction of success in further education seems to be marks from the secondary school.

(2) The second best instrument seems to be tests of aptitude for study of a general type, with measurements in several dimensions, or 'mixed' measurements.

(3) More specific tests and characterological tests seem to have less predictive value, although they may perhaps be of value in certain special forms of education.

(4) Combinations of marks and tests of aptitude for study seem to give more reliable predictions than marks alone. Adding further measurements to these does not seem to improve possibilities of prediction to any great extent.

(5) Efforts to improve methods of prediction should be aimed primarily at making marks, tests and criteria of success in studies more reliable.

Correlations between predictors and criteria at the 0·50 to 0·60 level seem to be feasible. It is doubtful whether much higher correlations than these can be expected for higher education in general. A question arising of itself is whether there is an optimal level for the correlation between predictors and criteria. Is it advantageous always to strive for the highest possible correlations, or is it unnecessary to go higher than, for example, 0·70?

We may reverse the question and ask, what will it imply if we achieve complete correlation between predictors and criteria? With a correlation of 1·00, the distribution of students will be exactly the same at entrance and leaving. If this occurs, there is reason to ask seriously whether the possibilities of development of the individual have been utilized in the best way. It may even be feared that the results at entrance have determined the whole of the later education and that this has thereby stagnated in a fixed pattern. If we are to avoid a selection result becoming decisive for the design of education, and instead encourage the development of new skills and interests, and the development of education as a whole, there is no reason to expect complete correlation. It may even be regarded as a disadvantage if correlations rise as high as 0·80 or 0·90. High correlations must never become an end in themselves. Far more important than that correlations reach a certain predetermined level is that all students are given an education suited to their aptitudes, and that none or as few as possible are unsuccessful. Drop-outs and course repeaters are often evidence of unsuitable selection and the shortcomings they reflect cannot be justified by saying that a high correlation is obtained between predictors and criteria of success for the few who complete their studies in the way intended.

9

Some Inquiries into the Problems of Real Assessment (Docimologie)

Françoise Bacher

Chef du Service de Recherches de l'Institut National d'Etude du Travail et d'Orientation Professionelle, Paris

The examination of the traditional methods of assessing knowledge has been the subject of numerous studies in France, a very full account of which may be found in *Examens et Docimologie* by H. Pieron (5).

These studies have a social interest in view of the part played by examinations and competitions in affording access to higher education and to a large number of careers. They are likewise of interest in the sphere of pedagogic research; indeed, the value of a particular method and the efficacy of tuition must be judged by their effects on the pupils concerned, and it is necessary to be able to appreciate objectively the knowledge acquired by the latter and the skills which they have themselves developed.

However, studies carried out on the traditional methods of marking have shown that several factors tend to reduce such objectivity.

CRITICISM OF TRADITIONAL METHODS

(1) *Comparison of Average Marks Awarded by Different Examiners*

Comparison of the marks given by different examiners on the same papers is most readily effected in experiments in which the same batch of papers – for which in the course of real examinations only a single assessment by subject matter would generally be appropriate for each pupil is submitted to several examiners.

However, in certain real examinations, it may be considered that different groups of pupils are comparable. Thus, in the case of the *baccalauréat* (the examination taken at the end of secondary schooling), the pupils are divided, in alphabetical order, among different examining boards. If, strictly speaking, there were no differences between these boards, the mean marks obtained by the pupils from the different boards should not vary by more than the sampling fluctuations. In point of fact, a study (7) relating to the *baccalauréat* of July, 1955 in the Seine Département showed that the variations of the means were statistically significant.

Seventeen examining boards were selected at random from all the *baccalauréat* boards in elementary mathematics and the mean markings were compared. For the written part of the mathematics examination the strictest board had given 5·81 out of 20 as the average mark, whereas the most lenient had given 9·06; in philosophy and in physics the average marks ranged from 7·00 to 9·30 and from 7·63 to 10·50, respectively. For the oral part of the examination the fluctuations were still greater; for example, the average marks for physics ranged between 8·30 and 13·00. Since an average of 10 out of 20 was the required pass mark, the proportion of passes varied widely between boards, in fact, from 30·7 per cent to 52·6 per cent.

(2) Comparison of the Dispersion of Marks Awarded by Different Examiners

To the effects of differences in strictness upon examination results must be added effects due to the dispersion of the marks. In many examinations, in fact, passing is determined by an aggregate mark made up of a weighted sum of partial marks. Theoretical coefficients are fixed for the different subject matters. But the real weights of the latter depend also upon the dispersion of marks for each subject so that, if these dispersions vary, the real weights may prove to be appreciably different from the assumed coefficients.

A study (3) carried out in five institutions in Paris in 1954 on an entrance examination for secondary education showed the following divergences: for a dictation test the theoretical coefficient was 3, whereas the real weight varied between 4·6 and 5·0; for a test of questions about dictation the theoretical coefficient was 4, the real weight between 2·9 and 4·0 ; for a test in writing a report on a text just read, the theoretical weight was 3, the real weight between 1·7 and 2·2; for a test in arithmetic the theoretical coefficient of 6 compared with a real weight varying between 5·6 and 6·8. There are, therefore, important divergences with regard to the forecast coefficients so that the weights of the different subject matters vary from board to board; moreover, it may be thought that on the average the weight of the most difficult tests to mark, where an element of appreciation was called for, i.e. those which involved the higher thought processes, tended to be lower, whilst the weight of the tests which were easier to mark, and which might have been expected to involve less elevated thought processes, tended to be higher.

(3) Study of the Correlations Between Marks

In addition to differences in the mean and dispersion of the marking scales used by different examiners, divergences have also been established in their classing of pupils. For example, in the June, 1955 baccalauréat, the correlation between written and oral examinations on the same subject (based on 1,049 passes) was only 0·38 for mathematics and 0·26 for physics.

In an experiment (6) in which sixteen teachers were asked to correct independently the physics papers of forty pupils who were in their last year of secondary education, the mean correlation between teachers was 0·81; in an oral examination (recorded) the agreement was weaker, the correlation being 0·73.

(4) Comments on the Assessment of a Year's Work

In the light of the above divergences, and also of the fact that in an examination the pupil is judged on the strength of one paper or of a small number of papers per subject on one occasion, it has sometimes been urged that examinations should be replaced by taking into consideration marks obtained throughout the year. The advantage is that appraisement of the pupil's success is then based upon a much greater number of tasks spread over a period. But this introduces a source of error which is even more important than the differences in strictness or criteria of judgement between teachers and the fact that pupils from different classes are no longer judged by the same tests, namely, the fact that the average level of *classes* is extremely variable, almost as much as that of the individual pupils. This feature has been verified, for example, in an inquiry on the position of pupils after four years of secondary schooling (9); a sample of about 10,000 pupils, representative of pupils at that level, were submitted to standardized tests in French and mathematics. From these general tests it was established that the average marks obtained by the pupils of the 406 classes examined varied considerably by class, from 26 to 58 (out of 80) for French, and from 8 to 38 (out of 44) for mathematics. The inter-class variance represented 43 per cent of the total variance in the case of French, and 28 per cent of the total for mathematics.

Another inquiry (8), carried out on pupils in their fifth year of primary schooling, showed that the teachers tended to judge the pupils in each class by comparison one with another, without taking account of the level of the class as a whole relative to a larger population (which they would generally have no means of knowing). In this way, two pupils having the same level of attainment according to a standard test, would be judged differently by their teachers, i.e. as relatively good if belonging to a backward class and as relatively bad if belonging to a more advanced class.

It is probable therefore that the use of average daily marks instead of examinations, in those cases where pupils from different classes have to be compared, would lead to still less objective marking, because of the differences in class levels, than would recourse to a common examination.

PROCEDURES FOR IMPROVING OBJECTIVITY IN MARKING

The foregoing findings have been substantiated repeatedly, and the main problem which has next to be faced is that of discovering some means of reducing the causes of divergent marking.

(1) *Adjustment of Marking Scales*

In principle, it is easy to effect an adjustment to the marks given by examiners by transforming their marking scales in such a way as to bring their averages and dispersions into alignment. But in real examinations, such an (algebraic) constraint is not admissible; the examiners may only modify their own marks. They may be given the opportunity to do this by being informed about the strictness of their marking compared with that of the other examiners, and this is a procedure followed in some examinations. In the course of a recent experiment (4), an attempt was made to estimate the effect of introducing a systematic adjustment for shifts in the mean marking. For this purpose, 150 examiners were asked to correct three papers (the same for all of them); they were then told what the distribution of marks had been for the examiners as a whole and asked to calculate the discrepancy between their own average marks and the general average. They were next asked to mark a new set of papers and to apply a correcting factor to their marks based upon the estimated discrepancy of the previous exercise. Under these conditions, it was found – contrary to expectation – that the adjusted marks showed as many divergences as the unadjusted marks. It should be noted that in this experiment the correcting factor was estimated from one series of marks and then applied to another series; it is possible therefore that the examiners were influenced, while marking the second set of papers, by the knowledge of their strictness or otherwise and of the adjustment they would have to apply to their marks; it is also possible that the correcting factor derived from the first set of markings was based on too few papers to provide a reliable measure of the teacher's customary strictness. In any case, this experiment shows that the adoption of the adjustment procedure in a real examination can give rise to difficulties which could not be foreseen because of the simplicity of the principle involved.

(2) *Determination of Common Criteria of Judgement*

The differences between examiners in their classification of pupils give rise to problems which are still more difficult to resolve. Indeed, they show that different examiners judge pupils according to different criteria. The construction of a ready-reckoner for standard marking, indicating the number of points to be given to each question and the weight to be attached to each type of mistake, should then bring about a closer agreement between examiners. In an experiment (1) with pupils in their fifth year of primary schooling, a comparison was made between the degree of agreement among examiners marking a given set of papers with that of examiners marking another set of test papers comprising free-choice questions for which a very detailed marking ready-reckoner had been established. The conclusion reached was that the existence of the ready-reckoner increased slightly the measure of agreement among examiners (the mean correlation coefficient was raised from 0·90 to 0·96 for a French test and from 0·94 to 0·97 for an arithmetic test). It was also concluded that improvements in the ready-reckoner would no doubt further reduce the amount of disagreement.

It is known that standardized achievement tests employing multi-choice questions push the procedure to the extreme; no room is left for the examiner's own personal assessment and marking is carried out quite mechanically. These tests, which enable pupils from different classes to be compared, can also be used in a more analytical way to reveal gaps in pupils' knowledge, by reference to the degree of knowledge displayed by pupils at the same stage of schooling. Thus, by noting the proportion of correct answers given to each question by a larger population, teachers are able to diagnose the strong and the weak points of their own classes (8). However, standardized tests are more easily constructed when one's concern is the acquisition of factual knowledge than when one is interested in testing the more complex mental processes. For example, writing ability can only be assessed by asking the pupil to express himself freely on a subject. One way of improving objectivity is then to take the average of several assessments made by different examiners. It is equally possible to make use of other types of standardized tests (in aptitude or creativity) which are less bound up with the acquisition of knowledge in a particular subject if the object of the examination is of a prognostic character – that is, if its purpose is not so much to assess the extent of the pupils' knowledge but rather to predict their aptitude for the pursuit of studies at a higher level.

TEACHING AIMS

When standardized tests are employed, the problem is no longer the attainment of objectivity in marking but the actual content of the test papers, and this can only be decided by reference to the original purposes of the examination and, in a more general way, to the teaching aims.

However, the determination of these objectives is far from being simple. It became evident, from inquiries among teachers about the attainments which seemed to them necessary for the pursuit of studies in a higher class, that the differences in their opinions were such as to preclude the drawing of any general conclusion (the inquiries were made in respect of the first year (2) and of the fifth year (9) of secondary education).

A new type of research, which the Institut National proposes to undertake, would involve investigating more directly whether different teachers hold varying concepts of the character of their teaching of the same subject at a given stage in the curriculum.

SUMMARY AND CONCLUSION

The existence of considerable divergences in examiners' marking of school papers leads to a search for methods by which the objectivity of their marking can be improved. Several techniques are available to this end: adjustment of the marking scales, the setting up of common ready-reckoners by which different marking criteria are standardized, and recourse to the averaging of several assessments. But these techniques do not allow the purposes of the examination or test to be fixed; these may be to detect gaps in knowledge, to control the learning process or to make a prognosis regarding the course of further studies. In a more general way, such techniques do not enable the aims of the pupils' education to be defined, although the definition of these aims constitutes an initial, fundamental problem. It is only after these aims have been defined that an attempt can be made to apply techniques designed to show whether they have or have not been attained. This is a field of research which has been little explored as yet.

BIBLIOGRAPHY

(1) J. Cambon, 'Objectivité de la notation des tests de connaissances à réponses libres'. *B.I.N.O.P.*, (1961), **17** n° 5, 329–334.

(2) J. Cambon and M. Reuchlin, 'Enquête sur les connaissances nécessaires aux élèves entrants en sixième'. *B.I.N.O.P.*, (1963), **19**, n° 4, 219–234.

(3) A. M. Guerbet-Seux, M. Reuchlin 'Etude sur l'examen d'entrée en 6e dans cinq établissements parisiens'. *B.I.N.O.P.*, (1958), **14**, n° spécial, 9–19.

(4) J. Pelnard, 'Rapport sur une expérience de docimologie'. To appear in *Les Amis de Sèvres*.

(5) H. Piéron, *Examens et docimologie*. (Paris, P.U.F., 1963), 190 pp.

(6) H. Piéron, M. Reuchlin, and F. Bacher 'Une recherche expérimentale de docimologie sur les examens oraux de physique au niveau du baccalauréat de mathématiques'. *Biotypologie*, (1962), **23**, n° 1–2, 48–73.

(7) H. Piéron, M. Reuchlin, F. Bacher, and M. Demangeon. 'Analyse des corrélations entre notations à une session de *baccalauréat*'. *Biotypologie*, (1962), **23**, n° 1–2, 17–47.

(8) M. Reuchlin, 'Enquête nationale dans les classes de cours moyen deuxième année'. *B.I.N.O.P.*, (1958), **14**, n° spécial, 21–97.

(9) M. Reuchlin, and F. Bacher, 'Enquête sur l'orientation à la fin du premier cycle secondaire'. Mimeographed report, (1964).

10

The Reliability of the Number-marking System: An Austrian Study*

Rudolf Weiss

Director, Paedagogisches Institut des Bundes fuer Oberoesterreich

Austrian teachers are obliged to give marks according to a five-grade mark system. A decree of the Ministry of Education defines the performances required for the different grades. An average performance has to be marked 'satisfactory' (3). We are going to call this definition of the Ministry of Education 'External Criterion'. This criterion would be adequate for marking if different teachers evaluated one and the same performance of a pupil by a standard approximately equal.

Another way of marking is to measure the marks by the average standard performance of the respective class. We call this procedure 'Internal Criterion'. In spite of all the deficiencies of this method – above all the lack of comparability of marks to those of other classes or even schools, every class representing, to some extent, a 'unity of marking', and, moreover, the fact that it is valid only for large groups – this internal criterion is reliable if the teacher succeeds in marking justly, i.e. uninfluenced by prejudices against the student. In other words, he should have the ability to apply and stick to his own subjective criterion of performance in an objective way, without being influenced by motives other than those of the pupil's performance.

Structure and Procedure of Tests

To examine the reliability of the external and internal criteria respectively, men and women teachers were asked to mark compositions and arithmetic tests.

The tested persons were given the following instructions:

(1) They were to apply the complete scale of marks (consisting of five grades), according to their judgement, without resorting to a vague medium 'precautionary grade'.

(2) In order to stay clear of any influence they were to avoid looking at the marks given by others and, above all, refrain from discussing the 'correct' evaluation with those sitting next to them.

---

* Detailed references to this study may be found in Rudolf Weiss, *Zeuzur und Zeugnis*, Linz, 1965.

(3) Men and women teachers not teaching those classes mentioned on the test papers were to mark the tests all the same, but to put their marks in parentheses. The specific purpose of the test was to examine to what degree the marking of the identical test paper would coincide among different teachers.

Two compositions were presented in typed form, containing all the spelling mistakes of the original. They were to be marked according to spelling, style and content. Furthermore, a general mark was to be given.

Whereas original school test papers could be used for the composition test it was more difficult to make up appropriate arithmetic test papers. In arithmetic tests the pseudo-criterion of the number of problems solved correctly in relation to the total number of problems is effective. In this case a similar assessment of marks is secured, which would, however, be based on a fictitious accuracy. The similarity of marks would not concern the student's performance, but the mathematical relation of the correct to the incorrect solution of problems. In order to avoid this pseudo-criterion and to require decisive marking also in arithmetic tests, we abandoned the system of 'correct-incorrect'. Instead, we used arithmetic papers with 'slight mistakes' – for example, the 'measure' required in the answer might be omitted, or errors might be made in addition. In marking such papers, which, in practice, occur more frequently than completely correct or incorrect results, it is possible to decide in three different ways:

(1) If the final result contains errors – no matter of what kind – it is incorrect. Pupils have to be trained in accuracy. Also in later professional life it is irrelevant *why* an error has been made, as the responsibility will have to be accepted.

(2) If the method in solving the problem is correct, but slight errors have been made, the problem has to be marked 'half-correct' or 'partly correct'. Also, in these examples there is a certain degree of performance which has to be considered in marking.

(3) Pupils are neither book-keepers nor bank officials. It is most essential for pupils to master the problems intellectually. If a problem has been solved correctly in this way, slight errors may be overlooked.

For one section of tested persons the *compositions* were preceded by the following introduction: 'Here are two compositions written by fourth-form primary school pupils. The first was written by an average pupil who is fond of reading comic strips; both parents are employed: the second is by a boy gifted in language whose father is the editor of a well-known daily newspaper.'

For the other section of tested persons, these characteristics were substituted: 'Here are two compositions written by fourth-form pupils of primary school. The first was written by a boy gifted in language whose father is the editor of a well-known daily newspaper: the second by an average pupil who is fond of reading comic strips; both parents are employed.'

One section of tested persons read the following introductory remarks to the *arithmetic tests*: 'This is the arithmetic test done by a pupil of fourth-form primary school. It was written by Fritz H., a boy gifted in mathematics and with an inclination for original solutions. How would *you* mark this test?' And the second test paper was prefaced: 'This is the arithmetic test done by a pupil of fifth-form primary school. It was written by Hans L., a boy of an average talent. The original test was strikingly untidy in handwriting and appearance. How would *you* mark this test?'

For the other section of tested persons these characteristics had been exchanged, i.e. positive for Hans L. (inclination for original solutions) and negative for Fritz H. (untidy appearance of original test).

This test, carried out with small groups of teachers in sixteen different places in Upper Austria, met with great interest. Not even one teacher refused to take part in the test. After the papers had been collected there were animated discussions among the tested persons about the 'correctness' or 'incorrectness' of the marks.

The marks of teachers without any experience in teaching those forms were eliminated. It had, however, been necessary to include this section of people in the test in order to prevent the other group from being influenced.

An evaluation was made of the compositions marked by 92 men and women teachers teaching the fourth form and of the arithmetic tests marked by 153 men and women teachers teaching the fourth form, and by 119 men and women teachers teaching the fifth form. The number of men and women was roughly the same.

The age-range of the teachers was very large – from 20 to 65.

Reliability of the External Criterion in Marking Compositions

A useful external criterion must be able to bring about rather corresponding ideas on the 'value' of a pupil's performance, i.e. identical tests must be marked more or less equally by differently qualified assessors.

The results of our tests were as follows: *Spelling* in both the compositions was marked by grades between 'very good' (1) and 'insufficient' (5). Concerning the style, the marks also ranged from 'very good' (1) to 'insufficient' (5) in the first composition, from 'very good' (1) to 'sufficient' (4) in the second composition. The *content* was marked from 'very good' (1) to 'sufficient' (4). Also the general mark in both the compositions ranged from 'very good' (1) to 'sufficient' (4). The extreme marking grades, especially 'insufficient' (5), occur less frequently than the medium grades, but not so infrequently as to call them 'exceptions' or 'errors'.

The four marks to be given (spelling, style, content, general mark)

FIGURE I

MARKING OF TWO COMPOSITIONS

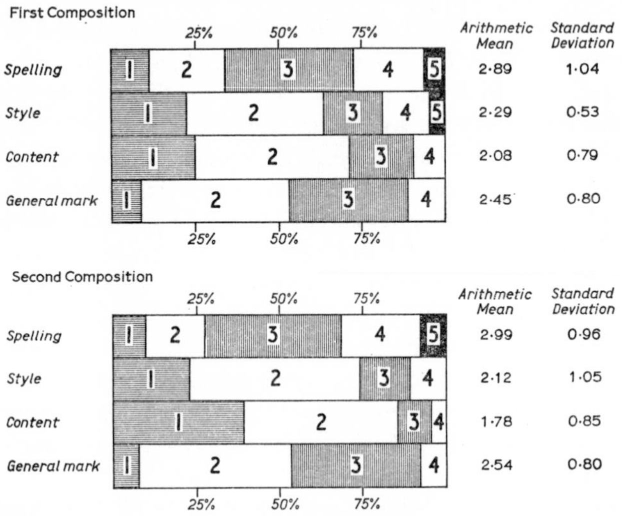

First Composition

	25%	50%	75%	Arithmetic Mean	Standard Deviation
Spelling				2·89	1·04
Style				2·29	0·53
Content				2·08	0·79
General mark				2·45	0·80

Second Composition

	25%	50%	75%	Arithmetic Mean	Standard Deviation
Spelling				2·99	0·96
Style				2·12	1·05
Content				1·78	0·85
General mark				2·54	0·80

differ from one another in the 'strictness of marking'. Spelling was marked most unfavourably (Arithmetic mean = 2·89 and 2·99 respectively); the complete marking scale had been fully applied. The marking of style was considerably more generous (Arithmetic mean = 2·99 and 2·12 respectively). The general mark did not represent an overall average of the marks given for spelling, style and content, but was influenced most strongly by the spelling mark and least strongly by the mark for content. This applies especially to the first of the two compositions.

Reliability of the External Criterion in Marking Arithmetic Tests

In the arithmetic tests the marks ranged from (1) to (5) in the fourth form, from (2) to (5) in the fifth form (no 'very good' (1)). In the fourth form the grades 'good' (2) and 'satisfactory' (3) occurred most frequently (83 per cent in all); in the fifth form, 'satisfactory' (3) and 'sufficient' (4) (81 per cent in all).

Although both the tests were set according to the same principles, the test for the fifth form showed a considerably stricter marking (Arithmetic mean = 2·56).

FIGURE II

MARKING OF TWO ARITHMETIC TESTS

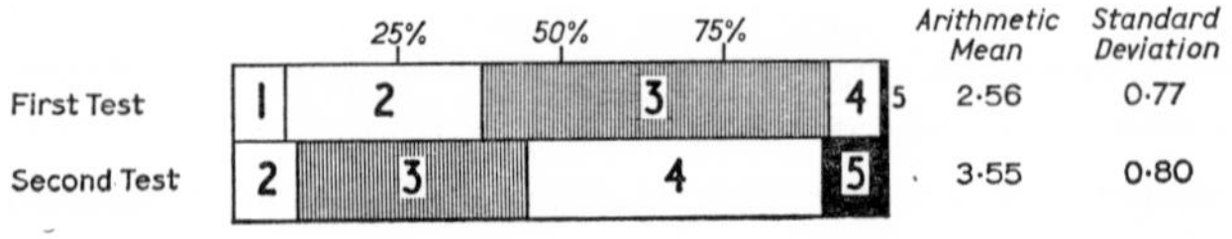

	25%	50%	75%	Arithmetic Mean	Standard Deviation
First Test				2·56	0·77
Second Test				3·55	0·80

Reliability of the Internal Criterion in Marking Compositions

The question to be examined is whether factors other than those resulting from efficiency are able to influence marking, such as positive or negative expectations caused by the presence of certain prejudices.

Marking was strongly influenced by the verbal hints put at the head of the compositions. Whereas 16 per cent of the assessors influenced by positive prejudice marked the spelling with 'very good' (1), there was not even one 'very good' (1) among those influenced by negative prejudice. On the other hand there are 11 per cent of 'insufficient' (5) influenced by negative prejudice compared with not even one 'insufficient' (5) influenced by positive prejudice.

The average marks differ by a full grade (A.M. = 2·35 against A.M. = 3·35). Also in the marks for style and content and in the general mark, this influence showed similar effects.

The differences are very significant throughout (P smaller than 1 per cent), except for content in the first composition (P smaller than 10 per cent).

FIGURE III

MARKING OF COMPOSITIONS UNDER POSITIVE NEGATIVE INFLUENCE

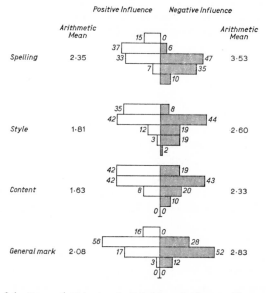

Reliability of the Internal Criterion in Marking Arithmetic Tests

Whereas an influence is clearly traceable in the fourth form (11 per cent compared to 0 per cent in the mark 'very good' (1); 5 per cent compared to 15 per cent and 0 per cent compared to 2 per cent in the marks 'sufficient'

(4) and 'insufficient' (5)), the degree of influence is very small in the fifth form. The deviation from the average range of marks, caused by prejudice is 'very significant' in the fourth form; not significant, however, in the fifth form.

FIGURE IV

MARKING OF ARITHMETIC TESTS UNDER POSITIVE NEGATIVE INFLUENCE

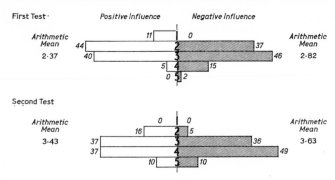

Summary

An examination of the reliability of marking compositions in spelling, style, content and general performance was attempted by having two compositions marked by 92 teachers; an examination as to the reliability of arithmetic marks was also attempted by having arithmetic tests marked by 272 teachers. Each of these teachers was experienced in teaching those forms from which the test papers were taken.

In the examinations we distinguished between external and internal criterion. External criterion was defined as the official marking degrees set up by the educational authorities, internal criterion was defined as the consideration of the average standard of performances of the respective class. The reliability of the external criterion is based on the fact that different teachers give equal judgement on equal performances on the grounds of precise wording and definitions. Apart from the disadvantages of the internal criterion, its reliability is proved if it is possible to apply the subjective criterion of performance without being influenced by motives other than those of the pupil's performance.

The examination of the external criterion has shown that the definitions of the educational authorities concerning the performances required for the different marking grades permit a very 'personal' interpretation. This statement does not apply only to compositions, for which it might even have been expected, but also to arithmetic tests.

The examination of the internal criterion showed considerable differences of marks in consequence of mere verbal hints, especially in compositions, and, above all, in spelling.

It may be conjectured with reason that in practice there is, moreover, considerably stronger liability to be influenced by the pupil's outward appearance, his actions and conduct, his way of speaking, knowledge about the performances of his brothers and sisters, and by the profession and the social status of his parents etc.

The number – marking system must, therefore, be considered extremely unreliable in marking compositions and, to a smaller extent, also in marking arithmetic tests.

Organization and Structure in Different Countries

Brian Holmes
Reader in Comparative Education in the University of London

There exists in England and Wales a 'wide range of examinations in use' (p. 110). In Scotland examination success has traditionally provided for any child, irrespective of the economic circumstances of its parents, a way up through 'a national system of education' (p. 120). For many years the problems associated with the running of examinations in France – a dominating influence on the whole system of education – have become 'more and more acute and less and less easy to solve' (p. 123). In Tanzania the structure of examinations is in process of transition from frequent selection to continuous assessment (p. 132). The traditional importance of school and university examinations as an agent of social mobility and professional success is increasing in the Federal German Republic (p. 140). In the German Democratic Republic examinations have a special role to play in the Socialist Unified Educational System as defined in the Act of 1965 (p. 146). Fears in the early days of the U.S.S.R. that examinations might 'foster formalism in teaching and get pupils into the habit of mechanical memorization of material, rather than promote a creative approach to study' have proved to be unfounded (p. 152).

In spite of these rather different foci of attention, the chapters in this section make clear that practically every country has a system of examinations which plays an enormous role in the operation of its national system of education. Sometimes, as in England and Wales, a great many agencies participate in the administration of various examinations. The system is largely unplanned, *ad hoc* arrangements being made to meet particular needs. In other countries such as France, the state is solely responsible for conferring examination awards, and the planning of examinations is part of a complex administrative machinery. Differences of opinion also exist about the effects of examinations on the schools. Rarely in any country is there consensus of opinion. Many teachers think they adversely affect teaching methods, circumscribe syllabuses and curricula, do little justice to many important pupil achievements and so on. Others consider that examinations exclude children unnecessarily from certain forms of education and curtail it for many. Admittedly, other educators, while deploring the restrictions placed on education by examinations, maintain that they offer the most objective way of selecting pupils for further education, of assessing what they have learnt and of providing incentives. These issues are referred to in all the articles, most of which show not only how examinations relate to the system as a whole, but reveal reform tendencies in various countries.

Traditional patterns of organizing examinations external to a school, can be discerned. Usually, children are assessed at the end of the primary stage of education when decisions are made about their educational future. The tendency is to modify the modes of assessment used; to postpone selection for the second stage of education; or, by re-structuring this stage, to abolish the need for selection altogether. The next point at which some kind of external examination is taken is towards the end of compulsory schooling. Success often leads to continued secondary education and may serve as an indication of occupational competence. At this point, special examinations and tests may also be given to assess occupational competence, but more frequently these are used after a period of technical training. However, examinations which give access to higher education and preparation for a professional career dominate most systems.

The expansion of educational systems has undoubtedly thrown a great strain on educational systems. The democratization of education has also made rigorous selection within a system unacceptable. Some of the problems of reforming the organization of examinations systems consequent on these changes are analysed in the chapters in this section.

11

England and Wales

Henry G. Macintosh
Deputy Secretary, Associated Examining Board

Daisy M. Penfold
Senior Lecturer in Statistics, University of London Institute of Education

The charts on pages 117–9 have been designed to show in outline the wide range and variety of examinations at present in use in England and Wales and to provide information which, together with the bibliography, may assist those interested in following further lines of inquiry. It will be seen that in many respects the system in England and Wales differs from the continental system. In the first place there is no nationally administered examination, and in the second place there is, at present, a variety of secondary schooling available. The two major examinations in the secondary field, the General Certificate of Education (G.C.E.) and the Certificate of Secondary Education (C.S.E.), have created at the present time a number of problems of general interest which arise in large measure through their being administered by twenty-two approved boards instead of one national board. These examinations have therefore been chosen for detailed discussion in this chapter.

The General Certificate of Education (G.C.E.)

The G.C.E. examination is today administered by eight boards approved by the Department of Education and Science, all but one of which developed historically from university interest in the qualifications of their prospective entrants. These boards can examine in any part of the United Kingdom, although in the course of time some of them inevitably have developed close connections with particular geographical areas. There is a wide range of subjects, each of which is examined upon a prescribed syllabus at two levels: the Ordinary (or O level), taken in the main at the age of 15–16, and the Advanced (or A level), taken in the main at 17–18. At either level a candidate may offer any number of subjects, but these need not all be taken at the same time. At O level, nine numbered grades are awarded, grades 1 to 6 being grades of pass. At A level there are seven lettered grades, grades A–E being grades of pass. In addition, at A level a grade O is awarded to candidates who it is considered would have obtained an O level pass had they been entered for that examination.

The establishment of the G.C.E. should be seen in the context of the new patterns of secondary education which arose out of the 1944 Education Act, two aspects of which are particularly important here. First, the Act envisaged secondary education for all, whereas prior to the second world war secondary education had been for the limited number who could obtain grammar school places, and secondly, it provided for the immediate raising of the school-leaving age to 15 and ultimately to 16.[1] This brought about not only a great increase in the number of candidates entering for the G.C.E. but also an increased awareness of the importance of the qualifications and certification which followed the successful completion of a school course. The increased entry was met in two ways: by the expansion of the existing G.C.E. boards, and by the creation of the Associated Examining Board, which is concerned with the preparation of a range of subjects and approaches to meet the needs of candidates now presenting themselves from a more diverse range of educational establishments.

The Certificate of Secondary Education (C.S.E.)

This examination was the outcome of recommendations contained in the Beloe Report (1958) which laid down certain criteria to which the new examination should conform. In summary these were: that the examination should be on a subject basis; that it should be appropriate for pupils at the end of the fifth year of a secondary school course; that it should be specially designed to suit the needs and interests of a range of pupils covering approximately the 40th to the 80th percentiles of ability, and finally, that the examinations were to be controlled by the teachers themselves – the standards, in the last resort, depending on their collective judgement. Unlike the G.C.E., the C.S.E., as finally set up, is not a pass/fail examination. Five grades are used to record performance in all subjects, the reference grades being Grade 1, which is the equivalent of a G.C.E. pass, and Grade 4, which a pupil of average ability 'might reasonably be expected to secure'. The C.S.E. is administered by fourteen regional boards, all of which can accept candidates from schools in their areas. The examinations are held once a year and are conducted in any one of three modes: Mode 1, in which the papers, based upon a prescribed syllabus, are externally set and marked; Mode 2, in which the papers are based upon the school's own syllabus but are externally set and marked; and Mode 3, in which the papers are based upon the school's own syllabus and are set and marked by the school, but subject to external moderation by the board concerned. Modes 1 and 2 were already in use in the G.C.E. but Mode 3 represented an exciting new departure in the form

---

[1] To be effected in 1972–73.

of the school-based examination and paved the way for considerable experimentation in examining techniques.

Problems and Scope of Examinations

The results of recent experiments which have underlined the lack of objectivity in marking in certain subjects, taken in conjunction with the rapidly expanding entry, have inevitably led to increased discussion upon, and interest in, the role of secondary school tests. These are designed both to measure achievement at a given point in time upon a defined subject-matter area and also to predict future success. This multi-purpose nature is emphasized on the chart and applies both to the C.S.E. and the G.C.E., although the former examination is less explicitly concerned with the predictive aspect. Three major issues which are common both to the G.C.E. and the C.S.E. may be highlighted. These are:

(1) the need to define objectives more clearly;
(2) the development of new testing techniques;
(3) the problem of comparability.

Objectives of Examining

Comparatively little thought has been given in England and Wales to consideration of the objectives of examinations or indeed of the school courses they evaluate. As a result, the use of the examinations for feed-back to the teachers in terms of providing a profile of skills relating to the objectives of the course has tended to be overlooked. Hitherto the majority of the questions in these examinations have been of the essay type and candidates have been required to answer four or five such questions out of a total of ten or twelve. This means that the questions have been multi-purpose and intended to elicit more than one skill or ability. As a rule no attempt is made, except in the roughest possible way, to assess the relative weighting to be given to these different skills or to establish whether the essay question is necessarily the best way of testing all of them. Recent curriculum reform projects such as the Nuffield Science have, however, made definition of objectives an integral part of their approach. With such developments, the need to ensure that measurement adequately reflects objectives becomes of paramount importance and the new Nuffield G.C.E. papers make use of scientific testing techniques for example, short-answer and multiple-choice questions which can be objectively marked and which aim at testing one skill at a time.

New Testing Techniques

Examinations Bulletins Nos. 1 and 2 of the old Secondary School Examinations Council (the body replaced in 1964 by the Schools Council for the Curriculum and Examinations), recognized and welcomed the challenge of the problems created by the fluid structure of the new C.S.E. examination; examinations Bulletins Nos. 3, 4 and 5 outlined principles of good examining, being concerned, respectively, with techniques of examining, objective type examinations and school based examinations; and Bulletins Nos. 2, 6–11 and 13, published between 1964 and 1966, contained details of trial examinations. All this left the reader in no doubt that this challenge was accepted with good will and enthusiasm on the part of Ministry, research and university personnel in the United Kingdom. Particular innovations at that time were the recommended use of scientific examining procedures such as are illustrated in the Mathematics papers of Bulletins Nos. 2 and 7 and in the Science paper of Bulletin No. 8, the latter including suggestions for a section on 'scientific thinking' and a practical test which can be to a certain extent objectively marked. Quite apart from their educational merits such trends are perhaps inevitable in view of the increasing numbers of candidates presenting themselves for examination. The suggestions in Bulletins 9, 10 and 11, regarding methods suitable for examining Oral English, Music and Home Economics, compatible with modern developments in these subjects, also appear to be of general interest.

The Problem of Comparability

Comparability can never be achieved in absolute terms. Moreover, its attainment in a very limited form may well only be at the expense of variety. Concern with comparability is, however, a major consideration since examination results are used as the principal means of selection for admission to the universities and professions as well as to a wide range of other employment. 'Comparability' as far as the G.C.E. boards are concerned implies that a candidate taking the same subject with two boards ought to obtain the same grade in both examinations. For the C.S.E. boards, however, 'comparability' implies not only comparability between boards but also comparability between C.S.E. Grade 1 and a G.C.E. pass. In addition, it implies comparability between different modes of examining in the same subject and between different tests on the same subject proposed by schools in the internal or school-based Mode 3. The main reason for C.S.E. concern over the problem of comparability lies not so much in the educational desirability or undesirability of achieving it but in the attitude of the user to an examination not yet fully established. The problem is a complex one since it seems clear from recent studies of inter-board comparability in the G.C.E. (as yet unpublished) that the major cause of discrepant results lies in the different types of problems posed by different boards in similar subjects. In order, therefore, to investigate problems of comparability it is necessary not only to look at the syllabuses, question papers and mark schemes involved but also to obtain the answer to such questions as: when the same candidate's performance differs on papers on the same subject, which board's approach more closely reflected the preparation; which set of results correlated most closely with the teachers' estimates; and finally, what was the motivation of the candidates? Did they really put an equal amount of effort into both papers? Research is needed into the development of a variety of moderating techniques, of which the work carried out by the National Foundation for Educational Research on G.C.E./C.S.E. Grade 1 comparability; work on agreement trials for Mode 3 C.S.E., and the provision of objective tests common to all or several of the boards in G.C.E., are but three examples. Because of limited space it is only possible to illustrate the first of these in any detail here. Schools Council Working Paper No. 6 (1966), Part 1, presents a statistical analysis of the results of a sample representative of different types and sizes of schools in an attempt to study comparability between seven G.C.E. and nine C.S.E. boards. Nine schools for each G.C.E. board and twenty for each C.S.E. board were chosen to give a stratified cluster of samples. Previous experience with 11+ norms in different counties suggested that there would be genuine variability in attainment in the different areas represented by the boards. The extent of this was investigated by obtaining scores for all candidates sampled in 1965 on a 100-item scholastic aptitude reference test and deciding upon a cut-off point corresponding to the lowest level of G.C.E. pass in each subject considered. This should correspond to the lower band of the Grade 1 C.S.E. in the same subject. If a board awarded Grade 1's significantly in excess of the proportion indicated by the reference test it might mean that that particular board was lenient and that its award of Grade 1's needed adjusting. Such a conclusion, however, could only be sustained if a similar pattern were repeated over a period of years. Teachers' forecasts of grades for their pupils were also invited, and these, too, were subjected to scientific analysis presented in detail in Part II of Working Paper No. 6. The assumption of a high relationship between the reference test and curriculum subjects is, of course, tenuous. Nevertheless, group results rather than those of individuals were in question and the subjects of the investigation were English, Mathematics, Science, Geography, History and French. These subjects are all taken by large numbers of candidates and are sufficiently academic in content to make such an assumption reasonable. On the evidence available, area standards often seemed to be variable, although the reasons for this need much fuller investigation before conclusions on such matters as lenience or severity can be drawn. A second experiment of the same kind in 1965, but on a smaller scale, was reported in Working Paper No. 9 (1967), using special subject reference tests in English and Mathematics to replace the scholastic aptitude test. Correlation coefficients as high as 0·78 were quoted to demonstrate the relationship between the mathematics reference test and both G.C.E. and C.S.E. grades, thus justifying the use of the former as a moderating device. Satisfactory, though lower, correlations were shown for the English sector and in both cases it was demonstrated that these were higher than those obtained with the scholastic aptitude test. However, the results of the larger scale repetition of this experiment in 1966 which may confirm these findings are not yet published. It is interesting to note that Report No. 6 states '. . . it is proposed to begin investigation on an entirely new reference test of attainment comprising a bank of items of known technical values and interrelationships from which boards could draw those which they considered to be valid calibrators of their own examinations'. It is possible that the reports quoted above will go down in history as a record of mere teething troubles but the fillip they have given to the use of scientific methodology in such situations is undeniable.

Conclusion

The comparative absence of any research reports on G.C.E. tests points, on the one hand, to the comparatively small amount of research that has hitherto been carried out and, on the other, to the fact that such work as has been done has not normally been published in a form which makes it generally available. To this the Occasional Publications published by the Joint Matriculation Board are a notable exception. In the last two years, however, the boards themselves have become more professional in the sense that they realize the need for properly qualified research workers and statisticians on their staffs. Virtually all G.C.E. boards are experimenting with objective and school-based tests. An inter-board research project in A level Physics has been undertaken and more limited projects in other subjects are also being undertaken by smaller groups of boards. The majority of C.S.E. boards have, from the start, processed their results on computers, and more than half the eight G.C.E. boards now do so. The greater availability of statistical information resulting from this has made awarding procedures more sophisticated. It has also made it possible for more research to be undertaken, the main problem here being the need for co-ordination so as to avoid duplication of effort.

Informed discussion on the many problems associated with secondary school testing in England and Wales is essential if solutions are to be devised for them. Only in this way can a situation be created in which undesirable backwash effects are kept to a minimum and in which the teacher and others concerned with the education of children receive the maximum amount of useful information.

BIBLIOGRAPHY

Secondary Education with Special Reference to Grammar Schools and Technical High Schools (The Spens Report), H.M.S.O. 1938.

Curriculum and Examinations in Secondary Schools (The Norwood Report), H.M.S.O. 1943 (reprinted 1962).

Half our Future (The Newsom Report). H.M.S.O. 1963.

Secondary School Examinations other than the G.C.E. (The Beloe Report). H.M.S.O. 1960.

Seventh Report of the Secondary School Examinations Council. H.M.S.O. 1963.

Examining at Sixteen + (Report of the Joint G.C.E./C.S.E. Committee of the Schools Council). H.M.S.O. 1966.

Schools Council Working Paper No. 6. Parts I and II: The 1965 C.S.E. Monitoring Experiment. H.M.S.O. 1966.

Schools Council Working Paper No. 9.: Standards in C.S.E. and G.C.E. English and Mathematics. H.M.S.O. 1967.

Schools Council Working Paper No. 12.: The Educational Implications of Social and Economic Change. H.M.S.O. 1967.

Examinations Bulletin Series, C.S.E. H.M.S.O. 1963—

J. A. Petch, *Fifty Years of Examining: The Joint Matriculation Board.* London, Harrap, 1953.

The J.M.B. – What it is and What it Does. O.P. 16. 1963 (Joint Matriculation Board, Manchester 15).

G.C.E. London. London University 1964 (University of London, Senate House, London, W.C.1.)

The C.S.E.: A Handbook for Moderators. D. R. Mather, N. France and G. T. Sare (London, Collins 1965).

STRUCTURE OF THE ENGLISH EDUCATIONAL SYSTEM

The degree of flexibility in transfers is much greater than a simplified diagram can illustrate. Transfers take place at all levels and ages but, for simplicity, arrows indicating possible transfers have been omitted.

Age	Year of Schooling				
24	20				
23	19				
22	18				
21	17	*Professional Training*	CNAA		*Professional Training*
20	16	University	HND OND	Further Education Advanced Craft or Technician ONC HNC	University Further Education
19	15				Industry Commerce
18	14				
17	13	Sixth Form	Further Education Craft Technician		Public School
16	12				
15	11	*Secondary* Grammar Technical Modern Comprehensive			
14	10				
13	9				
12	8				
11	7				
10	6	Primary School			Preparatory
9	5				
8	4				
7	3				Private
6	2	Infant School			
5	1				

OND = Ordinary National Diploma
HND = Higher National Diploma
CNAA = Council for National Academical Awards

EXAMINATION STRUCTURE IN ENGLAND AND WALES

It is important to emphasize that although this chart is intended to provide a reasonably detailed picture it does not include all examinations or all examining bodies.

Detail: Stage of education	Examining body	Name of examination	Main purposes
Primary	Local Education Authorities Tests normally supplied by testing services, e.g. GTRU, NFER	Selection examination for secondary education	Selection for secondary education Placement within secondary education
Secondary	Eight independent boards	GCE O level A level	Attainment as a terminal qualification and prediction for higher and further education
	Fourteen independent boards	CSE	Ditto
Further	CGLI/REB	Various operative, craftsmen and technicians qualifications	Attainment and/or prediction
	Various bodies, COP, RSA, etc.	Various commercial qualifications	Ditto
	Joint Committee of DES	ONC, HNC, OND, HND	Technician qualification
	Professional bodies	Associate/Fellow of body concerned	Professional qualification
Higher	Universities CNAA	Bachelor and higher degrees	Attainment
	Institutes of Education	Teachers' Certificates	Attainment
Other Examinations	Civil Service Commission	Various	Selection for Civil Service
	Defence Services	Various	Internal promotion and trade testing
	Various bodies e.g. NFER, NIIP, GTRU	Various	Guidance (a) within schools/colleges for attainment and selection (b) within schools for diagnosis and remedial action (c) end of school/college course for career guidance (d) within industry/commerce for promotion and selection

LIST OF ABBREVIATIONS USED

COP = College of Preceptors
CSE = Certificate of Secondary Education
GTRU = Godfrey Thomson Research Unit
NFER = National Foundation for Educational Research
CGLI = City and Guilds of London Institute
REB = Regional Examining Boards

Normal age of candidates	Type of test	Extent used	Changes contemplated
10–12	Objective Testing Verbal reasoning English Arithmetic	Nationally, but use for selection rapidly decreasing	Further developments unlikely
16 18 15 or 16	Largely narrative together with practical tests and elements of objective testing – internally or externally assessed	Upper 20 per cent of intelligence range Next 40 per cent of intelligence range	Increasing elements of objective testing and of teacher assessment
16 to 21	Largely external, narrative and practical examinations	Nationally	Possible introduction of objective testing
16 to 21	Ditto	Ditto	Ditto
18 to 22	Internally set and marked narrative examinations together with course work	Ditto	Possible use for admission to professional status
18 to 25	External narrative examinations	Ditto	
21 to 22	Internal narrative examinations	Ditto	Move away from written papers as sole terminal test
20 to 22	Largely internal, written and practical. Externally assessed	Ditto	
16 upwards	Written + interview	Nationally	Possible introduction of objective testing
16 upwards	Written + interview + practical	Ditto	Introduction of objective testing
7–22 7–22 15–22 16 upwards	Attainment + aptitude interview	Ditto	New British intelligence test

RSA = Royal Society of Arts
DES = Department of Education and Science
CNAA = Council for National Academical Awards
NIIP = National Institute of Industrial Psychology
ONC = Ordinary National Certificate
HNC = Higher National Certificate
OND = Ordinary National Diploma
HND = Higher National Diploma

12

Scotland

Douglas M. McIntosh
Principal, Moray House College of Education, Edinburgh

The foundations of a national system of education were laid in Scotland in the sixteenth century. Schools were established in each parish whereby every child, irrespective of the economic circumstances of his parents, was to be given the opportunity to travel along the broad educational highway leading to the university. From the parish schools in the Islands and Highlands, the glens and the cities of Scotland, children enrolled in the universities, and in 1867 the Argyll Commission on Education reported that Scotland compared favourably with any country in respect of the proportion of its inhabitants attending university, and that 16 per cent of the students were the sons of artisans and skilled labourers. It is perhaps not surprising that Scottish teachers developed a 'ruthless efficiency' in preparing pupils for written examinations and created a deep respect for them as a means of assisting with the learning process.

There were three stages at which major educational decisions had to be made. First, at the end of primary schooling when a pupil had to decide whether to proceed to secondary education which was in essence a preparation for university education. Secondly, at the end of the secondary schooling when the decision had to be made whether the pupil would proceed to university. Thirdly, after pupils left school and entered commerce or industry when they could obtain career qualifications by attendance at 'night classes' organized largely in schools in the evenings.

Examination barriers had to be surmounted to gain admission to secondary school and university. In the early stages, no clearly defined admission qualifications were necessary for evening classes: the wastage rate was high as success was achieved only by those who could survive the ordeal of a hard day's work followed by regular evening study. The provision of full-time courses for technological and technical training is a recent development.

Entry to secondary education was achieved in the early stages by passing a 'qualifying' examination: there was no question of limiting the numbers who passed because of the lack of provision. The early creation of a national system of education avoided the necessity for a large number of private schools such as exist in England, and the large majority of pupils in Scotland attended state schools. In England the 11+ examination raised hostility because of its selective nature, whereas the 'qualifying' examination and its successors were regarded more as standards to be reached in order to obtain entry to an academic secondary education. For those pupils who did not wish, or were judged incapable of profiting from, an academic education, the junior secondary school was created. It was, however, generally regarded as providing an inferior type of education and thus some form of comprehensive education was inevitable. Transfer tests, the successor of the qualifying examination, generally consisting of objective tests of Intelligence, English and Arithmetic, lost their significance and are being discarded. Attention is now concentrated upon the best means of assessing a pupil's ability in order to give the most efficient educational guidance.

For a small country with a secondary education which was essentially a preparation for university entrance, it was relatively easy to create a national system of examinations to mark the successful completion of secondary schooling. This was achieved in 1888 with the establishment of the Scottish Leaving Certificate. Originally it was a group certificate, gained only by passes in given subjects: failure to gain one of these subjects meant re-sitting all the examinations. The wide acceptance of the certificate for entrance qualifications to many professional and semi-professional careers has made it necessary for the group certificate to be abandoned. Now the value of the certificate is determined by the character of the endorsements which may be gained at any time.

The examinations for the Scottish Certificate of Education, as it is now called, are at two levels – 'O' (Ordinary) grade and 'H' (Higher) grade. Argument rages about the advantages and disadvantages of specialization at the school stage. Scotland has adhered to the pattern of a broad general education, and university entrance qualifications based on the 'H' grade certificate are normally obtained after five years' study at secondary school, the sixth year being devoted to a liberal form of education un-trammelled by examination requirements. The demand for some form of certificate for the sixth-year pupils has led to the introduction of a Certificate of Sixth Year Studies. This certificate, introduced in 1968, is not parallel to the English 'A' level as it attempts to cover a much wider range of ability.

National dependence on industrial efficiency has led to the recognition that all workers in commerce and industry must be trained, and thus day release has been introduced whereby workers are given the opportunity to attend local technical colleges during the day. Some employers, how-ever, still insist that day release should be accompanied by attendance at classes in the evenings and the Scottish tradition is still strong in this respect.

The certificates normally taken in the technical colleges are many and varied. National Certificates at the 'H' and 'O' standard are offered in many establishments, the higher standard being generally regarded as almost equivalent to university degree standard. Examinations of the City and Guilds London Institute are also popular for the courses with the more practical bias, and the Royal Society of Arts provides suitable examinations for those in the field of Commerce.

Technical college students may be categorized into four groups, technologist, technician, craftsman, operative; and there is a tendency to provide external examinations for all ranges of training. Unlike most academic examinations, however, which are multi-purpose, those provided in the technical colleges tend to be set for specific forms and levels of industrial and commercial training.

Entry into a wide variety of careers in Scotland is now dependent on a highly organized examination structure. The content and methods of teaching in the institutions which prepare for the examinations are largely influenced by the character of the examinations. Research and development is now being undertaken to ensure that the educational effects of the examinations are beneficial and that they measure the success with which pupils and students achieve the objectives of the prescribed courses of study rather than those determined by the examiners.

13

France

Louis Legrand
Director and Head, Département de la Recherche Pedagogique de l'Institut Pedagogique National, Paris

Among the difficult problems which preoccupy the educational authorities in France, that of examinations deserves special attention. Indeed, for some years the growing number of examinations and candidates has been causing local and national administrators problems which are more and more acute and less and less easy to solve. To give a clearer idea of the scale of the problem, let us recall that in France the state is solely responsible for the conferring of examination awards, or, in other words, the planning of examinations is part of complex administrative machinery. The examining panels are *départementaux* (belonging to the administrative departments, of which there are nearly a hundred in France), regional or national, but are not particular to any one establishment. Consequently there is a vast network of different subjects and examiners, working on a departmental, *académique* (examination board) or national basis; and consequently, too, a jigsaw of handwriting styles, correspondence, meetings and fees. It must also be remembered that school holidays in France begin on 1 July and last for two and a half months, and that these, together with the brief holidays at Christmas and Easter, leave only 180 days available for teaching. In such circumstances, for a greater part of the teaching profession to devote a whole month to examinations is dangerously to reduce the number of days available for real teaching of the vast majority of the pupils.

How has this come about? There seems to be a variety of causes.

First of all, the general increase in the number of pupils (200,000 more pupils of the same age each year since 1945), accompanied by a greater desire for education and an extended period of schooling, has certainly brought in its wake a considerable increase in candidates for the established examinations. This does not, however, seem to be the principal reason. Teaching reforms and the change in traditional orientation appear to be just as important.

Reforms in the System

Prior to the reforms adopted in recent years, the French teaching system was divided into parallel streams involving different types of teaching, and depending on different government regulations. Each stream had its own financial system and its own examinations. Elementary education thus included several examinations: at the end of compulsory primary education, the *certificat d'études primaires* (primary certificate) was sat by those children who either could not, or did not wish to, go on to higher grade studies. Then at the age of 15–16, the *brevet d'enseignement élémentaire* (brevet of elementary education) was taken by children who still received primary teaching, but who had entered more advanced courses, the *cours complémentaires*. Before the 1939–1945 war, elementary education even included courses at the level of the 'second cycle' (secondary – over 16) in what were called *écoles primaires supérieures* (advanced elementary schools) which prepared pupils for the *brevet supérieur* (advanced brevet).

In parallel to primary education, there developed the traditional secondary education, remotely descended from the Jesuit schools which had been taken over by Napoleonic decree. Entry to secondary schools was by an *examen d'entrée en 6e.* (entry examination at the age of 10–11). Seven or eight years' study led to the first part of the *baccalauréat* and, in the following year, to the second part: both these examinations, which were set by the *enseignement supérieur* (higher education authorities), constituted the qualifying examination for the universities.

Lastly, and more recently, the *écoles nationales professionnelles* (technical secondary schools) accepted pupils aged 10–11 who had passed an entry examination. After five or six years' study, pupils in these schools sat for *brevets d'enseignement industriel ou d'enseignement commercial* (brevets of industrial or commercial training) specifically related to the subjects studied. In addition, after the 1939–1945 war technical education developed short courses for pupils entering at the age of 14 after a primary education. These courses led to the various *certificats d'aptitude professionnelle* (proficiency certificates) in technical colleges.

The three types of education described above generally catered for pupils from different social backgrounds. But they often meant that pupils of the same age, especially in general education between the ages of 12 and 16, received much the same lessons.

The main object of educational reform has been to break down the barriers between different types of teaching, and to bring together pupils of the same age, hitherto scattered in different schools of the *premier cycle* (first secondary level: 11–16 years), in comprehensive establishments where there are at present great efforts to broaden the curriculum by the reorganization and amalgamation of previously existing courses. These are the *collèges d'enseignement secondaire* (secondary colleges), which bring together the classical and modern subjects of the traditional secondary schools; the modern subjects of the old *cours complémentaires* (advanced primary courses) which had already formed schools for more general education; the subjects studied by the final primary classes (12–14); and the subjects originally taken by pupils aged between 14 and 16 years in the old *écoles nationales professionnelles* (technical secondary schools). This amalgamation in comprehensive establishments is now going ahead and is accompanied by considerable modifications in the curriculum, with the aim of creating the greatest possible homogeneity.

This great change, amply justified for ethical and economic reasons, ought, of course, to have brought with it considerable modifications in the examination structure. But the reforming zeal devoted first to the educational structure and now to the definition of the syllabus and teaching methods, has not yet touched the examination system. So it continues as before, rendered even more complicated by the reforms outlined above. Thus it is still possible, at various stages of education, to find examinations belonging to the old types of education, which continue to exist in the completely different framework.

It should be explained that the reformers sought to introduce a system of orientation instead of the existing one of selection. It is now accepted in France that a child receives compulsory education up to the age of 16, and that during the last four years of his compulsory education he will be orientated successively towards entry to the *second cycle*, to courses and kinds of teaching which correspond to his abilities. This orientation, in theory, is not irrevocable. The various counsellors concerned with orientation at different stages are expected to advise parents but not to decide absolutely the course to be followed. The open nature of the orientation is balanced by an appeal system which allows parents to have their children examined when they are not in agreement with the recommended course. Thus the traditional system of examinations is further complicated by a new system introduced by the reformers themselves.

On the one hand, the amalgamation created in the *premier cycle* whilst retaining the various examinations of the old educational system, has considerably modified their function and the number of candidates. On the other hand, by introducing the system of orientation and appeal examinations, reforms have added to the traditional examinations new examinations which are often taken at the same stage and by the same pupils, but which, in fact, duplicate each other. The transitional period explains the proliferation of French examinations and their temporarily erratic character.

The Examination Ladder

Let us try to make the position more comprehensible by seeing, step by step, how one French schoolchild could be affected if he entered for all the available examinations.

At the age of 11, on leaving elementary school, the French schoolchild may wish to enter the first year of a course specializing in traditional classical and modern subjects. If the qualified local counsel favours the request, he will go straight into a course in the *premier cycle* specializing in those subjects. If, alternatively, he is considered unsuitable, and his parents appeal, he will sit for a qualifying examination. If he fails the examination, he will remain at an elementary school where reform has not yet penetrated, or will enter a comprehensive course in the *premier cycle*, but in a transition class. If the pupil has entered the first year of a traditional secondary course, he is reassessed at the end of the second year; if he is judged suitable, he is admitted on the basis of his school record to the third year. If unsuitable then, he will be directed either to a technical college for a short vocational training, or to a more practical third year in the same school. If his parents oppose this, the pupil will sit an examination to assess his ability. He may also, at the age of 14, and regardless of future plans, enrol for the *certificat d'études primaires* which is open to any pupil. This examination, originally intended for pupils leaving school at the age of 14, is, in fact, taken by nearly all French schoolchildren.

If our pupil has succeeded in entering the third year of the traditional secondary course (whether classical or modern subjects), his course will lead after two years to another examination, the *brevet d'enseignement du premier cycle* (brevet of the first secondary level, usually referred to as the B.E.P.C.), and to another reassessment. Almost all pupils sit for the B.E.P.C. at the end of their fourth year. Those for whom the orientation counsellor has recommended transfer to the fifth year, but for whom the parents reject the decision, will sit an examination to reassess their ability; an examination which is on the same level as the B.E.P.C., which covers the same subjects and which is marked by the same examiners. The pupil may also, if he wishes, sit for the old *brevet d'enseignement élémentaire*. It is still held, each year, and has a faithful following. Suppose the pupil to have entered the *second cycle* (second secondary level – over 16); he will spend either two or three years at this stage. If he takes the short vocational course of two years, at the end of this period he will take a new examination, the *brevet d'enseignement professionnel* (the vocational brevet). But this brevet has not in fact brought about the suppression of the old *certificats d'aptitude professionnelle* which are widely recognized in industry and commerce, and which are also taken by apprentices who have left school. If the pupil follows the long vocational course of three years, he will sit for the *baccalauréat des techniciens* or the *brevets industriels ou commerciaux*. There is nothing, however, to prevent him, after two of the three years, from taking the *certificat d'aptitude professionnelle*, theoretically intended for students taking the shorter two-year course. And he will usually do so. If the pupil has entered the 'second cycle' for the longer classical or modern course, he will normally reach the *baccalauréat* after three years. Recent regulations have suppressed the first part of the *baccalauréat*, but it is stipulated that if, unfortunately, he is judged unsuitable by the orientation counsellor for entry into the sixth year of his choice, he will again have to sit for a reassessment examination.

We apologize for the incomplete and tedious nature of this account. Many additions could be made: to mention but one, the assessment examination which pupils in receipt of a state bursary must take from time to time to prove their ability and to justify the continuation of the bursary.

The proliferation of French examinations is therefore to be explained historically by the superimposing of new examinations, based on new ideas, on old examinations which exist and continue to flourish. But the fact that the old ones do still exist and flourish makes a purely historical explanation unsatisfactory. The historical argument could be put forward if it were simply a question of a transitional period. But the incredible aspect of the situation is the astonishing vitality of theoretically out-of-date examinations, and also the enormous interest that more and more people show in them.

The Social Value of Examinations in France

This situation can only be explained by the social value given in France to examinations and the security which parents see in them. School studies are so long, and who knows if a child will reach the end satisfactorily? A paper qualification is always very useful; it opens many doors, even to the least skilled jobs, when a public sweeper needs to have at least the *certificat d'études primaires* (primary certificate); when salaries are often fixed according to the *certificat d'aptitude professionnelle* (proficiency certificate) or the *brevet d'enseignement professionnel* (vocational brevet); when advanced studies are impossible without the *baccalauréat*. All this explains the rush of pupils in traditional secondary courses for the *certificat d'études primaires* (primary certificate) at the age of 14, and for the B.E.P.C. (brevet of the first secondary level) at the age of 16; and, on the other hand, the rush of pupils in technical courses for the *certificats d'aptitude professionnelle* (proficiency certificates).

It is important to note that the creation of the new assessment examinations cannot be understood without appreciating the particular ethical attitude of the French to examinations. The French believe in examinations as the only means of impartial judgement. They are extremely wary of anything that could be a subjective judgement. Reformers have sought, for purposes of true orientation, to encourage evaluation by a pupil's school record, by his intellectual development, and by a psychological study of his personality. But this system is extremely suspect to the majority of Frenchmen. They smell privilege, political intervention, occult influences or even bribery. It is for that reason that official reforms have incorporated the appeal and reassessment system. This system, if not really useful or helpful, is psychologically reassuring in so far as it guarantees an impartial marking of numbered examination papers by anonymous examiners.

This social explanation is, nevertheless, very surprising when it is remembered that French examinations are still organized on very traditional lines. At all levels they consist of written and oral tests marked out of 20, and are subject to subjective factors. The papers are usually marked by an examiner working on his own, who is more and more cut off from proper preliminary meetings to decide a common standard because of the sheer volume of entries. Double marking, which used to be the rule at primary level, has been abandoned almost everywhere for similar reasons. The problems of *docimologie* (true assessment)[1] and their solutions are nevertheless well appreciated in France, and the work of the Institut National d'Orientation Professionelle (I.N.O.P.), among other organizations, has for some years sharpened awareness in the right circles of the drawbacks to solitary marking, and of the unfairness of decisions based solely on such marking. But the great majority of French teachers, particularly those with a literary background, are loath to accept any more general assessment of a candidate's abilities. The French teacher, both by tradition and temperament, attaches more importance to the power of synthesis, to good reasoning and to the organized expression of knowledge than to knowledge for its own sake, and systems of more general assessment seem to him, rightly or wrongly, to place detailed knowledge above general intelligence. For that reason, multiple-choice questions have as yet no place in France, and it is perhaps for that reason, too, that the statistical adjustments which were for a time applied to the examiners' marks in the *baccalauréat* have been abandoned.

It must be agreed that at the present stage of institutions and opinions, it would be extremely dangerous to introduce any system of more general assessment. The superabundance of examinations weighs ever more heavily on schoolchildren and on teaching methods. Whether as a passport to a job, or as a means of orientation, examinations impose a whole series of terminal essays as a preparation. The examination syllabus thus dictates the

---

[1] For a fuller discussion see pp. 95–100.

route courses must follow, a route marked at regular intervals by the inevitable periods of revision. There is little room for individual initiative on the part of the teachers, or for an individual rhythm of development on the part of the pupils. These factors contribute largely to the number of repeated years and to the number of failures which are both such a blot on our teaching system.

An impartial scheme for more general assessment, limited to rationalizing this situation, would make the curriculum even more demanding and would not take account of the population pattern in the examination results. In this way it would accentuate present faults and would mean a more impersonal but harsher selectivity. It seems essential, therefore, that France should considerably reduce the number of examinations and acquaint the teaching profession with the true significance of the results of research in *docimologie*. Towards this end, it is encouraging to note that in January 1968 an important report was submitted for approval to the appropriate departments and to the *Conseil des Ministres*. It proposes the foundation of a national institute of educational information and orientation; the definition of orientation methods by the creation of a body of teacher/counsellors; and the suppression of the secondary school entry examination at the age of 11 and of the appeal examinations. This is an important step towards long-awaited simplification in the system.

APPENDIX

The tables on pages 130–31 show the figures for examinations in the primary and secondary schools in France, based on 800,000 pupils of the same age in any one year (see *Informations Statistiques No. 95*, Ministère de l'Education Nationale, I.E.N.).

TABLE I: Elementary Education 1966

Candidates	Certificate d'études primaires (primary certificate)			Brevet élémentaire (brevet of elementary education)			Brevet d'études du premier cycle (brevet of the first secondary level)		
	Entries	Passes	%	Entries	Passes	%	Entries	Passes	%
Boys	304,357	232,039	76·2	3,223	370	11·5	175,508	124,127	70·7
Girls	270,909	217,269	80·2	4,560	968	21·2	212,985	146,775	68·9
Total	575,266	449,308	78·1	7,783	1,338	17·2	388,493	270,902	69·7

TABLE II: Technical and Vocational Education 1965

Candidates	Certificat d'aptitude professionnelle (proficiency certificates)	Brevet professionnel (vocational brevet)	Brevet d'enseignement industriel (industrial brevet)	Brevet d'enseignement commercial (commercial brevet)	Brevet supérieur d'études commerciales (advanced commercial brevet)	Brevet d'enseignement social (brevet in social studies)	Brevet d'enseignement hôtelier (hotel and catering brevet)	Brevet de technicien (technical brevet)	Brevet de technicien supérieur (advanced technical brevet)	Diplôme d'élève breveté des lycées techniques d'état (advanced diploma for pupils in state technical schools)
Entries	318,768	13,859	23,105	27,573	6,229	1,454	3,398	68	9,355	4,207
Passes	170,127	5,072	14,917	21,483	4,507	1,115	284	53	5,119	
%	53·4	36·6	64·6	77·9	72·4	76·7	71·4	77·9	54·7	

TABLE III: BACCALAURÉAT 1966

Category Candidates	Philosophie (arts)	Sciences expérimentales (science)	Mathématiques élémentaires (pure mathematics)	Mathématiques et technique (technical mathematics)	Mathématiques et économie (economics)	Total
Entries	91,962	63,621	44,884	9,595	2,358	212,420
Passes	47,329	34,028	19,379	3,933	1,170	105,839
% passes	51·5	53·5	43·2	41·0	49·6	49·8

14

Mainland Tanzania

R. C. Honeybone
*Professor of Education and Director of Institute of Education, University College,
Dar es Salaam*

J. K. Beattie
Research Fellow, Institute of Education, University College, Dar es Salaam

The structure of the examinations in the schools of mainland Tanzania
is still in the process of transition from a system containing frequent
selection examinations to a planned system where the aim is to offer
continuous periods in primary and secondary schools with the minimum
of interruptions by internal and external selection examinations. Table I
shows the educational system in mainland Tanzania and indicates the
various selection hurdles which existed at Independence in December,
1961.

TABLE I
SCHOOL SYSTEM IN MAINLAND TANZANIA

1 *Primary*[1]
  (a) *Lower primary* Standards 1 to 4 with selection at the end of Standard 4 (still
      existing in rural areas in 1967).
  (b) *Upper primary* Standards 5 to 7 (up to Standard 8 until 1967). Selection at the
      end of Standard 6 now eliminated. Leaving and selection examination at the
      end of Standard 7 (formerly Standard 8) for entrance to secondary school.

2 *Secondary*
  (a) *Forms 1 to 4* Selection at the end of Form 2 now eliminated. Cambridge
      Overseas School Certificate and selection at end of Form 4.
  (b) *Forms 5 and 6* Cambridge Higher School Certificate at the end of Form 6 used
      as basis of selection for the University of East Africa.

It is clearly much more effective educationally and more economical
to create a system which encourages every entrant to complete the full
course than to encourage wastage at frequent intervals. Selection at
Form 2 in the secondary school has already been eliminated and the policy
in the primary schools is to encourage all Standard 1 entrants to anticipate
a full seven-year course. The system has recently been streamlined by

[1] The normal age-range for pupils in primary schools in Tanzania is from about seven
years in Standard 1 to fourteen or fifteen in Standard 7.

TABLE II

		1961	1962	1965	1966	1967 Estimated
PRIMARY	Standard 1	121,386			154,512	169,200
	Standard 4	95,391		126,536	126,499	
			28%		48%	
	Standard 5	19,721	26,803		60,721	
	Standard 7	14,649			46,816	
	Standard 8	11,732			18,946	
	Total Primary enrolment	486,470			740,991	825,000
	Total Primary Leavers from Std.7 and/or Std.8	11,732		46,647	52,547	67,000
SECONDARY			41%		14%	13%
	Form 1	4,196	4,810		6,377	6,685
	Form 4	1,603		4,505	4,723	5,139
			18%		18%	19%
	Form 5	236	286		826	900
	Form 6	176		603	761	834
	Total Secondary enrolment	11,832			23,836	25,000
UNIVERSITY			54%		68%	68%
	Entrants to University of East Africa	60	95		410	517

Enrolments in schools supported or aided from public funds in Tanzania showing increases from 1961 to 1966, and proportions of pupils who can continue to further education at certain points in the system.

abolishing Standard 8 and redoubling efforts to make Standards 1 and 2 full-time and more intensive. However, as fees are still charged in the primary schools, wastage will no doubt continue to some extent although its incidence is now less severe than it was. The figures shown in Table II can, however, be misleading for the drop in enrolment from Standard 4 to Standard 5 is due to the fact that there are still insufficient schools and teachers to accommodate pupils who wish to proceed to the upper primary school. This problem is steadily being resolved by preparing an increasing number of more highly qualified teachers but it seems unlikely that teacher and school supply will be able to catch up with the demand for a long time.

Standard 1 at the moment accommodates only about 55 per cent of the child population. More accurate figures will become available with the publication of the details of the 1967 census. Table II shows that the decrease in the incidence of selection has been very marked but is not yet completely removed from within the primary schools. It also shows the increase in the total number of children in the schools and the greater possibility of a carefully planned curriculum for Standards 1 to 7 and Forms 1 to 4.

Examinations at the End of Standard 4

At the moment the examination for the selection of Standard 5 pupils still exists but the figures need to be treated with care. Since the figure of 48 per cent moving from Standard 4 to Standard 5 in 1966 (shown in Table II) is based on the enrolments in the whole country, and since all Standard 1 entrants in urban areas can now go through the seven-year primary course without selection hurdles, it follows that in rural areas the selection ratio is often lower than 48 per cent.

Selection at this level is organized by the Regional Education Officers, and is based on the results of regionally constructed tests. These examinations vary somewhat between regions but the general pattern is two tests each lasting one-and-a-half hours. Language, arithmetic, and general knowledge are covered in the tests. The tests are set in the form of short free-response and multiple-choice items and do not appear to have much backwash on the teaching in the lower primary school.

Selection at Standard 6 has now been eliminated in the urban areas and, as the figures show, plays only a very small part in the rural areas. In other words, as the need for selection decreases and finally disappears, the examinations assume less importance and finally disappear.

Examinations at the End of the Full Primary Course

Table II shows that approximately 13 per cent of those pupils who complete the full course of primary education can proceed to secondary courses in publicly financed secondary schools. The annual number of primary leavers has been inflated during the three-year period of transition from a system of eight years' primary education to a seven-year system, but with the expansion of the primary system it is not likely to fall below 60,000 in future, and will go on increasing. The high cost of secondary facilities suggests that expansion at the higher level will be limited to the nation's requirements for high level manpower. The basic general education of Tanzanian citizens is therefore envisaged as a seven-year primary course, regarded as an end in itself. Indeed suggestions have been made that as the term primary is now a misnomer, a new name should be formulated to carry with it the implication that the education provided is complete in itself.

At the end of the full primary course, pupils take an examination which was until recently known as the General Entrance Examination, but is now called the Primary School Leaving Examination. This examination is made up of four attainment-type tests. These are constructed by the Ministry of Education and responsibility for their printing and distribution to the seventeen regions lies with the Examinations Secretary of the Ministry. The tests are identical for the whole country, except that in the period of transition from a seven- to an eight-year system of primary education, separate tests were set for pupils completing their courses at the two levels. The organization of examination centres, invigilation, distribution of test papers within Regions, and marking teams is done regionally under the administration of the Regional Education Officers. Regional boards meet under the Regional Education Officers to select primary leavers to fill the regional quotas of secondary places. Selections are made on the basis of test scores in the Primary School Leaving Examination, and primary cumulative records are also considered.

The four tests which comprise the Primary School Leaving Examination are: Swahili Language, English Language, Mathematics and General Knowledge. The latter paper covers content from general science, geography, history and civics. The time for the English Language paper is two hours, while the other three tests are allowed one-and-a-half hours each. Each of the four tests is marked out of a maximum of 75 points. The form of the papers varies somewhat in the different subjects, but is very largely of 'objective' type. The General Knowledge test is entirely in four-part multiple-choice form. The language papers contain multiple-choice and short free-response elements, and the mathematics tests contain short free-response or multiple-choice items followed by a number of longer problems which are also worked on the test paper itself. The four papers are all taken on one day.

Printed marking schemes and cardboard keys to the multiple-choice questions are provided, and systematic checks are arranged to minimize the possibility of errors in marking or addition.

Prior to 1965 an investigation of the reliability of these tests was carried out by an officer of the Ministry of Education with the assistance of staff from teachers' colleges. Samples of the 1965 and 1966 examinations have been subjected to a full item analysis by the Institute of Education, in co-operation with the Ministry of Education, in order to obtain estimates of internal reliability together with information on the performance of each test item. A follow-up study of the 1965 examination is now being conducted by the Institute of Education to obtain an estimate of the validity of the test marks when used for secondary selection.

Tests containing various alternative content and item forms in mathematics and general knowledge have recently been tried out in parallel Swahili and English versions by the Institute of Education. Up to the present time, English has been the medium of instruction in the higher classes of the primary schools. In future, Swahili will be used as the medium of instruction throughout, though English will be introduced as a subject in Standard 1 instead of in Standard 3.

The small selection ratio from the top of the primary system to the beginning of the secondary course, leads to a rather high degree of competition among pupils who have traditionally regarded entry to secondary school as the key to success in life. Inevitably, the content and form of the tests used in selection have a considerable backwash effect on primary school teaching and learning. The most important problem in examining at this level may well be the construction of tests which are valid in terms of the objectives of primary education as an end in itself for Tanzanians, while at the same time ensuring that these tests yield marks which will have adequate predictive validity when used in selecting those pupils who have the ability to serve the nation's requirements for high-level manpower. Such tests are now being tried out as part of an Institute of Education research project.

Examinations in Secondary Schools

More relative progress has been made in the development of secondary school education than in primary school education as a result of the priorities established in the Five Year Plan, 1964 to 1969. This put the emphasis on secondary school expansion. Selection at the end of Form 2 had already been eliminated and a four-plus-two-year secondary system firmly established. It is hoped that by expanding the facilities for secondary and higher education, national independence in high-level manpower can be achieved as soon as possible. The figures given in Table II imply an increase of slightly over 100 per cent in total secondary enrolments from 1961 to 1966. This is quite remarkable when considered in relation to the very high cost of secondary facilities. No fees are now paid for education in public secondary schools and wastage between Forms 1 and 4 has practically disappeared.

At the moment all secondary school external examinations are organized by the University of Cambridge Local Examinations Syndicate and consist of the School Certificate taken at the end of Form 4 and the Higher School Certificate taken at the end of Form 6. But in the fourth year of secondary education, pupils take an additional major examination. This is set and marked on a regional basis. It corresponds fairly closely to the Cambridge Certificate examination which is described below, and its purpose is to provide information for use in selecting entrants for Form 5 of the secondary school, teachers' colleges and other training establishments. The necessity for this examination arises from the fact that results of the Certificate examination are not published until well into the next school year, by which time Form 5 pupils should be started on their new course work. A number of Form 5 places are held over so that some adjustments can be made after publication of the Certificate Examination results.

The Certificate held at the end of Form 4 is set and marked by the Cambridge Local Examinations Syndicate in England. Up to and including 1967 a full School Certificate was awarded to candidates who passed in six subjects including English Language. The Certificate was awarded in three grades according to over-all performance, and credits and distinctions were given for outstanding achievement in the separate subjects.

In 1968, the Certificate awarded will be known as the East African Certificate of Education, but the examination will continue to be set and marked for the time being by the Cambridge Syndicate. In addition to the change of name, there is an important difference of concept in the new Certificate. There will be no 'full' Certificate as such, but only one general type Certificate which will record actual performance. Candidates from schools will be required to *offer* a minimum of six and a maximum of nine subjects at one and the same examination on the first occasion when they take the examination. The subjects offered must include Swahili, English, Mathematics and at least one science subject. The most important effects of the new Certificate and entry regulations in Tanzania are likely to be: (a) that all secondary school pupils will have to follow a broad curriculum including the two languages, mathematics and an element of science throughout the four-year course and (b) that students will not suffer the stigma which seemed to attach to failure to obtain a full Certificate in the past. A student could formerly achieve excellent results in a few subjects, but fail to obtain a School Certificate due to weakness in others, and especially due to weakness in English Language. In such cases a General

Certificate of Education was awarded, but it did not carry the prestige of the full School Certificate. The new Certificate will be in the same form for everyone, and its value will depend on the grade of subject results recorded, and their relation to the form of further education or employment for which the holder may be an applicant.

Performance in the School Certificate examination has remained at approximately the same level throughout the period of rapid school expansion. In 1961, 53·5 per cent of the 1,612 candidates obtained full School Certificates and 213 were awarded General Certificate of Education. In 1966 there were 4,766 candidates, of whom 51·5 per cent obtained the full Certificate and 33 per cent obtained General Certificate of Education.

At the end of Form 6, pupils in the secondary schools take a further certificate examination. This has been known up to the present time as the Cambridge Higher School Certificate. As in the case of the Cambridge School Certificate described above, the award of the full certificate depended upon success in a minimum number of subjects, while an Advanced Level General Certificate of Education was awarded to those who achieved a lesser number of subject successes. In future, Higher School Certificates will not be awarded, but the grade of pass in each principal subject will be shown on a General Certificate of Education. School candidates are required to offer at one and the same examination, a General Paper, two Principal Subjects, and *either* a third Principal Subject or two Subsidiary Subjects. The General Certificate of Education will be awarded to those who pass in at least one subject at Principal or Subsidiary level.

The Cambridge examinations have often been criticized on the grounds that by publishing an external syllabus and offering question papers which tend to examine factual knowledge rather than understanding, they impose a rigidity on teaching in the secondary school, encourage rote learning and discourage real education relevant to East Africa. Recently there have certainly been many improvements and the supporters of the Cambridge system point to its flexibility and its readiness to accept local suggestions for improvements. They also point to the need in the past to create standards of international repute and to avoid any suspicion of corruption in administration.

In recent years, representatives of the Ministries of Education in Tanzania, Kenya and Uganda have met from time to time to formulate proposals to Cambridge; more recently, with the development of Institutes of Education, far-reaching suggestions for curriculum development and more appropriate examination papers have been made. Thus the position is being prepared for a gradual transfer to the newly formed East African Examination Council with a period of transition when questions in tune with a 'discovery' approach to teaching and more objective-type questions will be included.

The Cambridge-based examinations are organized in Tanzania by the Ministry of Education, which receives the applications, distributes question papers, transmits answer papers to England and publishes the results.

Other Examinations

Private individuals studying outside schools cannot enter for the Cambridge examinations in Tanzania. Instead, they take the University of London General Certificate of Education. Before entering for their full quota of subjects, they must take English Language by itself in order to qualify to offer the further subjects. A full pass achieved in English in this process of qualification can be recorded on the certificate awarded when further subjects are passed, without the candidate taking the English paper again. The Examinations Section of the Ministry of Education deals with six to seven hundred entries for the London examination annually.

The Ministry of Education also organizes examinations provided by various other bodies who award certificates for various forms of specialized technical and professional achievements such as the City and Guilds and the Chartered Institute of Secretaries, all based in Britain.

Summary and Conclusion

The Tanzanian educational system is essentially pyramidal in structure, with a broad base of primary education, narrowing down to a relatively small enrolment at the sixth form level. The foregoing account has been largely restricted to the public school system. It should be noted that there are also a number of unassisted primary and secondary schools. The former slightly increase the number of pupils eligible for selection to the public secondary schools, and the latter will shortly make a significant increase in the number of pupils entering for the East African Certificate of Education.

In the whole system, public examinations function as selection devices at the Standard 4 level, as leaving examinations and selection devices at the end of Standard 7, and as certification and selection examinations at the secondary levels. The need for examinations between Standard 4 and 5 will decline with the expansion of primary facilities to provide a full seven-year course for all pupils, but some form of publicly organized educational measurement at the end of Standard 7, Form 4 and Form 6 may well be permanent features of the system. The future is likely to show further developments in making examinations at all levels more truly educational and more fully relevant to the objectives of the country's social and economic aims.

15

West Germany

Karlheinz Ingenkamp

Director, Department of Educational Psychology, Paedagogisches Zentrum, Berlin

School and university examinations have for a long time possessed great importance for the professional career and the social rise of the individual. During the last decades their importance has increased still further, since, according to the German Federal Constitution, the sole criterion for admission to courses of higher education is the capacity and ability of the individual, and the school was given the task of selection on that basis. As a result, sociologists regard the school as 'a Central Bureau for deciding and directing the social status of the individual' or as 'a bureaucratic machine for distributing chances in life'.[1] These tasks of selection and placement can be fulfilled only imperfectly by teachers and school administrators. Although German psychologists and teachers in the early days made considerable contributions to the development and employment of objective tests (e.g. Ebbinghaus, Rieger, Ziehen, Lay, Meumann, W. Stern, Moede and others[2]), theories and methods of educational measurement have not established themselves in German schools. The testing and assessment of the pupils' performance during the school year and the examinations are carried out almost exclusively in the traditional manner. More objective test procedures have not been laid down for any examination, although their employment in various selection procedures has been recommended. In teacher-training, little attention is paid to methods of assessing performance and judging pupils' capacity. The prevailing attitude is characterized by a naïve confidence in the validity of the teacher's judgement; nevertheless for some time school marks and reports have been subjected to much violent criticism. In German schools there is a scale of marks ranging from 1 to 6; 1 is awarded for the highest achievement and 6 for the lowest. In particular, criticism has been directed against this attempt to give a satisfactory numerical assessment for complex achievements and against the effect of such assessments on parents and

[1] H. Schelsky, *Schule und Erziehung in der industriellen Gesellschaft* (Würzburg: 1957).

[2] Cf. Th. Marsolek, 'Historische Übersicht über die Testentwicklung in Deutschland unter besonderer Berücksichtigung der Schultests', in the pamphlet *Deutsche Schultests* (Weinheim and Berlin: J. Beltz, 1968).

pupils. Recently, there has been an increase in the number of published articles in which the validity, reliability and variations in standards of school marks and reports have been the subject of critical discussion.[3] In addition to the sources of error which arise because of differing subjective assessments, recent investigation has proved that whilst, on the one hand, marks awarded to the members of a particular class may possess some validity within that class, on the other hand, the marks awarded in different classes in the same grade cannot be compared. Equal work and achievement can be assessed in very different ways, depending on the average level of attainment in each particular class.[4] The teacher lacks a standard of comparison outside his own class, since the statement of aims and curriculum as officially laid down is not sufficiently precise for this, and the oral and written work is assessed with reference to the average attainment in the class. These differences and difficulties, which are present when attempting to assess the work of different classes, operate also in the selection of candidates for places of higher education.

The selection of pupils for the *Gymnasium* and *Realschule* constitutes the first general stage at which important decisions are made concerning their future education. Apart from insignificant exceptions this selection takes place in Berlin at the end of the sixth year; in the other Federal States (*Länder*) after the fourth elementary school class. The Ministers of Education of the German Federal States have laid down the principle that 'selection must not be decided solely on the result of an examination lasting a few hours or days', nor must the decision be left to the school the pupils are about to leave or to the institute of education to which they may be proceeding.[5] The latter may be the *Gymnasium* with classes 5 to 13 (in Berlin 7 to 13) or the *Realschule* with classes 5 to 10 (in some states from 7 to 10).

In accordance with a decree of the Ministers of Education, when pupils proceed from the primary school a detailed report must be provided by the school 'which gives an over-all picture of the individual pupils and expresses an opinion on their suitability for higher education in the particular type of school desired by the parents'. In addition an annual examination must be held to assess the suitability and performance of those pupils who have expressed a wish to be considered as candidates for higher education. 'This part of the procedure is based in general on written work and trial lessons'.[6] The Federal States may exempt from the

---

[3] Cf. A. Flitner, 'Das Schulzeugnis im Lichte neuerer Untersuchungen', *Zeitschrift f. Pädagogik*, no. 6, 1966. R. Weiss, *Zensur und Zeugnis* (Linz, 1965).

[4] K. Ingenkamp, *Untersuchungen zur Übergangsauslese* (Weinheim and Berlin, 1968).
K. Ingenkamp, *Zur Problematik der Jahrgangsklasse* (Weinheim and Berlin, 1968).

[5] From the *Beschluß der ständigen Konferenz der Kultusminister der Länder in der Bundesrepublik Deutschland* (8–9 December, 1960) (as formulated 23 March, 1966).

[6] ibid.

examination and lessons those pupils whose suitability is, in the opinion of the elementary school, beyond all doubt.

The decrees of the permanent Conference of the Ministers of Education can only provide a general framework. Details are defined by the individual states which possess authority in educational matters. Detailed administration and control of the two constituent parts of the selection procedure – the primary school report and entrance examination or periodic tests – therefore vary considerably in the individual states. At the same time, during the past few years it has been observed that entrance examinations and trial lessons are becoming increasingly less important. One significant reason for this may be ascribed to the violent criticism directed against this part of the procedure as a result of the findings of various scientific investigations. The entrance examination was usually conducted by the receiving school, i.e. by the *Gymnasium* or *Realschule*, and was limited to a period of one or two days. Of decisive importance were the written questions, essay, dictation and arithmetic examination, which were both set and assessed by the receiving school. Various investigations carried out with fairly small groups showed biserial correlations of 0·02 (Hitpass[7]) and 0·45 (Gebauer[8]) between entrance examination and school progress after six years. The most representative investigation covering the whole Federal area has been conducted by Schultze and others. Taking groups totalling in all 3,214 boys and girls, after five years they discovered parameter-free coefficients of correlation, which with a median $r_s = 0.33$ varied between 0·25 and 0·49.[9] Moreover, it was proved that the written papers set for the entrance examinations at different times and in different places revealed varying degrees of difficulty.[10]

As a result, there has been a tendency during the past few years to abandon the entrance examination and to fit it into the primary school curriculum and in general to attach greater importance to the assessment of the primary school. However, an investigation has shown that the assessments of the primary school teachers do not show any higher coefficients of validity than do the entrance examination conducted by the *Gymnasium* or *Realschule*. In an investigation which dealt with 2,226 pupils

---

[7] J. Hitpass, 'Bericht über eine 6 jährige Bewährungskontrolle von Aufnahmeprüfung und Testprüfung', in *Schule u. Psychologie*, no. 7, 1963.

[8] Th. Gebauer, 'Vergleichende Untersuchung über den Voraussagewert von Aufnahmeprüfung und Testuntersuchung für den Erfolg auf weiterführenden Schulen', in K. Ingenkamp (ed.), *Schulkonflikt und Schülerhilfe* (Weinheim, 1965).

[9] W. Schultze, (ed.), *Über den Vorhersagewert der Auslesekriterien für den Schulerfolg am Gymnasium*, Research Report No. 1, Max-Traeger Foundation, Frankfurt, 1964.

[10] E. Thomas, 'Vergleich des Schwierigkeitsgrades der Sexta-Aufnahmeprüfung in aufeinanderfolgenden Jahren', unpublished dissertation, Köln, 1964.

R. Ohlsson, 'Vergleich des Schwierigkeitsgrades der Sexta-Aufnahmeprüfungen an verschiedenen Orten', unpublished dissertation, Köln, 1964.

for the entrance year 1954, Undeutsch found a biserial correlation of 0·16 based on progress in their first year at a *Gymnasium*.[11] Here too, the most representative results are provided by Schultze and others, who with a median $r_s = 0·25$ calculated parameter-free coefficients of correlation of from 0·12 to 0·33 between the elementary school assessment and progress after five years at a *Gymnasium*. This low validity may be explained by the facts that no comparative tests are employed in the primary schools and that in the different classes there are extraordinary variations in standards. It follows, therefore, that the assessment of the elementary school cannot provide a solution to the problem of securing a valid and proper selection without the help of additional factors or criteria.

In various investigations, in particular in that already mentioned by Hitpass and Gebauer, it has been proved that group intelligence tests possess a considerably higher prognostic validity than either the primary school assessment or the entrance examination conducted by the *Gymnasium* or *Realschule*.[12] In spite of this finding the Ministers of Education merely decided that 'where tests are employed, they may be only carried out as additional to the existing prescribed procedure and only by experienced experts; in any case they should not interfere with the personal approach in teaching practice.'[13] The development suggested as essential by the findings of Hitpass and Gebauer, cannot, however, be arrested by such unconvincing decrees. Many teachers, of their own accord, already use tests to enable them to have a better foundation for their assessments of the work and progress of their pupils. In some education authorities' areas uniform tests are included in the selection procedure for transfer to the *Gymnasium*.

As a result of the selection procedures about 60 per cent of the pupils remain in the primary school (*Hauptschule*), about 20 per cent proceed to the *Realschule* and about 20 per cent to the *Gymnasium*. However, these proportions vary quite considerably in the individual Federal States. The primary school course (in the so-called *Hauptschule*) extends at present over nine years (formerly eight years) without any special examination at the end. The marks on the leaving certificate are based on the marks awarded by the teachers of the school. Nor is any universally compulsory leaving examination taken at the end of the tenth year in the *Realschule*. In some places at local level written papers were set, but marks on the leaving certificate are based chiefly or exclusively on the marks awarded by the teachers in the school during the last year or years.

---

[11] U. Undeutsch, 'Auslese für und durch die höhere Schule', in *Bericht über den 22. Kongreß der Deutschen Gesellschaft für Psychologie*, Göttingen, 1960.

[12] Cf. K. Ingenkamp, Collective Report 'Bewährung und Problematik der Übergangsauslese für d. Besuch weiterführender Schulen', in *Päd. Arbeitsblätter*, no. 11, 1965.

[13] *Beschluß der ständigen Konferenz der Kultusminister der Länder in der Bundesrepublik Deutschland*, op. cit.

If a pupil does not complete the course at school and later on wishes to obtain the Leaving Certificate of the *Realschule* (the so-called *Mittlere Reife*) he has to pass an examination set by a board appointed by the State Education Authority. This examination also includes oral and written tests of the traditional non-objective type. The same applies in the case of examinations which are taken at the end of a course of professional or vocational training.

In the *Realschule* and particularly in the *Gymnasium* a continual process of selection takes place as a result of the annual promotions to the next class or the repeating of a year by those who have to stay down. According to various computations it is estimated that only 20 to 35 per cent of pupils admitted to the *Gymnasium* reach their *Abitur* without having to repeat a year. The *Abitur* at the end of the thirteenth class is the Leaving Certificate of the *Gymnasium* and entitles those who pass to admission to any German university. The *Abitur* (also called the *Reifeprüfung* or Maturity Examination) can be taken at public or at recognized private *Gymnasien*. The examination consists of a written, oral and practical part (*Sport*). In the written part candidates have to take three (in Berlin four) papers, each of several hours. In each case an essay in German is prescribed; for the other subjects it depends on the type of *Gymnasium*. Thus, for example, in addition to the German essay at *Gymnasien* specializing in Modern Languages, two papers in the two foreign languages are required. At *Gymnasien* with mathematical-scientific bias candidates take one paper in mathematics and one in physics in addition. The actual responsibility for setting the questions varies in the different Federal States. In some the subjects are set by a central committee for all schools; in others the *Gymnasium* submits suggestions, from which the representative of the State School Authority, who supervises the whole examination, chooses the subjects to be set. The assessment of the candidates' work is likewise more or less centralized. Usually the examination work is scrutinized and marks assessed by the specialist teacher at the *Gymnasium*, then it is submitted to another specialist who acts as co-assessor and to all the other teachers of the *Abitur* class for their opinions, and is finally sent to the representative of the State School Authority for confirmation.

The oral examination is usually confined to subjects taken in the written part, to general knowledge and a further subject which the candidate is allowed to choose. The examination takes place in the presence of all the teachers of the *Abitur* class, under the chairmanship of the state representative. Candidates who have distinguished themselves by excellent work may be excused the oral examination.

The final result of the examination is based on the marks obtained by the candidate over the last two years at the school, and on the marks obtained in the written and oral examinations. Specific examination requirements are laid down by the individual states. Recent investigations, which have not yet been published, have shown that there are relatively considerable variations in the *Abitur* examination marks in the different states. The prognostic value of the *Abitur* marks for the assessment of school achievement is likewise extremely slight and probably does not exceed the validity of the selection for transfer to the *Gymnasium*. On this point proper investigations have not yet been carried out.

Candidates who have not attended or completed the full *Gymnasium* course up to the thirteenth class, may, if aged at least 19 years or over, apply to take the Maturity Examination for those not attending school (*Reifeprüfung für Nichtschüler*). They must take a written examination in four subjects and an oral examination in eight subjects. The proportion of failures in this examination is relatively high.

This survey has demonstrated that in no case within the schools themselves are examinations of an objective type prescribed. For the higher classes very few standardized tests are available. Not a single achievement test exists for the *Abitur* level candidate. Informal tests evolved by the form teacher are not customary in Germany.

The final examinations at the university and for civil service appointments, e.g. for teachers in *Gymnasien*, lawyers, etc. are framed in the traditional form as a combination of oral and written examinations.

It is true that one may already clearly observe a growing feeling of dissatisfaction regarding the limited reliability and validity of these traditional examinations. Here and there at nearly all levels of the education system, experimental tests are being conducted even for admission to university studies. Nevertheless standardized tests have, up to the present, not made headway to any notable extent except in the tests carried out at the admission stage to the primary school (*Einschulungsuntersuchungen*).[14] Here too, the same tests are usually employed and are taken at the same time at all primary schools within whole administrative areas. The prognostic validity of the procedure is on an average about 0·65.

The present picture is still determined by the dominance of the traditional, largely internal school examinations. At the same time, however, one may observe an increasing willingness to accept the use of objective tests, which are being employed more and more frequently by teachers, especially in the primary schools, to assist in providing supplementary information to help them better to assess their pupils' performance and progress.

---

[14] Cf. R. Meis, 'Deutsche Schulreifetests', in K. Ingenkamp and Th. Marsolek (eds.), *Möglichkeiten und Grenzen der Testanwendung in der Schule* (Weinheim and Berlin, 1968).

16

German Democratic Republic

Horst Möhle
Professor of Chemistry, Leipzig

The Act on the Socialist Unified Educational System passed in 1965 is at the bottom of the whole of the educational processes and is thus also the base of the demonstration of aptitude and proficiency checks, which form an organic whole with the system. Within this system examinations occupy a special place. In the main they come at the end of general, special and academic education; thus they consist of intermediate and final examinations. From the general principles laid down by law there emerge definite requirements as to their role towards society, theoretical foundation and practical execution.

The declared intention of our educational system is to ensure a high educational level of the whole people and to educate all-round and harmoniously developed personalities. Therefore, demonstrations of aptitude and proficiency testing are no longer, as they were in the past, a politico-social means to the end of excluding children, above all of workers and peasants, from higher education. Instead they are aiming today at the early discovery of endowments for certain occupations and callings, gifts of the most various kinds, so that they can be systematically developed and used to the full, with personal interests and those of society brought into line. Likewise such examinations ensure that every graduate will be assigned his job according to where his skills and abilities can be used most effectively. Furthermore, these examinations serve to provide an objective picture of the educational processes. For teachers, they are the yardstick by which to measure the effectiveness of their educational work. They afford pupils and students the possibility of making critical assessments of their performances and the results of their studying. Advances come to light as well as the dragging of one's feet. The feeling in the young people of their responsibility for education and self-education, their striving for high performances are to be encouraged. Evaluation of the examination results leads to measures aiming at encouragement for superior students and help for those staying behind. This renders the terminal examinations, in particular, occasions where our educational system is answerable to society. The interest of society is reflected in such final examinations as are held with the attendance of representatives from the public, for instance the parents' advisory council and the enterprise sponsoring, in a measure, the secondary school concerned. The principle underlying the whole of our social development, namely to use everybody according to his abilities and to rate him by his efficiency, holds equally good in the sphere of education. This principle of efficiency is part and parcel of the testing of aptitude and the proficiency checks.

A determining influence on content and methodical form of the demonstrations of aptitude and proficiency checks is exercised by the principles forming the mainstays of our educational system: the oneness of research, teaching and studies, the synonymy of training and education, the unity of theory and practice. The principle of the oneness of research, teaching and studies indicates that the subject of general, special and academic education must be a system of fundamental scientific knowledge which is in keeping with current findings, and that scientific recruits must, at all levels of the educational system, be familiarized with general and specialized research methodology, must be enabled to do their own research work and, eventually, be directly incorporated in research activities; this idea, in general terms, governs the objective of the demonstrations of aptitude and proficiency testing. Manifest in them is the need to prove that the examinee is able to utilize his fundamental knowledge, via generalized theories, of existing facts. A further demand made in these exams is the ability of the examinee to deduce from isolated phenomena, general laws and theories. However, the centre of gravity in these exams is ever more shifting towards finding out the scale of the examinee's capability to put to use general and special methodology and to think in logical and dialectical terms. The level and the advances made in the realization of scientific issues in practice and their formulation as a scientific statement of problems are to be tested, as well as the extent to which the examinee is working towards their solution, applying a scientific approach, and how far he is able to translate the results into practice.

Within the integrated educational process, the educational potential inherent in the subject matter is being made effective by the teachers at both technical colleges and institutes of higher learning. Also in the examinations, for instance, the statement of usable technical knowledge allows for conclusions on the examinee's outlook upon life in terms of the natural and the social sciences.

Lastly, the oneness of theory and practice is kept throughout this complex educational process. With the co-ordination of theoretical and scientifically productive work – true, it can reach its topmost stage only at university level – the results of the scientifically creative work of pupils and undergraduates continue to be evaluated according to how effectively they bear on practice outside the educational institutions; this partly replaces conventional examination procedure.

Written work on subjects which are significant for society, to be done in the practicals of shorter duration, in longer sections of the studies in the practical sphere, and also in the shape of diploma papers and kindred work, are rated according to their usefulness for science and society. The attendance at a secondary school, and studies at technical colleges and institutes of higher learning, considered by us as an assignment by society that is to a major degree in agreement with personal interests and desires, are thus appraised by such criteria as are relevant for society. The results of such work and examinations are at the base of the recognition by society of above-average achievements in the form of grants scaled to performance, and awards, such as special diplomas and medals.

Proceeding from these references to society *we apply the principle of uniformity* to the content of, and approach to, *the demonstrations of aptitude and the testing of proficiency* throughout our whole educational system. The latest knowledge in cybernetics, psychology and pedagogics is being made use of imaginatively. The syllabuses and curricula on the levels of the secondary school, the technical college and the university, ever better adjusted to the requirements made by society as these present themselves in the foreseeable future, feature a level of standards that is uniformly determined. The standards of the goal of the educational process are clearly defined, and from them emerge the standards of the single grades at school and the single academic years. This makes for evenly high requirements at all educational institutions of one and the same level, directed at the same aims as to content and method, in demonstrations of aptitude and proficiency. Therefore, the scientific recruit can pass through all the stages of the educational system without encountering difficulties, and change over from one institution to the next higher one. For the school providing general education it is possible to have one committee of specialists work out standardized requirements adjusted to the single grades, and standardized tasks for comparison of proficiency for intermediate and terminal examinations. Assessment and valuation can be made using standardized yardsticks. Overtaxing or undertaxing, overrating or underrating is excluded to a fair degree. Also, in this way, the same level is ensured for all pupils in schools both in town and in the country. The above-mentioned objective requirements and assessment scales go a long way in eliminating subjective factors, which, as is well known, are likely to make for undesirable consequences in education. Teachers and examiners can live up to their personal responsibilities, realizing that this accords fully with the demands made by society; their accountability for the moulding of young personalities is thereby not pressed into narrow confines.

Pupils and undergraduates showing particular proficiency and revealing specific interests get special encouragement in optional courses supplementing the standard classes from the ninth grade on, or in optional extracurricular group activities or optional lessons and in students' clubs. Individual syllabuses are provided for superior students. The training documents underlying this individual work will then serve the finding-out of attainments, i.e. in the examinations. To pass the aptitude tests and proficiency exams is the pre-condition for education to be continued with success on the next higher stage and for the personality of the student to be moulded. Content, form and methods of the examinations are being developed for the passing from primary school through the intermediate grades to the senior classes, and this pattern finds its parallel in higher education, where all stages of the system of studying – basic, subject, special subject and research studies – make adequate demands as to content and method in the testing of proficiency. For instance, the stage of basic studies is characterized by the fact that the fundamental knowledge in the arts and sciences and the special-subject knowledge, combined with the skill to apply general and special methodology, forms the main content of the pre-examination which concludes this stage of studying. It is a checking of proficiency, demanding from the student the solution of clearly defined problems, the self-reliant choosing of scientific methods being left to the examinee.

Since systematic advances in information reception, processing and application call for continuous feedback, routine testing of proficiency is being steadily extended. On the level of general education this is represented by viva voce checks during classes and the periodical writing of unseens; on the level of higher education by consultations of teachers, certificates of attendance as basic requirement for practical experimental work, seminars etc. This allows for the number of intermediate examinations to be reduced.

With the step-by-step switchover to complex non-programmed and programmed instruction at all stages of our educational system, feedback and control of advancements by the student himself are being added to. The working through the programmes, the algorithmic as well as the heuristic ones, allows especially for exact control of how the student applies the approaches and techniques of scientific work, including his logical operations. In these checks increasing use is being made of mechanical teaching gear, such as repeaters and examiners. However, in the final examinations we do not abandon personal communication between the examiner and the pupil, because what matters is not only the grading of the work done but also the rating of the student's attitude to work, and even the moulding of his individuality. Since proof of aptitude and checking of proficiency can refer to activities of a theoretical as well as practical content, teaching aids occupy in them an ever more important place. For instance in the science classes in secondary education, the experiment to be carried out by the pupil is frequently the subject or the foundation of the proficiency test. Also the use of audio-visual aids adds to the revealing potential of examinations.

Lastly the natural necessities and principles characteristic of our society and its educational system govern *how testing of aptitude and of efficiency is being carried out*. The standardized pattern of these tests at our secondary schools is ensured by official instructions, including the implementation of regulations and directions. Pride of place in these is given to the final examination at the ten-grade polytechnical secondary schools, which are attended by all children, and the matriculation examination at the twelve-grade (extended) secondary schools. On the level of the technical college and the university there exist directives aimed at the testing of aptitude for the taking up of studies, comprising aptitude tests and aptitude consultations, the outline examination regulation on questions of principle and the subject-governed supplementary regulations, referring specifically to the pre-examinations, major and graduation examinations at universities and similar institutes of higher education.

To meet special interests of the examinees and to give them a chance in subjects in which they are particularly proficient, the spectrum of subjects examined and compulsory for all pupils and students can include, for instance in the matriculation exam, an optional subject chosen from the sciences or from languages; students at universities are given the opportunity to suggest the subject-matter for their diploma work themselves. Since the examination has a function bearing on society, the examiners will so organize it that the examinee is able to give proof of a maximum of proficiency. Thus one can look forward to a psychologically favourable examination ambience. It is characterized by the examiner adjusting his approach to the assets of the examinee without dimming the essential features of an examination; this will help the pupil or student who develops an appropriate approach towards the checking of his proficiency to work without fear of the examination. Therefore, the examinations should be prepared with the end in view. For one thing, the future examiners will guide the student to the handling of problems of major concern and the pertinent literature. Adjusting the student at short notice to the narrow confines of calculated questions would be pedagogically pointless. Secondly, the examinees-to-be can consult their teachers and discuss with them their problems. Study groups of pupils and students to prepare their members for the examinations have proved a success.

Collective written work for complex subjects is in line with the current tendency for sciences to integrate into one whole. However, the requirement remains valid that it should be possible to rate the individual performance of each group member singly. Likewise, viva voce examina tions can be arranged as individual or group testing. With the latter, precise evaluation of the individual student's performance is a condition.

To put the pupil or student in a position where he can give a well-rounded answer he is allowed a brief period for preparation immediately preceding the oral examination. This preparation is followed by the examination proper in the form of a discussion. Work in the practical diploma papers and doctoral dissertations founded on theses is defended orally, so that the candidate can be rated according to the way he manages scientific discussion.

The evaluation of the performance shown in the examination refers to both the standard of the content and that of its linguistic expression. The performance is rated by marks ranging from 1 to 5, frequently based on a grading by points. When determining the final mark, the examiners duly consider whether proficiency tends towards the upgrade or downgrade. The performance is additionally labelled by verbal rating. The outcome of the examination is discussed with the examinee, and additional suggestions are made for his further studies. The regulations also allow for asking the candidate to make a self-assessment of his performance level. If the requirements of the examination are not met it may be repeated, provided the examiner sees a chance for the pupil to fill the gaps within a reasonable space of time.

Examination boards or committees are active on all levels of education; they are charged with ensuring that the examination regulations and the directions for the grading are adhered to. In addition, these committees will analyse the results of the examinations generally and in detail, in order to cover the advances made in the studies and uncover inadequate performances. A further responsibility of the examiners' board is to draw conclusions on the further development of the pupils' and students' approach to scientific work and on the raising of the level of the educational processes.

Testing of aptitude and proficiency are, in our country, owing to their relevance to society and didactics, a major subject of research in the theory and practice of pedagogics at school and university level. By means of this research it is intended to adapt examination practice, which is not, as yet, always satisfactory, to the needs emerging from that research, and it should step up further the effectiveness of the educational processes.

17

The Soviet Union

V. Strezikozin
Head, Curricula and Teaching Methods Department, Ministry of Public Education of the Russian Federation

PART I: EXAMINATIONS

Checking on pupils' knowledge by means of examinations has long become common practice in most countries. There was a period in the history of Soviet schools, however, when attempts were made to abolish examinations. When the new system of education was in the making, methods and forms were sought to overcome, in a short time, the formalistic and scholastic tendencies inherent in the pre-revolutionary Russian general education school. At the time it was believed that examinations foster formalism in teaching and get the pupil into the habit of mechanical memorization of material, rather than promote a creative approach to study. Experience showed that these fears were unfounded.

Re-introduction of examinations in Soviet schools was intended to raise the educational level of young people. This was prompted by the process of development of Soviet society, by the high level of industrialization and by the introduction of scientific achievements into production. These measures adopted a number of the decisions made by the Central Committee of the Communist party and the Soviet Government, which set schools the task of providing the children with a sound knowledge of the fundamentals of science necessary for the young people to take an active part in production and public activities.

Types of Examinations

Up to 1956 there were two types of examinations: end-of-year to transfer pupils to the fifth, sixth, seventh, ninth and tenth forms; and school-leaving – after a seven-year and after an eight-year course (incomplete secondary education), and after a ten-year schooling (complete secondary education). In 1956 in the Russian Federation and in several other Union Republics, examinations were abolished in all but the leaving forms. It was established that daily checking of the pupil's knowledge allows the teacher to form an objective opinion as to his level of academic achievement at the end of school year. A short examination once a year wouldn't add much to this evaluation. Moreover, preparation for examinations and the examinations themselves were a considerable strain on the pupils, especially in the junior forms.

Such an assessment of end-of-year examinations has not been unanimously accepted by Soviet teachers. In some of the Union Republics the Ukraine, Georgia, Kazakhstan, children still take end-of-year examinations.

Examination System

The system of examinations is established by the Ministries of Education of the Union Republics. They issue instructions on the order in which they are to be held, and for the work of the school examination commissions. Responsibility for the implementation of these instructions rests with the headmasters of schools, whose work is controlled by the local department of public education.

The pupils take exams only in the most important subjects in the curriculum. The end-of-year examinations, where they are held, include the Russian language (in the non-Russian schools there is also an examination in the native language), mathematics (in all forms) and some other subjects: physics, chemistry, geography, literature, a foreign language, history. In the Georgian Republic there are some distinctive features: here the subjects in which the pupils are to be examined are announced only at the end of the school year. In these conditions the pupils study the fundamentals of all subjects with equal diligence.

The amount of material to be tested at the leaving examinations after an eight-year schooling is not great. In the Russian Federation the pupils take examinations in the Russian language and mathematics (in the non-Russian schools there is also an examination in the native language). The leaving examinations taken at the end of the tenth form are in literature, mathematics, physics, chemistry, history, social sciences and a foreign language.

The coverage of material at the leaving examinations in different subjects is not the same. For example, the examination in the Russian language in the eighth form tests the pupils' knowledge of accidence, syntax, spelling, punctuation and style which has been acquired over the previous years; in mathematics, too, the subject matter may come from the syllabuses of lower forms, as well as from the eighth form. At the leaving examinations the subject matter comes from the last form, in view of its summarizing character. But in some subjects (literature, chemistry and others) the pupils are also examined in the subject matter coming from the ninth form.

In order to test the pupils' knowledge of theory and their skill in applying knowledge, there are written examinations in addition to oral ones (the Russian language and the native language for an eight-year school, mathematics in the eighth and tenth forms, and composition in the tenth form).

Examinations, both end-of-year and leaving, are not merely a means of assessing the pupils' knowledge. This is done by the teacher in the course of everyday work in the classroom: by calling on the pupils to give oral answers, by periodic written tests, by seeing how they are able to work independently in the classroom and at home. All this gives the teacher a sufficient idea of how the pupil is getting on with his studies. The importance of the examinations lies in the fact that they foster a responsible approach of the children to their studies, and at the same time they help them to systematize their knowledge.

Examinations in Soviet schools are, in a way, a public account by each pupil on the results of his work, an account not only to his teacher and to the school administration but to his classmates as well. This fact induces the pupils to study diligently and to acquire a better knowledge of the syllabus.

The examinations serve as a valuable check for the teachers on their own work and on the results of their teaching. The fact that the pupils are examined by a commission made up of several teachers is an extremely important factor. A commission is formed in every school which includes the subject teachers and their colleagues who teach the same or allied subjects. It is headed by the principal or his deputy. This system of holding examinations precludes any possibility of subjectivism or lenience in assessing the pupils' knowledge, since this is done by a group of teachers. On the other hand, the results of the teacher's work as seen from his pupils' oral and written answers, are made available to his colleagues who may openly pass their judgement on them. Therefore, it is only natural that the teacher tries to instruct every pupil to the best of his ability; hence, the educational value of examinations which stimulate the successful work of the pupils (and the teachers). Moreover, examinations are an important factor in solving a whole number of didactic tasks.

The process of instruction is not reduced to a simple accumulation of scientific information. Mastering any science at school must be done by studying the facts, phenomena and rules in a logical system that enables the pupils to master the laws governing this or that science. One of the primary tasks in education is the mastering of the system of scientific conceptions in which these laws are generalized and expressed; hence the importance for every pupil to systematize and generalize the entire material in studying any science. Examinations are important in achieving this aim. When the pupils write a dictation at an exam in the Russian language, provided the texts are chosen properly, it is easy to observe how they have mastered the basic laws of the language, as well as the laws of spelling and punctuation. For example, mistakes in the spelling of words with unstressed vowels, which can be checked by putting these words in other forms where these vowels become stressed, the omission, transposition and substitutions of letters (in junior forms) show that the pupils have not properly mastered the rudiments of phonetics, that they haven't developed skills and habits of analytico-synthetical work. Mistakes in the spelling of adverbs which must be distinguished from nouns, and mistakes in the usage of the Russian negative particle 'не' with verbs and other parts of speech show that the pupils lack a general understanding of the laws governing parts of speech, that they are unable to make a correct semantic analysis of words and sentences. At the examination in the Russian language the pupils show how well they understand the system of word-building, parts of speech, including the morphological way of word-building; their knowledge concerning the grammatical basis of the relation between words in a sentence is revealed, together with the syntactical role of all the parts of speech.

The end-of-year examinations in arithmetic in the fourth and fifth forms (where they are held) help one to get an idea of how the children are able to use their knowledge and skills in calculation, how they understand the relations between the component parts and the results of calculations.

The subject matter for leaving examination in mathematics may come from the syllabuses of the lower or higher grades so that the examination commission may check the whole volume of knowledge and skills acquired in arithmetic and algebra, trigonometry and geometry.

At the examination in physics in the tenth form the teachers can observe the pupils' understanding of the physical regularities which they have studied, their understanding of the physical basis of such phenomena as electrolysis and electrolytic dissociation, interference and diffraction of waves and light, the nature of spectra from the point of view of the theory of stationary and agitated conditions of atoms, their ability to explain from the point of view of electronic conceptions the material nature of the magnetic and gravitational fields, the nature of the conductivity of metals, complete conductivity of electrolytes, the relation between the temperature and resistance of metallic conductors, the origin of E.M.F. of electromagnetic induction.

The teachers examining school leavers in chemistry ask them to explain various chemical phenomena on the basis of the most important chemical theories and laws (the law of the conservation of mass, the periodic law of chemical elements, the electron theory, the theory of electrolytic dissociation, the theory of the structure of organic matter), to characterize the classes of inorganic substances, properties of organic combinations and to analyse various chemical reactions.

At the examination in literature, great emphasis is laid on how the pupils are able to analyse a work of art from the point of view of the unity of its idea-content, style and language.

Preparation for Examinations

We have chosen isolated examples, but they show what a high level of theoretical knowledge is required of the pupils. In order to achieve this high level the pupils are required to do a great deal of work to systematize and master the scientific information received.

The most important thing here is not so much the examination itself, as the preparation for it. If the preparation for the exam is properly organized, the pupil revises in his mind the subject matter covered earlier, re-thinks it for himself, and brings all the facts and knowledge into an orderly system, establishing the relationship between them. Such work is most fruitful when the pupil has already covered all the subject matter. At this stage of learning, when the pupil has accumulated a great amount of factual material, and when the general logical structure of the subject matter has become clear to him, the pupil is able to find a new approach to an understanding of the content of the different subjects that have been covered previously. At this stage he is able to grasp the most complex regularities, which are consistently revealed in the process of studying this or that particular subject at school.

Soviet teachers attach great importance to the preparation for examinations. It is considered necessary to announce the programme of the examinations well in advance. The way the questions are formulated requires of the examinees not simply to recount data stored in their memory, but, what is most important, to present these data in an orderly system, logically 'processed' in the pupil's mind beforehand.

Every year the questions for the examinations are issued four to five months before the examinations. This enables the pupils to see in what direction they should work to systematize and revise the subject matter in preparation for the exams. It might be feared though, that some of the pupils will learn the answers beforehand, answers prepared not independently, but with the help of teachers, parents, or friends. To avoid this the examiners are given the right to find out whether or not the pupil has learned the material mechanically by asking supplementary questions on the material.

Examination Questions

The wording of the questions in the examination cards is of great importance for the systematization of the subject matter in preparation for the examination. The questions are worded in such a way that they preclude any possibility of a 'local' or mechanical rendering of isolated facts.

Each question is aimed at finding out how the pupil understands this or that important scientific regularity, his ability to present it and to prove it on the basis of concrete facts and data.

Here are just a few examples to show how the questions in the examination cards are worded.

At the school-leaving examination in physics, for instance, the pupil gets the following assignment:

'The fundamentals of the molecular-kinetic theory and their experimental proof. Mass, velocity and size of molecules. How do molecules move in gases, liquids and solids?'

'Experiments and phenomena proving the complex structure of the atom. The discovery of the proton and neutron. The structure of the nucleus.'

'Law of Universal Gravitation. Gravitational constant. Derive the formula for the first cosmic velocity. Achievements scored by Soviet science and technology in the study of outer space.'

The examination cards for tenth-formers require of them, for instance, to characterize the chemical properties of metals known to them, in the light of the theory of the structure of the atom; to speak about the properties of aluminium and its alloys, on which their use is based; to describe the properties of unsaturated hydrocarbons in the light of A. Butlerov's theory concerning the structure of organic compounds.

The pupil is required to be able to generalize in the history examination, too, as the following questions show: 'Lenin's plan for the electrification of Russia and its implementation'; 'The reason for the victory of the Soviet Union in the Second World War and the significance of this victory for humanity'; 'Historic prerequisites for the victory of the October Socialist Revolution'; 'The advancement of science and culture in the U.S.S.R. Soviet achievements in the study of outer space'.

The ability to generalize and to prove is just as necessary in a Russian language examination for eighth formers when they are given an assignment of the following type: 'Pick out of a given text all the compound and complex sentences and explain why the comma is used in these sentences in each particular case'. 'The correct placing of the dash in simple and complex sentences'.

Some of the questions in the examination cards are formulated in such a way that in answering them the pupil is expected to generalize the subject matter and to draw on the knowledge acquired in learning the fundamentals of other sciences. For instance in a chemistry examination the pupils are asked to explain the significance of Mendeleyev's periodic law and periodic system for a dialectical materialistic understanding of Nature, for the development of science and production. At an examination in social sciences in speaking about matter and movement, a tenth former refers to scientific facts from the courses in physics, chemistry and biology. A school-leaver at an examination in physics used the knowledge acquired while studying chemistry, biology and social sciences in answering the following question, for example: 'Development of the theory of the structure of matter; cognoscibility of natural phenomena'. While solving the problem of calculating the forces applied to a system of bodies tied together and moving with a uniform velocity in a vertical or horizontal direction pupils make use of their knowledge of mathematics.

If the pupils are able to use their skills and knowledge in different situations with a view to solving various practical tasks, it means that their knowledge of the subject matter covered at school is good. This factor is taken into consideration at the examinations in most subjects.

As has been mentioned earlier, there are both written and oral examinations. The themes and problems that make up the content of written examinations are prepared with a view to discovering the pupils' independence of thinking and their ability to use their theoretical knowledge in a creative way.

Among the subjects for a written essay in literature suggested to the school-leavers, one will find themes that require an independent analysis of literary works that haven't been included in the curriculum, but have been read by the pupils of their own initiative. For example, the following themes: 'The Image of My Contemporary in Soviet Literature of the 1960s'; 'The Heroic Spirit of the Soviet People's Everyday Life and Work as Depicted by Contemporary Soviet Writers and Poets'; 'My Favourite Literary Character'; 'The Theme of Friendship and Struggle for Peace in Books by Progressive Writers Abroad'. The problems given to the pupils at an examination in mathematics are not merely a copy of those to be found in school textbooks – they require an original approach to solving them, independence of thinking and initiative.

Practical tasks are included in the oral examinations as well. At examinations in the Russian language (or native language in non-Russian schools) the pupils are given texts for a morphological, syntactical and phonetic analysis; at exams in mathematics the pupils are given problems and sums; at examinations in physics and chemistry the pupils are asked to prepare and carry out short experiments and to solve problems. These assignments and written works prepared with a view to originality and novelty of the requirements put before the pupils, and with a view to an independence of thinking and initiative on the part of the examinee in a new situation. It follows, therefore, that the practical assignments are given to the pupils only at the actual time of the examination.

Each examination card usually combines theoretical and practical questions. Here are a few examples:

Card No. 18 for Russian language examination in the eighth form

(1) Place the punctuation marks in a sentence with direct speech, given by the teacher. Put the whole sentence into indirect speech and make a syntactical analysis of it.

(2) Pick out the verbs from the same sentence and give their grammatical properties. Give the definition of a verb. Name the grammatical properties of participles and verbal adverbs and give their definition.

Card No. 12 for examination in mathematics in the eighth form

(1) Prove the theorem on the proportionality of segments of a straight line intersected by parallel straight lines.

(2) A problem on the equality of triangles.

(3) Plot the development of the planes of a right triangular prism and determine the area of its surface.

Card No. 21 for the examination in chemistry in the tenth form

(1) Fats, their composition, physical and chemical properties.

(2) The use of sulphuric acid in national economy. Properties of sulphuric acid on which its use is based.

(3) Experiment: obtain and collect a gaseous substance (as requested by the teacher); demonstrate experimentally the presence of this gas.

As can be seen from these examples, the examination cards only indicate the nature of the practical problem. The problem itself is made up by the teacher-examiner (the subject teacher) and is agreed upon by the examination commission, after which it is approved by the head of the school.

Assessment of Ability

Great attention is paid during examinations to finding out how the process of instruction develops the pupils' mental ability. One of the principal tasks facing the Soviet school is to develop the pupils' intellect. In solving this task, Soviet teachers strive to activize the work and study of children in order to help them master such mental activities in the process of education as analysis and synthesis, comparison and contrast, the establishment of objective links and relations between phenomena, the separation of the important aspects and features from the unimportant ones, logical conclusions, deductions, proofs and counterproofs.

Because all this is an integral part of the teaching process the assessment of the level of the pupils' development is carried out in the course of checking the pupils' knowledge, specifically, during examinations rather than by means of special tests of the I.Q. type. The logic in the pupil's answer to a question, his train of thought in writing an essay, substantiation of the chosen way of solving a problem etc., show his knowledge of the syllabus and his mental development.

Of course, all this does not mean that one must consider a regular checking of the pupils' knowledge to be of secondary importance. Of course examinations cannot rule out completely the element of chance – it may happen that a pupil with a far from excellent knowledge of the subject gives a perfect answer to the questions of the card he has been lucky enough to draw, or perhaps he may choose out of several themes for essays, the one he is familiar with. The insufficient amount of time at the disposal of the examination commission does not always make it possible for the examiners to make a completely objective assessment of the pupils' knowledge.

The most reliable system for checking on the pupils' work is regular testing thoughout the school year, which is carried out by a consistent and manifold study of the work of every pupil.

All these considerations are taken into account when the final marks are given to the school-leavers (at the end of the eighth and tenth forms). At the end of the final year at school every pupil gets three marks: the end-of-year mark (based on the results of regular check-ups made throughout the year), the examination mark and the final one. The final mark is based on the end-of-year and examination marks. This guarantees the objectiveness of the final, school-leaving mark which is entered on the school-leaving certificate. The highest mark is awarded to the pupil whose end-of-year and examination marks are excellent.

The reliability of the assessment of the pupils' knowledge at the examinations depends largely on their correct organization; this, in turn, is achieved by proper guidance on the part of the local department of public education and the heads of schools.

Organization and Supervision of Examinations

General supervision of examinations is provided by the Ministries of Education of the Union Republics in a centralized manner. This results in uniform educational standards, which increases the responsibility of teaching staffs of schools and local departments of public education for the results of the teaching process.

The fundamental requirements for the organization of examinations are laid down in special regulations approved by the government. In accordance with these regulations, and taking into account the specific conditions and tasks facing each Union Republic, the republican Ministries of Public Education adopt instructions regarding the holding of school exams. These instructions determine the conditions on which pupils are allowed to take examinations or to be exempted from them on account of their health; the list of examinations; the order in which the examination commissions are to be formed and requirements as to the organization of their work; the principal criteria for choosing the material for examination cards and written examinations, as well as the criteria for giving marks to the pupils at examinations.

The examination cards and the texts of the tests are approved by the Ministries of Education of the Union Republics. They are compiled on instructions from the Ministry of Education and under its guidance by specially appointed groups of educationalists and teachers.

School inspectorates of the republican Ministries of Public Education control the activities of the Ministries of Education of autonomous republics and territorial and regional departments of public education in organizing the examinations. Special attention is paid to the implementation of the instructions on examinations, to an objective assessment of the pupils' knowledge and to the fact that those pupils who get the highest marks are really worthy of them.

The district and town departments of public education play an important role in seeing that the examinations are properly organized. It is their job to discuss and approve the composition of examination commissions every year, they see to it that the time-table of the examinations is made up correctly and that preparation for the exams is organized properly. Exemption from examinations on grounds of health is also the work of the local department of public education. This is done on a representation by the school, and it is based on the report of the medical commission and on the decision of the teacher's council of the school. But only those pupils can be exempted who studied well throughout the school year.

During the examinations representatives of local departments of public education attend the oral and written examinations, see that the marks are impartially given to the pupils, that there are no violations of the time-table of the examinations.

The heads of local departments of public education arbitrate in those cases when members of the examination commissions could not reach a decision in assessing a pupil's knowledge. They also give final decisions on the results of the examinations or awards to pupils for excellent study and exemplary conduct if the teaching council failed to take a unanimous decision.

The organizational and control work of the local departments of public education is directed and coordinated by the Ministries of Education of the autonomous republics and by the territorial and regional departments of public education. They see that the preparation for, and the holding of the examinations are properly supervised by their staff inspectors. These bodies distribute the texts for written examinations through the local departments of public education.

The Ministries of Education of the autonomous republics and heads of educational departments of the autonomous regions and national districts make up and approve all the examination material (cards, texts for written exams) in the native language for the national schools of their republic, region or area.

It is the duty of the headmaster of a school and his deputies to organize the examinations properly. Long before the exams, the head of the school attends lessons and discusses them with the teachers concerned; the head sees that the subject matter is properly revised.

The discussion and adoption of practical assignments for examination cards (sentences for a grammatical analysis, problems in mathematics, physics, chemistry) is also one of the headmaster's duties. All this requires of him the proper qualifications and perseverance in work.

The order in which the examinations are taken and their time-table is also very important. Careful consideration must be given to such problems as a well-thought-out system of spacing examinations and rational work of the examination commissions. These time-tables are made up by the deputy head of a school responsible for the teaching process, and are approved by the headmaster. But of course, the main duty of the headmaster during examinations is to study the level of theoretical and practical knowledge of the pupils. The headmaster heads the examination commission at his school, and takes a direct part in checking the pupils' knowledge. This helps the headmaster to assess pupils' knowledge impartially and allows him to know better the results of teaching in his school. These observations also help to elaborate measures for improving educational standards. It is worth mentioning in this connexion, that examinations are an important factor in raising the teaching standards in each particular school and on a country-wide scale.

One of the main features of the Soviet school system is a uniformity of curricula, and hence, a uniformity of requirements of the knowledge and skills of the pupils. It is possible therefore to compare the results of examinations in different schools in various parts of the country, and to observe the shortcomings in the results of teaching, so as to determine and implement measures for eradication of these shortcomings.

In order to make a comparative study of the results of educational work at schools the Ministry of Education and local departments of public education make use of other means at their disposal, such as periodic tests based on uniform texts in different parts of the country. The results of these tests are studied, and recommendations are worked out to improve the educational process.

PART II: ASSESSING PUPILS' KNOWLEDGE IN SOVIET SCHOOLS

The schools are responsible to society for the general education of their pupils, whom they must bring up as socially conscious and responsible citizens. It is natural therefore that the school must make an all-round assessment of their knowledge when they finish school. This estimate is based on the teachers' observations of the pupils' academic progress over the years of study, their diligence, behaviour, pursuits and interests. The results of examinations are also taken into account. Examinations show how well the school-leavers are prepared for independent life and work, or for entering schools of higher learning.

The assessment of school-leavers' knowledge is of great social importance. It helps the pupil choose a road in life. His standard in this or that subject helps him choose which department of a higher educational establishment to enter, or what trade or profession to learn if he decides not to go on to college. Matriculation certificates given to school-leavers make it possible for universities and colleges, in enrolling new students, to take into account their academic standards. Factories and offices can also decide what jobs to offer school-leavers.

Since 1944 there has been a five-point system in Soviet schools for assessing the pupils' knowledge ('5' being the highest and '1' the lowest mark). This system is used for checking the pupils' knowledge and skills every day as well as for school-leaving examinations and final assessment of their knowledge.

The criteria for such an assessment with reference to each subject taught at school have been approved by the Ministries of Education of the Soviet constituent republics and are called 'Norms for the assessment of knowledge'.

The main criteria are as follows:

(1) The amount of scientific information, envisaged by the school curriculum in each subject, accumulated by the pupil.

(2) The degree of understanding of the material studied, of the relations existing between facts and phenomena; the ability to substantiate and prove scientific concepts and rules which the pupil uses in his oral answer or written work; the ability to make use of the most important aspects of logic (analysis, synthesis, classification, summarizing, conclusions, etc.).

(3) Soundness of knowledge, shown by the degree to which the pupil's oral answers are well based, complete and thorough, the speed and correctness with which the pupil solves practical problems relating to the subject matter covered.

(4) Ability to apply theoretical knowledge to the solution of practical tasks and problems of varying difficulty and in different circumstances.

(5) Correctness of oral and written expression as an indication of the pupil's intellectual development.

Let us see how these demands are applied in testing the pupils' knowledge in three subjects: Russian language, mathematics and physics.

The highest mark of '5' is given to a pupil for an oral answer in Russian language if he: correctly words and interprets the concepts and rules covered and is able to illustrate his answer by citing examples or thinking up his own examples: correctly analyses sentences and words from the the point of view of grammar, explains the spelling of words and punctuation marks; confidently solves practical problems devised to establish whether the pupil is able to apply the rules in practice; answers consistently and to the point, and expresses himself clearly and concisely.

In mathematics a pupil receives the highest mark if his answers conform to the following requirements and if he fulfills the accompanying practical tasks: the answers are absolutely correct, exhaustive, and the pupil shows a clear understanding of the rules, axioms and theorems; accuracy of enumeration and of setting down the conditions and the conclusion of the theorem being proved, correctness and completeness of the proof with respect to its logical construction and adduction of all data and all previous clauses, which it was necessary to draw on; consistency and correctness of setting down the proof, the high standard of the drawing; ability to apply the rules and theorems independently, correct choice of examples by the pupil to illustrate his answer; rationality in performing all the necessary operations and transformations, correctness and sub-stantiation of the manner in which the problem is to be solved; correct and comprehensive answer to the problem and checking its correctness, if required.

A pupil will be given the highest mark in physics if he: shows a correct understanding of the physical phenomena in question, knows the most important laws and theories, can prove them by concrete examples, and can use them in solving practical problems; gives an exact definition and interpretation of the main concepts, determines correctly the physical values and units and ways of measuring them; confidently and competently does physical experiments, illustrating his answer with drawings, diagrams, graphs, and correctly sets down the formulae making use of the accepted system of symbols; in answering shows independence of thought and good argumentation, and does not follow mechanically the contents and logic of the textbook; is able to find the relation between the various physical phenomena he has learned, and to make use of his knowledge of related subjects taught at school.

The 'Norms' envisage a lowering of the mark to '4' in those cases when the pupil, while showing a sound knowledge of the basic material, makes slight errors in answering the teacher's questions or in solving a practical problem. These could include an inaccuracy in working theoretical conceptions, rules, problems, etc., which the pupil, nevertheless, corrects himself at the request of the teacher. Other types of errors, which lower the mark to '4' are certain difficulties in applying knowledge in particular, not very successful examples to illustrate the answer, difficulties in explain-ing the results of a physical experiment, slight errors in drawings at geometry lessons. The pupil gets a '4' if in his answer or in doing a practical assignment he makes one or two careless slips (transposition of letters, slips in calculations, etc.).

A great deal of consideration is required on the part of the teacher when giving a pupil a '3', which, although a satisfactory mark, indicates a low standard of knowledge. Over-estimation of a pupil's knowledge must be avoided just as much as under-estimation. Special care must be taken when marking the pupil's work for a quarter of the year, half the year, for the whole year or for the whole course in the subject.

The 'Norms' in all subjects determine that the mark '3' is given only in those cases when, although the pupil displays a satisfactory knowledge of the material studied at school and, *in the main*, has acquired the skills and practical habits envisaged by the programme, his answers and solution of problems do not quite show soundness of knowledge, skills or independence of thought.

For instance a pupil's knowledge in physics is given a satisfactory mark ('3') if he correctly understands the essence of physical phenomena but displays certain flaws in learning major problems in the course of physics, which, however, do not hamper his further study of the subject matter. A pupil's mark is also lowered to '3' when he has difficulty in applying his knowledge to the solution of various problems without the teacher's help, in explaining concrete physical phenomena on the basis of the most important theories and laws, or in illustrating theoretical concepts with concrete examples of their practical application. The pupil gets the mark '3' if he has difficulty in carrying out experiments in physics (assembling set-ups, choosing the necessary instrument and making preparations for a physical experiment), although with some help from the teacher he overcomes his difficulty. A teacher of physics will give the mark '3' to the pupils who do not give a complete answer, limiting it in the main to a reproduction of the material from the school textbook.

In Russian language the mark '3' is given to a pupil for an oral answer if he displays a satisfactory knowledge and understanding of the subject matter in question, but he: makes one or two mistakes in formulating rules and definitions or in illustrating them with examples; is hesitant in his grammatical analysis, makes mistakes in determining grammatical indications of the parts of speech or syntactical peculiarities of sentences, finds it difficult to explain the spelling of words and punctuation without the teacher's help; hesitates in the practical application of rules of spelling and punctuation in carrying out practical assignments, and manages to cope with them only with the teacher's help; his answer is not coherent enough or consistent; makes a few mistakes in his speech.

From these two examples (one from the humanities, one from the natural sciences) it can be seen that the reasons for lowering a pupil's mark to '3' are as follows: incompleteness or hesitancy in answering, inaccuracy of formulations, insufficient independence of thinking and acting, mistakes in speech in answering questions.

The mark '2' is an indication of the pupil's unsatisfactory knowledge. It is given to the pupil if he is found to be ignorant of the greater part of the subject matter, if he is only able to answer leading questions put to him by the teacher – and hesitantly at that – and if in written tests he makes many bad mistakes.

The mark '1' is given to a pupil for an oral answer or written work if he shows that he knows absolutely nothing of the subject. For example, the pupil could not answer a single question put to him, or he gave a wrong answer to every one of them; he did not do a single assignment in his written work or did not even start doing them. It must be noted that the mark '1' is very rarely given to pupils.

Such is the approach to the testing of the pupils' knowledge and skills at Soviet schools. There exist special criteria for marking written work and laboratory experiments carried out by the pupils, which facilitates assessment of their knowledge. These criteria are based on the pupil's ability to use his knowledge for various practical purposes, which is evidence of the soundness of his knowledge and skills and of a flexible mind.

Naturally, the assessment of the school-leaver's knowledge is not the sum total of all the marks received by the pupil during his final year at school, but of the marks given him for the half-year, for the year and for the examinations. All these marks determine the standard reached by the pupil in the subject; they determine the final mark which is entered in the school-leaving certificate.

Neither the half-year nor the annual marks – still less, the final marks – should be the mean mark. Throughout the year the pupil's knowledge does not remain constant. That is why the final result of learning is extremely important, that is to say, the soundness of knowledge and skills of the pupil by the end of the final year at school. That is why, in giving the final marks to the pupil, great importance is attached to the results of the examinations and to the assessment of the pupil's knowledge at the end of the school year. At the same time, it would be wrong to disregard the pupil's academic progress throughout the year. If the pupil is inconsistent in his studies during the greater part of the year and tries to make up for it towards the end of the year, just before the examination period, even a perfect answer at the examination cannot guarantee a sound knowledge of the subject matter. Therefore, the giving of final marks requires a thorough approach and a synthesis by the teacher of all information at his disposal about the pupil's academic achievements. An analysis of the criteria adopted at Soviet schools for the assessment of the pupils' knowledge and the procedure of giving the final marks shows that this system of marking is flexible and thorough. The mark in the pupil's certificate of education is a concentrated reflection of the school-leaver's education.

The criteria for assessing the pupil's knowledge also orientate the schools to establishing the level of their intellectual development. Soviet educationalists do not believe it advisable to apply special tests to establish the pupil's intellectual level (I.Q.). Instead, their attention is devoted to the compiling of examination material designed to create the best conditions not only for the assessment of the pupil's knowledge but also for testing his intelligence.

We have stressed already, that in assessing the general educational level of Soviet children much attention is paid to their ability to use their knowledge and skills in solving various problems. Therefore, the effectiveness of the pupils' knowledge is also tested. In our opinion, this is an important factor, for only those pupils are ready to do their civic duties whose knowledge is not just 'dead stock', but a prerequisite for the successful application of one's energies in working for the benefit of the country. Only an ability to apply his knowledge in practice can help the school leaver to further his education at college.

The pupil's conduct is also taken into consideration when the pupil receives his matriculation certificate. Conduct is also assessed according to a five-mark system. If a pupil is given only a '4' for his conduct this is a serious factor of moral influence over him. It makes the public organizations at his place of work or study pay closer attention to his behaviour. Moreover, in some cases this mark is taken into consideration when applicants are enrolled at higher educational establishments, and also when applying for a job.

Of great importance, for characterizing the pupils' intellect and good standard of work, as well as for characterizing the pupils' civic maturity, is the system of rewards at Soviet schools. At the end of the eight-year school, pupils who have achieved excellent results in their studies and whose conduct was also excellent receive honorary certificates. They are an important factor in enrolling applicants at secondary technical educational establishments and help the teachers in the senior forms to develop the pupils' inclinations. The importance of rewards at the time of school-leaving is difficult to over estimate.

Pupils who have finished secondary school with excellent marks in all the subjects taught at school (except drawing, singing and physical training) and with excellent marks for their conduct are awarded a medal. Now, the question might be asked, why are the marks in drawing, singing and physical training not taken into account? In these subjects it is not enough for the pupil to show diligence and intellect; in some cases the pupils must be gifted (as in the case of singing and drawing), in others – the pupils' health is of no small importance. In this respect it would be unfair to apply the same requirements to all the pupils.

There is another category of rewards for school-leavers: honorary certificates for achieving excellent results in studying individual subjects. Such an approach to the assessment of the pupils' knowledge is extremely important: very often a pupil who has a real talent for mathematics, developed mathematical thinking and who shows a keen interest in studying mathematics, cannot achieve similar successes in studying the humanities. Whether this pupil thinks of continuing his education at college or university, or choosing a profession, it is only natural for him to take up mathematics seriously. The awarding of an honorary certificate to such a pupil for excellent progress in the subject is a great incentive for him. On the other hand, it is a good recommendation for entering the mathematics department of a university or college, and for being given preference as far as work requiring a knowledge of mathematics is concerned. Therefore, the rewarding of school-leavers for excellent results achieved in their studies is one of the many forms of orientating them professionally.

One must be extremely objective in giving awards to pupils. Even excellent pupils are not given medals and honorary certificates if their conduct is not model. The decision of the school examination commission concerning the excellent standard of pupils' knowledge is carefully studied by special commissions at the local educational department. They study the results of the oral examinations, written examination papers and other material testifying to the pupils' excellent academic standard throughout the school year. This highly principled and objective approach is all the more necessary since those school-leavers who are awarded medals get certain advantages in entering colleges and universities. They have only one entrance examination in the major subject, and if they are given an excellent mark they do not have to take all the other examinations.

The all-round assessment of the Soviet school-leavers' knowledge, inclinations and pursuits as well as their conduct in general is an imporant means of determining how they are prepared for life, and, by 'life' we mean productive labour and cultural activities and the young people's active participation in the further advancement of their country.

Selection for Education by Examination

Brian Holmes

Reader in Comparative Education in the University of London

The case studies in this section describe particular aspects of the use made of examinations in various countries to select children for further educational study. According to J. A. Valentine the major purposes of the College Entrance Examination Board in America are (1) to develop a programme of tests and examinations; (2) to carry out research; (3) to facilitate co-operative discussion among secondary schools and colleges and (4) to encourage the development of opinion regarding educational standards (p. 172). One major programme is the Admissions Testing Program which includes a scholastic aptitude test and subject matter achievement tests in English, mathematics, history, the social sciences and foreign languages (p. 173). The College-Level Examination Program provides national examinations to assess non-traditional college-level education and improve processes of admission, placement and transfer (p. 173). The Board's examinations, which are all based on psychometric theories and techniques, are used extensively in the United States.

J. de Bruijn shows how the system of education in the Netherlands operates as a continuous selection agency for higher education. He suggests that while social milieu, educational guidance, finance and ability affect selection, social background is becoming less important than the level of marks obtained in the various certificate examinations. The attrition rate is high – only 38 boys out of 1,000 leaving the highest grade of primary school complete university training; for girls the figure is 16 (p. 195). The maintenance of this system depends, to a considerable extent, on the conformity of curriculum within each school type.

At present, the U.S.A. appears to be the only country where objective-type examinations are used extensively.

Certainly, N. Cortada de Kohan, in Chapter 20, makes clear some of the difficulties of introducing objective tests into the school system of Argentina, in spite of a recognized need. Pressure on the universities, for example, has shown the need for entrance examinations which will eliminate the less able students (p. 199). Traditional examinations are not very helpful in this respect, but the preparation of objective tests runs into difficulties of translation, adaptation and standardization (p. 199). Expertise in test-construction is needed in any country proposing to move away from traditional-type examinations, but trained personnel are often lacking. In Argentina projects are in hand to develop tests for the primary, secondary and university levels of education, although many teachers and school administrators have yet to be convinced of the value of such tests. But they are undoubtedly one answer to the problems of rapid secondary school and university expansion.

The same problem is found in the U.A.R. Yusef Salah El-Din Kotb describes how the present main criterion for acceptance into higher education – the grade achieved in the general secondary school certificate – is harmful. Solutions proposed include the introduction of 'tests for differential aptitudes, skills, attitudes, and interests', the evaluation of community and social work (p. 207), and guidance programmes.

The unsatisfactory nature of traditional examinations is the focus of interest in K. Mellanby's article on access to higher education in Nigeria. It is a problem, he writes, common to all so-called 'under-developed' countries which, when they became independent, expanded university education but could still be faced with the task of selecting, for example, '200 university entrants a year, from a country with some 40,000,000 inhabitants . . .' (p. 208). The inadequacies of the secondary school system are made clear – another illustration of the close functional relationship between examinations and the scope and structure of primary and secondary education.

M. B. Lourenço Filho suggests that the practical collaboration of commercial and industrial firms helped to modify the traditional examination system of Brazil by the introduction of objective examinations for apprenticeships, educational guidance, and to discover the abilities of apprentices (p. 215). Problems due to rapid educational expansion have appeared in Brazil too. A vast project is under way to develop tests for the orientation of education and student selection (p. 216).

The most extensive change in India in the past decade reported by Snehlata Shukla, has been away from 'ambiguous questions asking mainly for reproduction of memorized material to be produced in large essays' to short-answer questions (p. 220). The reform gears examinations to stated instructional objectives, particularly at the secondary level.

K. Nakayama discusses how, in Japan, modern methods of testing have been introduced. The agencies and procedures used, which are described in some detail, offer prototypes for reform in systems as yet unstrained by examination systems appropriate to 'elitist' systems of education. More extensive use of objective tests appears to be inevitable with continuing expansion and democratization of school systems.

18

The United States of America

John A. Valentine
Executive Director of Examinations, College Entrance Examination Board, New York

The CEEB was formed in 1900 to establish uniform examinations, based on common syllabuses, for entrance to colleges that were to become members of the Board. For the secondary schools that prepared students to go to these colleges (twelve colleges in the beginning), the difficulties of coping with varying and conflicting entrance requirements set by different colleges were thereby eased. The Board, then as now, was a creature of its member institutions, controlled on democratic principles by them, without federal or state governmental authority. It has continued through the years to focus on problems related to the transition of students from school to college. It has grown, however, from a small association of privately-controlled colleges in the northeastern section of the country to a national educational institution composed of all major types of schools and colleges. The scope and nature of its functions and services have expanded, in response both to the extraordinary growth in the percentages and numbers of students going on to some form of higher education, and to the increasing recognition of the political, economic, social and educational variables that influence 'the great sorting process', as it has been called. Its name has become a misnomer, since it is no longer concerned exclusively with examinations, and the examinations (or 'tests') it continues to offer are designed for a variety of purposes, of which entrance or admission to a college is only one. The examinations themselves have been influenced by developments in the fields of psychology and statistics, and by changes in curriculum goals and organization. Use of external test scores, in conjunction with other information, in judgements about individuals made by themselves and by institutions, has been regarded as a more significant and acceptable objective than use of the tests to control teaching practices and standards. The unintended consequences, or 'side effects', of tests, however, for individuals, education and society, have been of increasing concern. A special Commission of the College Board is currently seeking to establish the kinds of tests, if any, that will be needed and possible ten years from now.

The Board is legally a non-profit educational membership organization, incorporated in the State of New York. As of spring 1968 its membership includes 782 colleges and universities, 238 secondary schools, and 88 educational associations. These member institutions represent a cross-section, although not a statistically accurate sample, of American education. Privately supported four-year liberal arts colleges are notably over-represented, and publicly supported colleges under-represented. Major policy decisions of the Board are arrived at by vote of the representatives of member institutions at an annual meeting presided over by the chairman of the Board.

The governing structure, in addition to the membership, consists of a Board of Trustees, officers, including a president, appointed by the trustees, a professional staff appointed by the president, and eleven permanent advisory committees. The chairman and vice-chairman of the Board, elected by the members for two-year terms, serve also as chairman and vice-chairman of the trustees. The president and former chairman are *ex officio* trustees, and the other trustees are elected by the membership for four-year terms. The ongoing affairs of the Board are managed by the trustees, with the appointed staff responsible for carrying out the directions of the Board of Trustees and of the president.

The purposes of the Board, as set forth in its charter, include:

(1) to provide for the continuance and development of a programme of tests and examinations;

(2) to provide for a continuing programme of research;

(3) to provide a medium for the co-operation of secondary schools, colleges, and other institutions of higher learning and for the discussion of their common problems; and

(4) to further the development of representative opinion with respect to educational standards.

In carrying out the first two purposes, concerned with examinations and with research, the Board depends heavily on Educational Testing Service – a separate and independent non-profit agency established in 1948 by the Board, the American Council on Education, and the Carnegie Foundation for the Advancement of Teaching.

Co-operation of secondary schools and institutions of higher learning (purpose 3) is a theme which finds expression in most of the Board's activities, services and programmes, since both school and college personnel are likely to be involved in their operation and periodic evaluation. The annual meeting of the Board membership in the fall, special colloquiums on college admissions and curricular change, and many regional conferences held each year, all provide open forums for the discussion by school and college representatives of problems of improving access to higher education. The Board's programme of publications also facilitates the exchange of ideas and information between schools and colleges.

The fourth purpose, the furthering of the development of representative opinion with respect to educational standards, has been achieved in recent years through the reports and recommendations of the Commission on Mathematics and the Commission on English.

The oldest and largest of the Board's testing programmes is the Admissions Testing Program consisting of the Scholastic Aptitude Test, and subject-matter Achievement Tests in English, mathematics, sciences, history and social studies, and in languages (other than English) commonly studied by American students. Most of the member colleges of the Board require applicants to take the Scholastic Aptitude Test (SAT), and many require them to take both the SAT and several (usually three) Achievement Tests.

Two programmes utilize tests derived from the Admissions Testing Program but for purposes other than use in selection decisions by colleges. A form of the SAT, known as the Preliminary Scholastic Aptitude Test (PSAT), is offered as part of the Board's programme of guidance services. It is taken by students a year or more before they complete secondary school education, and is intended to help them and their school counsellors make sensible college plans. Many colleges, through the Board, provide data on the SAT scores (which can be estimated from PSAT scores) of their applicants and entering students, and these data enhance the meaning and therefore the usefulness of the PSAT scores.

The Board makes available to colleges recent forms of Achievement Tests which are used in placing students, once admitted, in appropriate courses and levels of study.

The Advanced Placement Program includes examinations based on college-level courses taught in some secondary schools, and the results are used by many colleges as at least a partial basis for granting credit, or placement in a second-year course, or both, to entering freshmen. The point is to make the student's academic work more continuous, despite the discontinuities that abound between American secondary school and higher education.

The College-Level Examination Program, developed and offered within the last few years, is designed to serve a variety of goals: (1) to provide national examinations that may be used to evaluate non-traditional college-level education, including independent study and correspondence work; (2) to stimulate colleges and universities to become more actively aware of the need for and potential of credit by examination; (3) to enable colleges to improve procedures for admission and placement of transfer students; (4) to enable institutions to improve evaluations of their own programmes and students; and (5) to assist adults in advancing or improving their educational or professional status.

The international activities of the Board include two tests. One is a Spanish language Scholastic Aptitude Test, developed in Puerto Rico for use in the admission of students to colleges there and in countries of Latin America, and also in the evaluation of Latin American applicants to colleges in the U.S.A. The other is the Test of English as a Foreign Language, used by institutions admitting students from other countries.

All of the Board examinations have in common the application of psychometric theory and technique to their design, development, analysis, scoring and score interpretation. They are also generally similar in the way major policy questions regarding them are decided, and in the way ongoing work on their development and administration is organized and handled. The Admissions Testing Program serves as a convenient illustrative case.

The present structure of the Admissions Testing Program, consisting of the SAT and a menu of Achievement Tests, was set in 1942. The precipitating circumstance was the war between the United States and Japan, which resulted in many American colleges adopting an accelerated schedule of undergraduate study, starting early in the summer instead of in the fall. This meant that the results of the traditional June essay examinations, offered since 1900, were not available in time to affect admission decisions, and they were therefore withdrawn. Supporting circumstances were that colleges had had experience with the SAT since its introduction in 1927 and had found it useful. Some also had had favourable experience with multiple-choice subject-matter tests that the Board offered in April to help colleges judge the preparation of scholarship applicants, able and promising otherwise, whose school curricula were different enough from the syllabuses on which the essay examinations were based to make these examinations inappropriate. A more remote but relevant set of supporting circumstances included the force of the testing movement in the United States, and the congeniality of this movement with emphases in American education on general educational objectives, local control of curriculum, and an egalitarian philosophy.

The SAT and Achievement Tests are offered several times during the year at centres throughout the world, the SAT in the morning, the Achievement Tests in the afternoon. The SAT, a three-hour multiple-choice test, yields two scores, verbal reasoning ability (V) and mathematical reasoning ability (M). The Achievement Tests are one hour in length (the student may take as many as three in one afternoon session), and except for the English Composition Test, which may include a short essay, they also consist of multiple-choice questions. Students are guided by the requirements of colleges to which they intend to apply for admission in deciding which tests to take and when to take them. Standardized scores are reported, on a scale from 200 to 800, to colleges indicated by the student, and to his secondary school. 'Pass-fail' evaluations are not made or reported by the College Board.

The permanent advisory committee to the College Board for the Admissions Testing Program is the Committee on Examinations. It advises the president and the trustees on issues with respect to the organization, development, administration, and use of the tests. Depending on the significance of the Committee's recommendations for the Board membership, they may be acted upon finally by the staff, the trustees, or the membership itself.

For each test the president appoints a committee of examiners, which serves as a source of advice to the staff and the Committee on Examinations. The Achievement Test examining committees also participate in ongoing development of the tests along with members of Educational Testing Service. In the case of the SAT, the committee is composed of leading psychologists in the field of educational measurement. The committees for the Achievement Tests include professors and teachers selected on the basis of subject-matter competence, interest in curriculum, and representation of significant points of view. They work closely with specialists at ETS familiar both with the subject and with test technique.

The development of each new form of a test starts with determination or review of the domain of knowledge and ability that the test will sample, and the number of questions to be included in each category of knowledge and ability so as to construct an adequate sample. The number of questions of various types, of various degrees of difficulty, and with various degrees of power to discriminate between generally high-scoring and low-scoring students are also decided upon. Guiding considerations include need for a test that will be fair to students with different curriculum preparation, need for new test forms to serve interchangeably with recent earlier forms, and need for a distribution of scores that will differentiate among students at all levels of proficiency.

Many more questions are written than will eventually be needed. Questions are reviewed and edited extensively before being tried out or pre-tested on a group of students comparable to those who will eventually take the final test. The analysis of pre-tested questions affords information about their difficulty, discriminating power, and clarity or ambiguity, and contributes to their acceptance, refinement or rejection for the form in process. In the assembly of the final, operational form, some questions will be included from one or more earlier forms to permit appropriate conversions of raw or original scores to scaled scores. Once assembled, the form will be finally reviewed before being readied for printing and administration.

In the interest of fairness to all students, steps are taken to ensure that some students do not have advance knowledge of the questions, and that the testing conditions for all students are uniform. Booklets describing the tests, including sample questions, are made available to students at the beginning of each testing year.

Whatever merit the tests may have as a result of the knowledge, skill and care that go into their development, administration and scoring, they have ultimate social value only if the scores are interpreted and used with knowledgeable awareness of their meaning and limitations. It is difficult to determine the extent to which this condition prevails. It is fairly evident that the scores are properly understood by some admissions officers, school counsellors, students and parents, and misunderstood, in a minor or major way, by others. It is reasonable to assume that the community of enlightened users is expanding, as a result of increased opportunities to gain the necessary background of experience and information. Whether the gains from sensible use sufficiently offset the damage done by misuse and abuse of test scores is a matter of controversy.

The tests are most likely to be used to the advantage of the student when they are considered in the perspective of other relevant information about the abilities in question, when the margin of error surrounding them is taken into account, when the norms available for their interpretation are used knowingly, when whatever predictions they afford on empirical grounds of future academic success are understood, and when what they fail to measure as well as what they do measure is appreciated. Under these conditions, the tests may justify themselves on the grounds that they enable the student himself, and those advising him, to reach judgements that are more truly informed than they would be without the test scores in the picture.

The possible unfortunate consequences of the Board tests that are cited by critics include intense and crippling anxiety, unjustified feelings and judgements of limited potential which serve to block further development, too much emphasis on glibness and superficiality of thought and too little on profundity and creativity, corruption of teaching objectives and practices, and sharpening of social class distinctions. The extent of these consequences is more a matter of impression than of fact, but serious concerns about them are expressed by some thoughtful observers of the American scene.

In addition to concerns about the misuse of the admissions tests, and their unfortunate side-effects, there are concerns that the tests in their present form are simply outliving their appropriateness and usefulness in the face of changing social, educational, and technological circumstances.

The limited supplementary information they provide may not be necessary as school-based information becomes more complete and manageable. The emphasis they place on selection, and therefore exclusion, is increasingly out of place as educational opportunities expand, setting a premium on guidance and placement. Common, uniform examinations for all students make less sense as teaching becomes more individualized, and computer-based tests, that adjust to individual differences, become a reality. Overwhelming dependence on reading, and an abstract verbal ability generally is out of joint as learning through other media than words and the development of perceptual and kinesthetic as well as cognitive skills assume more prominence.

To undertake a thorough review of the Board's testing functions in American education, to consider possibilities for fundamental change in the present tests, and to consider what kinds of tests and programmes may be needed a decade hence, the Board appointed, in 1967, a Commission on Tests to conduct a three-year study and to make recommendations to the Board. The Commission is composed of teachers, administrators and writers representing various types of experience with tests and points of view regarding them. Its plan includes the holding of a series of open meetings in different areas of the United States, to gather evidence from various interested individuals and groups, and it has heard already from a number of critics of the tests. In line with its intention to operate in the public view and in the public interests, periodic reports[1] of its findings will be made generally available.

BIBLIOGRAPHY

Frank Bowles, *The Refounding of the College Board, 1948–1963.* (New York: College Entrance Examination Board, 1967.)

College Entrance Examination Board, *A Report to the Trustees: The Organization and Functions of the College Entrance Examination Board.* (New York: College Entrance Examination Board, 1964.)

College Entrance Examination Board, *Charter and Bylaws.* (New York: College Entrance Examination Board, 1966.)

College Entrance Examination Board, *The College Board Today.* (New York: College Entrance Examination Board, 1967.)

Claude M. Fuess, *The College Board: Its First Fifty Years.* (New York: Columbia University Press, 1950.)

---

[1] Interested readers should write to the College Entrance Examination Board, 475 Riverside Drive, New York, New York 10027, U.S.A.

19

The Netherlands

J. de Bruijn
Head, Department of Educational and Cultural Statistics, Central Bureau of Statistics, Netherlands

The subject 'Selection for Higher Education' is socially relevant and of current interest. Indeed, more than ever before, education – and notably higher education – is considered as one of the social and economic factors that contribute to changes in society.

First of all there is the economic aspect: the factor 'labour' has acquired a new dimension, viz. the educational attainment of the gainfully occupied population. Our society – characterized by accelerated industrialization, automation and highly increasing research activities – needs more and more university graduates, particularly scientists and engineers. However, the change in the social structure also requires more consideration for the welfare of man. This implies an increasing demand for medical men, psychologists, sociologists and teachers.

Then again there is the social aspect. Many socially backward groups – labourers, residents of rural districts, some religious groupings – feel a strong need for social emancipation. They often take considerable pains to enable their children to occupy a higher rank in the social scale. The most appropriate way to achieve this is thought to be a better and more prolonged education than they themselves enjoyed. One of their ambitions is to let their children have a university education.

Finally, sociological research has shown that the level of education attained is highly decisive for the pattern of leisure time. This will be more fruitful and varied as the educational attainment is higher. And in a society in which leisure time continues to take up an ever more prominent place and is becoming a world apart from work, development of personality is justly considered to be most important.

These three summarized aspects of the social framework of our subject show, on the one hand, a great social demand for university graduates and, on the other hand, a strong need for higher education in the various social groupings. Therefore it is important to study the road which leads to the group of the university graduates – the method of selection.

This subject was broached *i.a.* by Dr Frank Bowles in his book *Access to Higher Education*. In the introduction he states: 'Admission to higher education is not a single administrative act, performed when a student moves from secondary to higher education, but a process which extends over a period of years during which a series of selections determines those students who continue towards the goal of ultimate entry to higher education' (pages 25–26). When following up his ideas he says that '. . . admission to higher education is a process which takes place in systems of education in all nations, commencing at or before entry to secondary school and continuing through stages until enrolment in higher education is complete' (page 61).

For one country, the Netherlands, this chapter will describe and – in so far as the statistical material permits – quantify this process.

In this selection process the following phases can be distinguished:

A. The transition of the highest grade of primary education to secondary education which prepares for the university;

B. the school career at the secondary education level;

C. the transition of those holding a certificate of secondary education to higher education and the choice of branch of study;

D. the study-record of the higher education.

We shall show that in each one of the above mentioned phases a continuous selection takes place. Various factors determine this selection. Some of them are: the social milieu from which the student comes, his talents, his financial situation, the guidance in matters of study-possibilities. Moreover, the selection may vary with the sexes whilst the extent of selection can change in the course of time. Unfortunately the available statistical material is insufficient for a systematic quantifying of the influence of each one of the factors in each phase. Before we describe the four phases of the selection process we present first:

I. A Brief Description of the Educational System in the Netherlands

Under the system of education in the Netherlands at the time of writing – in 1968 a new system comes into operation – the transitional phase from primary to secondary education is extremely important: here the first and most essential selection takes place. The boy or girl who has completed primary education has – generally speaking – three possibilities for continued education at the secondary level:

A. *Secondary Grammar Schools* (v.h.m.o.) – This group includes some forms of education which – with some exceptions – prepare for university studies and for higher vocational training courses, and also for professional occupations. The duration of study is 5–6 school-years. The school-types belonging to the v.h.m.o. show relative differences in their programmes of study, either as from the beginning of the study or after one or more years of joint schooling. Finally they result – for our purposes – in four diplomas:

(1) the diploma gymnasium-α strongly stressing the study of Latin and Greek;

(2) the diploma gymnasium-β, devoting attention not only to the classics but also to mathematics and sciences;

(3) the diploma 'Hogere Burgerschool-A' (HBS-A), in which the three modern languages and economics play an important part;

(4) the diploma 'Hogere Burgerschool-B' (HBS-B) emphasizing mainly the modern languages and mathematics and sciences.

These four diplomas all carry the right to take university examinations, although not every diploma gives access to all faculties.

B. *The Junior Secondary Education* (u.l.o.) – This type of school offers general education and largely functions as a preliminary education for the secondary and semi-higher vocational training courses. The duration of the study is 3–4 school-years. The diploma does not give access to university examinations.

C. *The Junior Vocational Education* – This complex of school-types – duration of study between 2 and 4 years – prepares either for (semi-) skilled work in trade, industry, agriculture and navigation, or for simple female occupations.

This brief outline of the Dutch school system has been somewhat simplified. We have given the impression that only education mentioned under A. (the v.h.m.o.) would give access to the university examinations. This is not quite correct. It is, for instance, possible to pass via the u.l.o. (school-type B) on to the v.h.m.o. (school-type A), and thus arrive at the adequate previous education for the university. It is also possible to follow a university education based on a certificate obtained from some semi-higher vocational training school. These semi-higher educations will not be discussed here. Studies undertaken via these schools are indeed detours, which lengthen the preceding schooling by about two years, because the programmes of study are completely different from those of the v.h.m.o. Up to 10 per cent of the freshmen of the higher education come to the university by these detours. Consequently this simplification causes but little distortion in the quantitative aspect of the selection process.

II. The Selection Process

The selection process itself is outlined as follows:

A. *The Transition of the Highest Grade of Primary Education to Secondary Education which Prepares for the University.*

(1) *General Remarks* – Table I shows that only 20 per cent of the boys and 17 per cent of the girls continue their studies at the v.h.m.o. after

TABLE I

DESTINATION OF THE PUPILS WHO LEFT GRADES 6 AND HIGHER OF THE PRIMARY SCHOOLS

Year	Total leavers		of which (percentages) went over to				
	Absolute figures	Percentage	Secondary grammar schools	Junior secondary schools	Vocational schools*	Other education*	No further education†
Boys							
1961	116,000	100	16	31	39	10	3
1962	111,000	100	17	30	40	9	4
1963	109,000	100	18	30	40	9	3
1964	109,000	100	19	30	40	8	3
1965	108,000	100	20	30	41	7	2
1966	107,000	100	20	30	41	7	2
Girls							
1961	112,000	100	13	34	39	12	2
1962	106,000	100	13	34	39	11	2
1963	105,000	100	14	34	39	11	1
1964	105,000	100	15	34	38	11	2
1965	105,000	100	17	34	37	10	1
1966	103,000	100	17	35	38	10	1

* Exclusively full-time education.　　† Part-time education included.

SOURCE: Central Bureau of Statistics. Basic material derived from 'Flows within the educational system and entry into the labour force, 1936, 1956, and 1961–1966' (*Matrix*).

Y.B.E.—7

completing primary education. Evidently the selection is very marked in this phase. However, in the past years considerable changes occurred because the percentages continued to increase. They are also different for boys and girls. Even though the girls are still behind the boys, they are rapidly catching up.

(2) *Social Selection* – The social composition of those admitted to the v.h.m.o. greatly differs from that of the pupils of the highest school-year in primary education and – primary education being compulsory – of the younger generation of the population. In this phase of the selection process fundamental decisions are made. The share of the higher social groups and the middle-class employees is relatively higher, whilst that of the labourers is considerably lower.

TABLE II

Pupils of grade 6 of Primary Education and Pupils admitted to Grade 1 of Secondary Grammar Schools, by Sex, by Social Status (Percentages)

	Grade 6 primary education		Admission to grade 1 of secondary grammar schools	
	Boys	Girls	Boys	Girls
Higher class	7	6	24	20
Middle class:				
salaried	19	17	31	38
independent	21	22	20	18
Lower class:				
administrative	9	10	8	9
labourers	41	43	16	15
Soc. status unknown	2	2	1	1
TOTAL	100	100	100	100

Source: Central Bureau of Statistics. From *Educational flows, Sample-survey 1964*.

Other statistical material shows that since World War II a social democratization is evident. Since 1949 the numbers of pupils admitted to the v.h.m.o., coming from the higher social milieus, increased by 24 per cent, and from the lower classes by 82 per cent. The most marked increase however was that of the middle class, by 124 per cent. This shows that democratization goes by phases.

This type of school was originally attended to a large extent by the 'upper classes', but after the war the middle groups became most predominant. It is very likely that in the next phase of the acculturation process the lower employees and workers will assume this position.

(3) *Influence of the Geographical Situation* – An urban situation – see Table III – stimulates the afflux to the secondary education which prepares for the higher education. Undoubtedly the social-milieu factor has a (veiled) influence.

Other data, however, indicate that the isolation of the countryside is an independent factor which impedes the flow towards the v.h.m.o. Indeed, the number of rural schools for elementary education from which in three successive years not a single pupil passed on to the v.h.m.o. (mainly concentrated in the cities) is remarkably high. As other than socially lower-class groups also live in the country, a lack of efficient guidance – caused by a geographical and cultural isolation – will definitely have an influence on this phenomenon.

TABLE III

PUPILS ADMITTED TO GRADE 1 OF SECONDARY GRAMMAR SCHOOLS (1964), IN PERCENTAGES OF THE NUMBER OF PUPILS LEAVING GRADE 6 OF PRIMARY EDUCATION, BY DEGREE OF URBANIZATION, BY SEX.

Coming from	Boys	Girls
Rural districts	16	9
Urban districts	17	12
Cities	25	21
TOTAL	21	16

SOURCE: Central Bureau of Statistics. From *Educational flows, Sample-survey 1964*.

(4) *Influence of Difference in Talents* – The question arises whether the considerable differences in admission patterns between the social groupings are completely or largely determined by social selection. To what extent are the differences in talents within the social groups co-determinants? This point has been studied by the Netherlands Central Bureau of Statistics in close co-operation with the Sociological Institute of Leiden University and the Netherlands Institute of Preventive Medicine. The survey is as yet insufficiently advanced to make quantitative statements. So much is certain however, that the relative number of intelligent youngsters is considerably higher in the upper classes than in the lower social groups. Consequently selection based on intelligence would lead to appreciable differences in the social composition of the younger generation of the population and that of the v.h.m.o.

3. *Selection During the Secondary Education*

(1) *General Remarks* – Not all pupils who start the v.h.m.o. education gain the school certificate. In the Netherlands educational system a great

part is played by those who end their education prematurely or who complete it with a delay of one or more years.

Thanks to a statistical method – the so-called cohort-analysis – at which each pupil is individually followed during his school career, the educational statistics can exactly determine the selection within the v.h.m.o. and study its various aspects.

TABLE IV

Study Results of the 1949-Generation, by Sex, in Percentages (Total v.h.m.o.)

	Boys	Girls	Total
	Qualified persons		
Without doubling classes	21	27	24
After doubling classes	31	26	29
Total qualified persons	52	53	53

Source: Central Bureau of Statistics. From *Statistical Investigations on Education and Leisure*, Volume 1, 'Analysis of Student Performance', page 12, upper part only.

The results of this cohort-analysis (see Table IV) show that only 24 per cent of those admitted to the first grade of the v.h.m.o. take their final certificate within the normal time, that is to say, without retardation. It further shows that 29 per cent terminate their study successfully with retardation. Thus it appears that just over half of those who were admitted survived the selection within the v.h.m.o. It is noteworthy that these figures show a very constant picture for the different generations: otherwise, there are few differences in time.

(2) *Social Selection* – It appears that the selection process does not show the same trend for all social milieus. It is, however, worth while to follow this selection process from a sociological as well as from an educative standpoint. A sharp contrast is apparent between those who take their diploma without retardation and those who gain it after one or more additional years. In the first category the percentages are – at least for the boys – more or less identical for all social groupings, namely about 22 per cent. However, considerable differences appear for those with a retardation of one or more years. As against 40 per cent of the boys from the upper classes who gain their diploma in the end, there stand only 23 per cent of the boys from the working classes. There are reasons other than educational to account for these differences. Undoubtedly the financial situation of the parents plays an important part when, immediately after an incurred retardation, the question arises of whether or not study should be continued.

TABLE V

THE QUALIFIED PERSONS OF THE 1949-GENERATION BY SOCIAL STATUS, AND SEX, IN
PERCENTAGES OF EACH SOCIAL STATUS (TOTAL V.H.M.O.)

	Without doubling classes		After doubling classes		Total	
	Boys	Girls	Boys	Girls	Boys	Girls
Higher social status	21	29	40	32	61	61
Middle social status:						
(a) Salaried	22	30	35	25	57	55
(b) Independent	20	24	26	22	46	46
Lesser social status:						
(a) Clerical personnel	25	22	29	23	54	46
(b) Labourers	22	26	23	16	45	43
GRAND TOTAL	21	27	31	26	52	53

SOURCE: Central Bureau of Statistics. From *Statistical Investigations on Education and Leisure*, Volume 1: 'Analysis of student performance', page 12.

These above-mentioned differences in positive study results – and thus in selection between the various social groups – imply that the social composition of the pupils who gain their diplomas is different from that of the original first-graders – the upper class increased whilst the lower class relatively decreased. The following table quantifies these shifts.

TABLE VI

THE PUPILS OF THE 1946-GENERATION OF SECONDARY GRAMMAR SCHOOLS BY SOCIAL
STATUS (PERCENTAGES)

	Higher social status	Middle social status	Lower social status	Total*
When admitted in 1946	28	50	20	100
After obtaining the leaving-certificate (with and without retardation)	33	48	17	100

* Including 'Social status unknown'.

SOURCE: Central Bureau of Statistics, March 1956. Special investigation, *Study results on Secondary Grammar Schools by Social Status*, Table 5.

(3) *Selection According to Talents* – A survey of the positive study results according to intelligence or talents is being carried out, as we mentioned before. Results are not yet available. Nevertheless other material – also taken from the cohort-analysis – offers an indication which gives some idea. They should be handled with a certain degree of caution.

TABLE VII

QUALIFIED PERSONS OF THE 1949-GENERATIONS BY AGE WHEN ADMITTED, BY SEX,
IN PERCENTAGES OF EACH AGE (TOTAL V.H.M.O.)

	Without doubling classes		After doubling classes		Total	
	Boys	Girls	Boys	Girls	Boys	Girls
11 years of age and younger	33	39	48	38	82	77
12 years of age	27	32	39	32	66	64
13 years of age	20	25	30	23	49	48
14 years of age	13	18	21	13	35	32
15 years of age and older	9	10	9	8	18	18
GRAND TOTAL	21	27	31	26	52	53

SOURCE: Central Bureau of Statistics. From *Statistical Investigations on Education and Leisure*, Volume 1: 'Analysis of Student Performance', page 12.

Noteworthy is the close relation between the gaining of a certificate – be it with or without retardation – and the age at admission to the first grade of the v.h.m.o. For the boys 81 per cent of the youngest complete their studies successfully, but this can be said of only 18 per cent of the oldest. Girls show an analogous picture. Statistically speaking this admission age can be interpreted as an indicator of eventual retardation during the elementary education. And, where large numbers are concerned, a connexion may be made (with the necessary reservation) between the retardation during the elementary education and intelligence.

C. *Transition of Students Holding V.H.M.O. Certificates to Higher Education and the Choice of Branch of Study*

(1) *General Remarks* – The Netherlands educational system does not have any administrative selection processes for admission to higher education. There are no entrance examinations; not a single faculty has a *numerus clausus* or a *numerus fixus*. It is not even necessary to possess a v.h.m.o. certificate to enroll as a student. The certificate is, however, required for the passing of university examinations. This is the reason why the group of students, enrolled at the universities without a v.h.m.o. certificate, is limited.

(2) *Transition of Certificated Students to Higher Education in General* – The figures in Table VIII show that – regarding the totals only – a relatively increasing number of secondary school graduates of the v.h.m.o. continue their study at the higher education. The differences between the

TABLE VIII

PERCENTAGES OF PUPILS WITH LEAVING-CERTIFICATES FROM SECONDARY GRAMMAR SCHOOLS IN FOUR CONSECUTIVE PERIODS OF THREE YEARS, WHO WENT OVER TO UNIVERSITY EDUCATION, PER CERTIFICATE, BY SEX

Period	Certificate				Total
	Gymnasium-α	Gymnasium-β	HBS-A	HBS-B	
Men					
1954–1956	69	85	19	47	48
1957–1959	69	86	24	56	54
1960–1962	72	90	27	59	56
1963–1965	80	93	36	65	62
Women					
1954–1956	61	64	7	29	34
1957–1959	66	76	8	34	40
1960–1962	66	72	10	35	39
1963–1965	71	76	11	42	43

SOURCE: Central Bureau of Statistics. From *Regional Differences in the Transition from Secondary to University Education, and Choice of University and Faculty by First-year University Students* (1963–1965).

numbers of men and of women continuing their education are marked.

Considering the transition-percentages for the various types of certificates (for the characteristics see p. 179–80) it appears how great these differences are: while 80 per cent of the male persons with a certificate gymnasium- and even 93 per cent of those with the β-certificate continue their studies at the university, these percentages are considerably lower for those with a certificate HBS-B and even more so for HBS-A. The two last-mentioned groups are also increasing; again, especially the certificated persons with a diploma HBS-A. The increase in the transition percentage of all diplomas combined should thus be largely ascribed to the growing interest in the higher education of those in possession of a HBS certificate.

(3) *Social Selection* – Social selection also enters into the transition of the v.h.m.o. to the higher education.

As in the preceding phases of the selection process, the upper social milieu increased whilst the lower one decreased.

The social selection in this phase can also be elucidated in another way. More than ten years ago the Netherlands Central Bureau of Statistics studied the connexion between the performances at the final examinations – judged from the marks obtained at that examination – and the subsequent choice of branch of study, for all the v.h.m.o. diplomas in question. The survey only concerned boys.

TABLE IX

PUPILS WHO PASSED THE FINAL EXAMINATION OF SECONDARY GRAMMAR SCHOOLS
(1957–1958) AND FIRST-YEAR UNIVERSITY STUDENTS (1958), BY SEX, BY SOCIAL
STATUS (PERCENTAGES)

	Those who passed the final exam. at grammar schools		First-year university students	
	Men	Women	Men	Women
Higher class	29	41	45	66
Middle class:				
salaried	27	26	25	17
independent	25	21	21	14
Lower class:				
administrative	6	4	3	2
labourers	13	8	6	2
TOTAL	100	100	100	100

SOURCE: Central Bureau of Statistics. From *Educational flows, Sample-survey, 1964.*

By combining the relevant subjects of the final examination and the obtainable marks, 'performance-types' were constructed. The expression 'performance-type' instead of 'intelligence-type' was chosen on purpose in order to express that the level of the marks obtained at the final examination is not only determined by intelligence but also by application, perseverance, etc.

In this way 15 performance-types per certificate were established, of which No. 1 indicated the highest and No. 15 the lowest type. By applying this typology to the secondary school graduates of two successive years 60 groups were formed – 15 performance-types for each one of the four diplomas. Finally, the extent to which these groups continued their studies at the higher education was investigated. The results were as follows:

Of the 'best' (performance-types 1–3 inclusive) having a diploma gymnasium-α, gymnasium-β or HBS-B, each time between 90 and 95 per cent passed on to the higher education, but not more than 50 per cent of those with a diploma HBS-A.

Of the 'weakest' (performance-types 13–15 inclusive) about 70 per cent of those with a diploma gymnasium-α or -β enrolled in a university. For those with a diploma HBS-B and -A these figures were about 30 and 10 per cent respectively.

These figures permit, first of all, the following interpretation. On the one hand, there is a group of parents who – at the time when they choose for their son an education at the gymnasium – already intended to let him continue at the university. Indeed, after gaining the diploma the son is sent to the university, regardless of his performance at the v.h.m.o. On the other hand, there are parents who made their son follow a HBS education and left his future more open for further decisions. The results obtained at the final examination determined to a far higher degree the decision on the future study.

The results permit another still more drastic interpretation. Taking into consideration that the gymnasium recruits its pupils largely from the upper social milieus (44 per cent from the upper social level, 6 per cent from the working classes), which is not the case for the HBS (18 per cent from the upper levels, 20 per cent from the working classes), it can reasonably be concluded that motives of social prestige do play an important part in the decision to take up a study at the university.

Although the survey has not been repeated since 1955, it can be assumed that notably the middle groups are adapting themselves to the aspirations of the upper social levels. The following may serve to corroborate this assumption:

In the first place, we have seen in section II A under 2 that in the last years the relative share of the middle social levels has increased most rapidly. No important shifts were noticed in the social structure of the school types – gymnasium and HBS. The number of pupils of the HBS showed the highest increase. The frequency distribution of the final examination marks, and thus of the performance-types, remained constant during a series of years. Finally, as shown in Table VIII, the transition percentages of those with a certificate of the HBS-B and HBS-A were the ones which increased most markedly.

All these factors together give reason to assume that in the field of education – as in other sectors of society – the differences between the higher and the middle social grouping are fading away.

(4) *Choice of Branch of Study* – Social factors also influence the prospective student's choice of branch of study direction. In the Netherlands, research on that score is still in its initial stage and thus has not yet resulted in clear conclusions. Therefore we have to confine ourselves to a statement on the results of the various influences as they are manifested in the actual social composition of the faculties (Table X, p. 190).

Table XI shows, on the one hand, that the selection on and after leaving the elementary school up till the enrolment for the university education is far-reaching and thus has a quantitatively strongly reducing influence, and, on the other hand, that the barriers at the different levels gradually lose their importance in the course of time. This also appears from the increasing percentage of students whose fathers had no university education.

TABLE X

First-year University Students, by Social Status, by Sex and by Faculty, per 100 First-year Students of each Faculty (1964–65)*

	Higher class		Middle class		Lower class		Total	
	Men	Women	Men	Women	Men	Women	Men	Women
Theology	34	71	51	24	14	5	100	100
Arts	33	57	53	39	14	4	100	100
Medicine	50	51	43	45	7	4	100	100
Dentistry	44	56	52	31	5	13	100	100
Veterinary science	30	50	66	38	3	13	100	100
Mathematics and Natural science	31	51	51	42	18	7	100	100
Engineering	30	53	55	44	15	3	100	100
Agriculture	27	64	64	35	8	2	100	100
Law	50	58	43	38	8	4	100	100
Economics†	34	57	54	43	13	—	100	100
Political and Social sciences‡	30	50	57	44	13	6	100	100
Psychology	27	47	58	46	15	6	100	100
Pedagogy	11	56	69	38	20	7	100	100
Geography	27	48	58	45	15	7	100	100
Others§	32	75	59	25	9	—	100	100
TOTAL	35	54	52	41	13	5	100	100

* Exclusively students of Dutch nationality and under 35 years of age. † Including econometrics. ‡ Excluding Psychology and Pedagogy. § i.e.: actuary science and central combined department: Philosophy. SOURCE: Central Bureau of Statistics. From *Statistics on University Education 1965–1966*, page 31.

TABLE XI

First-year Students at University whose Fathers did not obtain a University Degree, by Faculty, per 100 First-year Students of each Faculty (1954–55 and 1964–65)*

	1954–55		1964–65	
	Men	Women	Men	Women
Theology	79	78	83	57
Arts	85	57	87	67
Medicine	67	67	71	70
Dentistry	66	50	73	56
Veterinary science	82	83	85	83
Mathematics and Natural science	76	53	86	74
Engineering	79	58	88	68
Agriculture	75	50	86	57
Law	65	54	75	70
Economics†	86	78	90	76
Political and Social sciences‡	77	55	89	76
Psychology	84	64	90	76
Geography	80	67	96	59
Others §	—	—	98	65
TOTAL	77	59	85	70

* Exclusively students of Dutch nationality and under 35 years of age.
† Including econometrics.
‡ Excluding Psychology and Pedagogy.
§ i.e.: actuary science, Pedagogy, and central combined department: Philosophy.
Source: Central Bureau of Statistics. From *Statistics on University Education 1964–65*, page 28.

This phenomenon shows that the university graduates form an ever less tightly closed group. To an increasing degree the youngest generations are continually being supplemented by students from social groups in which the parents are not university-educated.

D. *Study-career in Higher Education*

(1) *Freedom of Study* – It also applies to university education that not all those who start a study bring it to a successful conclusion. Undoubtedly the results of study at the Netherlands universities are co-determined by the relatively great measure of freedom the student often enjoys. This applies to the attendance at lectures and practical training courses, and often also to the time at which examinations are taken. To a certain extent the student is free to choose his own tempo. It should, however, be mentioned that – mainly due to the strongly increasing number of students in all faculties, this freedom has become ever more curtailed in recent years. Characteristic is an increasing study-guidance.

As has been shown under 1 of section C, there is no selection for admission to higher education, based on the results obtained during the previous education. This implies that it is unavoidable that there will be a number of less talented students amongst the freshmen. This evidently acts adversely on the average study-results. Many give up their study before passing the final examinations, and the duration of study is widely divergent.

(2) *Determining Study-results and Duration of Study* – In order to determine the useful effect and the duration of study the method of the cohort-analysis is also used for this branch of education: a card is assigned to each individual student as soon as he begins his study; on this card, a number of data are entered, such as sex, choice of branch of study, year of birth, age at which the final v.h.m.o. examination was passed, certain marks gained at that final examination, occupation of the father (= social milieu). During the study the card is kept up to date as to immatriculation and possible change of faculty, the examinations successfully passed and the time at which they are taken.

TABLE XII

Achievements after 13 years for the Final Examination of the Students of the 1948–50 Generations, all Fields of Study, by Sex, in Percentages of the Number of Students of each Faculty of the named Generations at the Entry of University Education

Field of study	Male	Female
Theology*	83	n.a.
Arts (including History)	58	33
Medicine (excluding Pharmacy)	69	52
Dentristry	63	n.a.
Veterinary science	65	n.a.
Mathematics and Natural science (including Pharmacy)	59	36
Engineering	57	n.a.
Agriculture	51	n.a.
Law	68	54
Political and Social sciences	30	22
Psychology	49	29
Geography	56	n.a.
Economics	51	n.a.

* With the exception of the students at the Calvinist University at Amsterdam and at the Roman Catholic University at Nijmegen. In the faculty of theology the 'kandidaats' – examination is considered to be the final examination.

n.a. = These data are not available because of too small absolute numbers.

Source: Central Bureau of Statistics. From: *Statistical Investigations on Education and Leisure,* Volume 1: 'Analysis of Student Performance', page 28, Table 2.

Of particular importance for our purpose is the question of which factors determine these achievements. During the past years the Netherlands Central Bureau of Statistics have studied the influence of some quantifiable determinants, which are mentioned under 3 and 4.

(3) *Influence of the Social Milieu* – It is particularly noteworthy that – but for a few exceptions – the social milieu from which the student comes no longer has any influence on the results of his university study. Apparently this factor has lost its influence as far as the university study is concerned.

(4) *Influence of the Marks Gained and the Age at which the School Certificate was taken* – It appears, on the other hand, that the study-performance during the preliminary training at the secondary level – the v.h.m.o. – determines to a considerable degree the success of the university study. The level of this performance at the v.h.m.o. can be expressed by means of:

(*a*) The age of the pupil when taking the school certificate. Statistically this may be interpreted as an indicator for the degree of retardation during the v.h.m.o. years.

(*b*) The level of the marks gained at the school certificate of the v.h.m.o. which is an indicator of the 'quality' of the secondary school graduates.

TABLE XIII

INFLUENCE OF AGE WHEN THE V.H.M.O. LEAVING-CERTIFICATE WAS OBTAINED ON THE ACHIEVEMENTS, AFTER 13 YEARS, FOR THE FINAL EXAMINATION. PERCENTAGES OF THE NUMBER OF STUDENTS IN EACH FACULTY PER GROUP OF AGES AT THE ENTRY OF UNIVERSITY EDUCATION. STUDENTS OF THE 1948–50 GENERATIONS, SIX MAJOR FIELDS OF STUDY, BY SEX, EXCLUSIVELY FOR THE STUDENTS WITH A V.H.M.O. LEAVING-CERTIFICATE

| Field of study | Age when v.h.m.o. leaving-certificate was obtained | | | | | |
| | Male students | | | Female students | | |
	18 years and younger	19 years	20 years and older	18 years and younger	19 years	20 years and older
Arts (incl. History)	70	60	60	46	31	29
Medicine (excl. Pharmacy)	80	68	58	61	53	29
Mathematics and Natural science (incl. Pharmacy)	65	56	43	41	27	31
Engineering	66	53	42	n.a.	n.a.	n.a.
Law	76	71	63	69	49	33
Economics	58	48	37	n.a.	n.a.	n.a.

n.a. = These data are not available because of too small absolute numbers.

SOURCE: Central Bureau of Statistics. From: *Statistical Investigations on Education and Leisure*, Volume 1: 'Analysis of Student Performance', page 32, Table 5a.

TABLE XIV

INFLUENCE OF THE LEVEL OF THE LEAVING EXAMINATION MARKS IN COMBINATION WITH THE AGE WHEN LEAVING-CERTIFICATE WAS OBTAINED, ON THE ACHIEVEMENTS FOR THE FINAL EXAMINATION IN ENGINEERING. PERCENTAGES OF THE NUMBER OF STUDENTS IN EACH LEVEL PER GROUP OF AGE AT THE ENTRY OF UNIVERSITY EDUCATION. STUDENTS OF THE 1948 + 1949 GENERATIONS, EXCLUSIVELY FOR THE STUDENTS WITH A HBS-B CERTIFICATE*

Level of leaving examination-marks†	Age when leaving-certificate was obtained		
	18 years and younger	19 years and older	Total
Level 5	77	74	77
Level 4	71	65	69
Level 3	66	53	59
Level 2	56	41	49
Level 1	36	26	31
TOTAL	65	51	57

* Those with a Gymnasium-β certificate formed too small a group to be analysed successfully.

† For Engineering two groups of examination marks were combined to compose five levels: the group mathematics, natural science and chemistry, and the group of modern languages (French, German and English).

For the first group the examination marks were separated like this: levels 5 and 4 = average 8 and more, levels 3 and 2 = 7 or $7\frac{1}{2}$, level 1 = $6\frac{1}{2}$ or less. For the second group: levels 5 and 3 = 7 or more, levels 4 and 2 = 6 and less, level 1 = no distinction for language marks.

The distinction between levels 5 and 4 resp. 3 and 2 therefore is caused only by the difference in marks for modern languages. Level 5 is the best level, Level 1 the lowest.

SOURCE: Central Bureau of Statistics. From: *Statistical Investigations on Education and Leisure*, Volume 1: 'Analysis of student performance', page 33, Table 6.

It goes without saying that – when studying the influence of the certificate-marks on the results of the university study – the choice and evaluation of these marks differs accordingly to the faculty. Thus, for the faculties of mathematics and the physical and technical sciences, the marks gained for mathematics are primarily important, and for the faculty of literature, the languages.

For the inquiry into the results of the study at the university the age at which each student took his school certificate v.h.m.o. as well as the marks he gained have been recorded. The results may be seen from the preceding tables. These tables show us that:

(a) The *younger* the students when taking their school certificate v.h.m.o. (statistically those with less retardation in their preliminary education) the *better* the results of their university study.

(b) The *higher* the relevant marks gained at the school certificate (or the level of performance during the preliminary education) the *better* the results of the university study.

III. Final Conclusions

In the preceding sections we have analysed, step by step, the consecutive phases in the process of selection from the end of the primary school to the final examination in university education. Table XV gives a survey of the results of this continuous selection.

TABLE XV

Decrease in Number of Pupils/Students in each successive Phase of Education, starting with 1000 Pupils in Primary Education, by Sex

Phase of education	Boys/Men	Girls/Women
Grade 6 of primary education	1000	1000
Admission to grade 1 of secondary grammar schools	200	170
Those who passed the final examination at the v.h.m.o.	104	90
First year students at university education	64	39
Those who passed the final examination at university education	38	16

Source: Central Bureau of Statistics. Figures based on percentages of Tables I, IV and VIII of this article, and on percentages calculated from 'Analysis of Student Performance', pages 28 and 35.

This table shows that of 1,000 boys leaving the highest grade of primary school, 38 complete university training; for the girls this is 16. Influenced by several factors – the educational system, social factors as social class, intellectual horizon, financial situation, etc., and finally also the potential intellectual capacities – a very rigorous process of selection is demonstrated in this flowing through the educational system.

It must be stated clearly that the figures just given only have a global character – they are not the results of one empiric longitudinal statistical study, in which the pupils are followed during the whole course of study. The figures are the results of an estimate, based on empirically found coefficients with regard to transitions and study-results in the year 1966. This necessary restriction, however, does not detract from the inference.

Another restriction must – especially in international comparisons – be taken into account. The results are also influenced, as has been said before, by the Dutch educational system. Several types of education, such as the teachers' training for primary schools and schools for higher technicians, social workers, etc., in the Netherlands are not incorporated in university education, but are regarded as semi-university education.

TABLE XVI

SHIFTS IN PERCENTAGES OF SOCIAL MILIEU IN THE VARIOUS STAGES OF EDUCATION

	Higher class	Middle class		Lower class		Total*
		Salaried	Independent	Administrative	Labourers	
Men						
When leaving grade 6 of primary education	7	19	21	9	41	100
When being admitted to grade 1 of the v.h.m.o.	24	31	20	8	16	100
When having obtained the leaving certificate of the v.h.m.o.	29	27	25	6	13	100
When being enrolled for the first time to university education	45	25	21	3	6	100
When having passed the final examination of university education	45	25	21	3	6	100
Women						
When leaving grade 6 of primary education	6	17	22	10	43	100
When being admitted to grade 1 of the v.h.m.o.	20	38	18	9	15	100
When having obtained the leaving certificate of the v.h.m.o.	41	26	21	4	8	100
When being enrolled for the first time to university education	66	17	14	2	2	100
When having passed the final examination of university education	66	17	14	2	2	100

* Including: Social milieu unknown.

SOURCE: See Tables II and IX respectively.

Other countries, e.g. the U.S.A., often have a different system. The structure of our educational system, when compared to other countries, therefore has a tempering influence on the relative size of the numbers of the highest level, i.e. the group of university-trained persons.

We can draw another inference: the shifting in the structure of social origin, based on the occupation of the father.

It is clear that the proportion of the higher social class is steadily growing while, especially, the labourers' class is decreasing. These data must be interpreted with great caution. From what has been said before in this article it is evident that in this process of selection social factors and intelligence play an essential part, but that statistical material now available does not allow an insight into the influence of each of these factors separately. At the moment it is impossible to give a table analogous to Table XVI, showing the shifting in intelligence-structure. Further study is necessary, not only for scientific, but also, equally, for social reasons.

The development of modern society, briefly mentioned in the introduction to this article, implies a great demand for and a great supply of university-trained persons. It is to be hoped that the present trend towards the removal of social barriers will continue, to enable us to make the best use of all our intellectual resources.

20

Argentina

Nuria Cortada de Kohan
Professor of Statistics Applied to Psychology and Sociology, University of Buenos Aires

Tests are not very extensively used in the school system of Argentina. School marks are used as the main information about children and they are obtained with essay-type or oral-type examinations. In our country we have encountered some difficulties in using objective achievement tests. These tests and the possiblity of their gradual introduction into Argentina are the subject of this article. I shall not make reference to other types of tests such as those measuring intelligence, aptitudes, interests and personality which have been discussed elsewhere; suffice it to say that some of them have been standardized and are extensively used by psychologists for guidance purposes and in clinical settings.

Some of us, however, have long been convinced of the need to introduce objective achievement tests. We thought that this procedure would help not only to evaluate more properly the knowledge of the students but would also help teachers to become aware of the fallacies and deficiencies of the methods of essay and oral examinations generally used. It seemed to us that our education system suffered from verbalism and rigid discipline formalities together with a great emphasis on obtaining information mainly from rote memory processes rather than by higher learning behaviour. Usually there is not enough scope for personal criticism and practical application of the theoretical knowledge to the living everyday 'matter of fact' reality. The youngsters who finish secondary school absorb quite a lot of practical information but – and I believe this happens also in other Latin American countries – they are not ready to apply efficiently the knowledge they possess. Sometimes they fail at university or even, without failing, drop out, not because they are incompetent or ignorant but because they do not have the autonomy and creative thinking required at that level. The distance between what the university requires and what the secondary school provides is too great in all fields.

Many people in our country think that our educational system is in need of fundamental revision. (1) This has been one of the reasons for the recently introduced organization of a centre for Educational Research sponsored partly by the government, partly by Unesco.

The problems involved in the change of curricula, together with the guidance of students are numerous, not only at the primary level but also at the secondary level, the universities and higher educational levels. There are problems related to the rapid increase of applicants for secondary and higher education because of the general growth of the population, the spread of general education bringing schooling to segments of population which were formerly, by tradition, deprived and also because of a new awakening among the lower classes, who are discovering that education is the way for fast moving from the lower to higher strata of the society. This increase of student population has not been opposed by administrators at the secondary level, at which entrance examinations are generally very easy or even non-existent, whenever there are enough vacancies. However, the universities are faced with an increasing number of applicants and handicapped by very tight budgets; at the same time they are under pressure to accept as many students as possible. The result of this pressure was that university administrators did not dare to talk about entrance examinations, especially at the public or national universities. However, a tendency can be detected now that shows the need for entrance examinations. Here we face two major problems. First, the process of a fair elimination of the applicants and secondly, perhaps more difficult, the distribution of the acceptable students among the different specialities of the university. There are no comprehensive and reliable manpower studies indicating the need of trained manpower in different disciplines and giving estimates of the future needs in various fields. The knowledge of students applying for entrance to the universities, concerning the nature of education in eac hfield and the types of job possibilities related to those fields is so incomplete and misleading that vocational interest cannot be a sound basis for their placement.

Against this background the traditional type of examinations cannot be very helpful and the development of a useful battery of tests is sometimes very difficult because administration of such programmes is costly, and planning is beyond the reach of most institutions.

In view of all these problems our efforts have been directed towards the very limited aspect of trying to introduce objective testing, or at least, for teacher-made tests. (2) We also have tried to promote a change of attitude in those teachers and professors who hold administrative positions in the system.

The first problem we met was to find personnel who could help in the technical areas. The possibility of translation, adaptation and standardization of tests of achievement is quite limited, because in this field one has to look at the subjects of actual curricula and specific programmes of the country in question. Influenced by the methods that I had the opportunity to learn while following the ETS Workshop for Foreign Scholars in 1962,

I organized in 1963 a local workshop for advanced pupils of the Department of Psychology and the Department of Education of the University of Buenos Aires. There I taught the fundamental statistical and psychometric tools and we started the construction of an achievement battery of tests of the multiple-choice type for the subjects taught in secondary schools. This first group of students organized themselves as an informal team and with great enthusiasm started the construction of different tests according to their own interests and abilities, and also, the opportunity of access to the schools for trying out the items.

Part of my work has been facilitated by my position as Director of the Department of Vocational Guidance of the University – held until recently – and the opportunity of having a rented IBM 805 scoring test machine, calculating machines, and the use of a rotaprint for the printing of experimental materials. The fact that I teach Statistics at the University was a great help, since I had the opportunity of knowing many students of Psychology, Education and Sociology who were interested in learning and applying the techniques of test construction.*

The tests we are trying to construct are directed to the three levels of the educational system: primary school, secondary school and university. We have limited ourselves to the multiple-choice type which permits the use of the standard IBM answer sheet.

Primary level: We are working on the construction of a battery of tests to measure achievement of children when they finish compulsory schooling, that is, around twelve or thirteen years of age. This battery has three tests: Language, Arithmetic and Geometry, and General topics (which involve History, Geography, Natural Sciences, etc.). Each test has 50 items, the time for each being a two-hour period with a short resting time in between. We have worked on these items with teachers who are experienced in primary school curriculum. (3)

Secondary education level: We started constructing a battery for five main fields of knowledge: Spanish Language and Literature, Mathematics, Zoology, Botany, Physics, Chemistry and Anatomy, Geography, History and Civic Instruction, Psychology and Logic. We tried to have the items necessary for four parallel forms with the same specifications. However, it was too ambitious a project and when we tried out the test on a selected random sample we found that the tests were much too difficult. So we started all over again, concentrating on one subject at time, and we are now analysing the items for a test of Spanish Language and Literature. (4)

---

* Among the people who helped me most I shall mention E. Adamosky, C. Cuidet, A. Casullo, S. Frondizi, M. Segre, M. Carro and A. Bertoni. Many of them now have their own projects and are teaching test construction to other new groups. I should like to acknowledge my gratitude to them.

University level: We have designed a project which includes the administration of a verbal and mathematics aptitude test to all entering students to different departments and colleges of the University of Buenos Aires. (5) The first form of the test was tried at the School of Mathematics and Natural Sciences and at the School of Philosophy. While it is a test of aptitude we know how difficult it is to separate completely achievement and aptitude tests. Unfortunately the project has not been carried on by all the schools and is moving very slowly because of budget and administrative problems.

The testing of achievement at the University has been organized in different courses, mainly in statistics where we constructed a test that I have been using for my own pupils as a partial examination or quiz at the middle of the course and at the end of the quarter. I have now tried more than 200 items of which I know the discriminatory level and their difficulty. Since our pupils are quite inexperienced in the multiple-choice type of test we tried to find out if there was a change of attitude related to the subject after the first objective multiple-choice test was taken in the course. The findings show some positive results, although we have only provisional data. (6) Professor Kaufman has also constructed a test in General Psychology with good results as far as the analysis is concerned. (7) Casullo *et al.* (8) (mainly professors from the Department of Architecture) last year constructed a test for entrance courses at the University, which they are analysing.

Some of the difficulties encountered in our projects are related to the scarce financial resources we have. But we also consider very important the sceptical attitude which we found in some people, especially among the secondary schools' administrative staff. Many professors and principals of the schools resent objective testing as a procedure *per se*. The fact that these tests are machine scored seems to be misinterpreted by teachers and pupils alike. That is why we have been spending a lot of our time organizing workshops at the local level. The pupils taking these courses generally have become a very positive help in their own areas. However, we think that in five years we have at least been rewarded to the extent that we have been able to gather a group of enthusiastic students and teachers who have been working with increasing interest.

As a summary I shall emphasize some points which indicate the need for a large-scale testing programme in Argentina:

(1) There is a general awareness of the need for revision of our school system, mainly related to curricula and evaluating techniques.

(2) We are facing a tremendous growth of school population at the secondary and university level.

(3) We are faced not only with the problem of selection of candidates for university level, but also with the need for a planned distribution among the various fields of study.

(4) There is an urgent need for manpower studies giving estimates of the future needs in various fields.

(5) We lack trained personnel in the field of educational measurement.

(6) We need an urgent change of attitude on the part of the school administrators as regards objective testing.

(7) We have paid attention simultaneously to the construction of tests of achievement for the primary, secondary and university level. But we lack sufficient financial support. At the present we are focusing on problems related to personnel training in educational measurement and attitude scales construction.

BIBLIOGRAPHY

1. N. Cortada de Kohan, 'Sobre la necesidad de introducir las pruebas objetivas en la Universidad' (*Actas de las Segundas Jornadas Universitarias de Humanidades.* Mendoza, Argentina, 1964, p. 473.)
2. N. Cortada de Kohan, 'Objective Achievement Testing – Need and Difficulties for their use in Argentina, (*Proceedings of the IXth Congress of the Interamerican Society of Psychology.* Miami, U.S.A., 1964, p. 565.)
3. N. Cortada de Kohan, E. Adamosky, and A. Casullo. 'Una prueba objetiva de rendimiento escolar para la escuela primaria' (*Revista de Sanidad Escolar*, Buenos Aires, Argentine, 1966. Vol. X, 24, p. 37.)
4. N. Cortada de Kohan, and C. F. Cuidet. 'Test de rendimiento para la enseñanza media' (*Trabajos de las 5as. Jornadas Uruguayas de Psicologia de Montevideo*, Uruguay, 1965.)
5. N. Cortada de Kohan, 'Test Verbal y Matematico "Princeton" ' (*Trabajos de las 4as. Jornadas Uruayas de Psicologia*, Montevideo, Uruguay, 1964.)
6. N. Cortada de Kohan, 'Changes of attitude towards Statistics after objective testing'. Read to the *International Workshop on Possibilities and Limitations of Educational Testing*, sponsored by the Pädagogisches Zentrum, held at Berlin, 22 May, 1967.
7. F. Kaufman and V. Prosdocimi, 'Prueba objetiva sobre el temario de Psicologia General,' Buenos Aires, Argentina (unpublished).
8. A. Casullo, *et al.*, 'Prueba objetiva de rendimiento del curso de ingreso de la Facultad de Arquitectura.' Buenos Aires (unpublished).

21

The United Arab Republic

Yusef S. El-Din Kotb
Vice-Rector, Ain Shams University, Cairo

Historical Background

Early in this century, enrolment for higher education in Egypt was no problem for any student who could afford to pay for tuition and fees. In fact, the vacancies in higher education were greater than the actual number of students applying for them. As a result, merely to pass the general secondary school examination was in itself enough to allow the student to enrol in higher education. Most of the masses, however, were deprived of this opportunity for financial reasons.

In the second half of the present century, a marked change took place. The impact of the increasing social demands as well as the growing consciousness of the importance of higher education resulted in marked reduction in tuition and fees to allow greater numbers to enrol for higher education. After the 1952 revolution, a radical step was taken, namely education at all levels became free, and was consequently available to a larger number of the masses. Moreover, financial grants were provided for gifted students to help them continue their higher education. These factors led to a marked increase in secondary and higher education enrolments. The following table shows the increase in the general secondary school and university enrolments from 1925 to 1966:

Year	No. of students in general secondary schools*	No. of students in universities†
1925–26	17,000	3,400
1945–46	75,000	14,000
1965–66	650,000	130,000

* These figures include students whose ages range between 12 and 18 years.
For 1965 the number of students includes those in preparatory school.
† These figures do not include students in higher institutes not affiliated with the university.

Need for Criteria for Admission to Higher Education

(1) As a result of the increasing number of students who wished to apply for higher education, and in view of many limiting factors that impeded

the acceptance of such numbers, it was felt that there was a need for a criterion to select students qualified for enrolment in higher education.

(2) Moreover, statistics show that in spite of the fact that the number of enrolments in higher education trebled between 1951 and 1963, the percentage of the secondary school graduates accepted in higher education has decreased year after year. The percentage in 1951–52 was 69 per cent whereas in 1962–63 it was 49 per cent. These two factors led to a need for setting up a criterion for higher education entrance.

(3) Most of our secondary school graduates show definite interests and preference for certain faculties and colleges such as medicine and engineering; very few show interest in other colleges such as teachers' colleges. This is primarily due not to their actual interests but to other incentives like better payments and promotions in certain professions. This factor raises another problem, namely bitter competition between students for joining certain faculties within a given university.

(4) A certain prestige is attached to the older universities. This factor contributes to the attraction of greater numbers to the older universities rather than to the new ones, which necessitates a certain criterion to ensure appropriate distribution amongst different universities.

(5) Because of greater prestige attached to the universities when compared with higher institutes not affiliated with the university and because better payment and promotion is provided for university graduates when compared with higher institute graduates, there is a marked tendency to enter universities rather than higher institutes. This factor adds to the problem of the criterion needed for appropriate distribution of secondary school graduates between universities on the one hand, and the higher institutes on the other.

The Main Criterion for Higher Education Entrance

The main criterion accepted for higher education entrance is the grade achieved by the student in the General Secondary School Certificate. This has been carried out through a co-ordinating Bureau for Admission established in 1956 to co-ordinate admission to different university colleges and higher institutes. The number of students admitted to each faculty is determined by the Supreme Council of Universities according to state central planning. The same system holds true for higher institutes and training centres as well.

In view of all the above-mentioned considerations, students with the highest grades mainly join the faculties of engineering and medicine, whereas those with the lowest grades join training centres.

Since the final examination of secondary schools is the only criterion used at present for higher education admission, it follows that this examination is of paramount importance in the life of students, parents and school teachers. In fact, it becomes a sort of a life and death problem in the family life.

Despite the fact that this system has contributed to the equalization of educational opportunities, since selection is based on the result of a final examination as an objective measure, it has, nevertheless, very serious limitations.'

The Effect and Influences of the Final Secondary School Examinations

(a) In view of all the above-mentioned considerations it follows that the final examination has become an objective in itself, and therefore the whole process of education has been affected by this view.

(b) This final examination is mainly an achievement test. Therefore, it does not measure in the least any attitudes, ways of thinking, interests, and skills which are actually of equal importance in the educational process. This encourages students to neglect all these aspects, and to exert all their efforts towards memorization.

(c) Private lessons in almost all subject matter are prevalent since each student wishes to have better grades. This phenomenon has very detrimental effects upon students and teachers, and parents as well, and it tends to make the student more dependent on others. In addition it leads to student negligence of school life. Moreover, only those who can afford payment for private lessons can make use of it and this in itself undermines the principle of equality of educational opportunities.

(d) Since the academic and social future of students depends on this final examination, most of them show worry, anxiety and minor neurotic symptoms.

(e) The family social atmosphere manifests increasing tension prior to the final secondary school examination. Parents become as much involved in this vital problem as their own children. Consequently, there is a marked increase in tension, worry and anxiety levels in the family atmosphere in general.

(f) Since some faculties provide better careers (financially and socially) for their graduates, most secondary school graduates prefer these faculties to others. However, only those who get the highest grades are admitted to these faculties. It is noteworthy that some of the able students are tempted to join these faculties because of their higher status and prestige, without taking into consideration their actual capacities and interests. Consequently quite a number of such students fail to continue their higher education, despite their higher grades in the final secondary school examination. Several follow-up studies on secondary school examination show that it is not the best predictor for university success.

(g) Many students who could have contributed most to certain fields such as technology and arts have been deprived of such opportunities because of low grades in the final secondary school examination.

(*h*) Many of those who feel most capable when compared with their peers in certain fields that depend primarily on talent such as music, art, dramatics, feel inferior and may lose their self-confidence when not admitted to higher education because of their low grade level in the examination.

(*i*) Some students who pass the final secondary examination with low grades usually go through the whole process more than once, hoping for better grades. This phenomenon creates many problems such as greater class density, inequality in entering higher education and repetitive failure.

Examinations in Higher Education

After the student is admitted to the university, his life becomes loaded with a constant flow of examinations. When the number of students was limited, students were known personally to their professors. Evaluation was therefore made mainly on the basis of personal contact with their professors, who were almost entirely responsible for grading.

When the number of students increased markedly in recent years and the ratio of students to the teaching staff increased, it became almost impossible to grade students in the same way. Examinations therefore assumed a dominant place in the life of university students in accordance with this change in the density of students in higher education.

Students are graded now on a scale ranging from excellent to very weak. The scale is as follows: Excellent, Very Good, Good, Pass, Weak, Very Weak. The students must get a grade of at least Pass. A general grade of Excellent or Very Good entitles the student, regardless of his socio-economic level, to a grant during the academic year after obtaining such a grade. All university graduates are employed by the government regardless of the general grade they may get in their final examination. This is done in an effort to give every graduate the right to employment and to make use of all the educated human resources in the country. However, a minimum general grade of Good in Bachelor's Degree is generally required for post-graduate admission.

Future Outlook

Three main considerations determine the future outlook concerning the improvement of the examination system.

(1) Appropriate consideration should be given to work and production rather than to the attainment of university certificates. This new outlook would encourage students to apply to different faculties and higher institutes as well as to training centres instead of clustering around certain institutions. In fact, more positive incentives should be created to en-

courage secondary graduates to join the hitherto neglected technical colleges and training centres in order to meet the great need for graduates from such colleges and centres at the present stage of our development. This will result in better distribution between the universities on the one hand and the higher institutes on the other, as well as between the different faculties within a given university.

(2) With this new outlook towards the main objective of higher education, the examination system should be reviewed. It should include important aspects other than memorization of facts and information. This means that there should be tests for differential aptitudes, skills, attitudes, and interest, and should depend on other types of evaluative measures such as participation in community development projects, social work and the like.

(3) A programme of vocational and educational guidance should be initiated based on the study of general ability, differential aptitudes and interests, to help students choose types of education appropriate to their abilities and interests.

These three main considerations should be viewed as a whole since they are inextricably interdependent on each other.

22

Nigeria

Kenneth Mellanby

Director, Monks Wood Experimental Station; Member, Inter-University Council for Higher Education Overseas; First Principal, University College, Ibadan

Even in a 'developed' country, with reasonably uniform educational standards, examinations present many problems, as other articles in this volume clearly show. Even where these problems have been carefully investigated, authorities differ in their assessment of the value of different types of examination and in the nature of their proposals to improve the situation. In those parts of the world with no tradition of examinations and with only the rudiments of an educational system, the situation is even more complicated, particularly when it is bedevilled by politics, as may occur at the end of an imperial era, and before the introduction of self-government and an autonomous educational system.

My experience in 'under-developed' countries, at a period when Higher Education was just being introduced, and when political changes were proceeding with breakneck speed, may be of some interest in showing which problems are universal, and which are peculiar to less advanced communities. I shall confine myself mainly to an account of my experience in Nigeria between 1947 and 1953, when I was concerned in the creation of the University of Ibadan, but I shall also refer to events in other tropical countries with related problems.

In Nigeria I was concerned with an attempt to select the best candidates, in the hope that these were the people who would, in the future, give the best performance at the end of a further course of study. Specifically, I had the problem of selecting 200 university entrants a year, from a country with some 40,000,000 inhabitants, and with (by Western standards) a disproportionately high percentage of young people of the age groups usually considered suitable for university entrance. There were also many older men and women who had previously been denied the chance of applying for admission to a university, but who believed themselves capable of reaching graduate status successfully. With this huge pool of potential candidates, it should have been possible to select a student body of the highest calibre.

All universities which practise selection find it difficult to distinguish between the mediocre candidate who has been well taught in a good school (or, for that matter, skilfully crammed, which may or may not be the same thing) and the boy or girl of greater ability and potential who has been badly taught. In Britain there is a great difference between the best and the worst secondary schools. In Nigeria, the situation was infinitely worse. The best grammar schools were on a par with many in England. The worst had hardly emerged from the Dotheboys Hall pattern. The buildings were ramshackle and unsuitable, the staff was untrained and inexperienced – perhaps one external London graduate who had qualified by correspondence, and one or two teachers with the lowest local certification. Such schools might be run for commercial gain, but others had sponsors with the highest motives and intense religious motivation. Their main advantage was the keenness of their students.

Under these circumstances, it is clear that we should have had an ambitious programme of research into the methods of selection. In the event, we did no such thing. We relied, for our initial screening, on the Cambridge School Certificate results. This was at least an objective test, and one accepted by the Nigerians. Unfortunately it enjoyed, if anything, too much prestige. It was generally believed, and, even when not believed, it was stated with considerable vigour, that anyone who had the appropriate passes-with-credit which exempted them from the pre-1949 'matriculation' standards had an unalienable right to admission to a university in Britain, and so we had no reason to demand any higher qualifications. However, we clearly had to select by some means, for even in Nigeria the number of individuals with reasonably good school certificates far exceeded the number our infant university could admit.

Our first method was to give a second examination in five subjects, similar to the School Certificate but, in theory, at a higher standard. We also interviewed the candidates. This was a continuation of the policy followed for selection for the old Higher College, a government institution of sub-university standards. The results were disappointing. When, four years later, these students sat their final B.A. or B.Sc. examinations, only about a third of their number was successful, though many did in fact qualify later. However, it was clear that we had not managed to select the *élite* which had been our original object.

To those with racist views, these results were a confirmation of their beliefs. It was suggested that, as regards academic learning at least, the Nigerian was clearly 'inferior' to the European. However, further experience suggested that this was not the real explanation, and we had simply not made anything like the best selection from the material available.

As the number of applicants for admission increased, we decided to try to simplify the admission procedure. It was clear that any change would be unlikely to be for the worse! Therefore, we decided to do without the interview, even though many members of staff shared the belief with their opposite numbers in Britain and elsewhere that they could somehow spot the genius by this personal contact. The number of papers was cut to two, and more reliance was put on the Cambridge School Certificate. All this had at least the desirable result of reducing our labours; it also seemed to be more efficient as a selection method, for the subsequent degree results improved considerably.

The only serious attempt to assess the value of the entrance examination was that, for some years, all candidates were also subjected to the Raven Progressive Matrix test. In Britain this has been found to be useful in the initial screening of candidates for commissions in the forces, but to be of little value in university selection, as even the unsuccessful candidates tend to be in the top 10 per cent of total population. Our Ibadan entrants gave a different picture. A substantial proportion obtained high scores, similar to those entering British universities, but nearly half the scores were well below the level expected of grammar school pupils in Britain.

This result was most unexpected. Where so few pupils went to grammar schools, they might have been expected to cream off the brightest individuals from the whole population. If this was indeed the cream of Nigeria's youth, the prospects of university education were bleak. However, the explanation seemed to be that selection at the grammar school level was not selective as we would understand the term. Although few boys and girls obtained a secondary education, there was a great element of luck in their admission. Being in the right place, with the most acceptable religious background, and with a parent or sponsor able to pay the fees were sometimes the most important reasons why an individual went to a particular school. We soon found that masses of more able children were passed over.

As the years went by, the selection, as measured by the results at university degree examinations, improved considerably, so that they soon compared quite favourably with those in British universities. But I do not think that we at the university level were responsible. The change was in the schools, which were admitting more children and training them so much better.

The results of our entrance examinations always showed a considerable range of marks above the 'cut off' point, below which no one was admitted. I compared the final degree marks with those obtained in the entrance examination on several occasions. There was no significant correlation. (Several who obtained quite high marks failed their finals, several who scraped in got high grade passes.) I realize that similar results have been obtained in Britain, where 'state scholars' have often disappointed, but we found the results surprising. It was interesting to note that the matrix figures gave a different result. They were well correlated with subsequent university performance. No individual obtained a good degree who had not a high matrix score, and no one with a matrix score below the level expected for a university entrant in Britain ever obtained a creditable degree. Admittedly some students with good matrix results failed their finals, but the correlation between the matrix scores and degree marks was highly significant. I think therefore that we might have evolved a better selection technique – provided that was a desirable object.

As mentioned above, the political situation may have its repercussions on the examination system. In Nigeria, as in India and other parts of our former Empire, there were times when those responsible for some of the institutions of higher education were identified with the 'colonial oppressors' and it was deemed politically meritorious to try to outwit the examining authorities. Even in Britain security is not always perfect; it was much more difficult to maintain overseas. However, there is a code in these matters. There have been incidents reported, particularly from some Eastern countries, where examination papers have been stolen. These have then been widely circulated, giving everyone an equal chance. There have been reports of student strikes where the authorities, discovering that there has been a leak, have changed the papers so that candidates have complained that they have, unfairly, been made to sit the 'wrong' examination!

At Ibadan, our security was, probably by good luck, reasonably good. There was, however, one instance where papers were stolen. One of our clerks was the culprit. He made the mistake of selling the papers to three candidates for £20 each – a large sum in 1950 in Nigeria. However, it proved a good investment, as the buyers all did brilliantly. Unfortunately they were unmasked, on information laid by others who had not been so dishonest (or who may not have had £20). It was generally agreed that to steal papers for gain in this way was quite wrong.

It is clear that we missed useful opportunities for really fundamental research on the question of examinations. However, the surprising thing is that under such different circumstances, the system used in Britain worked reasonably well, and fitted in to a scheme which brought a valuable university education to so many students. It has enabled many to proceed to other countries for post-graduate studies, and has helped to bring Nigeria and other developing countries into the world-wide system of Higher Education.

23

Brazil

Manuel B. Lourenço Filho
Emeritus Professor of Education, Universidade do Brasil; Founder and Director, Instituto Nacional de Estudos Pedagógicos, Ministério de Educação, Rio de Janeiro

For very many years the aims, objectives and methods used in examinations continued unchanged in Brazil. Even fifty years ago the work of the majority of pupils was examined in exactly the same way as had been the case during the Empire. The Empire came to an end in 1889, and examinations had varied little from those employed in the Jesuit 'colleges' which existed until 1759, the year in which the Portuguese Government expelled the Jesuits from their dominions. It is only comparatively recently that there has been any questioning of traditional forms of examinations and that minor attempts at reform have been made. However, there has been rapid development in the past few years.

The pattern of traditional examinations was as follows. At the end of each scholastic year, pupils were submitted to oral or written examinations or both, the object being to discover the extent of knowledge acquired from the curriculum, whether from oral teaching or from written or printed textbooks. The examination could be on a single subject, or could include questions on a variety of subjects; in every case the questions would be taken at random from the items in the syllabus. In secondary or high schools, examinations were permitted twice a year so that a pupil who failed the first time could take the examination a second time. The examining body was a group of teachers chosen by the government authority, and the results were final with no appeal.[1]

The value of these examinations in themselves was more especially shown at secondary school level. Young people could present themselves for examination whether they had attended a school or not, and could take the examination in single subjects (preparatory examinations), or in a group of subjects corresponding to finals in the humanities (*exame de madureza*).

The fact that this system was used for so long showed a steady and consistent pedagogic philosophy in accordance with the general idea concern-

---

[1] Primitivo Moacir, *A Instrução e o Império* (3 vol.) Editora Nacional, 1938, and *A Instrução e a República* (7 vol.) Ministério de Educação, Rio, 1941 and 1942.

ing the function of education in society and in the training of teachers. Not necessarily peculiar to Brazil, this philosophy expressed an intellectual understanding of the forms and mores of education. It derived in part from the principles of the *Ratio Studiorum*, invigorated and even extended in government schools with ideas from the '*Ilustração*' movement, by which a country's progress was advanced through an enlightened minority or an *élite* of scholars educated in the arts and sciences, although the majority of the population remained ignorant.[2]

This philosophy was also linked with the social life of the country for ecological and economic reasons; population dispersal over wide areas, subsistance agriculture (cattle rearing and farming in greater or smaller plantations, based on a negro slavery which was only abolished in 1888). It was only natural that these schools should be few and they should be selective in order to produce the 'educated' minority conforming to the ideas of the period. Also it was quite understandable that selection should be by way of examinations on textbooks used in the schools.

In each school the pupils were selected for promotion from one grade to another by means of 'entrance examinations', of varying difficulty. Teachers approved of this system because it followed their own training, and their appointment had been made as a result of public examination or competition when applying for positions in government schools. Throughout the whole of the nineteenth century, no reference was made in any pedagogic work to the examination system as a subject which might be questioned, and it is remarkable that during the Empire only one document discussed the matter. This was not written by a professional educationist, but by a politician, Rui Barbosa, and appears to deal with a teaching project presented to Parliament. His criticism of examinations, however, was more indirect than direct inasmuch as it attacked more especially the teaching methods employed in the country, classifying them as 'unintelligent and uncouth' and instruments which 'made the young into imbeciles'. This attack made no impression on Parliament and the matter was never even debated, but it is certain that in the long run it has had great influence on Brazilian pedagogic thought in this century.[3]

Writings condemning traditional examinations and practical suggestions for their substitution only began to appear after 1920. The first intelligence tests and special aptitude tests were carried out by teachers interested in the new psychological methods of education, by doctors dedicated to problems of mental health, and later by technicians preoccupied with problems of the organization of labour – particularly those

---

[2] Roque S. Maciel de Barros, *A Ilustração Brasileira e a ideia da Universidade*, Universidade de São Paulo, 1959.

[3] Rui Barbosa, *Obras Completas*, vol. X, nos. 1, 2, 3, and 4. Rio de Janeiro: Ministério de Educação, 1947.

connected with professional selection. Experiments of this kind were made in São Paulo, Pernambuco, Ceará, Minas Gerais, Bahía and Rio de Janeiro, giving impetus to publications on mental and comprehension tests of the 'multiple choice' and 'lacunae to be made good' types. A course (open to the public) held in 1927 by French specialists in applied psychology influenced the pursuit of these initial studies, enabling them to be placed on a firmer basis.[4]

In 1931 the first governmental service of applied psychology for education and system of objective examinations for apprenticeship were established by the education department of the State of São Paulo. This body did its utmost to develop the idea that the acquisition of knowledge should, amongst other factors, be according to the capacity of the pupil, which should be assessed by the teacher. At the same time there were experiments in educational orientation and adaptation of new methods. More continuous experimentation under objective control in the special field of educational tests was later carried out in the Institute of Education in Rio de Janeiro, the centre for teacher training in the former capital. This experiment lasted from 1933 to 1938, and 150 teachers and over 4,000 students took part.

The results of this research impressed the Federal authorities responsible for the recruitment of civil service personnel and, as a first step, a special commission was organized to study the subject. Later, in August 1938, a special body was set up – the selection division of the Administrative Department for Public Service. In order to prepare the material needed by this division, the Minister of Education created the National Institute of Pedagogic Studies which was also charged with general aspects of school reform.[5]

The work developed by this institute was shown in reforms in various branches of secondary education decreed by the Federal Government between the years 1942–44. Express reference was made to the need for objective study of the pupils and the advantages of creating services for the orientation of education. It should also be noted that at the same time two autonomous bodies were created with the collaboration of sponsoring agencies from industry and commerce: *Serviço Nacional de Aprendizagem Industrial* (National Industrial Apprenticeship Service) and *Serviço Nacional de Aprendizagem Comercial* (National Commercial Apprenticeship Service). These bodies were set up to look after the training of industrial apprentices and technical assistants in commerce, and each established services for applied psychology and centres for the preparation of objec-

[4] Henri Piéron, *Psicología e Psicotécnica* (Summary of a Course), Tip. Siqueira, São Paulo 1927.
[5] Instituto Nacional de Estudos Pedagógicos, *Sete anos de atividades*, Rio de Janeiro Ministério de Educação, 1945.

tive tests, so that the abilities of the apprentices could be more clearly identified, and a more complete understanding of their former heterogeneous education obtained.[6]

The creation of these services, with the practical collaboration of commercial and industrial firms, is illustrative of certain changes in social and commercial life which were taking place throughout the country. World War I caused import difficulties which brought about the opening of many factories, the initial phase of a great industrial movement which followed after World War II. As new opportunities arose for industrial employment, it became necessary to train skilled and semi-skilled workers rapidly. In this way the concept of selection and professional direction found a practical field of application.

In 1947, the Getúlio Vargas Foundation, created three years previously for the purpose of studying the problems of rational organization of labour throughout the country and the development of new methods connected with it, became responsible for establishing an Institute of Selection and Professional Direction (*Instituto de Seleção e Orientação Profissional* – ISOP). Once organized and available to the public, the services of the Institute, for which both foreign and national specialists had been engaged, were warmly acclaimed by those interested in such problems, including educationists. Now, after twenty years of uninterrupted work, the Institute constitutes a centre for study and practical work, outstanding amongst those of a similar nature in Latin America.[7]

Other forces also began to work for such a development, and for a completely new attitude towards examinations. From 1939 onwards faculties of philosophy, science and letters had been established in the country, expressly for the training of teachers for primary and secondary education. In these courses, the subjects of pedagogy and psychology were now studied at university level where previously this had not been the case. Furthermore, the social and economic changes which were tending to modify the closed structure of Brazilian society, in conjunction with the population explosion of the last twenty years (about 3 per cent per year), created a demand for education at all levels, particularly at the secondary and higher levels. Even in 1933 the total number of pupils in secondary schools was less than 100,000 and in higher education the figure did not reach 30,000. Since the end of that decade the numbers have increased very rapidly and today the number of pupils in secondary schools is over two millions; in higher education the number is 200,000. It should

---

[6] M. B. Lourenço Filho, 'A psicologia no Brasil', in *As Ciencias no Brasil*, Vol. 2, Ed. São Paulo: Melhoramentos, 1955.

[7] Fundação Getúlio Vargas, *Vinte anos de atividade*, 1944–1964, Rio, 1966, and also 'Arquivos Brasileiros de Psicotécnica' (19 vols. published 1948 to date).

also be noted that the kinds of teaching at each of these levels have also increased to meet the new demands of the labour market.[8]

With the old system of 'entrance examinations' still continuing, schools have had to face much more difficult tasks with the growing numbers of candidates. Many institutions at secondary and university level have tests employing increasingly improved techniques in these examinations, and have even made use of computers for the more rapid verification of results. Various schools are also using objective tests to determine the yearly promotion of students, and a few, for admission to certain courses, are trying out experimental questionnaires for the assessment of aptitudes and personality development.

In the universities attempts are also being made to transform the actual academic structure, not only to meet demands for the better orientation of students, but also for the greater utilization of the resources of these centres of education, in installations, equipment and teaching staff. It should be remembered in this connexion that Brazilian universities have developed from existing schools, with little modification of methods, i.e. the schools did not establish general, basic courses to precede the studies for graduation. Social needs, together with greater technical requirements previously not envisaged in the traditional examinations, now call for new solutions.

This demand has partly been met by the Getúlio Vargas Foundation (the same body which founded the *Instituto de Orientação e Seleção*) by setting up a vast project, in collaboration with the Ford Foundation, for the development of tests and psychological research in the organization of education. The principal objectives are these: (*a*) to contribute towards the aims and purposes of Brazilian education through the dissemination of information about tests and educational methods in general; (*b*) to institute a centre for the development of tests to encourage the production of research material for the orientation of education and student selection for universities and other educational institutions.

American and Brazilian specialists have been working together on this project for about a year. Their practical work comprises the construction and checking of a battery of tests of 'educational development', with the object of defining the standard of education acquired in school or in other ways, among adolescents with educational levels corresponding to the second cycles of secondary studies. The existing tests for general aptitude at this level are as yet very few. It is not intended to assess the proficiency of students in isolated subjects, but to determine what standard may be expected in more long-term projects in languages, mathematics, physics, biology, and social studies. The comparative study of the correlation of

[8] M. B. Lourenço Filho, 'The explosion of Education in a Latin-American Country Brazil,' *The World Year Book of Education 1965*, London: Evans, 1965.

the results of this battery of tests with results of first-year university studies on the one hand, and with results from secondary schools on the other, and the actual entrance examinations, should serve as a basis for assessing the methods of selection in operation until now.[9]

Thus it can be seen that in the field of school examinations, whether by pressure of social demand or by the adoption of more clearly defined technical standards, many changes have already taken place and others are in train. All are working towards new horizons in the philosophy of Brazilian education, leading to a new understanding of the functions of work in schools, and, with this, to the modification of existing methods of teaching.

It is true that at present all the developments so far are very unevenly distributed throughout the country, reflecting as they do, the varying social and economic conditions, and it should also be stressed that some of the principles governing the examination of pupils' work in secondary schools, which still exist officially, are contrary to trends already freely accepted by a great many educators.

Nevertheless, the new examination methods and the influence of the growing movement of reform in various aspects of educational organization show that, on the whole, progress is indisputable.

---

[9] Instituto de Seleção e Orientação Profissional (Comissão de Estudos de Testes e Pesquisas Psicológicas), *Os testes no diagnóstico escolar*, Rio de Janeiro: Fundação Getúlio Vargas, 1967, and report supplied by Professor Ruth Scheeffer, Co-ordinator of the Commission.

24

India

Snehlata Shukla
Department of Psychological Foundations, National Institute of Education, New Delhi

Committees and Commissions which have, from time to time, reported on the system of education in India, invariably recommended changes in the system of examinations. As, however, these constituted only a fraction of all the recommendations – and possibly for some other reasons too[1] – they failed to make any major impact, even on thinking, let alone any active steps introducing changes. In the early 1950s, however, the problem received more attention from both educationists and administrators. Two factors may be considered responsible for this sudden spurt of thought and action in this area. Criticism, assessment and experimentation with examinations in the English-speaking Western world over the last five decades, had by this time registered some successes and caught the attention of many Indian educationists, some of whom had either studied or travelled abroad. Secondly, the changed political circumstances of Independence since 1947 meant that a greater variety and complexity of responsibilities were to be expected from the citizens of an independent and industrializing nation. It was felt that the examinations which evaluate the citizen's education should, to some extent, provide assessments on these variables and influence instruction in desired directions.

Objective Tests

The critique of examinations can conveniently be analysed into dissatisfaction with its form, content and organizational control.

With a large number of reports (among them Hartog's *Examination of Examinations*) emphasizing poor *reliability* of scoring as well as poor *validity* of essay examinations, the first move to catch momentum in this country, as elsewhere, was a shift to objective-type questions. However, attempts to introduce changes in internal examinations conducted by the institutions themselves met with failure because of the fear of the ultimate (public) examination, which continued to be of the essay type. Internal or house examinations should, it was often felt, be similar to external ones in

---

[1] Notably, *Calcutta University Commission* (1917–1919), University and Secondary Education Commissions, 1949 and 1953.

order to establish their own 'validity' as well as to serve as good preparation for the latter. Attempts to introduce changes in public examinations were, in their turn, sporadic and frequently given up under fire of criticism without adequate trials. One important source of failure was strong resistance to changes which were sometimes seen as ideas from the West not easily acceptable right after independence from colonial status, and, on other occasions as upstart Americanisms not acceptable to British-trained men. There was, too, sheer limitation of the amount and level of skills available. We come finally to the failure to bring about other supportive changes – e.g., the cut-off points for passing or for placing students in I, II, or III division ought to have been changed but were not.

Internal Assessment

Another change that was attempted at this time was the promotion of internal assessment by the schools themselves and adding its contribution to assessments at external examination towards the over-all evaluation of pupil performance. It was felt that because of some inherent restrictions, written essay-type external examinations given by a distant central agency once every few years could assess only some of the outcomes of education. Many others could be assessed over a long range of time by teachers themselves. This idea, giving greater prestige and authority to the teacher as it does, has been welcomed, by and large, by the teacher community. However, the general public, especially employers, have been reluctant to accept it and there has sometimes been resistance on the part of students, who fear that objectivity may be lacking, or that too much additional work would be involved. Their fears are not completely groundless. The pressures of castes, communities and personalities; inter-institutional rivalries; the difficulties encountered by the average teacher in carrying out his job adequately and with professional integrity (either for want of skill or through inability to assume the role of objective evaluator *vis-à-vis* pupils in his own face-to-face group) are only some of the variables which arouse suspicion and opposition towards a basically good idea. The fears become all the more important when one is conscious of the power of the 'grade' in India. Gradings (or divisions obtained) in our centrally controlled public examinations tend to become very powerful determinants of access to a great variety of jobs and to all higher education. Even employers or agencies which conduct their own selection tests, e.g., the Public Service Commissions of the State and Central Governments, the railways and other enterprises, use grades earned in the public examinations for initial screening of the invariably large number of applicants. Their own tests are often patterned on those of secondary- or degree-level public examinations. There are few institutions which would disregard these grades to any extent. Even with all this, internal assessment has made some room for itself. In many places it is recorded side by side with marks obtained in public examinations which, incidentally, are also used by institutions for scaling their assessments. A very limited attempt has been made to help teachers to further their skills in evaluating students' achievements.

Changing the Content of Examinations

The most extensive change that has been attempted in the past decade – since Benjamin Bloom's recommendations[2] on the subject – is in the *content* of examination questions. It would not only render the external examinations (whose strength in the Indian educational situation is given due recognition in this scheme of reform) a more comprehensive evaluation of outcomes of education but would also become a powerful instrument to influence the teaching-learning process in the classroom which is invariably directed to achievement in final examination. An Examination Reform Unit set up by the then All India Council for Secondary Education (now part of Department of Curriculum and Evaluation in the National Council of Educational Research and Training) has, supported by some State Evaluation Units, undertaken extensive activity in this area. This movement is directed towards making examinations more valid in that the questions should not only require information acquired but tap basic understanding and also test for applications to, and interpretations of, new situations. The need to give due weight to both the contents and objectives of the subject has moved examiners to ask a larger number of questions than has been the norm so far. The main trends have been away from ambiguous questions asking mainly for reproduction of memorized material to be produced in large essays, towards specific questions requiring brief answers demonstrating comprehension, analytical ability and practical application of principles. Put crudely, the move is from objective tests to objective-based tests. The new reform movement does not rely on any particular form of the question; instead, it stresses the content of examinations being geared to stated instructional objectives.

The problem is being attacked from three directions. Members of the Boards of Higher Secondary Examinations who have authority at decision-making levels are being persuaded through conferences and discussions to introduce desirable changes. Examiners are being trained in writing better questions and pools of questions are being built up for use by them on request. Teachers and teacher-educators are being made aware of the total programme so as to expect these changes in the final examinations and modify their teaching to suit these needs. The latter are being provided with relevant literature and a limited amount of training

---

[2] See *Evaluation in Indian Secondary Schools* (All India Council for Secondary Education, 1958). Also, for the technical bases there, Bloom's *Taxonomy of Educational Objectives*.

to write good examinations as well as to put evaluation (assessment) to more comprehensive use.

Prospects and Problems

Some of the success or otherwise of this effort is, of course, dependent upon its relation to the sheer scale and magnitude of the task. There are over 900,000 examinees in over twenty Secondary School Examination Boards at the high school leaving level each year, involving a few thousand examiners and over 26 thousand secondary schools in which instruction is being carried on throughout the year in the high school alone. Seventy universities examine over 2,000 affiliated colleges in which over a million students study and prepare for university examinations. It will be appreciated that success must, in these circumstances, necessarily be partial and slow in coming.

Reforms in examinations have mainly been confined to the secondary level. Though there has been occasional talk of introducing reforms at college university and primary school levels, the progress recorded at either of these two levels can be considered negligible. At the higher level, the reasons are that (i) the academic community is more resistant to change; (ii) the fact that the movement originated with educationists does not carry sufficient weight; and (iii) the limited amount of money available is being utilized for more urgent needs, such as raising teachers' salaries so as to attract talent away from the civil service or setting up equipment for science teaching. The committee on the subject set up by the University Grants Commission a few years ago concentrated largely on problems of internal assessments. The Institutes of Technology and Agricultural Universities have introduced the semester system and internal grading on a more substantial scale with some measure of success. In universities proper, innovations of this kind have sometimes run into resistance from students. At the primary stage it has made no impact because (i) the examination at the end of the primary stage is hardly given any importance beyond its use for admission to secondary school; (ii) sheer magnitude of numbers as well as the quality of teachers and pupils involved seem to suggest futility of effort.

There has been some debate about the scheme of priorities as between reforms of examination and reform in methods of instruction. The critics have compared beginning at the examination end with placing the cart before the horse, but the opponents argue that only a change through the most powerful agent can be effective and that with this strategy the methods of instruction will change at a much faster rate than with any other. It is interesting to note that some effort has recently been put into preparing model curricular material to help improve methods of instruction alongside improvement of examination. Predictably, the effort has faced problems of sheer size, the mechanics of transplanting any centrally conceived educational measures into the educational system of states exercising constitutional rights on the subject, and resistance/indifference of the poorly paid and poorly trained teacher who is at the core of the whole educational process. However, if the needed change in instruction does not keep pace with changes in evaluations and grading, unrest among student communities could follow.

25

Japan

Kazuhiko Nakayama
Instructor, Graduate School of Education, International Christian University, Tokyo; Member of Research Staff, Educational Test Research Institute

The modern theory and methodology of tests as a means of educational evaluation were introduced in Japan at the beginning of the twentieth century. Based on the theory of objective standardized tests, several kinds of tests such as intelligence tests, scholastic achievement tests, personality tests and aptitude tests were constructed and used experimentally by educators and institutes or associations for educational research. Such tests had been well developed and had achieved practical usability by the beginning of World War II. However, the war suspended further development of tests and testing institutions.

Since World War II the development of educational tests has continued, but the institutionalization of tests in Japan may be said to be still in the stage of development.

The present state of development of educational tests, their administration and agencies that administer such tests will be summarized in the following account.

Standardized Tests

At present, twenty-seven private agencies publish standardized educational tests. Most of the agencies that publish the tests are profit-making publishing companies. Many of the tests bear the names of famous scholars as editors or constructors of the test. However, the tests are in reality edited by the publishers.

Tests published are: 83 intelligence tests, 59 personality tests, 12 vocational guidance tests, and 483 scholastic achievement tests. Among these, there are questionable ones, the content of which or the validity and reliability of which are doubtful. Though standardized, in some of the tests the selection of the norm groups seems to be inadequate for the test to be called standardized. Consequently, the tests which could dependably be used as standardized tests might number only half of the total number reported above.

The reason why so many standardized tests exist may be that in the original school record form, which is made uniform for elementary, lower and upper secondary schools throughout Japan, there is a column for recording the results of standardized tests. Also, though a pupil is not required to take such tests, the teachers are encouraged to use the results of intelligence tests and other standardized tests for the guidance of pupils. Therefore, these tests are purchased by the school, and administered and scored by the homeroom teachers.

Here it must be noted, as a unique feature in Japan, that such tests, their keys and manuals are sold on the open market, and anyone can buy them. Therefore, if one knows beforehand that he will be given an intelligence test or a personality test in the screening for admission to school or for employment, he can practise taking the same test or a similar one. Even technical guide books for such preparation are published.

Methods of Screening for Educational Institutions

For screening, one of three methods or a combination of them can be used. (1) Applicants may take entrance examinations prepared and given by individual institutions. (2) Applicants may take one examination prepared and administered by one organization. (3) The institutions base their judgement on student's grade records, the number of credit hours earned and kinds of courses taken at the previous institutions. In Japan, screening is done at the times of entering the upper secondary school and the university.

At the screening for admission to the upper secondary school, a combination of the second and third methods is used. The screening is based on the result of achievement tests and the grade report from the lower secondary school. The achievement tests are constructed by each prefectural Board of Education. Third year (ninth grade) pupils in lower secondary schools take a uniform test given in their prefecture. The Board of Education administers the examination. In some prefectures the results of tests are said to be analysed and their reliability and validity studied. However, how many prefectures actually do this is not known at present.

Screening for admission to the universities: all universities, with almost no exception, use the first method. Certain private universities which have their own 'attached' upper secondary school or which are of very low standard, apply the third method. This does not mean that there has not been any attempt to administer a common examination to all the applicants throughout the nation. In order to avoid having able persons fail the screening by applying to an institution with a large number of applicants, the nation tried twice (for six years from 1902 to 1907 and for two years in 1917 and 1918) to screen applicants on a national scale by giving a uniform examination to all applicants throughout Japan and placing them in appropriate institutions according to their performance on the test. However, such nationwide examinations were soon abolished, for the reasons that they were difficult to administer and manage and that they tended to infringe upon the autonomy of individual higher education institutions.

At present, all universities construct their own tests and give an entrance examination once a year. All those wishing to enter a university are required to take such an examination. The screening is done on the basis of applicants' performance in the examination. Usually, test items are constructed by a 'Test Construction Committee' appointed by the president of the university from its faculty members. The names of the committee members are not known to those outside the committee.

After the entrance examination is over, the tests are made public. However, in a very few cases, those tests are analysed and their reliability and validity are tested. As for the content of the tests, there are two steps of checking. First, the university's test construction committee should have checked the content of their tests before they are administered. Second, after the entrance examination, copies of the tests are sent to the Ministry of Education, where they are examined by small committees organized by the Ministry for each subject, as to whether the content of the tests are within the range described in the national Course of Study. The results of the examination by the committees are published in a pamphlet by the Ministry of Education and sent to individual universities. Only extremely poor test items are noted in it. Consequently, it does not have any great effect on the actual test construction. Before the war, all the tests used at screening examinations were of essay type. After World War II, it was decided, on the advice of Civil Information and Education Section (CIE) of the Occupation Army's General Headquarters, to use objective tests in the screening examinations. Since then, objective tests have been used.

However, in the last few years, there has been criticism against tests of the recognition type being included among objective tests. The points of argument are: (1) Since there are correct answers included in the answers to the questions, students could be successful without having correct understanding or knowledge. (2) The test puts undue weight on measuring fragmentary knowledge which is mechanically memorized and fails to measure the ability to recognize relationships between facts, to analyse, to compare, integrate and make judgement, or the ability to think productively and creatively, etc. (3) Such methods of screening set the framework for the pupils' learning habits and motivation for learning. They make efforts to obtain fragmentary knowledge of information, numbers, definitions and the like, but do not try to take a bird's eye view of the contents, to interpret them or to build up their own ideas and opinions. They are not good at doing the latter. (4) As a result, they lack ability to build up their ideas and write a paper. Their ability in composition is low.

(5) Evaluation by teachers becomes mechanical. They make tests with little effort, so that there are those who are not clear as to what they measure. Some teachers use published tests instead of making tests by themselves.

In order to solve such problems many persons have come to believe that so-called 'written-type tests', to which a student writes an answer himself, should be used instead of choosing an answer. The written-type test is a combination of recall-type test, objective-type tests, and essay-type test. Table I shows the types of achievement tests used for upper secondary schools in the last ten years. The study is made on tests in science given in ten prefectures.

TABLE I

TYPES OF SCHOLASTIC ACHIEVEMENT TESTS IN SCIENCE
FOR UPPER SECONDARY SCHOOL ENTRANCE IN 10 PREFECTURES

Test type		Year					
		1957		1966		1967	
		No.	%	No.	%	No.	%
Answer-choice type	True–False	12	4·6				
	Multiple-choice	152	58·0	123	49·6	90	40·8
	Matching	71	27·1	33	17·3	10	4·6
	Ordering	2	0·8	3	1·2	3	1·4
	Sub-total	237	90·5	169	68·1	103	46·8
Written-answer type	Simple recall	7	2·7	22	8·9	33	15·0
	Completion	18	6·9	45	18·1	61	27·8
	Graph or Picture drawing			9	3·6	9	4·1
	Essay			3	1·2	14	6·4
	Sub-total	25	9·6	79	31·8	117	53·3
	Total	262	100·0	248	100·0	220	100·0

The same trend is seen in screening examinations for universities. While until 1966 no essay-type test had been given, in 1967 many universities gave essay-type tests. Moreover, not a few universities gave all examinations of written-answer type. Since this phenomenon of increased use of written-answer type test for screening in 1967 was applauded in mass-communications and welcomed by teachers, it is expected to increase further in 1968.

Educational Test Research Institute

The higher institutions limit the number of students to be admitted each year in spite of the strong desire of the large number aspiring to universities and colleges. Hence, selection for university entrance is a very serious educational and sociological problem in Japan.

In accordance with the recommendation presented by the Central Educational Council, an advisory organ to the Minister of Education, the Educational Test Research Institute (ETRI), on which the author serves as a research staff member, was established in January, 1963, through the co-operation of upper secondary schools, higher educational institutions, boards of education, and the Ministry of Education.

The aims of the Institute are: (1) to study and establish methods of obtaining highly reliable information regarding the scholastic aptitudes and the scholastic achievements of candidates for university entrance; (2) to administer nation-wide objective tests by adopting such methods; (3) to improve the entrance examination system; and (4) to give better guidance for pupils in selecting their future careers. The organization of the Institute is shown below.

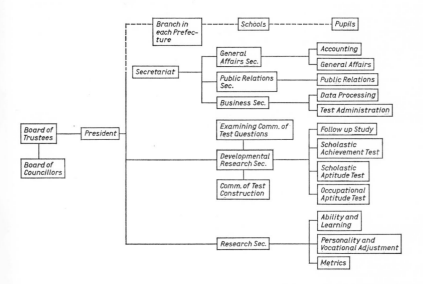

To realize its aims, the Institute constructs the following five kinds of tests: Scholastic Aptitude Test, Scholastic Achievement Test, Occupational Aptitude Test, National Merit Scholarship Test, Entrance Examination Test for National Technical Colleges. The last two tests are constructed at the request of National Merit Scholarship Board and National Technical Colleges' Association and are administered by them.

The numbers of pupils who took the ETRI tests are shown in Table III. On the average, a pupil takes about four subjects in the Scholastic Achievement Test. This means that more than one million answer cards will be

TABLE II

ETRI Tests Administered by ETRI in 1967

Name	Aim	Subject	Administered in:
Scholastic Aptitude Test (for second and third years of upper secondary schools)	To measure scholastic aptitude for universities To contribute to the improvement of screening system of university entrants	Verbal reasoning and Non-verbal reasoning	June
Occupational Aptitude Test (for first and second years)	To measure occupational aptitude To contribute to occupational selection and guidance of jobs	General Aptitude Basic Scholastic Aptitude	June
Scholastic Achievement Test (for second year)	To measure scholastic achievement in subjects learned at school To contribute to selection and guidance of future plans	Japanese Language (modern and classical), Mathematics (Math. I), English, One can select from 3rd year subjects	November
Scholastic Achievement Test (for third year)	To measure scholastic achievement in subjects learned at school To contribute to the improvement of screening system of university entrants To contribute to the selection and guidance of future plans of individual pupils	Japanese Language, Social Studies (5 subjects), Mathematics (3 subjects), Science (4 subjects), Foreign Languages (English, French, German)	November

TABLE III

Number of Pupils who Took ETRI Tests, 1963–1967

	Kinds of test						
	Scholastic aptitude		Scholastic achievement		Occupational aptitude		
Year	2nd school year	3rd school year	2nd school year	3rd school year	1st school year	2nd school year	3rd school year
1963	198,311	124,379	198,311	124,379	—	—	—
1964	232,453	90,424	133,727	92,912	140,100	142,301	—
1965	180,957	76,175	139,101	124,967	126,961	118,880	14,009
1966	180,962	76,493	101,360†	121,282‡	237,494		
1967	20,826	88,321	154,045	53,287	84,711	88,506	7,864

† 3.2 } Average number of subjects taken by a person
‡ 4.1 }

sent back to the ETRI office at once for scoring. For scoring, the ETRI and UNIVAC (Universal Automatic Computers) in Japan have developed a new optical card reader for computers that reads about three hundred and eighty answer cards per minute. All processes for scoring and report making is handled by computers.

As was mentioned in the section on Scholastic Achievement Tests for Screening (p. 225), many criticisms have been raised against objective-type tests. ETRI tests are no exception. For the improvement and analysis of tests, ETRI is currently conducting the following studies:

(1) *Check against Random Guessing*—All ETRI tests are of multiple-choice or matching type, so that the whole process of scoring and analyses can be computerized. The objective test forms being not entirely free from chance scores, each test is carefully designed to minimize the probability of guessing the correct answer by increasing the number of alternatives or combinations of possible responses.

A non-chance range of scores is calculated for each test with the aim that more than 95 per cent of the individual scores will be in the effective range. The checking of chance scores is also explored in relation to item difficulty, intercorrelations and 'response biases' in uncertain decision. Several other factors undesirably involved in objective test forms are being studied.

(2) *Item Analysis*—Dividing the examinees into three groups with respect to their total scores, (the upper and lower 27 per cent and the middle groups), item difficulty, discriminative power and factor structures for each group are determined, by which the items and test constructs are evaluated.

(3) *Structure Analysis*—Whether the response structures properly correspond to the content structures, as intended by test makers, has been examined by the use of factor analysis and other correlational methods. Response patterns are studied by listing the successive pairs of item responses by tracing various groups of individuals who made a correct response to a given item in relation to their responses to other items.

The findings are used to improve test items in the light of the mutual dependency among items suggesting to what extent the solution of a given item relates to the solution of other items.

(4) *Study of Norm Groups*—It has been found that there are positive correlations between the test averages of groups of examinees and the sizes of the groups at various testing places. There are a number of small groups of examinees, most of which have been found to be unstable, drifting in number and level of achievement and generally poor in test averages. This study is concerned with the adjustment of those groups in selecting the most appropriate samples of students and schools for norm development. Several pilot surveys are being made to relate various factors, such as school curricula, proportion of the students entering

colleges and so on, with the group achievement. General criteria for establishing a norm group are being examined. A longitudinal systematic survey of groups of examinees under varying conditions is being planned.

In addition to the above studies, ETRI is conducting research in developing personality tests for normal people and in follow-up study of those who took ETRI tests and enrolled in a university. The subjects of this follow-up study are 12,000 in number and are enrolled in 157 departments of thirty-seven universities. Those who became Seniors in April, 1967 are the group who took the first ETRI tests. Therefore, only interim results have been obtained.

ETRI is an institution similar to the Educational Testing Service (ETS) in the United States. ETRI hopes that their Scholastic Achievement Test will be used as an aid to screen students seeking admission to college just as the College Entrance Examination Board Achievement Test is used in America. The ETRI's tests are highly evaluated as being good tests by university professors, upper secondary school teachers and specialists in testing. However, from the very beginning, the Japan Teachers' Union has vigorously objected to the ETRI test. They tell the pupils not to take the test. Their reasons for opposition are: (1) Though it is a private organization, it was originally established by the advice of the Central Education Council. Therefore, it plays a role in government's manpower policy to serve the 'capitalistic social system'. (2) Imposing a test made by such an organization is equivalent to imposing a uniform government-made curriculum throughout the country. This means state control over education. (3) Since the testing is nation-wide, the form of text necessarily becomes objective, which to them is undesirable for pedagogical reasons. (4) If many universities start using the test, students will begin to prepare for the test in addition to preparing for the entrance examination. Thus, students will have a heavier load to prepare themselves for entrance to college (which is the opposite to what has been claimed by ETRI). (5) As long as so few universities adopt it as one of the information sources for screening, it is not much use for students to take the ETRI test.

Universities hesitate to adopt the ETRI test for the following reasons: (1) For the same reasons [(1) and (2)] given by the Japan Teachers' Union, it is said that the autonomy and authority of the university will be hampered by adopting the ETRI test. (2) It is only a very few years since the testing was started. Therefore, there is no decisive evidence of its effectiveness and predictability. (3) Since it is a nation-wide uniform test, the test necessarily becomes objective. This is against the recent tendency in testing. The result of the ETRI test cannot be trusted as a whole, because the ETRI test is not constructed, nor administered, nor scored by individual universities. (4) Studying the test scores of those admitted to universities, the ranking of the individual universities can be made numerically clear. In 1966, one university and one junior college, and in 1967, eighteen universities and junior colleges made use of the ETRI test scores as one of the data for screening candidates to their universities. In 1968, thirty-seven universities and junior colleges are expected to use the test score. Though the number of institutions making use of the ETRI test is gradually increasing, no famous university is going to use it in 1968. In 1966, one national university and in 1967 one famous private university used the ETRI test for their first screening. After screening applicants by ETRI test scores, they invited twice as many applicants as were to be admitted finally to take the second screening tests which were constructed and administered by the respective universities. In both universities, a small group of students, who advocated the same way of thinking as the Teachers' Union, caused confusion on the campus by such actions as the occupation of the administration building. Consequently, these universities stopped the ETRI test after only using it once. Now it is generally considered that famous universities will not adopt the ETRI test for some time in the future. This is seen in the decrease in the number of high school students taking the ETRI test.

Economic and Social Effects of Examinations

Brian Holmes

Reader in Comparative Education in the University of London

The effects of education on social class structure, economic development and political stability have been studied recently by social scientists using increasingly sophisticated techniques of research. They have concentrated attention on formal education in industrial and developing countries. It is important, however, to realize, as Rosemary Firth points out, that young people have to be initiated into adult society whether that society be a small non-industrial traditional society or a complex modern technological society. The rituals of initiation differ, Western examination systems are ritualized (p. 236) and results can determine the occupation, status and salary of individuals for the rest of their lives.

Considerable attention has recently been given to the economic outcomes of education and L. Emmerij analyses the effects of examinations on the economy while admitting the difficulties of measuring these links, through either the manpower or the rate-of-return approaches (p. 243). Manpower needs do not govern social demand for various types of education. Educational planning should be more concerned than in the past with the factors that govern demand. By implication it is clear that examination success, unless closely related to a realistic economic structure, will not enhance progress. In other words, economic pressures have not yet modified examination systems and until they do the phenomenon of a growing group of unemployed and unemployable graduates will persist.

This analysis is continued in a somewhat similar vein by J. Capelle who sees the French *baccalauréat* as part of a system of higher and more selective examinations which set apart, on a national scale, an *élite* whose members form a kind of 'mutual aid' society (p. 261). The system, he writes, provides the country with academically brilliant leaders while harming others. Does it contribute to political instability, however? Capelle questions whether the professional diplomas really guarantee professional proficiency (p. 263). For a time at least, they do accurately indicate potential: subsequently the diploma holder has to acquire real professional ability.

H. Leibenstein indeed regards certificates, diplomas, degrees and licences as 'skill labels' (p. 267). Many skill-labelling schemes (degree courses, etc.), are economically wasteful and career proficiency in many cases would have been improved if the number of years of education actually spent acquiring the label had been different. Examinations are important determinators of the label, but the label may bear little relation to the tasks which have to be performed. One reason is that examination systems, controlled by educationists, invariably lag behind occupational requirements.

W. R. Niblett analyses and compares in England and the U.S.A. the extent to which the classification of results in degree examinations influences the identification of an intellectual *élite*. He suggests that in the U.S.A. the aim is to train a professional *élite* – functionally useful as technologists, scholars and administrators (p. 277). When it is remembered that only 6 per cent of the small group graduating from English and Welsh universities obtain first class degrees, the extent to which the classification of degrees establishes an *élite* (whose future for the most part is assured) is clear.

The English system was carried to many African countries. S. H. Irvine analyses the relationship in Africa between examinations, wastage and high-level manpower. He points to the high cost, and selection, though valuable, does not effectively reduce wastage.

The desire for academic qualifications persists in Japan, too, in spite of changes since World War II. S. Wada traces this to the *samurai* tradition and their love of learning. 'This insatiable thirst for knowledge and education on a national scale has no doubt produced Japan's amazing industrial and economic developments' (p. 294). Its effects on political stability in the 1930s needs to be examined, since economic progress at the expense of democracy may be a price few nations wish to pay.

In contrast, K. C. Mukherjee suggests that the examination system in India has strangled economic growth (p. 300). In Iran, too, according to Iraj Ayman, examinations have shaped or limited 'the rate of social change and progress' (p. 302). Since the war in Indonesia, writes I. P. Simandjuntak, the educational system has been directed towards ensuring an expansion of educational opportunity 'solely according to ability' (p. 318).

Examinations in most countries tend, in short, to be the agencies of selection of an intellectual *élite*, members of which may be included in the political, social and economic *élite* groups, but the extent to which they test knowledge, aptitudes, and attitudes appropriate to the performance of leadership functions in the modern world, is obviously in doubt. The need for reform in broad social terms is apparent from these articles.

26

Examination and Ritual Initiation

Rosemary Firth
Lecturer in Education, University of London Institute of Education

It is difficult for us in the twentieth century to see education except as a formal activity which goes on in special places, like a school, college or university; or examination as other than a written test of ability, actual or potential. But if we want to explore the theme of examinations comparatively, and to see its relationship with the educational system of more than one country, we must adopt a wider view of education. We need to look beyond the philosopher's view that 'education can have no ends beyond itself', and try to see it in relation to social ends which may differ from society to society. To the social anthropologist, education is one of the ways in which a society maintains its cultural identity. Technical skills and accumulated knowledge must be handed on, but an attempt must also be made to impose the patterns of behaviour and the values of the past on each succeeding generation, as well as to train them for the future.

A Comparative View of Examinations

Not only societies untouched by Western influence, but European society itself in past centuries had very different ways of doing this. The education of a gentleman in the seventeenth century was partly attained by attachment to the sovereign's court, and in the eighteenth and early nineteenth centuries by travel abroad with a tutor. The learning of certain skilled trades was by apprenticeship in the family of a master of that trade, and skills of agricultural production, hunting and fishing may still be learnt in simple societies by imitation, play and practice, in addition to formal instruction.

Granted that we should expect very different methods of teaching the skills required in a small non-industrial, traditional society; by what methods should we expect them to recognize the difference between the acknowledged and experienced specialist, and the novice under training? For this is at bottom what an examination does for any educational system: it divides those who may practise from those who may not, those privileged to exercise a skill from the mass of unprivileged, the initiated, as we say, from the uninitiated.

Into what then is it that a person is initiated? What does initiation do for those who organize it, those who watch it, and those who undergo it? To what extent are initiation rites mainly formal or mainly symbolic? These are matters with which anthropologists have always been much concerned; for they have implications for every society, and reflect currently held ideas about the nature of social relations, in particular the integration of the individual with the group.

In studying initiation rites and socialization in other societies, we may perhaps see examinations in Western society in a different light, as performing latent or hidden social purposes from their manifest, or publicly admitted ones. This may clarify some aspects of the actual as opposed to the stated nature of the examination system. For the anthropologist is interested in finding out the difference between what people say happens and what can be observed to happen. It is in analysing the discrepancies between these that he gets his most fruitful insights into the workings of the society he is looking at.

Education as Role Learning

The basic task of the educational system in any society is training in institutionally acceptable forms of behaviour. Not only has the child to learn how to speak, act and think in the traditions of his society, he also has to learn how to *feel* in that society. He has to discover who he is in relation to the people surrounding him, and how he must behave to them. Not only has he to acquire some skills, he has also to appreciate which skills he may appropriately acquire. In some societies men and women both learn to weave, but each weaves a different kind and width of cloth. In all societies some tasks are preferred, some essential and some forbidden to each sex; and similarly there are behaviours appropriate to different age groups, and between different kin groups.

It is here that Ralph Linton's concept of role and status, first developed in 1936, is useful in understanding how we learn to behave in society. Since status develops in groups, and roles are exercised in relationships, it is possible to look at them as parts played by an actor in a certain social setting. The setting defines the part to be played, and limits the way it is played. The role we play, if not actually given, has always to be recognized by society.

It is here that the classical study of van Gennep on what he called 'rites of passage', has illuminated our thinking about the way critical stages of life are socially defined. He showed that birth, puberty, marriage, parenthood and finally death in all societies, classical and Christian, as well as primitive, have been marked by ritual or – as some prefer to call it – ceremony. The ritual calls attention, in a striking manner, to changes in social status and to acceptance of new social roles.

Put into a modern idiom, Meyer Fortes has shown that a person does not just step into a role, or acquire a status as he might a garment, but that they are conferred upon him by society. The ceremony of conferring this new garment upon a person is only performed at the stage when it is supposed that he will be able, or has learnt, to wear it with decorum. The graduation ceremony will illustrate this analogy. It is a rite which endorses what has gone before, the final sign that the candidate has left the general company and has shown by study and by examination that he is fit to be incorporated in the select group of academics. The act of the chancellor in draping the hood over him seals the pact between the admitting university and the young student in public view.

Ritual and Role Changing

It was an essential part of van Gennep's theory that rites of passage eased a transition from one to another social role, and that they did so by a threefold action: separation rites to remove an individual from his old group, transition rites while he is on the threshold, and finally incorporation rites as he acquires new status.

Thus both mother and new-born child must often be separated from ordinary household contacts and kept hidden until special purification rites, by washing, fire or other ceremonial, enable both to be safely brought back into contact with family and neighbours. The Christian service of the churching of women as well as infant baptism are relics of such rites in our own society.

The bride who goes veiled to church and who must be carried over the threshold of her husband's house after a honeymoon period of seclusion, as well as various funeral and mourning sequences for widows practised until quite recently in this country, are other modern examples of public rites still used to help in the adjustment of new social and emotional relationships.

Birth, marriage and mortuary ceremonies usually test and testify to the candidate's ability in role play. In many marriage ceremonies, some attempt is made to determine that the bride is fit for the marriage, by the calling of banns, by ritual demonstrations of virginity, and in other ways. Delay between birth and rites for the new-born give time for the child to show its likelihood of survival. Wakes allow for public scrutiny of the dead, and in mourning both the widowed and other bereaved have opportunity in which to come to terms with their new situation.

But it is undoubtedly in the rites of initiation into adulthood, or puberty rites, that we find the most interesting conjunction of mechanisms which both test, and attest to, a new social situation.

Operations of male circumcision as part of religious ceremonies to indicate manhood are widespread in Africa and elsewhere; painful cutting of other parts of the body, as in tattooing, knocking out of certain teeth, of piercing the earlobe or nostril, have been performed in Australia, Oceania and many other parts of the world. These acts form part of a whole series of rites to mark change in status; and what they really do is to admit a new group of young persons into responsible adulthood. The rites affirm that after certain things have been suffered by the young, the older members will admit them to social equality.

Circumcision rites stress adult sexuality. The ability to bear without flinching the pain of decorations incised into the skin of an initiate show that he can stand upon his own feet and manfully shoulder adult burdens. In many Australian tribes, traditional ceremonies last through several years of adolescence. The novice, well supported by male kin, was subject to anxiety-producing treatment such as seclusion in a dark hut, privation of food and rest, while he was taught the secrets of the social group. Separation from his mother, who wept for him, was often violent. The intention of all that was done was to make a momentous change in his life. He is to be cut off from the past by a gulf he can never recross, and henceforth be a man, instructed in the sensible duties which devolve upon him as a member of his community.

Each such cycle of activity has one broad aim. It makes public that a change of status has occurred. It says something of importance to the rest of society about the youths, and it makes both the young and their elders feel differently about each other. It is in the power of ritual to make people *feel* differently after its performance, that it eases the transition of status. In societies where there is no written word, the public nature of the performance sets a seal of capacity upon him, which serves as his graduation diploma.

Rituals of Examination

I have argued that in marking the transitional stages in an individual's life, these personal rituals are part of his social education, and that in addition they give important information to the rest of society.

But I have yet to show that written examinations as we know them can usefully be regarded as such rites. Indeed we in the West declare most firmly that they are not symbolic, but a genuinely functional method which will enable us to distinguish the able, skilled and intelligent in action and thought. It will be readily agreed that any given act may serve more than one purpose. It can, in Edmund Leach's phrase, *do* something as well as *say* something, as the clothing we wear may keep us warm and announce our occupation or sex at the same time. But what is said, and what is done, may be differently interpreted by actor or onlooker.

The way in which Western examinations are held are quite ritualized. They take place in a special hall, with special paper to write on, and sometimes special dress is required. There is a set time, elaborate preparation of the candidate, formal overseers and an atmosphere of gravity, impersonality and secrecy. Like the Australian initiate, the candidate is kept in the dark as to the precise tests he has to undergo. He may feel that he has not only to show knowledge, but to display it in set ways expected by the examiners and indicated by the form of the questions. After the ordeal, there is a period in which he is in limbo, neither graduate nor student. The results are published with a certain amount of ceremony, and may even be handed to him in a decorated folio sometimes inscribed in the 'secret' language of the classics.

The result of the examination can determine his future place of training, his job, salary, status and social esteem for the rest of his life. This is what it can do for him. But what does it *say* to him, and to his examiners? It says that he is able to conduct himself with dignity and quietness under stress; to keep the rules of the intellectual discipline in which he was trained, to rely upon certain acceptable methods of procedure, as logical reasoning, or citation of authority, or avoidance of *ad hominem* arguments; to understand the value of inquiry, or of experiment, or of technical skill, rather than of eccentric originality, or personal iteration, or 'magic' formulae; or whatever it is that the examiners appear to require and respect.

But if he is successful, his subsequent performance may be as much influenced by his feelings of success and approbation as by any actual skill he demonstrated during testing.

A good illustration of what a rite is said to do, compared with what it can be observed to do, is to be found in a fascinating description by Audrey Richards of an initiation rite for young girls in central Africa.

A Girl's Puberty Ritual

A matrilineal society, the Bemba, have ceremonie. for the initiation of young girls, with a cycle of rites of mounting importance and tension which last several weeks, and are witnessed by a crowd of women and older girls. Usually a wedding follows closely after. The rituals are regarded as a teaching device for the girls, they proclaim the legal obligations of men and women to each other, and help to enforce the duties entailed in marriage. But perhaps more important than all else is their function of giving confidence to individuals and groups in carrying out their social duties.

A bowdlerized account given to Dr. Richards by local women before she had witnessed the event went somewhat as follows: 'Oh, they take the girl into the bush. Then she has to jump over a hoop of branches. Then she is carried back to the village by her father's sister. The women make a lot of beer for their daughters. Then they pretend the bridegroom comes and shoots at a mark in the wall. The women clap and cheer. The girl is given sacred pottery figures. She is rubbed with oil, and presents are given to the elders.'

In fact the ceremonies were of extreme intricacy and emotional tension, involving symbolic aspects of the whole culture. So bald a description came no nearer reality than would an account of an honours history examination as writing on a piece of paper a few dates, with the events related to them.

There were interesting differences in the accounts given by various groups of people when asked directly about the meaning of the rites; just as I imagine rather different versions of the nature and purpose of examinations would come from parents, school teachers, employers, university staff and the pupils themselves.

The men said, of course the rite was necessary; without it no man would marry a girl; she would be just a 'piece of rubbish', an 'uncultivated weed' or an 'unfired pot'. The women were more specific. The rites 'make the girl grow', they make her 'a woman as we are'. The girl herself, although in an emotional state during which she is highly suggestible to the general emphasis on marriage and child-birth, may have very little idea of what is actually done. Her attitude was, it must all be gone through 'because it is the custom'. Only later, the more inquiring asked for clarification.

Although rites representing various domestic and womanly duties were part of the ceremony, teaching, in our sense, was markedly absent. The girls were sometimes directly forbidden to look on; their heads were often wrapped in blankets, and no attempt at explanations was offered. Besides, as Dr. Richards points out, the girls already know how to cook, garden and care for children, and have some sexual experience.

But while witnessing all that went on, and directly noting the reactions of participants, Dr. Richards concluded that the rite was a real test in the eyes of the performers. Mothers showed great anxiety lest their daughters fail to do correctly all that was demanded of them, and the girls were often reduced to tears of anxiety and confusion.

But in the end, whatever doubts and fears she originally felt, the girl knows she has jumped the branches successfully, caught the insects in her mouth and killed the chickens, as she was required to do.

At the end of the rite, the initiates appeared one morning and knelt outside Dr. Richards' tent. They were washed, their hair cropped, and wore shining new white cloths around them. Although meek and submissive, they were alive and responsive again. 'When I remembered the dirty, frightened and exhausted creatures who had been badgered and pushed through the ritual weeks, and compared them with these demure and shy young brides, I began to understand the meaning of a rite of transition.' The modern Western teenager has no such tangible proof to show that she is a grown-up, and may behave like one. Is there anything in our educational system to link up with these notions?

Rites which Accept and Rites which Reject

I have tried to show some similarities between public examinations in the West and initiation ceremonies in primitive society. The things taught and tested in primitive society are, of course, more general and less specific than those of our examination system. But there is a more profound difference between them which I must now stress. Western examinations serve to exclude as well as to include. For whatever the theory, it is not easy to fail young people at initiation. Society cannot stop them from growing up, unless, of course, the ordeal is so severe that death results, and this may have occasionally happened in the past.

If we understand the difference between rituals of examination as accepting some and rejecting others, while rituals of initiation normally pass all candidates through, perhaps we can appreciate why such frantic efforts are made in countries unaccustomed to Western educational methods to distort the system so that everyone must pass. We can also see something of the social value of a degree or diploma in the marriage market of India, or the scramble for clerical jobs in Africa and elsewhere. In such situations, the examination is seen basically in its symbolic and not in its technical terms.

There are other things which we might understand by pondering the resemblances and differences. Initiation rites are normally non-competitive. Is the trend towards increasing use of non-competitive examination for school leavers in line with the more diffuse practice of other societies? Is the value placed on continuous assessment part of the same trend? Our system is becoming increasingly anxiety-ridden. Primitive rites also arouse anxiety but they have built-in procedures for allaying it. Does this help us to understand the conflicts in student-staff relationships in a system which fails to make clear to the candidate how far, and in what respect, his tutors fill the supporting role which is always provided for the novice in initiation?

Examination and Transformation

I began this paper by describing education as the business of integrating the individual into his society, and as a process by which continuity is maintained between the generations. Margaret Mead has shown that one of the most striking features of modern education is the need 'to create discontinuities', to turn the child of the peasant into a clerk, the farmer into a lawyer, the illiterate into a literate.

Initiation rites concern themselves with the discontinuities of life. It is therefore perhaps no accident that the economic and social needs of our modern educational system demand rites to clarify these discontinuities.

The conventional view of examinations is that they facilitate movement between educational levels, and that they do this by roughly assessing the suitability of the candidate by testing ability and received knowledge. This is a technical view.

My view is that in a society which tends to break education into a number of discontinuous processes, to detach people from their background and to train *élites* at various levels, examinations can also be seen as rites which serve to validate the process of exclusion, as well as to demonstrate the grounds of inclusion, for those permitted to be initiated. From a sociological viewpoint, however faithfully or unfaithfully they reflect knowledge or ability, they also serve as a charter for the broad patterns of our manpower selection.

I think it is no accident that the higher we go on the educational ladder, the more an examination approximates to a rite of inclusion; the lower we go, to a technique of exclusion. Few candidates who finally present for it, are permitted to fail for a higher doctoral examination.

To conclude, our examinations have many of the traits of initiation rites. No one who has congratulated an apprehensive new graduate can fail to see that for many, the passing of this test was indeed a rite of transition, which has transformed him.

It is only as he proceeds up the academic ladder, that the student begins to discount examinations; unlike the initiation tests of primitive society ours seem to form an almost endless series, of which the candidate at the lower levels is hardly aware. To many, university examination is still that gate by which he first enters the sacred groves of learning.

BIBLIOGRAPHY

M. R. Allen, *Male Cults and Secret Initiations in Melanesia* (Melbourne University Press, 1967).

Arnald Van Gennep, *Rites de Passages* (Paris: 1909; London: Routledge & Kegan Paul, 1960).

Max Gluckman (Ed.), *Essays on the Ritual of Social Relations* (Manchester University Press, 1962).

W. D. Hambley, *Origins of Education among Primitive Peoples* (London: Macmillan, 1926).

Ralph Linton, *The Study of Man* (New York: Appleton Century, 1936).

E. R. Leach, 'Ritual' in *International Encyclopaedia of the Social Sciences* (New York: Macmillan, 1968).

Margaret Mead, 'Educational Emphases in Perspective' in *Anthropology a Human Science* (Princeton: D. Van Nostrand, 1964).

R. S. Peters, *Education as Initiation* (London: Evans, 1964).

A. I. Richards, *Chisungu, a Girl's Initiation Ceremony* (London: Faber & Faber, 1956).

27

Effects of Examinations on the Economy

Louis J. Emmerij
Educational Investment and Development Division, OECD, Paris

This chapter is about the relation between the expansion of examinations and tests on the one hand and the economic and technological development of our society on the other. The renaissance of the economics of education is now about ten years behind us. At the end of the 1960s, looking back over the past decade, many controversies which have shaken the specialists as well as the not-so-specialists, do not appear to be of such a dichotomic nature as some suggested them to be. There have been those who wanted at any price to distinguish between the so-called quantitative aspects and the so-called qualitative aspects, and there have been those who insisted on defining what I would like to call 'exclusive' approaches to the quantification of the effects on the economy of educational expansion patterns. The first distinction is based on an exaggeration of the difference between quantitative and qualitative aspects because so many quantitative factors have qualitative implications and also because more and more factors can be quantified which were before considered as purely qualitative and not liable to rigorous measurement.[1] The second distinction – that between 'exclusive' approaches to quantifying the economic objectives of education – has been and, to a certain extent, still is more disturbing because of the very definite viewpoints adopted by a certain number of economists on this issue. I am, of course, referring to the so-called manpower approach versus the rate-of-return approach to measuring the educational implications of economic development prospects. This controversy was still very much apparent in the 1967 issue of the *World Year Book of Education* which dealt with Educational Planning, and more particularly in the Editors' introductions to the various parts of the book.[2] Because, after all, the possibility of measuring the relationship between the economy and the educational system is of primordial importance to the subject under consideration in

---

[1] In all fairness it must be said that this controversy is to no small extent due to the extreme quantitative approach adopted in many educational planning documents of the early 1960s.

[2] *World Year Book of Education* 1967, *Educational Planning*, see for example p. 86, pp. 135–138, pp. 240–241.

this chapter, I will devote the first section to that problem. In a second section the expansion pattern of graduates and school-leavers is examined as well as the question whether this is in line with the needs of the economy. In a final section I will go into the problem of factors that might explain any discrepancies between the economic needs and the supply pattern of graduates as it results from the educational system.

I. PROBLEMS IN MEASURING THE LINK BETWEEN EDUCATION AND THE ECONOMY

It would be superfluous to explain once more in detail the methods used in the manpower approach and those adopted in the rate-of-return approach. For this we can refer to the 1967 *World Year Book of Education* and to the specialized literature in this area.[3] It is, however, essential to examine the critique addressed to each of these approaches. The main criticisms addressed to the manpower approach centre around the absence of cost–benefit analysis and, consequently, of a way of choosing among alternatives, and around the fact that the results of projections based upon this approach are liable to large margins of errors. The rate-of-return approach is objected to as being a marginal concept applied to average values. It is also argued that it would be mistaken, in many societies, to assume that factor prices are equal to productivity or opportunity costs, and that the use of cross-section material concerning earnings, age and qualifications to predict future earnings ignores the dynamics of sectoral and occupational structure.[4]

Certain critics tend to mix technical and conceptual arguments. Surely the fact that the results of the projections are so uncertain is a technical matter which could be improved to a certain extent when more and better data and additional insight into the underlying causal relationships become available. But this should not enter into the discussions on conceptual issues and vice versa. At the first level of conceptualization, the question is whether education has an economic contribution to make; in other words, whether education is one of the factor inputs of production. If the answer is no, then all approaches to measure this contribution have to be rejected as irrelevant. There is practically nobody left under the sun who holds this extreme position. At a second level one comes down

---

[3] For the manpower approach, see H. S. Parnes, *Forecasting Educational Needs for Economic and Social Development*, OECD, 1962. For an evaluation of this approach, see R. Hollister, *A Technical Evaluation of the First Phase of the Mediterranean Regional Project*, OECD, 1966. For a relatively sophisticated integration of this approach into an educational prospective plan, see *Education, Human Resources and Development in Argentina*, OECD, 1967. The rate-of-return approach is clearly set out in Mark Blaug's 'The Rate of Return on Investment in Education in Great Britain', *The Manchester School*, Sept. 1965. For a critical view, see Stephen Merrett, 'The Rate of Return to Education: a Critique', *Oxford Economic Papers*, Nov. 1966.

[4] See Stephen Merrett, op. cit.

to conceptual differences between the two above-mentioned approaches. The manpower approach is indeed situated in a Leontief universe where a network of technological relationships and coefficients is spread and where prices do not enter. On the other hand, the rate-of-return approach puts all its eggs in the wage basket and ultimately will say that each person or group of persons will earn the salary it deserves. . . . The conceptual framework of this approach holds more or less true according to the country under consideration. It would obviously be foolish to adopt such an approach in a country like the U.A.R. where, since 1961, the government has bound itself by law to employ any university graduate from whatever faculty or with whatever specialization, within one year from graduation, at a fixed and relatively high salary. This may be an extreme situation but it is a well-known fact that the salary structure in many (and particularly in developing) countries does not necessarily reflect the countries' actual hierarchy of skill needs. Some advocates of the rate-of-return approach would then suggest the use of shadow prices, as is often adopted in economic planning, when one has the impression that certain prices are distorted through imperfections in the market mechanism. But in the present case, how else can one determine the shadow prices for salaries of the various skill and/or educational categories other than by finding out their relative priority in terms of economic development needs? Thus we are back at the manpower approach. Let us, however, suppose that we have detected a country in which all the conditions are fulfilled for the rate-of-return approach to be perfectly valid. In that case it remains nevertheless true that, because one examines *present* salary differentials, one can only expect short-term signals from which no long-term conclusions can be drawn. This is obviously a serious drawback in the field of educational policy and planning, since it simply is not feasible to change directions every year unless one is in the presence of a perfectly flexible educational system.

After these remarks on the rate-of-return approach, one should add immediately that the results of a manpower-approach projection, based upon technological relationships, hang indeed in thin economic air, not only because of the absence of an optimalization procedure but also because in most cases very little evidence is presented in these studies as to the problems of the 'transition period', i.e. of how to get from the present occupational and educational structure of the labour force to the required one. The only indication presented in these studies, in the most favourable of cases, refers to the expansion of the various levels and branches of education necessary to reach the occupational and educational targets. However, very little or no attention is being given to the functioning of the labour market in general and to the salary and wage structure in particular. This is obviously an absurd position because it could and will degenerate into a situation in which the manpower-educational planner would forecast time and time again, say, more technical school graduates, whilst the bulk of the youngsters keep preferring to opt for the general secondary schools in order to enter white-collar occupations. Why? Because the incentives schemes, the salary structure, the social status attached to certain jobs push them in that direction. We are faced here with exactly the opposite kind of difficulty to the one noted above with regard to the rate-of-return approach.

The above remarks clearly point to the desirability of combining both approaches by adopting their soundest aspects. This would mean projecting the occupational and educational structures of the labour force through the manpower approach, but having this accompanied by a thorough study of the actual functioning of the labour market mechanisms with specific attention to wage and salary differentials. Such an analysis would allow an indication of what needs to be changed in terms of incentives and relative wages and salaries in order that the 'technological' manpower projections can get their feet on economic ground.

A final note on these conceptual issues: attacking the manpower approach merely on the grounds that it is a Leontief concept is equivalent to attacking a major piece of economic innovation which has rightly been considered as one of the basic findings in applied economics of this century.

All the rest is technical feasibility. Now nobody would deny that major difficulties have been and will be encountered in quantifying the economic objectives of education and, conversely, in assessing the economic contribution of educational supply patterns. But on this technical level as well, progress is gradually being made. In a recent OECD publication[5] the possibilities and limitations of using international comparisons on the macro-economic and on the sector level is examined in view of projecting the occupational and educational structures of the labour force in a given country. This was done by quantifying the relationship between the occupational and educational coefficients on the one hand with a certain number of explanatory variables on the other. These variables represent indicators reflecting levels of economic and technological development reached by the countries or economic sectors under consideration. The relationships were quantified by using regression analysis. This study clearly shows all the technical difficulties inherent in the manpower approach, but it nevertheless indicates for which occupations and in which sectors forecasts can be made with a fair amount of accuracy.

At the same time research is going on with regard to testing the above type of relationships on the micro-economic, i.e. on the establishment

---

[5] *Occupations, Education and the Economy – Possibilities and Limitations of an International Comparison Approach*, OECD, 1969.

level.[6] In the United Kingdom a pioneering study has been undertaken in eighty establishments of the electrical engineering industry which has also thrown light on the question of the link between occupations, education as well as career patterns and salaries on the one hand and the economic performance of the establishments on the other.[7]

Gradually, therefore, and as more and better data become available, new insights are being won which makes the quantification between the economy and the educational system something less than a completely hopeless task.

II. EXPANSION PATTERN OF EXAMINATIONS IN RELATION TO ECONOMIC AND TECHNOLOGICAL CHANGE

The above rather abstract discussion was considered necessary because, without a reasonable amount of certainty as to the feasibility of measuring the link between economic and educational development, not much meaning could be attached to the presentation that follows.

It has become a truism to observe that enrolments have increased at a very rapid speed during the last fifteen to twenty years or so. Together with this upward trend in enrolments, we have witnessed important increases in the numbers of graduates and school-leavers, although not necessarily of the same order of magnitude because of changes in the retention rates and variations in the effective duration of studies, as well as because of the time-lag between entry and graduation.

Table I indicates for a certain number of OECD countries the evolution of enrolments and of first degrees delivered at the university level (i.e. excluding post-secondary non-university education). The data are presented in index form, taking 1952 equal to 100. This information quite clearly shows the acceleration of the expansion that has taken place in the second half of the period under review.[8]

Some reasons for this expansion are: (i) the postwar upward change in birth-rates in most countries; (ii) a change in the taste of education viewed as a consumer good resulting in an increase in the so-called social demand for the higher levels of education, and (iii) the growing needs of the economy for better and more educated personnel. It must be stressed, however, that the first factor (the demographic one) has only played a minor role in the observed changes in enrolments. This could be, and has been, shown by taking for example the pre-war enrolment *rates*

---

[6] The OECD has set up a special project in this respect.

[7] This is the Industrial Manpower Project of the Unit for Economic and Statistical Studies on Higher Education at the London School of Economics, University of London.

[8] The apparent stagnation of the Yugoslav enrolments between 1961 and 1965 is due to a switch from university to post-secondary non-university enrolments (Vise Skole). These latter schools doubled their student number during these five years: from 31·6 thousand in 1961 to 63 thousand in 1965.

TABLE I

EVOLUTION OF UNIVERSITY ENROLMENTS AND OF FIRST UNIVERSITY DEGREES IN SOME OECD COUNTRIES: 1952–1965

(1952 = 100)

	U.S.A.		FRANCE		ITALY		SWEDEN		YUGOSLAVIA		TURKEY	
	Enrolm.	*Degrees*	*Enrolm.*	*Degrees*	*Enrolm.*	*Degrees*	*Enrolm.*	*Degrees*	*Enrolm.*	*Degrees*	*Enrolm.*	*Degrees*
1952	100	100	100	100	100	100	100	100	100	100	100	100
1956	127	93	110	141	93	111	128	122	127	118	148	100
1961	171	121	146	200	118	108	204	178	223	209	222	160
1964 (5)	236	162	242	228	158	130	355	248	220	238	250	216

SOURCE: Provisional data elaborated from the *Quantitative Analytical Survey of Current Expansion of Higher Education in OECD Countries*. The final version of this Survey will be published by the OECD in 1969.

and applying these to present-day age-groups, and by comparing the enrolment figures thus obtained with actually observed student numbers. The differences which such a comparison shows are due to the factors mentioned under (ii) and (iii) which in turn have been stimulated by policy measures in the field of education, such as the extension of compulsory schooling, the trend towards comprehensive schools at the secondary level, school location, fellowship policy, etc. This 'enrolment explosion' is not confined to the OECD member countries but is practically universal.

TABLE II

EVOLUTION OF ENROLMENTS AT THE THIRD LEVEL IN SOME
DEVELOPING COUNTRIES: 1950–1964
(1950 = 100)

	Ghana	Ecuador	Peru	India
1950	100	100	100	100
1955	360	142	105	169
1960	1409	227	194	272
1964	1832	303	290	273

SOURCE: *Statistical Yearbook 1965*, Unesco, Table 15

Table II gives data for one African and two Latin American countries as well as for India. The data refer to enrolments only and include all types of post-secondary education, both university and non-university. It is interesting to note that three out of four countries selected have experienced growth rates in enrolments analogous to their OECD counterparts, particularly if the slight difference in the period of time covered is taken into account. The case of Ghana is, of course, due to the very low base-year figure: according to the Unesco source cited in the table, there were 210 students in Ghana in 1950. This figure had increased to 3,848 in 1964. This explains the extraordinary high index figure for that year.

So far we have given a rapid over-view of the acceleration in enrolments and in degrees awarded which has been observed everywhere in the past decades and particularly in the past ten to twelve years. This was done for third-level and university education only because an expansion at this level presupposes, normally, an even bigger expansion at the lower levels coupled with an increasing social demand. As such, the expansion of third-level education can be considered as being significant for the educational system as a whole.

However, the two tables above refer to *global* enrolments and *total* number of first degrees awarded. When one reasons in terms of the manpower link of education, the stress is very often laid on scientific and

TABLE III

PROPORTION OF UNIVERSITY ENROLMENTS AND OF FIRST DEGREES IN SCIENTIFIC AND TECHNOLOGICAL SUBJECTS
IN SOME OECD COUNTRIES: 1952–1965

as a % of total enrolments and of total first degrees

	U.S.A.		FRANCE		ITALY		SWEDEN		YUGOSLAVIA		TURKEY	
	Enrolm.	Degrees	Enrolm.	Degrees	Enrolm.	Degrees	Enrolm.	Degrees	Enrolm.	Degrees	Enrolm.	Degrees
1952	—	20·9	26·4	n.a.	27·9	26·9	32·0	35·2	40·8	n.a.	5·8	7·1
1956	—	20·5	30·8	37·5	27·2	27·8	30·0	35·3	37·8	41·3	5·7	9·3
1961	—	22·4	39·9	55·3	26·7	27·7	31·0	35·3	40·3	40·9	5·4	11·8
1964 (5)	—	20·3	36·1	49·0	25·7	27·5	29·0	35·5	41·0	40·9	6·4	7·7

SOURCE: See Table I.

NOTE: Owing to the system of student options and composite courses at the undergraduate level the distinction of science students in the United States is impossible. Science and technology includes natural and exact sciences, engineering (and in some cases architecture) and agronomy.

technical personnel and hence on the science and technological branches of the educational system. It is, therefore, of interest in the context of this chapter to examine what proportion of the rising number of university enrolments and of the first degrees awarded is concerned with science and technology and how this proportion has developed in time.

This is shown in Table III for the same OECD countries listed in Table I and they refer therefore again to university enrolments only (excluding post-secondary non-university education). The first striking aspect of this table is the fact that the proportion of students in science and technology has remained fairly stable during the period under review. The same is true for the proportion taking a first degree in science and technology. The only exception to this rule is France. The second aspect worth underlining is the fact that the United States has a lower proportion of graduates in science and technology than any other country in the table except Turkey, which has strikingly low proportions indeed.

At this point it is necessary to mention that the U.S.A. has obviously much greater numbers enrolled, both in absolute as well as in relative terms (i.e. relative to the school-age population). In 1964 total university enrolments in the U.S.A. amounted to around 33 per cent of the 20–24 age-group; the enrolment rate as thus defined and for the same year was 11·5 per cent in France, close to 9 per cent in Italy, nearly 11 per cent in Sweden, and 7 per cent in Yugoslavia.[9] Consequently, the relative over-all educational effort is much bigger in the U.S.A. than in Europe. It is in the above context that the relatively low proportion of science and technological graduates in the United States has to be interpreted.[10] It remains true, nevertheless, that the important inflow of scientists and engineers into the United States (the so-called Brain Drain viewed from the 'donor' countries) may point to the fact that the U.S.A. should step up its efforts in the field of scientific and technological education.

Some comparable information for the four developing countries already mentioned above is presented in Table IV, showing graduates only, but covering total third-level (post-secondary) education.

A word of caution must be sounded before commenting on these figures. The figures for India exclude natural sciences which, for reasons beyond our comprehension, have been included with humanities. Moreoever, both for India and Peru only two figures are available – for the years 1957 and 1960. In general the period of time covered in this table is a relatively short one. This is particularly disturbing in the case of Peru where the two figures available vary considerably. It would look as if

---

9 This would become 10 per cent if all post-secondary enrolments had been considered.
10 For a more detailed discussion on U.S.A.–Europe comparisons, see *Analytical Report on Technological Gaps*, OECD, 1968, Chapter A: Educational Aspect.

TABLE IV

PROPORTION OF THIRD-LEVEL GRADUATES IN SCIENCE AND TECHNOLOGY
IN SOME DEVELOPING COUNTRIES: 1957–63
(as a % of total graduates)

	Ghana	Ecuador*	Peru	India†
1957	3·0	24·5	10·6	5·6
1960	6·3	25·1	20·5	6·8
1963	4·4	24·0	n.a.	n.a.

SOURCE: *Statistical Yearbook* 1965, Unesco, Table 20.
NOTE: For definition of science and technology subjects, see Table 3.
* Includes pharmacy.   † Excludes natural sciences.

the Latin American countries have a proportion of science and technological graduates which comes close to those observed in Europe, whereas
Ghana, in spite of rapid increases in total enrolments (Table II), has not
been successful in attracting relatively more students into the science and
technology subjects. India probably falls somewhere in between: it could
indeed be expected that, if natural sciences were included, their proportion
would rise to some 10 to 15 per cent. The striking aspect again is the
stability of this proportion (with the obvious exception of Peru) in spite
of rapid increases in total enrolments, a stability already observed for the
OECD countries when we commented on Table III.

It will be clear that the enrolment rates for these developing countries
are lower than those observed for the OECD countries: using the same
definition as above they amounted to 0·8 per cent for Ghana; 2·5 per cent
for Ecuador; 5 per cent in Peru, and 2·6 per cent in India. (All these
figures refer to 1964 or nearest year.)

One of the more interesting pieces of information obtained through
Tables III and IV related to a relative stability in time of the proportions
of enrolments and graduates in science and technology, in spite of the
important increases in total numbers enrolled and first degrees awarded.
Now it is a well-known fact that the manpower-educational planners
have been insisting not only on the necessity of having bigger numbers
enrolled, but above all on a shift towards science and technology in
higher education, and towards the technical and vocational branches in
secondary education. I know of no educational planning document
which tried to relate the educational system to the economic and
technological environment that concluded with a note of satisfaction
with regard to the present proportions, and current trends, of pupils and
students in the technical subjects. This phenomenon can be observed in
industrialized as well as in developing countries. Table V presents projections made for a few industrialized countries.

TABLE V

Projections of Enrolments in Science and Technology as a
Proportion of Total University Enrolments in Some
Industrialized Countries

Countries	1965	1970	1975	1980
France*	34·0	—	40·5	—
Italy	27·5	—	41·3	—
Sweden	28·3	40·8	—	—
U.K.	44·1	47·8	49·1	53·2

Source: *Analytical Report on Technological Gaps*, op. cit.,
Table 17.

Note: The small changes for the base year compared to those
given in Table III are due to slight definitional alterations.

* Period 1964–1973.

Table V speaks for itself. All these countries forecast a considerable
change in emphasis away from humanities and towards science and
technology. Even in the United Kingdom where this proportion is
already high, the forecast wants even more, leading up to more than
50 per cent of all university students reading science and technology
in 1980.

Analogous results could be shown for other countries. For example,
in the case of Yugoslavia and Turkey the educational planning reports
elaborated in the framework of the OECD's Mediterranean Regional
Project also put much emphasis on this switch towards science and
technology.[11] This holds true to an even greater extent in the case of the
developing countries in Africa, Asia and Latin America.

Summarizing what we have said so far in this section, we must note
that the quantitative expansion of degrees awarded (and of examinations
in general) has been impressive everywhere. However, according to
existing manpower studies, there is too little emphasis on science and
technology and they forecast rising and sometimes rapidly rising proportions in these subjects. At the same time we have observed a tendency
for these proportions to remain stable in the past. This leads us perforce
into the last section which will deal in general terms with the problem of
incentives and wages.

Before doing so, some remarks are in order concerning secondary
education, since the discussion has been almost exclusively centred
around the university, although we have explained why. There is of
course a close interrelationship between what happens at the secondary

---

[11] See *Education and Development: Yugoslavia and Turkey* (Country Reports), OECD, 1965.

level and what we observe at the higher level of education. If there is an imbalance at the university level between science and technology graduates on the one hand and graduates in humanities on the other, this imbalance can very often be found back at the secondary level. If we take the enrolments in the general versus the technical secondary schools, we frequently find similar results to those shown here at the university level. But the problem is more complicated because we have to take account of the various streams inside the general secondary schools. This raises the whole area of science and mathematics teaching in secondary schools, the trends towards comprehensive schools, etc., etc. In the framework of this chapter it is impossible to go into these questions, but we thought it essential to mention them. A recent survey in Ruanda revealed that of all pupils enrolled in second-level education (8,500), half were taking Greek and Latin in the classical stream of the *lycée*.

III. OBSTACLES TO BALANCED EDUCATIONAL GROWTH PATHS

There are a certain number of factors that may explain why at a given point in time, or during a certain period, the output structure of the educational system in terms of graduates does not correspond with the requirements of economic and technological development. These factors might be grouped under the following headings:

(*a*) factors related to the internal dynamics of the educational system;

(*b*) factors related to the labour market.

The cynic may of course argue that the reason why one observes discrepancies between the forecast (i.e. the desirable) and the actual development of the educational system lies in the fact that the forecasts are wrong! This may very well be true. But I would like to view the problem in this section from a different angle. My point of departure will be: suppose we are dead certain about the economic-technological desirability of having more trained people in a certain speciality at a given point in time. What may be the difficulties in getting them?

(*a*) *Factors Related to the Internal Dynamics of the Educational System.* A disequilibrium may occur because of the long gestation periods inherent in the educational process. This phenomenon is of course closely linked to the degree of flexibility of the educational system, and to the level of sophistication of educational planning going on in the country under consideration. For example, if at a given point in time the authorities 'feel' that there is a need for training more sociologists and an important campaign is started to attract more secondary school graduates into the relevant university departments, one runs a risk of rapidly overshooting the target because of a deficient timing and spreading of the expansion pattern. There is indeed a danger of running into some kind of a cobweb mechanism: if the campaign is successful, graduates start pouring out of the university after five years or so and after a while it may happen that from a period of shortage one falls into the other excess of oversupply. Social demand will react with a time-lag and demand for places will go down, which may result some time later in a feeling of shortage, etc., etc. Unless one disposes of a completely flexible system, one cannot stop a movement overnight once it has taken momentum in the educational system. This is what one might call the lethargy inherent in most educational processes. It is another reason for stressing the importance of taking a long-term view in educational policy and planning; this also shows the importance of educational and vocational guidance.

(b) *Factors Related to the Labour Market: Incentives and Wages.* It will be clear from what has just been said that *ad hoc* measures in the field of educational policy may be one of the reasons for an unbalanced educational growth path (unbalanced with respect to economic needs). Although it is therefore true that the integration of manpower aspects into a prospective educational plan is a necessary condition, it will very often not be a sufficient condition. This is so because educational and manpower plans tend to put much too little emphasis on motivation, attitudes, incentives and wages. This is particularly serious in the case of developing countries. We join here our remarks made in the first section of this chapter concerning the fact that the manpower projections hang in thin economic air, and we could now add that they also frequently ignore social constraints. All this may result in a continuous development of the educational system according to past trends and patterns, whereas the signals given by the manpower forecasts remain in the realm of wishful thinking. We have therefore interpreted the obstacles related to the functioning of the labour market in a wide sense, including not only such economic incentives as wages and salaries, but also social incentives such as the status of certain occupations, the prestige of government service, etc.

W. Arthur Lewis drew attention many years ago to the lopsided salary structure in many African countries. It may be of interest to quote one paragraph from his stimulating paper:

The situation is particularly acute in Africa, where senior administrative salaries have a considerable premium above similar salaries in Europe, in order to attract European recruits. In consequence, the range of personal incomes is wider than anywhere else in the world; much wider than in Asia, where senior salaries are only about a half of their European equivalents. Now that Africans are taking over the top administrative jobs, they are asking, in the name of the sacred principle of non-discrimination, to be paid the same salaries as Europeans, as if it were necessary to spend 50 per cent more on them to attract them away from Europe. Many African politicians have stamped on this ridiculous proposition, which handicaps development by making it unnecessarily expensive, and also merely substitutes the yoke of the African B.A. upon the neck of the African peasant. The ultimate outcome cannot be in doubt, but much passion will be expended on the way.[12]

A situation as described above is not only expensive in monetary terms, but is not well geared either to the economic needs of the society because in general it is not the *type* of studies followed that counts, but rather the *level* attained. A more precise example in this respect has been given in a recent paper concerning the situation in the U.A.R.

In 1961, the socialist measures were taken, and the responsibility of the Government to achieve the goal of full employment was established firmly. This commitment was absolute in regard to University graduates. The Government decreed that all those graduating would be employed, regardless of their specialities or the need for them. They would be hired at the 7th category allotted to University graduates. This commitment was less firm for secondary school graduates. By February 1968, several thousands of the 1965 technical secondary school graduates have not yet been employed, while University graduates are hired within a maximum of one year of their graduation.'[13]

The above is clearly an extreme example of the absence of economic pressures within the system. Wages are out of touch with the realities of the economic and technological environment, and the blanket guarantee of employment for university graduates from whatever faculty maintains redundant surpluses and keeps the system suffering from the shortages.

These economic incentives (or lack of incentives) are very often reinforced by social incentives, such as the status of certain occupations, the attitude towards manual labour (created frequently by the very fact of obtaining some years of formal education), etc.

It is therefore clear that indicating the future manpower needs is not sufficient. Educational planning should be more concerned than it has been up till now with the factors that govern social (or individual and family) demand for the various types of education. This necessitates a careful study of the factors mentioned in this paper. It will at the same time go a long way towards reconciling the various 'approaches' to educational planning.

---

[12] W. Arthur Lewis, 'Priorities for Educational Expansion', *Policy Conference on Economic Growth and Investment in Education* (1961), OECD, 1965 (second printing), p. 37.

[13] N. A. Shaat and M. A. Mustafa, 'A Working Paper on the Effect of Wages and Salaries on Manpower Development and Allocation in the U.A.R.', paper presented to a Seminar on Manpower Planning organized jointly by the OECD and the Institute of National Planning, Cairo, February 1968 (mimeogr.).

28

Sociological Aspects of Examinations

Jean Capelle

Professor of Education, University of Nancy; formerly Director General, Ministry of Education, Paris

In a world which is ever becoming more realistic and competitive, the idea of a disinterested culture is a dream which is still cherished by certain idealists, but for the great majority of young people and for their parents, the essential purpose of education is to supply knowledge and skills which will bring with them calculable advantages. The appropriate training is recognized by diplomas granted as a result of methods of evaluation of varying types which are called examinations. In this category we include psychotechnical tests. It is because of this state of affairs that examinations have become of such great social importance. They determine the structure of our society, they decide what grade of position shall be held by any individual both in state and private concerns; on them depends the way in which children progress in their school careers, and finally they influence promotion in the chosen profession. Each stage in the life of the modern citizen is marked out, controlled, certified by examinations which form a means of regulation and classification accepted by all as the best spur for competition and the fairest way of giving to each one his due. This has been so much accepted that were examinations and diplomas to be discontinued society would find itself in an unimaginable state of chaos from which it would be difficult to emerge. For all these reasons it can be considered that, in spite of the criticisms levelled at it, the examination system in a modern country forms an essential part of the social order and political stability.

Sociological Aspects of Examinations

We shall not discuss examinations which are organized by teachers themselves as part of the educational course; they form part of the teacher's stock-in-trade and are used as a stimulus for the pupils and also as a means of forming a provisional assessment. They are not very important for they are not decisive. In this paper we shall consider only the examinations which take place at the end of each stage of studies and of which the purpose is either to recognize that the work in this particular stage has been satisfactorily accomplished or to guarantee that the pupil has the necessary aptitude to embark, with some hope of success, upon a more advanced stage. The first type produces final diplomas, the second provides a qualification for further education.

This distinction between the two types of examination cannot always easily be made, since certain diplomas claim to be both final and qualifying: such is the case with the French *baccalauréat* which keeps changing in form, but each year is used to examine more candidates. It is both – officially, anyway – a recognition that a course of secondary studies has been successfully completed and a certificate of aptitude for university studies. Nevertheless this distinction is particularly necessary at the moment when members of the general public, better informed as a result of measures taken to make education more widely available, are inclined to think that every certificate gained is a proof of the ability of its holder to go on to more advanced studies.

It is because of this impression that the pupil at the *collège technique* who passes his final examination which, for example, qualifies him as a mechanical fitter is more and more inclined to consider this diploma as a guarantee of his ability to enter a *lycée technique*. In the same way the technician working in an office for industrial studies, who has just left a *lycée technique* is more and more ready to assume that his next step should be entrance to a *grande école* or to a university, with a view to becoming eventually a qualified engineer.

Doubtless, in a democratic society, no path should be a dead end. Nevertheless, final diplomas, when they are specifically meant to bear witness to the fact that the holder is qualified for some particular job of work, should lead to this sort of work and not to a further course of full-time education for which, in any case, the diploma gives no guarantee of adequate preparation. It is while carrying on their vocational activity that those who have the desire and the aptitude should find, thanks to the facilities offered by the 'parallel' school and to favourable conditions provided by the laws concerning work and leisure, the surest means of promotion capable of satisfying even the highest ambitions.

Having made this point – and it is an important one, since an entire policy of vocational promotion may depend on a full understanding of it – it is necessary to note that diplomas are surrounded by a magic aura in the eyes of the general public; he who holds a diploma is one of those who 'have knowledge'. The pursuit of the diploma corresponds to a democratic vision in which everyone joins the social class of the 'top people'. But until all citizens have become 'top people' those who hold diplomas are considered as having climbed up some of the rungs of the social ladder.

The *baccalauréat* brings with it an obvious social distinction. In a certain village cemetery one can read the inscription: 'Here lies X who passed his *baccalauréat*.' The deceased had been the intellectual aristocrat of the village.

The respect in which the *baccalauréat* is held among ordinary people does not come only from the fact that it marks a certain social advance; it finds further justification in the fact that the fortunate holder of this certificate has automatic right of entry to university faculties and can thus enjoy the material and social advantages which go with the status of being a student engaged in advanced education.

It is interesting to observe the activities of an almost ritualistic type in which the candidates for the *baccalauréat* take part at the end of the examinations. The traditional *monôme* (rag) and the ceremonies which go with it are reminiscent of initiation ceremonies in primitive societies, the only difference being that the behaviour of these young examination candidates is much less disciplined and less rich in inner meaning.

More serious is the fact that it is generally thought that luck plays a major role in examinations, and further, that this idea is found to be quite acceptable. The language of games of chance as well as that of statistics is normally used in connection with the *baccalauréat*, not only in everyday conversation, but also in the terminology used by the administration. It is the belief in the fundamental element of luck which justifies the organization of the *baccalauréat* for a second time each year – a typically French docimological phenomenon – usually called the 'second chance' examination for candidates who were not 'lucky' enough to pass the first time they sat for the examination. It should be noted that this very choice of words in so far as it is justified – and it is, alas, only too often true, as numerous inquiries and studies have clearly shown – exposes a weakness in an established procedure to which, however, the general run of parents remains very attached.

Thus it is acknowledged that luck forms an integral part of a method of evaluation which tests pupils once in each subject (it is the estimation at a single point on an advancing curve which, for each subject, is like so many teeth of a saw) and which is entrusted to examiners who, and this is a point about which the authorities make certain from the beginning, do not know the candidates personally. At the same time, surprisingly enough, this procedure is considered to be the best guarantee of fairness. To admit that a choice in which chance is all-powerful is more just and objective than a choice made as a result of the general responsibility of the teaching staff and of individual teachers who know the candidates whom they have trained, reveals a very low opinion of the objective power and ethical principles of teachers!

Of course, both the brilliant and the very weak scholars receive, in spite of the element of luck, the just recognition of their merits or their weakness; but in the case of many candidates, it may well be open to question whether there is really a way which makes it possible to divide them into two groups: that of the chosen and that of the rejected! It is even possible that this problem admits of no solution, because beyond doubt, it is a false problem.

Let us suppose that the candidates for the most recent *baccalauréat* examination were to be divided into three sections: those whose average is above 12/20 (they pass): those whose average is below 8/20 (they fail outright); and finally those whose average is between 8 and 12. This third section, which certainly includes more than half of the whole number of candidates, is subjected to the mechanical procedures of the examination and is divided into two groups, almost equal in number, those who pass and those who fail. Let us further imagine – this is simply an intellectual exercise – that this group be submitted to a game of chance, those who pass being chosen by the toss of a coin. Can we be absolutely sure that this new way of division between those who pass and those who fail would be less just than that which was in fact used? We have to make an effort to convince ourselves that it is essential for us to be sure of this.

Thus the problem remains: a method of evaluation must be found of which the objectivity would be guaranteed by the assessment of a sort of balance sheet (instead of an evaluation made at a given point) and by the moral and professional integrity of teachers.

In any case, as the wider spread of education makes a grammar school education possible both financially and geographically for more and more children, ambitions become more and more intensely focused on the *baccalauréat*. The education provided for pupils between the ages of fifteen and eighteen ought really to satisfy a wide diversity of tastes and aptitudes and should meet the needs of society. Instead of this ideal state of affairs, the general run of pupils concentrates increasingly upon the bottleneck of the *baccalauréat* as if the crossing of this barrier were the sole means of salvation. A very real shortage of pupils wanting to be trained to become qualified workers and technicians is becoming apparent among young people of less than eighteen years of age. This shortage may well become more acute in the next few years as a result of the greater awareness of the possibilities of social advancement by means of the *baccalauréat*.

The prestige of the *baccalauréat* is mainly the result of the belief that unless you have passed this test you can only hope to engage upon subordinate types of work. It does not go so far, however, as to set apart, on a national scale, an *élite* whose members pride themselves on having passed the *baccalauréat* examination. There are higher and more selective examinations, resulting in the formation, by those who have been successful, of a sort of mutual-aid society in which the members support each other; some people allege that they are like freemasons. Thus those who are successful in the competitive examinations for the *grandes écoles* are not only assured of certain advantages in their future careers but they join an aristocratic club, that of the former pupils of the *Ecole X*; a club which is jealous of its distinctive features and in which the members foster among themselves, in spite of the element of competition which may arise during a man's career, a spirit of solidarity of which the preferential character is generally overestimated by those who are not members of this sort of club. Many of the *élite* of the country were trained in such establishments, whose names, which enjoy a very high reputation, frequently feature on visiting cards. For example, the following qualifications carry with them much more prestige than university degrees:

> *ancien élève de l'Ecole Normale Supérieure* (Special College of Education)
> *ancien élève de l'Ecole Polytechnique*
> *ancien élève de l'Ecole Nationale Supérieure des Mines de Paris*
> *ancien élève de l'Ecole Centrale des Arts et des Manufactures*
> *ancien élève de l'Ecole Nationale d'Administration*

This method of selection and classification of a large section of the *élite* of the country, which provides them for the rest of their lives with the title of 'former pupil' of a *grande école* has a darker side: the failure in the competitive examination for admittance to one of these highly esteemed brotherhoods is bitterly felt by many, albeit discreetly, and sometimes for a very long time. A man whose career has been outstandingly successful, may still feel bitter at the age of fifty because earlier he failed in the entrance examination for the *Ecole Polytechnique*. The *grandes écoles* have the merit of providing the country with a supply of potential leaders who are without any doubt brilliant academically but they also have the drawback of doing great and unjustifiable harm to others. But this is not the place to launch an attack on the system of the *grandes écoles* and their so-called privileges. The high degree of selectivity of the *grandes écoles* acts as a counter-balance to the absence of selection for entrance to a university; it helps to show how important a part quality must play in any well-balanced policy for a democratization of education.

Adaptation of Examinations to Needs

Consideration will now be given to the conditions which must be satisfied for entry into the professions for the practice of which it is essential to hold certain qualifications.

If a man wishes to engage himself in vocational activities he has to satisfy ever stricter and more exact regulations. Detailed lists have been drawn up of the different types of work included in each profession, of the different grades of knowledge corresponding to each of them and of the different ways in which these grades are recognized.

Educationists and the people who make use of the services of those engaged in these professions are equally concerned in the elaboration of a system of examinations which will give a firm guarantee of the proficiency necessary for the different responsibilities inherent in any particular position. A distinction should be made, with regard to paper qualifications for various professions, between their practical and intrinsic value.

(1) *Practical Value*—Certain professional diplomas allow their holders to carry on a given profession; others are really guaranteed appointments to professional posts.

In the first category must be placed diplomas which are demanded by the regulations which govern the exercise of certain professions. Thus, the diploma of doctor of medicine is necessary for the practice of medicine: it does not guarantee patients. The university diploma in pharmacy is required by a dispensing pharmacist if he wishes to practise. The *licentia docendi* (a degree qualifying its holder as a teacher) has for a long time meant that the holder could teach in a secondary school. The possession of a certificate of professional proficiency (C.A.P.), of a technician's certificate or of an engineer's diploma does not guarantee a job, but these certificates do ensure that their holders will be paid a minimum guaranteed salary in accordance with collective union agreements.

In the second category are found diplomas of proficiency, the possession of which means permanent employment in a particular post. Such is the case in all recruitment examinations whose aim is to fill posts in the civil service. They usually take the form of competitive examinations in the sense that the number of posts to be filled is fixed in advance and their aim is to select the best candidates from among those who satisfy certain prerequisite conditions. The type of tests set in these examinations is directly determined by the nature of the occupation to be carried on. The recruitment of employees in the administration of the Post Office, beginning with the first secondary certificate (B.E.P.C.) or the *baccalauréat*, that of secondary school teachers, beginning with the Teachers' Diploma (*licence d'enseignement*), that of cooks in the nationalized colleges, like that of professors attached to faculties of medicine, are only a few examples of posts which are filled in this way. Between the Teachers' Diploma (*licence d'enseignement*) and the C.A.P.E.S. (certificate of proficiency in secondary school teaching) there is as great a difference as there is between recognition of a capacity to teach and the appointment to a permanent teaching post. Success in the competitive examinations for the *grandes écoles* does not bring with it legally a guaranteed appointment to any particular post; but because of the prestige which is attached to these establishments it can indeed be considered that the certificate of entry to a *grande école* ensures an enviable and permanent post. This almost certainly is only because of the very small number selected; but this small number gives rise to the charge of Malthusianism which is from time to time levelled against the *grandes écoles* – which establishments do not seem to be greatly disturbed by it.

Doubtless no one will question, at least in principle, that it is necessary to set up in one way or another a system of examinations to measure candidates' ability to undertake certain types of work, and competitive examinations to distribute posts according to merit. But is it possible to do this with complete efficiency and justice? How can it be guaranteed that these standards will be maintained throughout the duration of a professional career, especially in those cases where appointments to posts are made for life?

(2) *The Intrinsic Value of Diplomas*—A diploma bears witness to the fact that the person who holds it has certain official ability. On the other hand, this same person, in the exercise of his profession, possesses real ability. What correspondence is there between official and real ability? Are these two skills equal, or if there is inequality between them, in which direction does it lie? Official ability is rigid, because its content has been defined once and for all, at a certain fixed moment. Real ability develops by the practice of one's profession: any comparison between the two abilities is therefore difficult to establish.

Two sorts of problems arise:

(*a*) How can the real value of the official ability be guaranteed?

(*b*) How can real ability be officially recognized?

Let us consider the first problem. Official certificates testifying that the holder has certain professional proficiency are usually awarded either by boards made up of teachers who are also professionally qualified – as in the case of the diploma for a doctor of medicine – or by mixed boards comprised of teachers and people engaged in the relevant profession. Certificates testifying to professional ability, technicians' certificates and, at least in principle, engineers' diplomas are awarded by such mixed boards.

Can it be said that these official diplomas are a guarantee of real professional proficiency? Yes, but only for a certain time: they bear witness to the fact that the holder has potential ability, that is to say he has the necessary aptitude to acquire within a short time actual, real professional ability. The time required will depend upon the effectiveness of the period of initial training. Here is to be found a difficulty with which each professional sector deals in accordance with its traditions. It can be thought that in France this extremely important period of transition from guaranteed potential ability to the real ability necessary to carry on one's profession efficiently is far too often treated much too lightly and left to chance. As far as this question is concerned the method used in Britain is interesting and without a doubt very successful. The young engineer who has just been granted a diploma by a university must, for at least two more years, still be systematically supervised at this period by members of the profession itself, before he is granted, by the professional body, the final certificate testifying to his official and real ability. This is done by admitting him as a member of a 'professional institute'. Consideration should perhaps be given to a widespread application of this method of solving the difficulty at this particular moment when the systematic training provided by a school or university needs to be more closely connected with the acquisition of basic knowledge. The profession would then have to undertake a more effective share in the application to actual working conditions of the general and professional training received by the young candidate at school or at the university. Doubtless the relationship between the professions and the education system ought to be made more effective and functional so that official diplomas more closely correspond to a systematic evaluation of needs. The Commission on Diplomas for Engineers set up in France as a result of the law of July 10th, 1934, concerning conditions governing the granting and use of the term 'qualified engineer' is not sufficiently powerful either to be of help to the development of the relationship between teachers and those in the engineering profession, nor to ensure a measure of control over the adaptation of training to needs.

Finally comes the question of how to give official recognition to professional proficiency actually acquired in the course of carrying on professional duties. How is its value to be measured in each individual case, as the person's career progresses? These are not the least important of the problems to be found in the wide subject of promotion of workers, itself a part of the sector which concerns continuous education.

In the first place it is a question of maintaining, or of adapting to circumstances, the real value of official diplomas. Doubtless it may become necessary in the future to consider that diplomas of proficiency should be granted for a certain limited period only – and this is, in fact, already done in the sector of atomic technology. But at the same time attention must be given to the establishment, for all those concerned, of conditions by which they may keep up or further their knowledge and to define the methods by which they may periodically be reassessed. This gives rise to delicate moral and technical problems, for the candidates must be kept up to scratch and their further development must be encouraged, but, in addition, care must be taken not to create an atmosphere of instability which could be more of a worry than a help, nor should adults have to sit for examinations of a scholastic type. At a time when life in our society is already regimented and to a certain extent made more rigid by an abusive use of examinations, the entire country must not be plunged into a paralysing atmosphere of acute examination fever. The question, however, remains: the doctor, the engineer and the teacher must keep up with modern trends in order properly to fulfil their professional responsibilities and the need to be up to the minute in the changing world must not only be urged and favoured, but, to a certain extent, controlled. Moreover, and this is only just and right, any skills acquired while carrying on professional duties, thanks to the personal efforts of the individuals concerned, must be eligible for official recognition. Of course, it is usual in most societies to reward, by moral and material advancement, those employees and others who work with them who have been able to improve their real ability. This recognition is only within the industrial concern; it remains linked with the evaluation made by the latter. It ought to be made more objective in character, to be made official, either by making it easier for those concerned to prepare for the official examinations provided for by the normal system of education, or by setting up special diplomas.

'Higher grade' technicians who have been trained while in regular employment and who are real master technicians, deserve recognition, and so do those who, in addition, have acquired a sound scientific training. In the sector of health it is perhaps regrettable that doctors, concerned with the protection of the sphere for which they are responsible, have, no doubt rightly, in practice maintained a sort of vacuum around themselves. Women nurses are the nearest to them; as for male nurses, they are usually only the manual labourers in the general life of the hospital. Now these are people who have vocations and talents but who are not suitable for advanced scientific study and yet they can be of real service and can make a complementary contribution to medicine which can be of great value. The control of official recognition of these talents when they do exist, would make it easier to eliminate charlatans, for recognition would be granted to real technicians, capable of being, in certain conditions, medical auxiliaries. Among the 'bone-setters' there are certainly people whose services, suitably guided, are worthy of recognition. Many of these are at present publicly denigrated, even though, secretly, they are often consulted.

Incidentally, how can we fail to be worried when we think of certain under-developed countries which will only accept doctors of medicine, trained according to standards normal in economically developed countries at a time when they are producing doctors of medicine in numbers which fall pitifully short of their needs? These small numbers are produced at an astronomical cost. Medical technicians, suitably trained for current needs, somewhat similar to the 'medical health officers' of former days, could well satisfy urgent demands.

To conclude, where our own society is concerned, first priority should be given to the necessity of making clear the value of diplomas so that their temporary nature may be better understood, and of making a study of methods of evaluation of a more continuous sort which would be less a matter of luck, less likely to produce traumatic effects and more acceptable for adults than traditional examinations. The result would be suitably adapted procedures – such perhaps as the method of examination by assessment, which reports on a whole period of activity and passes judgement on the ability of the candidate to follow any particular course – and a real deontological outlook on the part of teachers towards the responsibility which they must accept in assessing their pupils, whether they be children or adults.

Another important need is the development, with the help of public opinion and the organization of institutions, of means of ensuring – at all stages and in every sector of professional activity – the enduring nature of actual proficiency and the promotion of the best workers to senior positions.

Modern countries have successfully tried to make public opinion accept the fact that while scientific research is inevitably hazardous and expensive, nevertheless, increasingly large sums of money have to be invested in research. It is now time to make the general public realize how urgent and far-reaching the problem of continuous education is, if they are to face up to the fierce competitive spirit of modern society and to contribute more effectively to the progress of science, to the need of justice for men and to their aspirations towards happiness.

29

Economics of Skill Labelling

Harvey Leibenstein
Andieloft Professor of Economics and Population, Harvard University

I. Economic Values of Skill Labelling

Some of the processes of education, whether they be formal schooling, on-the-job training, or some form of experience, result in formal and informal processes of skill labelling. The most obvious examples are certificates, diplomas, degrees and licences. Occasionally associated with such labels are formal titles of address such as Doctor, or other means of establishing status such as initials after one's name. From a personal viewpoint, such labels have an obvious economic value and are frequently eagerly sought after – sometimes more so than the education or skill that they represent. In addition, in the very imperfect market for human skills, such labels serve the function of evaluating individuals' capacities to perform certain services. Labels greatly facilitate the practice of expertise, or of specific skills, in a market of inexpert buyers. Even in markets where the buyers are expert, or may readily become expert in judging skill performance, labels serve a useful economic purpose because they eliminate the necessity of testing degree of skill on every occasion in which the service is sold. From a personal and a social viewpoint, skill labels are useful social inventions.

We will ignore, for present purposes, the degree to which labels may be acquired or used in a fraudulent manner. While this would certainly be an interesting subject in its own right, it probably does not significantly detract from the economic value of skill labelling.

The significant question is not whether, in some general sense, skill labelling as a process is worthwhile. This seems to be obviously true. Rather, what may be looked into is whether the degree and type of skill labelling that exists at any one time is optimal.

II. The Skill-labelling Component in Returns to Education

In recent years economists have calculated rates of return to education in various countries. In most instances the returns to primary education are high; and in many instances the returns to higher education are also relatively high, while the returns to secondary education are usually lower than either of the others, and in some cases are very low. An interesting finding in this connexion is that the returns to the final year of education of a specific type, for example the last year of high school or the last year of university, as compared with previous years, is frequently twice as large as the return to the other years. The likely inference is that the return for the last year is not only the return to the schooling but is attributable to the fact that completion of the last year confers on one a broad skill label which the previous years do not. Nevertheless, we should not presume that the measure of the value of the skill label rests entirely on the differential between the last year of education of a given type and the previous years. Rather, it is quite possible that most of the return to many types of education should be attributed to the fact that the educational process operates as a complex funnelling system in which people are classified in accordance with various skills and abilities. This would be one way of explaining the fairly high rates of return to various types of education of a liberal sort which are frequently unrelated or only marginally related to the exact work that individuals undertake. While we can measure, in some sense, the personal returns to education, we do not know at the present time which detailed components of schooling have an economic value. It seems likely that the skill labelling part of the process is one of the components involved.

III. On the Economic Efficiency of Skill-labelling Schemes

The actual skill-labelling schemes in use are, to a considerable degree, arbitrary and depend to a great extent on historical accidents, borrowing from other countries, and the gradual evolution of some types of labels which may have meant one thing in their initial context but which mean something different today. The years of education of different types depend, for the most part, on historical precedence. It seems likely that there is considerable economic waste in the labelling system in use compared to that system which would be best from an economic viewpoint. For instance, the number of years spent in higher education are usually arbitrary and, as far as one can see, frequently unrelated to the work performed by recipients of that type of education. If, under the American system, people normally have four years of university training and these individuals afterwards choose a wide variety of occupational careers, it seems likely that the variety of careers could have benefited from very different numbers of years of education than those actually spent. It is probably true that the same could also be said for the types of education received. While to some degree this is likely to be somewhat less true of professional training than the liberal arts and science type, it is notorious that many aspects of professional training are looked upon as being wasteful by practitioners in later years. Finally, that part of the labelling scheme that is likely to be least satisfactory is the implication of quality of performance to be expected from one possessing the label. It is rare that the label in any way indicates the degree of skill, given the range of skill possessed by those bearing a similar label.

At least two considerations enter into formulating an optimal arrangement. On the one hand, the larger the number of labels the better the economy would be able to fit specific skill capacities to specific tasks. On the other hand, a labelling scheme that is too detailed and too complex becomes very difficult to operate because a high degree of expertise is then required in judging the content and implications of different labels. Clearly, some balance has to be achieved between these conflicting requirements.

We must also remember that quantity and quality in skills are substitutes for each other, and that social and economic waste occurs if the degree of substitutability is not appreciated. For example, a very high-quality medical student, who has received only three years of medical schooling, may be the equal of a somewhat lower-quality student who has received the standard four years (in the American scheme). In the rigid labelling scheme that exists today, the one with three years of training cannot utilize any of his training whatsoever, while the one with four years is able to do so. In this case the rigidity of skill-labelling schemes could lead to considerable economic waste. This is especially likely to be true in various skills where, along the way, people receive useful training but where there may be fairly high drop-out rates at various points.

There are also a number of dimensions of skill which are frequently not tested at all in some types of skill labels. For example, many skill labels deal mostly with formal schooling and say nothing about the value of subsequent experience. Others say little about the payoff to the recency of education, or quality of education, or grade of work done by the student, and so on. There are many other qualitative aspects of skill which come to mind which are not in any way implicit in the skill-labelling procedures in use.

In many areas skill labelling is tied up with formal schooling. In many cases it would be less expensive to relate skill labelling simply with a process of testing, regardless of the means of obtaining the skill. The obverse of the coin of higher standards is an increase in the rigidity of obtaining the skill. It is likely, although there are no detailed studies in this area, that the general trend has been towards an increase in the rigidity of skill labelling rather than the reverse. The social loss in having rigid skill labels is that it makes various substitutes for a given skill, except the one formally labelled, almost potentially valueless. What is desired in periods of rapid technical change is that the substitution possibilities should be appreciated so that lower-quality substitutes can be used where there is a scarcity in the higher quality formally-labelled skill. Substitution increases the possibility for the supply of skills to increase as demand increases. The rigidity frequently goes beyond the mere fact of quality substitution. The label and its economic payoff is usually awarded only to those who obtain the skill through some well recognized and orthodox procedure. As a consequence, those who have the skill in question, or who could obtain it through unorthodox means, but who have not, for various reasons, obtained the label, may in fact be of equal quality or of higher quality than those who have the label in question. As a consequence, the procedures of skill labelling should be constantly under review.

In fact, skill-labelling procedures have an institutional life of their own. Frequently, those who determine the qualification for the label have a self-interest in setting unnecessarily high standards, or in limiting entry to the skill. Thus, there is frequently a conflict between the institutions that determine the system of skill labelling and the economic value of the skill-labelling scheme.

If skill labelling is to be treated from an economic viewpoint, then we cannot treat each particular label in isolation. Rather, it is the set of labels and the degree of substitutability that they imply that is the important economic element. This view is of interest since, from time to time, reforms are suggested and considered for specific skill labels, but these are treated on a one-at-a-time basis rather than in relation to the other labels that, in part, imply skills that are substitutes for each other.

30

Classification of Results in Degree Examinations in England and the United States

W. R. Niblett

Professor of Higher Education, University of London Institute of Education

It is hoped to show in this chapter, by some considerations of degree examinations in England and the U.S.A., that systems of classifying results incorporate presuppositions about both the nature of a university and the kind of society into which its graduates are going.

Practice in Medieval Times

Examinations for university degrees in the Middle Ages in Europe and in England were oral and the degrees awarded were with few exceptions unclassified. In medieval universities at each stage in the examining procedure, examiners and candidate came face to face. No doubt a curriculum largely composed of language, oratory and philosophical argument may have been most appropriately tested orally by 'disputation'. But clearly the examinations themselves were more than intellectual tests alone. There was an element of social ceremony, even of display, built into them, and failure was uncommon. They were neither so external nor so competitive as in later times: in a medieval society there seemed little reason why they should be.

The earliest recorded example, so far as is known, of dividing students into classes or grades was in the University of Louvain, where as early as 1441 masters were graduated in three classes, in each of which the names were published in order of merit: *rigorosi* (honours men), *transibiles* (pass men) and *gratiosi* (men given a pass as an act of charity). The names of the few who failed were not publicly announced. In Edinburgh, a century or so later, the names of candidates for honours at the mastership level were arranged in five classes, those in the lowest being awarded only a bare pass.

Eighteenth- and Nineteenth-Century Practice

The system of disputing in the schools at Oxford and Cambridge continued till the eighteenth century, though often in form only. Examination of any kind for first degree purposes was indeed, for a period at Oxford, entirely perfunctory; but in Cambridge some written examinations were introduced in 1722 and in 1747 the first classified 'Tripos' list was published – in mathematics, which was the only subject to be classified either at Oxford or Cambridge until the nineteenth century. The success-ful candidates were graded into Wranglers, Senior Optimes, Junior Optimes and Pollmen or Passmen, the names in each class being pub-lished until 1909 in order of merit, but after that in alphabetical order. In 1824 a Classical Tripos was introduced and it was not until then that any examination paper was actually printed. After the arrival of a degree in classics, some more brilliant students attempted to prove their dis-tinction by taking 'double honours' – sitting for their examination in classics a year or two after their examination in mathematics.

At Oxford in 1800 new Public Examinations Statutes introduced both written examinations for degrees and classified honours degrees, though for many years after that the majority of students continued to read for pass B.A.s, the minimum requirements for which were so low as to be a standard in name only. Basically if a student was studying for honours he was studying with an examination in mind; and students who were at a university for social purposes tended to regard those reading for honours as their social inferiors. But by the middle of the nineteenth century occasional complaints could be heard both in Oxford and Cambridge that examinations had come to dominate teaching and that a good many students sought not to be educated but to get a high place in the honours list.

The entry of the University of London into the field in 1838 as an examining body and the fact that from 1863 onwards it began to award honours degrees in a range both of arts and science subjects added to the competitive element. At the 'modern' universities in big English cities founded during the latter part of the century, classified honours degrees were given from the start in arts, science and applied science subjects and though the proportions of candidates opting to take them was at first not large, it steadily increased – a circumstance owing something to the continuing growth of industrialization in the country, with its concomi-tants of competitiveness and personal ambition. The idea of classifying degree results owed much to the need for encouraging students to work, but something also to the growing scientific spirit of the age – which encouraged a looking for results and results that could be measured. But it is noteworthy that even in the 1870s when the foundation of a university in Manchester was being advocated, *The Times* thought the danger to be that its degrees, though attainable with honours, would count for little because they would carry no social status with them. The principle of proof of merit by examination result, however, very much went with the stirrings against privilege of the growing middle class; and the intro-duction of competitive examinations in 1872 for posts in the highest administrative grades of the Civil Service, with half the marks awarded upon the results obtained in them and only half on interview, was significant. Admittedly it was difficult for those who had not done well in mathematics or classics at Oxford and Cambridge to gain entry. But the idea of a university as a place chiefly for the leisured or the detached was beginning to give way to a more democratic concept of its function, and some of the key Oxford teachers of the later nineteenth century were men profoundly concerned with the social and political problems of contemporary life.

The direction of progress in the civilization of Europe from the seventeenth century onwards has in general been towards the further individualizing of men; and the process of classifying university degrees can perhaps be seen as an English contribution within this sequence. University students became less and less treated, as once they were, as members of a group with a right to a degree as a result of years spent as members of a university community (their *alma mater*); instead it came to be agreed that they ought to be judged and classified 'fairly'. University examiners were thus increasingly required to become more external in their attitude, and to grade candidates on behalf of society, of the nation, indeed of civilization itself, so that their ability and qualifications could be more objectively depended upon. The nation was in course of evolution from aristocracy to meritocracy.

The Twentieth Century

By the early years of the twentieth century, with the spread of secondary education in Britain, and the rapid enlargement of the boundaries of knowledge itself, education at universities even for a first degree was becoming less general and more specialist for almost all candidates. 'Double honours' now, if attempted, were usually taken in related subjects rather than in ones so dissimilar as classics and mathematics. Universities were becoming more highly selective in entry and increasingly thought of as training an *élite* which could use its intelligence with skill and a backing of expert knowledge. And so degree examinations (especially where high honours were concerned) ought, it was argued, to test intellectual ability and thoughtful mastery of subject matter. Little test was included of the personal qualities of candidates nor was overmuch attention given to amount of sheer information amassed.

The theory of undergraduate education in the first part of the twentieth century held that in so far as general education continued to take place during university years – and it was accepted that this was important – it should be given in two main ways: through personal contacts between tutor or professor and student, residence in college or hall, and mixing with contemporaries who had themselves been selected as above average in intelligence; and through the clear apprehension of principle which came from mastering a specialism 'in depth'. It was this mastery which classified honours degree examinations were supposed fairly to test. A candidate taking an 'honours' course normally specialized in one subject only for an appreciable part of the three or four years he spent in studying for his B.A. or B.Sc., the one or two other subjects he might take being subsidiary and often dropped altogether in the final two years. The discipline of mind which specialist study involved had, it was held, a certain generality of application. The good honours student would come to an understanding – wide in its application – of the importance of seeking the truth through thick and thin. So that a first class honours degree in almost any single subject indicated something like first class perspicacity, intelligence and scholarly promise. At Oxford the 'Greats' and 'Modern Greats' degrees were in combinations of related subjects but most others were in single subjects. At Cambridge the 'Tripos' system enabled different subjects to be taken for Part I and Part II but each in itself was normally in one field.

By 1950 over 70 per cent of university undergraduates in England and Wales were reading for honours degrees, their final examinations – often taken by means of a series of three-hour written papers in sequence, with a small oral element only – being highly competitive and normally classified into First, Second and Third class Honours, the Second class being divided into a first and second division. The First class was usually kept very small (it amounts to some 6 per cent of those graduating), though usually smaller in arts than in technological or science subjects. By 1962, 86·6 per cent of the undergraduates in the arts and social sciences were proceeding to classified honours degrees in the universities of England and Wales generally[1] and 98·4 per cent at Oxford.[2]

A further inducement to candidates to read for classified honours degrees was the increased number of scholarships available for higher degree work and the growing prestige of research. For no one was normally allowed to go on to study for an M.A., M.Sc., M.Phil. or Ph.D. unless he had already taken a First or a good Second class honours B.A./B.Sc.

The confidence in many universities that the intellectual and academic standard required to gain a 'First' or a 'Second' bachelorship in every subject was approximately the same hardly stood up to test.[3] Nor is it probable that universities were as equal to one another as they liked to

---

[1] *University Development 1957–62*, Table II.
[2] Franks Report, Table 156, Vol. II, p. 176.
[3] cf. C. W. Valentine, *The Reliability of Examinations* 1936 p. 191, and Robbins Report, Appendix 2(A) pp. 150–151.

assume in the standard required for the various classes of honours in the same subjects.

It is to be noted that the English attitude to the classified honours degree even now still has an element of the aristocratic, even perhaps the snobbish, about it – though now the aristocracy concerned is an intellectual, not a social, one. For it is not the reward of hard work only or of sheer knowledge amassed. This is not equally the case in the United States.

American Practice

In the U.S.A., each student during his course for a first degree, which normally lasts four years, takes enough subjects to give him about 120 'semester hours', or 180 'quarter hours', of credit. He gets credit for attending lectures and classes in his assorted subjects – his attendances (in many universities though not all) being recorded – and for doing work in connexion with these. Each course is marked usually by A, B, C, D, E or F grades, and a student must obtain grades of at least an acceptable minimum in each of his subjects if he is to gain his degree. In many State universities entry to college courses is not highly selective and 'drop out' rates in the first and second years of the course are high – sometimes as high as 66 per cent. A student's grade averages form an essential part of his academic record, a transcript of which must be passed on to another university if at some stage or stages of his course he wishes to transfer. In many places it is possible to get a degree *summa cum laude, magna cum laude* and *cum laude*, if one attains the requisite grade average. But these are mainly recognitions at the graduation ceremonies themselves and no stigma attaches to not having such a distinction. Some of those who obtain these distinctions, however, will mention the fact in their letters of application for entry to a graduate school. In a considerable number of colleges the highest academic honour for a graduate in liberal arts is election to the *Phi Beta Kappa* fraternity; this distinction, which is awarded to perhaps 3 per cent of their undergraduates on average, is based primarily on the grades a student earns, though some consideration is given to other qualities.

In the colonial period of university development in America students were sometimes divided during their courses into several categories – at Yale, for example, *optimi*, second *optimi*, *inferiores* and *peiores*; at William and Mary 'first in their class', 'improving respectably', 'making little improvement' and 'learning little'. But such rating scales did not resolve themselves into classes for degrees. Harvard was one of the first universities to provide an honours classification: there, under Lowell, from the 1920s onwards a student could, if he wished, sit for an honours final examination designed to test, not his knowledge of his separate subjects, but the power to see relationships between the parts of his studies

Swarthmore, under Aydelotte in 1922, began to allow students to take honours separately from the pass students if they were considered by their tutors fit to do so. They concentrated their work in a single field. But though some colleges followed their example in these measures, both Harvard and Swarthmore, in encouraging classification at the first degree level, were imitating English practice, not inaugurating a new American tradition which has generally 'taken over'.

The basic American system of first degrees, with its multiplicity of possible offerings and combinations, has more flexibility than the English, but absence of final 'classes' is in accord with the American disinclination overtly to label a man's intellectual attainments. Even the term 'grades' is perhaps less socially conscious or divisive than 'classes of honours'. But in many colleges there is a tendency to work within a fairly fixed range of proportions for the various grades; so that a student can raise his position only at the expense of his fellow students. The emphasis for many tends to be on securing a sufficiency rather than upon excelling. The practice of checking students' attendance at classes and giving them relatively frequent tests are realist devices to ensure that justice is done. But they tend, in general, to put the emphasis on adequacy rather than excellence. There is nothing like the stigma attached to being 'a drop-out' from an American university that there still tends to be for those who fail at any stage during a first degree course in an English university.

In America, more than is yet the case in Britain, there is a sense in which university education proper is postgraduate – with, in many of the better universities, a robust selection of students to be allowed to start upon higher degree courses in spite of there being no categorization into Firsts, Seconds and Thirds. Masters' degrees have been awarded by examination or by thesis in most American universities since the 1870s; but Yale was the first to give a Ph.D., as early as 1861 (compare its intro- duction in English universities only in 1918). It is not possible in the United States to obtain a Master's degree 'with distinction' as it is in a number of British universities, though the Mastership is now very often given, as increasingly in Britain, as a result of passing a written examin- ation – possibly supplemented by an oral test – instead of by thesis. A growing differentiation in some of the most distinguished universities is between the 'terminal' Master's degree and one which is 'on the way' to a Doctorate. The Ph.D. degree itself is very definitely intended to mark out the man who is genuinely knowledgeable in his field, and to be a guarantee of research expertise.

But in the American tradition there is in fact much less attempt than in England to identify an intellectual *élite* as such. The aim rather is to train and underwrite a professional *élite* – made up of those able to serve the community usefully as technologists, scholars and administrators.

The explanation of the lack of desire in the U.S.A. to identify in the English way either a social or an intellectual *élite* is to be sought in the anti-aristocratic strands present in United States society generally and the strong tendency to make a proved capacity for long-maintained, reliable hard work a considerably greater social asset than cleverness. Normality is respected; to get the reputation for being an egghead or a snob can be disastrous either to one's advancement or to any hope of being really trusted. In addition, there is a powerful desire not to classify a man at one stage of his life in a way that might give him either a permanent privilege or a permanent handicap. The emphasis is on the free promise of future achievement rather than upon pride or regret at what has been achieved at an earlier stage.

There are tendencies in American degree-giving practice which may indicate the coming of a more hierarchical pattern. 'What's your current grade-point average?' is an increasingly significant question for the man hoping to get into graduate school. But the course remains the fundamental American unit of educational progress and the predominant emphasis at every stage is upon proving that satisfactory or more than satisfactory work has been done. Little is given in the way of a bonus, as it is in the English classification at first degree level, for showing intellectual power or promise; in America it is realized actuality that counts most.

31

Examinations and the Economy: An African Study[1]

S. H. Irvine
School of Education, University of Ontario

Examinations in Africa have usually served two purposes. They hav signified the end of one phase of education and have also been used as a screen for applicants for the next phase. Only recently have large-scale studies in West Africa (Kane, 1967; Schwarz, 1961, 1963), East Africa (Silvey, 1964; Vernon, 1966) and Central Africa (Heron, 1966; Irvine, 1964, 1965, 1966, 1967) been organized to consider selection apart from certification. Similarly, the work of Ashby and his colleagues (1960), Harbison (1964), Hunter (1963), consultants to Unesco (1961) and the Manpower Survey in Rhodesia (1964) have indicated the primacy of defining economic goals, assessing manpower targets in relation to these goals and planning educational strategies to achieve the targets. Aims and methods of investigation, availability of data and timing of research are seldom close enough for psychologists, economists and educators to work in concert to assess how efficiently examinations meet the declared aims of educational policy. For example, wastage is an accepted phenomenon of manpower planning in the education systems of developing countries. Knowledge of the psychological and social correlates of wastage, especially in the secondary school system, could produce educational strategies to diminish its severe economic effects. In order to be able to assess the consequences of examinations in an interdisciplinary way, at least three basic studies are required: a census, a manpower survey and a scientific investigation of selection systems. Conveniently, three such studies took place in Rhodesia in 1962 before the dissolution of the Central African Federation. The data gathered then and in subsequent years, while following the 1962 end-of-primary-school cohort through the secondary system, are the basis of an empirical study with two main aims:

---

[1] This article was prepared while the author was a United States Public Health Service Visiting Scholar in the Personality and Social Behavior Research Group in 1967–68, while on leave from the University of Bristol. He wishes to thank Miss Susan Koch, who prepared the tables and checked the data, and his colleagues at Educational Testing Service, Princeton, specially Dr. N. Frederiksen, Director of Research.

(*a*) to study the effects of the African school and examination system in relation to the production of high-level manpower;

(*b*) to examine curricular emphasis in examinations at the end of the secondary school in relation to economic needs.

I. Examinations, Wastage, and High-level Manpower

Given the initial entry to a primary school system, it is possible, where all births are registered and school-entry ages are regulated by law, to follow the age-group through the system and estimate how many emerged at the end. But in Africa one cannot state with certainty that any school intake is homogeneous by age because of the backlog of educational provision and uncertainty about ages. It then becomes necessary to estimate the age-range in any output year and the proportions in each age-group. One can then, for a single age-group, estimate the proportion of pupils achieving an educational qualification, provided a population census has been made. Such a procedure, unlike others, takes account of the usual annual increase in provision of places. If one has an agreed lower level of attainment for recognition as high-level manpower (HLMP), then the exercise has valuable extension as a method of estimating unit cost. Unit cost can then be made to vary with strategies of selection and school treatment of individuals selected.

The working out of this model is seen in an example. In 1962, a study was made of selection systems at the end of primary school (eight years of education, called Standard 6) involving African pupils in Rhodesia. Over 1,800 pupils, in the ratio of two boys for every one girl, were sampled from a population of 16,700. The sample yielded good fits for the population by sex, examination results, type of school attended and rural and urban school ratios. We assume for this study that the reported ages of the sample did not differ significantly from those of the population and that the proportions of children in the reported age-groups did not differ over a five-year period. Although the assumptions made are important in evaluating possible sample error in the example given, they do not alter the rationale for using the model to estimate wastage in an age-group. In the sample, proportions of 0·099 were aged seventeen or over, 0·288 were sixteen, 0·311 were fifteen, 0·240 were fourteen and 0·062 were thirteen. Table I shows that these proportions were used to estimate the numbers of children born in the period 1947–48 (averaged out to represent an age-group for one year) who came through the endpoint in the primary school system during the period 1960 to 1964. From records it is possible to estimate proportions of wastage from first to second year of secondary education, and from success ratios at examination points. Records for Standard 6 results in Rhodesia exist from 1928; for Junior Certificate (JC) from 1957; and for Cambridge School Certificate

TABLE I

PROGRESS OF 1947–48 AGE-GROUP TO HIGH-LEVEL MANPOWER (HLMP) LEVEL ALLOWING FOR AGE DISTRIBUTION: RHODESIA 1960–64

Age: born 1947–48	Year	Standard 6			HLMP Pool			HLMP Product		
		Total (000s.)	Est. Prop.	Number (000s.)	Other*	Form 1	Form 2	J.C. Pass	C.S.C. Pass	Other
13	1960	12·0	0·05	0·60	20	130	120	80	30	20
14	1961	14·2	0·25	3·55	110	780	700	490	200	100
15	1962	16·7	0·31	5·34	160	1,140	1,060	740	300	150
16	1963	21·1	0·29	6·12	180	1,350	1,210	850	340	160
17	1964	23·1	0·10	2·31	70	510	460	320	130	60
Total born (000s.) 1947–48		79·5	Standard 6 Pool	17·92	540	3,940	3,550	2,480	1,000	490
Prop. of 1948-born		1.00		0·225	0·007	0·050	0·045	0·031	0·013	0·006
Prop. of Previous Ed. Standard				0·900 Std. 5	0·030 Standard 6	0·220 Standard 6	0·900 Form 1	0·700 Form 2	0·400 Form 2	·003 Std. 6

NOTES: The upper five rows of the table estimate the numbers attaining Junior Certificates for the age-group born in 1947–48. The lower three rows show totals, estimated proportion of the age-group and of the previous educational standard respectively, e.g. 3,940 attain Form 1. This is 0·05 of the age-group and 0·22 of all those reaching Standard 6.

* Teacher-training, technical-training and domestic-science students.

(CSC) from 1948. For example, the Form 1 entry for 1960 to 1964 was calculated at 22 per cent of the previous year's Standard 6 entry. By applying this to the proportion of the age-group estimated in the Standard 6 class for any one year, the number of HLMP students in the age group can be gauged. Wastage between Form 1 and Form 2 is nearly 10 per cent, while the JC pass rate has been held constant at 70 per cent since 1961.

In line with the Manpower Survey's recognition of the African HLMP educational base line in Rhodesia as Form 2, the table shows that the age-group's HLMP product is just on 3,000, adding JC passes to the students who have undergone professional training for two years' post-primary school. The total expenditure on education for African children was, for the ten-year period following 1955, approximately £37 million, and the bulk of this has been on primary education. If one accepts this as a rough total estimate of cost of producing the HLMP for the age-group, the cost is £12,300 per person. Suppose one were to eliminate wastage between Form 1 and Form 2 and produce a further 300 qualified persons, even to the point of subsidizing each of the 500 drop-outs by £100 over the two years and thus increasing costs by £50 thousand. So small is the number of HLMP products that the average cost per person still drops to £11,200, even with a financial subsidy for potential drop-outs.

This strategy assumes that the major component of wastage is lack of money, but it may not always be. Table II opposite shows the results of tests applied to 231 pupils in Standard 6 and Form 1, the local survivors[2] at form 2 of the original 1962 sample. As 291 pupils in Form 1 were tested, this left a cohort of 60 pupils for whom test results at Standard 6 and Form 1 were available but who had not survived to Form 2. A comparison of means for the two groups is presented in Table II below. In the primary school tests, the two groups do not differ significantly except in English tests, favouring the Form 2 group. Clearly, however, they are differentiated at the end of Form 1 in all subjects. The sex ratios in the two cohorts were very close, ruling out sex differences as a factor. The only difference found was in greater proportion of drop-outs who had attended schools of poorer quality. This leads to the most compelling finding of the study, which is discussed in detail below.

However well we may define manpower targets and construct selection devices to screen manpower available to meet these targets, the treatments given to pupils after they have been selected will be as important factors as any. Indeed, selection can be maximally efficient only when treatments are homogeneous. One of the tasks in evaluating the efficiency of selec-

---

[2] We originally identified 329 in Form 1 in schools readily accessible. A further 33 were found outside the region but could not be tested. The proportion of the 1962 sample in Form 1 was 0·195, differing for the population figure of 0·202 for that year by only 0·007.

TABLE II
DIFFERENCE BETWEEN JUNIOR CERTIFICATE AND DROP-OUT GROUPS
RHODESIA 1963–64

	Std. 6 Experimental Tests						Std. 6 Examinations				Ment					Form 1 Tests					
	SNV	SNA	Raven	NB Read	NB Vocab	NB Spell	Eng 1	Eng 2	Arith 1	Arith 2	Arith	HCA	GNS	Total	REC	GK	Eng	Alg	Geom	Arith	Total
SD_c a	2·4	2·4	8·7	2·6	3·4	2·1	5·7	5·3	12·6	15·3	3·0	5·0	4·2	7·0	7·4	11·7	10·3	5·7	9·2	5·1	23·0
SD_w b	2·3	2·9	8·6	2·8	3·6	2·2	6·1	5·2	10·5	13·5	4·3	3·3	4·0	6·6	8·3	10·2	7·8	5·7	9·8	4·8	22·1
M c	18·7	18·6	33·8	13·5	21·9	9·3	30·9	52·3	78·4	56·8	19·0	36·2	36·6	61·3	60·3	46·0	69·6	19·9	33·7	35·8	158·8
M_w d	18·4	18·0	32·0	12·6	20·8	9·0	29·4	50·6	81·0	59·8	18·3	35·4	36·2	60·5	59·2	44·2	63·8	16·8	30·1	33·8	144·4
$\lvert D_{c-w}\rvert$ e	0·3	0·6	1·8	0·9	1·1	0·3	1·5	1·7	2·6	3·0	0·7	0·8	0·4	0·8	1·1	1·8	5·8	3·1	3·6	2·0	14·4
t f	0·86	1·42	1·39	2·17	2·06	0·92	1·66	2·17	−1·58	−1·44	1·44	1·20	0·66	0·80	0·90	1·14	4·64	3·62	2·48	2·74	4·31
sign† g	NS	NS	NS	S	S	NS	NS	S	NS	NS	NS	NS	NS	NS	NS	NS	SSS	SSS	S	SS	SSS

NOTES: Rows a and b give standard deviations of tests, c and d contain the mean scores for the certificate and wastage groups and e, f, g, reflectively the differences t and significance levels for each test respectively.

* Significance: NS p > 0·05; S p < 0·05 > 0·01; SS p < 0·01 > 0·001; SSS p < 0·001.
Abbreviations: For full details see Irvine (1965).

*SNV—Spiral Nines Verbal Ability
*SNA—Spiral Nines Abstract Ability
Raven—Raven's 1938
*NB Read—Normal Battery Reading
*NB Vocab—Normal Battery Vocabulary
*NB Spell—Normal Battery Spelling

Eng 1—English Composition
Eng 2—English Usage
Arith 1—Arithmetic Processes (Mechanical)
Arith 2—Arithmetic Problems
Ment Arith—Mental Arithmetic
HCA—History and Current Affairs
GNS—Geography and Nature Study
Total—Total of Std. 6 Tests
REC—Scaled Headmaster's Estimate

GK—General Knowledge
Eng—English Usage and Comprehension
Alg—Algebra
Geom—Geometry
Arith—Arithmetic Processes and Problems

*Supplied by N.I.P.R. Johannesburg.

tion systems is to assess the influence of school differences on individual differences. To complete such a task, an estimate of school efficiency in passing examinations over a period of time is necessary as well as some estimate of individual differences prior to entry at any one point in time. Previous work by Irvine (1965) had shown a correlation between school quality and individual achievement in criterion tests to be in the region of 0·4, but more detailed evidence became available after the institution, in 1963, of grades of certificates awarded at the end of primary school. These grades were used to select African pupils in Rhodesia for places in the secondary schools. There were five grades in all, of which the first three contained approximately 11, 14 and 18 per cent of all the Standard 6 students. Two years later the students took the Junior Certificate examination and it was possible to relate the grades awarded in the primary school in 1963 to their success or failure in that Form 2 examination in 1965.

It was also possible to trace the success of schools in gaining Junior Certificate passes in the years 1963 and 1964. The rank correlation between percentage passes gained by the schools for these two years was 0·71, suggesting a definite and persistent table of school success ratios. There were 39 schools in all and examination of the scatterplot of percentage passes for the two years showed that three main groups of schools emerged, categorized as follows:

Grade A Schools—Single-sex, denominational boarding schools built on Crown Land with long-serving staff, offering four-year courses.

Grade B Schools—Schools, mainly boarding, sharing some of the characteristics of the A schools, but including non-denominational government schools and schools in small urban centres.

Grade C Schools—Schools either in large urban areas or on European farm land, non-boarding and mixed-sex with a high proportion of staff with short terms of service in these schools.

On the basis of these findings, schools were classified for 1965, before the examination results were known, on the hypothesis that there would be a continuing relationship between school type and examination success. A table of probabilities of Junior Certificate success for school types and individual primary certificate grades was constructed when the results were available. Table III shows the combined effects of school quality and individual differences on Junior Certificate success.

The most immediate finding is the relative lack of success of students rated in the top 11 per cent of the Standard 6 examinees, who go to Type C schools where the probability of passing Junior Certificate is 0·54. Their lack of success is all the more startling when compared with the success of students who were awarded Grade 3 certificates but went to

TABLE III

PROBABILITIES OF SUCCESS (P_s) IN JUNIOR CERTIFICATE BY SECONDARY
SCHOOL TYPE AND PRIMARY GRADES (RHODESIA 1965)

School Type	1963 Standard 6 Grades			
	Div. 1	Div. 2	Div. 3	Total
Type A	0·914 (446)	0·875 (223)	0·895 (64)	0·900 (733)
Type B	0·846 (301)	0·718 (312)	0·608 (138)	0·749 (751)
Type C	0·543 (173)	0·335 (206)	0·265 (165)	0·380 (544)
Total	0·822 (920)	0·659 (741)	0·504 (367)	0·705 (2028)

Ratio of success over schools and individuals $P_s = 0·705$
Over all schools for Div. 1 and Div. 2 pupils $P_s = 0·749$
Over all pupils for Type A and Type B schools $P_s = 0·824$
Over pupils in Div. 1 and 2 and school Types A and B $P_s = 0·844$

Type A and B schools. This confirms the writer's (1966) hypothesis that individual differences can be largely overlaid in developing countries by different school treatments. The differences in probability of success within school types for different grades of entry are far less than differences between schools for the same grade of entry. In terms of probabilities, between-school differences are at least twice as large as within-school differences. Table III shows what would happen if both entry of pupils and types of schools were regulated. The pass rate for the population at Junior Certificate is 0·70. If entry were restricted to Grade 1 and 2 passes at Standard 6 level and the students were sent to all types of schools, the probability of success would rise to 0·75. If one allowed all of Grades 1, 2 and 3 to proceed only to schools of Types A and B, then the probability would rise to 0·82. This means that, for this sample, increasing the strictness of the selection ratio would have half the effect of ensuring treatments of Types A and B for all those within the presently represented range of ability.[3] If we combined these effects of selection and treatment,

---

[3] The psychologist will note that the regression lines for the correlation between Standard 6 results and the pass/fail criterion at Junior Certificate will differ in slope for the three major school types. There is virtually no correlation in Type A, a small correlation in Types B and C where individual differences probably exert most influence in a relatively adverse environment.

then one could expect a pass rate of 84 per cent in Junior Certificate compared with 70 per cent at present. These proportions, to revert for a moment to the cost of producing HLMP, can readily be combined with the figures in Table I to produce a cost-efficiency index for different strategies of selection and treatment.

The results presented above lead to the following general conclusions about the effect of selection examinations on the production of HLMP.

(1) In African countries, emphasis on primary education with a large wastage component produces a great majority of people who are employed in the economy below the minimum HLMP education requirement. From an economic point of view the return for the investment must be regarded as limited.

(2) Those who reach HLMP level do so at very high relative cost.

(3) The drop-out in secondary schools is an extremely critical factor in assessing the overall HLMP cost; and an important step is to eliminate wastage as completely as possible until students gain the minimum HLMP qualifications. If this means financial subsidy, then that is some evidence to show that at the secondary stage an increase in costs over a small number of students actually reduces overall costs.

(4) Although selection systems are valuable, their effectiveness in reducing wastage due to misallocation of pupils is nullified by systems where large differences in school treatments are found.

These conclusions lead to the formulation of a tentative strategy for maximizing HLMP production in secondary-school systems such as the one under review. The priorities appear to be: (a) reduction of wastage by every possible means; (b) upgrading of schools by in-service training for teachers and improvements in school facilities, such as study halls and subsidized meals if necessary; and (c) improvements in selection systems.

Finally, examinations are seen in this context as arbiters of economic investment in human resources. Universal primary education is a severe strain on the economics of such investment because so few are left from an age-group to provide the economic growth point for the vast majority who participate in the economy as if their educational skills had never existed. Each examination is a barrier that is erected essentially on foundations that are academic and intellectual. It would seem essential that examinations should in some respects demand from the population skills that were to be realistically related to the ecology of man in his environment. A qualitative assessment of examination trends forms the second part of this paper.

II. Values, Examinations and Economic Goals

Examinations at the end of secondary education represent the formal educational skills that pupils in the HLMP group carry with them into the economy. The study of a country's examination system from a curricular viewpoint then gives the information necessary to evaluate the outcome of education in relation to economic goals. There has been a continuing insistence in both colonial and post-colonial eras that the transmission of skills in schools should be directly related to environmental conditions and economic targets. Since the days of the Phelps-Stokes reports, agricultural and technical skills have been particularly emphasized for African countries with a primary-product economy and which seek to develop self-sustaining secondary industries. Rhodesia is a good example of such countries, being primarily agricultural, with some mining, and with a modest secondary consumer product economy. Moreover, the insistence on education related to community needs has been a feature of reports and commissions of inquiry in education since the first official report appeared in 1925. In spite of this emphasis, the actual entries by African students for subjects in the Cambridge School Certificate examination show an interesting order of popularity. Table IV shows these subjects' entries and the percentage passes at 'O' level for the years 1965 and 1966 and gives the rank orders of entries and passes. The compulsory English-language paper comes first, followed by the informational subjects.

Readers familiar with examination entries in Britain for the same examination will note the similarity in the patterns for Rhodesia. To account for the similarity in terms of the ease with which one can teach certain subjects by chalk and talk methods and a few textbooks (essentially a cost criterion) compared with the difficulty of providing equipment for technical orientation, is not sufficient. For example, the studies of occupational prestige carried out by Mitchell and Epstein (1959), Mitchell and Irvine (1966) and Hicks (1967), in central Africa, show a great similarity in the ranking of occupations among African groups and between African and European groups. Those requiring evidence of continuous formal education are valued highly. Those of a technical and agricultural nature tend to be ranked low.

The writer carried out a 'utility' study of school subjects[4] and the rank order of utility has been related to the rank order of popularity for the Rhodesia Cambridge School Certificate entry. The results are in Table IV, and the correlation is 0·61. The studies of prestige and utility seem together to indicate a strong tendency towards a value system operating among cultures that place high esteem on achieved status based on formal education. There is little evidence to show that material economic needs or policy statements expounding them have much effect on what students study and why they study.

---

[4] An inventory of school subjects was listed and Likert five-choice scales of utility were completed for each school subject by 346 African students in the Copperbelt of Zambia.

TABLE IV

SUBJECT ENROLMENT AND PASSES ON THE AFRICAN CAMBRIDGE STANDARD
EXAMINATION: RHODESIA 1965–66

Subjects	Enrolment				% Passes				Combined 1965–66			
	1965	rank	1966	rank	1965	rank	1966	rank	pass rank	entry rank	entry rank	util-ity*
Eng. Language	895	1	1,028	1	66	6	51	15·5	10	1	1	2
Eng. Lit.	710	4	896	3	57	9·5	65	7·5	8	3	—	—
Shona	598	7	692	6	57	9·5	53	14	13	6	5	5
Latin	354	9	315	9	39	15	50	17·5	16	9	8	13
Zulu	141	11	127	14	51	13	58	11	14	12	—	—
French	51	15·5	132	13	20	21	24	20·5	21	14	14	14
History	794	2	904	2	58	8	61	10	9	2	2	9
Geography	674	5	785	5	75	3	65	7·5	4	5	4	8
Bible Knowledge	561	8	667	7	60	7	70	3	5	8	7	4
Biology	147	10	279	10	72	4·5	69	5	3	10	—	—
Health Science	92	13	146	12	42	14	85	1·5	7	13	9	1
Mathematics	747	3	856	4	55	11	56	12·5	12	4	3	3
Gen. Science	608	6	658	8	79	2	85	1·5	1	7	6	6
Add. Gen. Science	86	14	43	18	35	16	22	22	20	15	—	—
Physics	14	21·5	48	16·5	93	1	69	5	2	20	—	—
Chemistry	33	18	78	15	72	4·5	56	12·5	6	16	—	—
Add. Math.	51	15·5	31	20	24	21	42	19	19	18	—	—
Physics with Chem.	138	12	161	11	54	12	62	9	11	11	—	—
Woodwork	42	17	48	16·5	33	17	69	5	15	17	10	7
Needlework	32	19	41	19	31	18	51	15·5	17	19	11	10
Art	15	20	17	21	13	22	24	20·5	22	21	12	12
Metalwork	14	21·5	12	22	29	19	50	17·5	18	22	13	11
Spearman ρ	ρ = 0·95				ρ = 0·64				ρ = 0·45	ρ = 0·61		

* Utility as determined from Zambia Utility Study conducted in 1960.

Clearly, the examination system could become a tool for change. Just as
some West African countries have removed the English-language pass
criterion for University entry, so others could insist that certain subjects
deemed to be in the economic interest should be compulsory, or at least
elective. The educator shrinks from this as a denial of the student's
personal expression, based on an economic touchstone of educational
propriety. Nevertheless, there are ways in which choice can be exercised
within electives from groups of subjects that would do as little or as much
harm as being asked to choose, for example, between either German and
French or Physics and Chemistry – but not between German and
Chemistry, since the timetable and teachers cannot be stretched that far.
But the government that wills such changes must also will the means,

namely, equipment for teaching technical skills and opportunity to exercise them out of school in an expanding economy. For example, in 1966, the *de facto* Rhodesian administration announced a plan to expand secondary education to include 50 per cent of all primary leavers, of whom three-quarters would have an 'ecological' form of secondary education, the remainder to have an academic course. In 1967,[5] a follow-up of 342 Form 4 1966 African school leavers showed, from 272 returns, that 113 were students in tertiary education, 120 were unemployed, and only 39 were earning in the economy. It is also virtually impossible for African boys to be accepted as apprentices after Form 2, because of strong traditional resistance from the white trade unions. Hence, policies alone will produce little unless the economy can absorb educational output, although there are historical examples of educational overproduction being absorbed in emigration. However, Africa hardly seems ready for such mobility at technician and sub-professional levels. There are instances of the movement of educated Africans outside their language areas arousing resentment, rivalry and tribal hatreds that education has singularly failed to diminish. Examinations, in a sense, represent a microcosmic system of values and it seems, in African context, that the values represented are often in direct conflict with those of economic necessity. If one rejects economic necessity as a touchstone, then one must look to a general education as the base for future specialization, and some may consider an early vocational orientation in secondary education to be essential for developing nations where time seems short.

Summary

The whole of this paper suggests that the economies of many developing countries are bearing a very severe burden because of the amounts being spent on primary education in relation to the numbers effectively in use at HLMP level. Examinations, the arbiters, may not be wholly effective in producing educational efficiency by homogenizing groups of students for maximum success. A great deal of their success seems to depend on school quality and wastage is severe. Secondary examinations seem to produce entry patterns that are consistent with a highly diversified economy in a typical developed country, but are inconsistent with policy statements for Africa, and other developing nations. This anomaly is hypothesized as mainly due to the emergence of a sytem of educational values that will doubtless lead to conflict between student aspirations and the policy of governments that might wish, on economic grounds, to use examinations as a tool for curricular change.

---

[5] Approximately one-third of the national output in 1966.

BIBLIOGRAPHY

Ashby, E. *et al.* (1960) *Investment in Education.* (Lagos, Nigeria: Govt. Printer).

Harbison, F., and Myers, C. (1964) *Education, Manpower and Economic Growth.* (New York: McGraw-Hill).

Heron, A. (1966) 'Experimental studies of mental development in conditions of rapid cultural change'. *Proc. XVIII Int. Congress Psychology*, Symposium 36, Moscow.

Hicks, R. E. (1967) 'Similarities and differences in occupational prestige ratings'. *African Soc. Res.*, **3**, 206–207.

Hunter, G. (1963) *Education for a Developing Region.* (London: Allen and Unwin).

Irvine, S. H. (1964) 'Ability testing in English-speaking Africa: an overview of predictive and comparative studies'. *Rhodes-Livingstone J.*, **34**, 44–55.

Irvine, S. H. (1965) *Selection for Secondary Education in S. Rhodesia.* Faculty Paper No. 4. (Salisbury: U.C.R.N.).

Irvine, S. H. (1966) 'Towards a rationale for testing abilities and attainments in Africa'. *Brit. J. Educ. Psychol.*, **36**, 24–32.

Irvine, S. H. (1967) 'A four-year follow-up of secondary school selection procedures in Central Africa'. *Proc. Int. Conference on Educ. Testing*, Pädagogisches Zentrum Berlin.

Irvine, S. H., MacArthur, R. S., and Brimble, A. R. (1964) *The Northern Rhodesia Mental Ability Survey.* (Lusaka, Zambia: Inst. for Soc. Res.).

Irvine, S. H., and Mitchell, J. C. (1966) 'Social position and the grading of occupations'. *Rhodes-Livingstone J.*, **38**, 42–54.

Kane, G. (1967) 'Tests of Selection for Secondary Schools in Mali'. *Proc. Int. Conference on Educ. Testing*, Pëdagogisches Zentrum, Berlin.

Mitchell, J. C., and Epstein, A. L. (1959) 'Occupational prestige and social status among Africans in Northern Rhodesia'. *Africa*, **29**, 22–40.

Rhodesia (1964) *Final Report of the April/May 1962 census of Africans in S. Rhodesia.* (Salisbury: Govt. Printer).

Schwarz, P. (1961) *Aptitude Tests for Developing Nations.* (Pittsburgh: American Institute for Research).

Schwarz, P. (1963) 'Adapting tests to the cultural setting'. *Ed. Psych. Measmt.*, **23**, 673–686.

Silvey, J. (1964) *Selection for Secondary Schools in Uganda.* (Kampala, Uganda: E.A.I.S.R.).

Unesco (1961) *Final Report of Conference of African States on Education in Africa.* (Paris: Unesco).

University College (1964) *The Requirements and Supplies of HLMP in S. Rhodesia 1961–1970.* Occasional Paper No. 3. (Salisbury: U.C.R.N., Dept. of Economics).

Vernon, P. E. (1966) *Selection to Secondary Schools in Tanzania.* Unpublished Report to Tanzania Ministry of Education.

32

Japan's Academic Career-Cult

Shuji Wada
Assistant Professor, Faculty of Education, Kyoto University

Educational Changes in Post-war Japan

In the course of the democratization of post-war Japan carried out under the American occupation, the former European type of school system was re-formed on the model of the American '6–4–4 single-track system'. The most radical change took place in higher education; *teikoku-daigaku* (Imperial University), fifteenth through seventeenth years of education and *kōtōgakkō* (university preparatory higher school), twelfth through fourteenth years, were abolished on the pretext of their being highly exclusive institutions for the privileged few. All post-secondary and higher educational institutions of different character and origin were rather mechanically combined and raised to *daigaku* status, thirteenth through sixteenth years, legally equal to the pre-war university. As a result, the quantitative development of secondary and higher education has been remarkable along with the economic development of the country; Japan has now 369 four-year *daigaku* and 451 two-year *tandai* (junior college) and in 1967 the percentage of the entrants to the upper secondary schools by age-group was 74·5 per cent, and 23·6 per cent to university and college.

But many new *daigaku* have expanded so rapidly without proper facilities and followed the administrative and instructional practices of the pre-war university that they betray their weakness and have lost their own characteristics and reputation. In addition, 70 per cent of *daigaku* are private and as they are largely financed by tuition and entrance examination fees, they very often admit large numbers of students beyond their educational capacity. On the other hand, the beautiful slogan of 'equal opportunity in education' was interpreted as easy promotion to higher institutions, and the single-track system gradually began to aim the whole of education towards university preparatory goals, pushing vocational courses and schools into the shade. These circumstances helped a few of the old government universities to stand higher in public estimation and make their entrance examinations even harder.

It is difficult to understand why such fanatical concentration on university entrance came from this system unless we know the history of the *élite* and of the position of the school in Japan. The most popular interpretation of present confusions in Japan is based on the idea of incompleteness or of lag in modernization supposedly caused by such remnants of past 'feudalistic' society as authoritarianism, hierarchy and 'face-morality' – all lacking an inner sense of individual responsibility. But this is not entirely true if we consider Japanese feudalism according to the concepts of those in Europe or of primitive caste-society.

Some Characteristics of Japanese Feudal Society

It is true that Japan was an isolated, feudalistic class-society governed by the military class (*samurai* or *bushi*) for almost three centuries. But we must not overlook the fact that her feudalism was not during times of war, but in peacetime. Moreover, before that time, in the fifteenth and sixteenth centuries, Japan had experienced periods of ambition, adventure and power, and of great upheaval. Those who could govern and win admiration and devotion from the public in these times of deep uncertainty had to have moral superiority besides mere military power. So originated the relation between leaders and subjects in terms of personal solidarity and mutual trust in an existential situation. Hence, the ideal of the *samurai* was solely to be a reliable person, honest, upright, and the keeping of promises became their creed. So-called *giri* was not a matter of reluctant conventional submission, but of deep sympathy and loyalty towards persons or the community who trusted them. As they highly appreciated purity of mind divorced from self-interest, they valued righteousness and fairness in judgement, thoughtfulness and courtesy even to their opponents. In this sense, the way of *samurai* (*bushi-dō*) was not a mere glorification of power and bravery, but a maintaining of dignity and self-respect as a responsible person in daily life.

After the restoration of peace and the establishment of the feudal caste-system in the seventeenth century, the *samurai* class lost its meaning as a military power and they were required to be more moralistic and rational under the influence of Confucianism, which was the moral bulwark against which the Tokugawa Shogunate justified its reign. In Confucian ideas, class distinctions were based on grades in morality, governing could only be legitimate in so far as it was reasonable, and the governor needed to discipline himself and his family, to abstain from dissipation, and to cultivate virtue before he could rule others. Thus the *samurai* gradually turned into non-militaristic, well-organized, disciplined, administrative officialdom, but became powerless in actual life because of their complete inability with regard to productive labour. On the other hand townsmen (*chōnin*) took the leadership in social and cultural life by the middle of the seventeenth century and those among the *samurai* who were drawn to arts and sciences were delighted to admire and learn from scholars and artists of the town. Especially, in the eighteenth century, among the lower-class *samurai* whose living conditions were no different from the common people and who could communicate and live together with them at ease, there came to exist a kind of ex-caste intellectual society including the *samurai*, the *chōnin*, priests, doctors and village-headmen.

Love of Learning

In many respects, feudal Japan was different from other class-societies. Whether the *samurai* could be equated as the privileged class corresponding to European nobility is a question. Their numbers including their families came to nearly 10 per cent of the total population, and a majority of them were, as a matter of course, not well off. More than that, we should remember their special respect for morality and learning. After the middle of the Tokugawa Period, the feudal system met many difficulties associated with gradual changes in economic and social life, and the Shogunate and clan-governments became eager to find men of talent and so established schools for their youth to cope with their increasing problems. Interest towards the practical arts and realistic knowledge including Western sciences (termed *rangaku*) grew slowly. Being menaced by the intrusion of Western Powers in the East, their educational concerns were accelerated; by 1830 there were no clans without a school and clan-government schools for *samurai* youth (*hankō*) established during the Edo period numbered 223, some of which were opened to the public towards the last days of the Shogunate. In 1856 the Shogunate called the competent *rangaku* scholars together and founded the first national institute for Western learning, the predecessor of Tokyo Imperial University, the present University of Tokyo.

This training and the cultural background of the governing class proved to be a great boon to Japan when she had to open herself to the world later. Modern industrial society demands men of rational thinking, with planning and organizing faculties, and the spirit of free enterprise, which were certainly unfamiliar to the common people of a closed, static, conventional, agricultural society. Fortunately, Japan could foster modern industry making good use of the ex-*samurai* class who lost their place but also set themselves free from the taboo of profit-making by the fall of the *ancien régime* in 1868. In order to survive and take an active part in the changing society, they rushed to the newly established higher institutions to get the key to the new civilization, knowledge. The percentage of ex-*samurai* students at the University of Tokyo in 1878 was 75·5 per cent which shows their great concern for learning at that time.

Although merchants, artisans and peasants had to work under the *samurai*, they were never entirely abject slaves. If a man had been excellent enough, whether a carpenter or a theatre-player, he could win high respect as a master from the public, for it was believed that any human work – improving one's fencing technique or celebrating the tea ceremony – could be equally a way to the Absolute as far as it was ultimately concerned and done by both heart and soul. This idea of transcendence and the lack of mobility in social classes helped them to concentrate their energies on refining their work, and made them loyal and diligent in their calling. Concerning education for commoners' children, temple schools (*terakoya*) and other private schools had developed all over the country and enjoyed considerable public support. It is said that in 1873, 1,128 *terakoya* existed in Tokyo alone.

Appearence of Academic Career-Cult

Such being the case, Japan already had rich human resources for morally inspired, progressive leadership and fairly literate, diligent labour power at the threshold of modernization, and it could be said that Japan's rapid progress was made by the astute use of her feudal tradition, especially the love of learning among the people. For securing national independence, the Meiji Government endeavoured to catch up with advanced Western countries by introducing Western science and technology as well as Western institutions. In 1872, the first national education system was initiated and higher education was opened to all the people for a broad development of national leaders. As modern education in Japan was very practical and centralized under the national plan, the graduate of higher institutions was naturally able to progress to the higher positions of state. Moreover, the utilitarian philosophy emphasizing development of human abilities as essential to economic and social improvement, advocated by leading spirits like Yukichi Fukuzawa, encouraged many parents to educate their children and send them to the university which seemed to the average person an opening to all honours and privileges they could never have in the past. As early as 1881, students from among the commoners accounted for half of the total enrolment at the University of Tokyo. In fact, in Japan schooling has functioned effectively as a pipeline to social mobility. At the time of writing 37 per cent of political, 24 per cent of business, 18 per cent of the top academic and cultural *élite* in Japan are from the former farming class, and 90 per cent of the entire leading *élite* appearing in the Japanese equivalent of *Who's Who* are university or college graduates, of whom a third are graduates of the University of Tokyo. Generally speaking, modern Japanese schools developed along the lines of *hankō* in character and were open and egalitarian during compulsory education.

As a necessary component in the process of a hurried Westernization, both the Meiji Government and the public held a common faith that knowledge is power and education is the best investment. This insatiable thirst for knowledge and education on a national scale has no doubt produced Japan's amazing industrial and economic development, and still continues to produce this effect. But, however ready Japan was for modernization, the fact that it was begun by foreign initiative led to the deterioration of its later development. Modern Japan has always kept the West as her ideal and tried so hard to catch up to this 'complete' model that she failed to consider herself. The more Japan became Westernized, the more she forgot herself, while her traditional foundation rapidly degenerated. The unconscious conflict with the departed past began to bend her course when she was commonly acknowledged as a modern powerful state in the world through the Russo-Japanese War and World War I. The appreciation of loyalty and diligence certainly inspired organizations and strengthened productivity a great deal, but after establishment of a bureaucracy, it transmuted to the custom of life-engagement in a firm or an enterprise and promotion through long service, which decreases the opportunity of moving upward by means of merit and endeavour. The initial engagement and ranking for employment in most avenues practically determines the final position where one's career will end. Here the nation-wide fanatical concentration on academic careers – more exactly, on admission to better universities, appears as the only and major competition of one's life. By concentrating on the education of their children, parents became more selfish and short-sighted for 'their share at the trough' and less interested in commitment to the advancement of the commonwealth, which at least was a common purpose of the people in the Meiji era. After the tragic reaction of super-nationalism and its disastrous fall in World War II, this current produced radical egalitarianism and uniformity of education under the decentralization policy of the American occupation.

It could be said that the present confusions of Japan are not all necessarily the fault of feudal society itself, but largely come from her rapid Westernization without regard to her own traditional background. The common people loved learning, but modern schools and education were not an indigenous development, but were set up as complete, but foreign, models to which the nation ought to adjust as fast as possible. It is no wonder that in the process Japan formed an authoritative, standardized attitude towards education and formed the habit of using much of her energy and diligence for learning and receiving other patterns and institutions instead of creating her own.

We might indeed say that this habit is not very recent, but rather a distinguishing national trait strongly connected with the geographical situation of Japan as an isolated, insular country. Fortunately or unfortunately, the Japanese had never been under foreign occupation until 1945, so they were far less suspicious towards foreign influences and had a poorly developed sense of national community. For a long time, Japan had

TABLE I

ENTRANCE EXAMINATIONS IN JAPAN*

Purpose of examination	Description of examination at present	Age at which normally taken	Extent used	Contemplated Changes	Testing organizations
1 Testing for selection to Upper Secondary Education	Achievement test (3 to 9 subjects) Reports from lower secondary school physical examination	15	Widely	Reducing examination subjects to 3 (Japanese, mathematics, English)	Each establishing body (private, municipal, prefectural, national)
Higher Education	Scholastic examination (generally includes 5 subjects) Reports from upper secondary school physical examination	18	Widely	Introducing recommendation from upper secondary school principal for the very able. Nōken Test	Each university and college (private, municipal, prefectural, national)
Graduate Studies	Scholastic examination interview; college graduate thesis (occasionally)	22 and older	Widely		Each graduate institution (private, municipal, prefectural, national)
2 Testing for educational standards	Certificate for comparable scholastic attainment for college candidates	18 and older	Rare		Ministry of Education
3 Testing for information	Nōken Test (scholastic aptitude and achievement)	17 or 18	Not widespread†		Educational Test Research Institute

* Though private schools and experimental schools attached to National Teachers' Colleges are often selective at the age of 6 or 12, they are not mentioned here because of their small weight in compulsory education; the percentage of private school pupils is 0·5 per cent at elementary, and 2·9 per cent at lower secondary level in 1966.

† Not popular and has become a political issue.

to understand the foreign world only through the images of imported luxuries, so that they easily idolized it and sacrificed themselves to adopt it. Nevertheless, they did not notice that their ideal foreign world was but, in effect, the product of their own idealism. Japan should now learn to know her own place after contact with the diversity of the West and after 100 years of rapid Westernization.

33

The Examination Stranglehold in India

K. C. Mukherjee

Lecturer in Comparative Education, University of London Institute of Education

The major universities of India were founded over a century ago on the model of the University of London. When the three universities of Bombay, Calcutta and Madras were founded in 1857, an entrance examination became prevalent as a gateway to the university. Students could only get into the three universities after passing the entrance examination which was later changed into Matriculation and School Certificate Examination. The universities became primarily examining bodies; their main function was to conduct examinations. Teaching was started later and research was conducted still later. Besides the entrance examinations, the main universities also held various other kinds of examinations throughout the year, mainly between March and June and again in October. One of the largest sources of income for the universities was derived from examination fees.

From the beginning, the examination system became very rigid and strict. The results of the Calcutta University were most criticized. In the entrance examination of 1858 in Calcutta 66 per cent of the candidates were unsuccessful. In the same year in the same university 85 per cent of students failed in the B.A. examination. Some universities took pride in the fact that the percentage of success of their students had been very low. Thus they boasted of the strictness of their examination.

While it may be argued that a university which fails a large number of students raises the standard and prestige of its examination, it also shows that their teaching standards are deficient. The existence of a high rate of failure of examinees should be a matter of educational concern rather than pride, as is shown in many Indian universities, because it is conducive to a great national wastage of the human and financial resources of an underdeveloped country.

From 1902 the examination system has been the constant target of severe criticism and was recognized as one of the worst features of Indian education. Even from as early as 1881, some commission reports and studies have pointed out the abuses of examinations. Teachers, students and educationists alike have complained that examinations have become the sole aim of education. All instruction is subordinated to examinations, extinguishing all initiative in the students. Indian examinations, it has been said, are 'capricious, invalid, unreliable and inadequate' and 'tend to corrupt the moral standards of university life'. The student's sole aim has been to pass the examination and to get the stamp of success from the universities. Indeed, Indian markets and bookshops are flooded with 'notebooks' and 'question and answer books'. Even the names given to notebooks, e.g. *Short Cut to Success, Sure Pass, Made Easy, Touch and Pass*, explain the corrupt standards of examinations.

The University Education Commission (1949) was convinced that the most urgent single reform in university education in India should be the examination system. The deficiencies and harmful consequences of this evil in Indian education have been clearly understood for a long time but unfortunately the character of the examination in India has remained unchanged for the last fifty years.

Examinations rightly designed and intelligently used can be a useful factor in the educational process. But in India, where reform is most urgent, the system has remained unchanged for many years. Nor is there much evidence of that willingness to undertake reform which is exhibited in other countries where the defects of the system are less great.

Fortunately there has been a wealth of research on testing measurement and evaluation done in Western countries. The West's objective of testing intelligence and aptitude could be modified and adapted to reform the age-old system of examinations in India. The University Education Commission made detailed suggestions for conditions of a good examination. Among these are various kinds of tests: intelligence and achievement tests, aids in selection and counselling of students, tests as aids to the teacher and as checks on quality of work, 'half-mark attainment', recommendations regarding objective examinations and for the correction of evils now existing in the examination system, with a warning that 'without these there is danger that India's higher education will fall into chaos'!

The high priority given to the examination, plus the overcrowding of classes, lower the standard of the teaching. Lecturing too frequently takes the form of reading, at dictation speed, from a textbook, or the giving out of set answers to set questions – and frequently, when students sitting for the examination find the answers they learned by rote do not tally with the questions on the paper, they walk out *en masse*, declaring that the paper is 'too stiff'.

It is too easy to lose patience with Indian university students, but, for the majority, their condition is tragic. A vice-chancellor of an Indian university recently wrote 'The sleepless nights they spend on the eve of the examination often have disastrous consequences on their health as well as on their performances at the examination. Many are unable to stand the physical and mental strain that last-minute efforts involve and either fall ill at the time of the examination or get confused in the examination hall'. Nowhere in the world do so many students adopt various malpractices as they do in India. Mr. S. R. Dongerkery, Vice-Chancellor of the Marathwada University, said 'In spite of the penalties by way of rustication of students for a period and cancellation of their results which the University imposes on students found guilty of malpractices at its examinations, the instances of such malpractices do not show any tendency to decrease. The malpractices assume various forms and disclose ingenuity on the part of the erring student which is worthy of a better cause.'

The University Education Commission rightly said that the chief purpose of the present examinations is not organically related to the actual process of education. They are a means whereby a hallmark of competence is given which employers, public and private, may recognize as a more or less reliable indication of the possession of a certain intellectual and, perhaps, moral quality and of certain types of knowledge and skill. A B.A. or M.A. degree is a kind of passport for jobs.

With the current economic crisis, economic pressure exists with extreme poverty. As a result, the insistence on a university degree as the minimum requirement even for minor posts of a clerical nature has put a premium on a number of evils which have come to be related to the examination system. It has subjected teaching to examinations, thus making it virtually impossible to provide true education and to develop genuine interest in expanding educational horizons and has created temptations to cheating, corruption and favouritism. The obsession to obtain, by hook or by crook, as it were, a ticket in the lottery of job-securing has overshadowed the good aims and purposes of education which a good examination should aim at.

In India there is today an all-embracing influence of the examination. Social prestige also increases with the passing of examinations. Even the values of the future brides and bridegrooms increase in the marriage market to a great extent. The possession of a degree determines the social, matrimonial and financial prestige of young Indians. The following advertisements from the recent 'matrimonial' columns of Indian dailies make it evident!

(1) Rich parents of a B.A. handsome boy of 27 with flourishing business want beautiful slim B.A. bride from a good family. Correspond Box . . . Calcutta.

(2) Wanted a suitable Bengali match for a Ghosh Kulin girl of 23 years with an M.A. degree. Apply Box . . . .

(3) Wanted a suitable match for a Sindhi doctor. Doctor preferred but an M.A. degree in English will be considered. Apply with photo. Box . . . Madras.

(4) Wanted a vegetarian match for a Brahmin girl with a first class M.A. in Sanskrit. Apply with photo to Box . . . Allahabad.

It is needless to write that examinations should be designed chiefly with educational ends in view. The introduction of a sound system of examination with the necessary modification and adaptation will prove a great boon to Indian education.

34

Examinations as a Determinant of National Development

Iraj Ayman

Professor of Psychology and Director, Institute for Educational Research and Studies, National Teachers College, Tehran

Although examinations have combined educational and social effects, in Iran for many centuries it was the social significance of examinations which was more prominent. As far as educational objectives are concerned, examinations are conducted for the assessment of competence, achievement, and individual differences. They have other educational advantages, and can be used as a teaching device or as a regulatory or disciplinary measure. The social effects of examinations also are varied and numerous. They can be regarded as a measure of distinction, and they can cause either setbacks or accelerations in individuals as well as social progress. Strangely enough, they can also be used as a social motivational factor. Historically, in Iran, it has always been the social effects of examinations which in one way or another have been pronounced in society.[1]

Examinations can serve as a factor shaping or limiting the rate of social change and progress. In a way, they are regulating the pace of development. From the point of view of economic or of human development, we can see that manpower training and utilization is a decisive factor. What is manpower development other than individuals going through an educational or training process? The main characteristic of such a process which makes it organized, systematic, and relates it to its purpose is a carefully spaced set of examinations. In other words, we require people to take certain examinations in order to prove that they are qualified for assuming certain responsibilities or performing certain jobs. On the basis of such examinations we divide the work to be done according to the manpower available. This classification of manpower and classification of work determines the pace and even the direction of any social or economical development project. Therefore, no matter whether we are interested in keeping the *status quo* or in introducing certain changes, we always limit our operations to the type, nature and variety of examinations. This has been the social role of examinations in Iran.

---

[1] Issa Sadigh, *A History of Education in Iran.* (Tehran: National Teachers College, 1962.)

Traditional Examinations

A classical viewpoint of examinations in Iran is its discriminatory nature. An examination was always regarded as a means of proving one's distinction, innocence, or expected achievement. A famous Persian poem reads 'it is nice to have the examinations performed so that the guilty be ashamed'. This particular verse embodies the philosophy and nature of classical examinations. It is something that one tries in order to prove something to others. There is no force, regulation, formality or universality attached to it. Examinations were looked upon as a demonstration performed by certain volunteers to create admiration and applause. It was the final phase of a training or educational process. It was done mostly for others to notice, and not for the examinee or examiner, who were both completely assured of the end result well in advance. Therefore, traditional examinations in Iran were occasional tests for the assessment of individuals' qualifications. By its very nature, they were mostly performed in an oral or performance manner so that the jury as well as the audience could see and enjoy the occasion. If they were related to knowledge, they took the form of eloquent oratory, and were interupted from time to time by loud applause from all those present. If they were performances they were like shows or contests with all the usual environmental arrangements.

There are no records showing that any formal examinations of a specific type were performed for very distinctive purposes such as the examinations for entry into civil or military service as in some other countries like China.

Formal Examinations

Formal examinations were introduced in Iran with Western-type education towards the end of the nineteenth century.[2] As a distinctive feature of modern education, examinations were conducted under very strict discipline almost as precise as a military control. They were and still are considered as barriers on the route a pupil should cover. The pupil therefore, is expected to pass over the barrier to show that he has gained enough competence through his learning. In this sense, examinations are performed as a device for elimination, those who fail being looked down upon and considered unfit for academic pursuit.

One has to try as many times as possible to pass through these barriers in order to prove himself capable. In other words, an individual life in Iran is nothing but a long series of examinations starting around the age of six or seven, repeated several times every year up to the time he wants to enter some kind of government or official service. As every school year is divided by examinations, school terms or semesters are nothing but

---

[2] op. cit.

seasons for examinations. Students are always concerned about how the examination will take place and what will be required of them. That is the first question at the beginning of every course put to the teacher or instructor. Everybody is concerned with what that instructor will be planning to ask at the time of examination. After they manage to get this goal clarified, they start working backwards to try to see how they can reduce this load over the intended period before the time of the examination.

Another characteristic of these formal examinations is the general request for postponement. No matter how the date for the examination is fixed and even if it is arranged beforehand by the general consensus of the students, there is always a request for postponement of the date. This shows the fear of failure which is so entrenched in the minds and souls of the students, that no matter how well they are prepared to answer the questions, they do not feel confident enough to accept the challenge. It is interesting to note that the feeling, behaviour and reaction towards examinations does not change with the age of the student, but is a universal pattern overshadowing the life of everybody. The only freedom from this constant anxiety and horror comes when one is either forced to leave school or decides to escape this hazardous road to graduation.

Until very recently it was only the government sector which was paying much importance to examinations. In other words, our civil service as well as any other governmental employment is completely based on formal education and the type of certificates people hold. That is the decisive factor. It decides at what level one can enter the service, how fast one can be promoted, and more or less to what levels he can attain. Recently, some organizations in the private sector which are becoming larger and larger, and, necessarily, more bureaucratic, have decided to follow the government example by asking for diplomas and certificates for certain positions. This has forced an increasingly larger number of people, including adults, to go to schools and colleges to try to earn more and higher certificates and degrees as a pass for promotion and a guarantee for a better position and a better life.

As is expected, formal examinations are a process where formality and procedure are more important than the content of the examination. What everybody is concerned with is how the examination session is conducted. Usually, very little attention is paid to the formulation of the questions and problems or the procedure for scoring and interpreting the results, as though, if the session were pompous and formal enough, everything else could be assumed to be equally correct.

Emergence of Educational Testing

Certain limitations embodied in traditional examinations have gradually caused us to reorientate our assessment technique. Historically speaking, it was not the desire for objective evaluation which encouraged certain authorities to give way to testing, it was rather the headaches and problems they were facing in using traditional examinations for certain purposes such as competitive examinations for scholarships or selection of applicants for certain training programmes or for certain jobs. Three difficulties were the inadequacy of examiners to conduct examinations of a large number of applicants; the urgency of having the results known as soon as possible; and last but not least, the need for easily defending the examiners' position in view of the final results. Therefore, testing was introduced as the easiest eliminatory device which could relieve the responsible authorities of most of the headaches of the old type of examination. Until 1953 test development and testing in Iran was by and large limited to entrance examinations of the National Teachers College and certain experimental studies by the students of that college for instructional purposes. All of these efforts were mostly done out of curiosity and for novelty – not for any other administrative reasons.[3]

In 1953 a Testing and Vocational Guidance Unit was established as the result of joint project between the Iranian Government and U.S. Technical Operation in Iran (Point IV) for the improvement of selection and placement of personnel in Iran. As one of its first activities the unit started to develop and standardize psychological as well as educational tests and measurements. The first battery of tests included the Persian standardized version of the *Army General Classification Test*. This effort was followed by the formation of the Personnel Management and Research Centre at the University of Tehran in 1954 and the National Institute of Psychology in 1958.[4]

Both of these institutions were the natural outcome of the 1953 project and were totally engaged in development, standardization and administration of tests for educational as well as administrative purposes. Over the past fifteen years more than 200 tests have been developed and close to one million individuals have been tested by these institutes.[5]

In the early 1960s, other centres and institutes were established by the Ministry of Education and the National Teachers College, as well as by universities and other government organizations, for the purpose of reforming the examinations and developing more objective techniques. At the present time there are more than eight independent units engaged in this type of activity. There are aptitude and achievement tests in the Persian language available for various school levels as well as other scales

---

[3] M. B. Hushiar, *Experimental Psychology* (Tehran: Sherkat-e-Mat buaat, 1938,) pp 581–86.
[4] *Monthly and Annual Report* (University of Tehran: Personnel Management and Research Center, 1954–59.)
[5] *Annual Reports* (National Institute of Psychology, 1963–64.)

and measures for assessment of interest and personality traits. As the result of all these efforts there is a change of attitude taking place among educators in Iran. It is hoped that the next few years will witness the wider application of objective techniques for educational evaluation in Iran.[6]

Types of Examinations

Examinations in Iran are usually performed in one of the following three forms – written, oral, and performance. Although written examinations are becoming more and more common, still, in certain cases, oral examinations have their own place. Some school subjects at primary or secondary level should be examined orally. This principle is even adhered to at the higher levels of education; for example, at the Faculty of Law there are certain subjects which should always be examined orally and there is a very detailed procedure on how to decide which subjects should be examined orally each year. Oral examination is also essential for the selection of employees of some particular positions such as professional positions at the Ministry of Justice. Written examination is important because a document is produced which can be kept and referred to from time to time. There are, of course, questions of economy in time and cost as well as the type of examiners used which give more preference to written examinations. In the case of performance or practical examinations, there should be a board of examiners. The use of some kind of external examiners on these boards has always been the rule in order to prove the objectivity and impartiality of the examinations.

Oral and practical examinations, because of their similarity to the classical type of examinations in Iran, still have their appeal and authenticity. It is believed that one cannot perform as freely in a written examination as in an oral examination. This is because the elements of impressing the onlookers have always been important factors in successful examinations.

From an entirely different point of view we can classify examinations in Iran into two types – ordinary and final. An ordinary examination is an examination conducted by teachers or schools for the purpose of the assessment of the students' progress. These examinations have no formal significance outside the schools and are regarded as an internal matter. On the other hand, final or official examinations are controlled and designed by some outside authority – for example, the Ministry of Education. Final examinations qualify the individual for a certain level of education, and entitle him to receive a certificate or diploma. Final examinations are the end result or the dividends of various levels of education. It is through the final examinations that one passes from one level of education to another.

---

[6] William Lightfoot, *Educational and Vocational Guidance in Iran* (Tehran: Unesco, December 1959) (mimeographed).

There are at the present time, one final examination at the end of primary education, another at the end of the ninth year of secondary education and the third at the end of the twelfth year of secondary education. Other final examinations are given at the end of any professional or college course. In the case of final examinations, because the teachers and principals are not responsible and authorized only to conduct, evaluate and report the results, these examinations are regarded as a measure of performance by various educational institutes. Many schools concentrate only on helping the students to pass through these final examinations; after all, this is what everybody wants from going to school. Ordinary examinations, as a result, are becoming less and less strict and are more educational in nature. The less they are related to certification, the more helpful they become in the educational life of students.

A unique feature of educational examination is the repeat examination. That is to say when a candidate fails in the examination he can work on his own for several months, usually during the summer vacation and then take the examination again. These repeat examinations are so deeply rooted in the educational system that even at the universities one can make use of them to get the grades and fulfil the course requirements. It has created a right and a reputation which is unlikely to change.

Birth of Vocational Guidance

Rapid and consecutive social changes in Iran have so modified the way of living in both urban and rural areas of the country that everyone is motivated to have a better life and specially seek a better life for his family and his children. In order to achieve this end more than anything else, the educational system is the target of people of various walks of life. It is not only the ordinary man who uses the educational ladder for progress and promotion; even governmental and private organizations appeal to training and education in order to solve their many problems. Therefore, it is not only the number of people asking for education which is increasing but the amount of education sought by each individual is also on the increase. The situation is becoming more difficult because of the fact that not many parents can be totally responsible for the education of their children. They do not have either the time or the knowledge to perform such a task. They look towards the schools to care for their children now, and to provide a better future for them. The con-fusion is more tense because of the increasing variation in jobs and specialities, in hobbies and activities. There are less family relationships and associations. Everybody is trying to find new opportunities to fill his free time and also wants to have the type of specialization which gives him confidence and security. Parents as well as teachers are becoming more and more bewildered on what should be given to every individual. National development is being hampered by misconceptions in the mind of the people and a balance between the education of academicians and technicians cannot be kept. Vocational training and technical jobs are not regarded highly enough to be pursued. Everybody wants to receive university education and this has a detrimental effect on agriculture and industrial development. Proper guidance of students to various vocations and careers is becoming vitally important. All this has forced educational authorities in Iran to become more and more serious about vocational guidance.

The first effort in this line started in 1956 when the Personnel Management and Research Center was asked by the Ministry of Education to develop a battery of tests for the vocational guidance of secondary school students, and Unesco was requested to send vocational guidance advisors to Iran.[7]

These efforts continued until 1960 when the nucleus for vocational and educational guidance was formed in the Ministry of Education, and were disrupted during the next few years. The force of economic development in Iran has put so much pressure on educational authorities that very recently they have planned a new system of education which is going to have a specific period of guidance somewhere between primary and secondary education. The intermediate period is a three-year programme which starts at the age of eleven and goes from grades six to eight. It is hoped that in a variety of comprehensive-type schools all children will be tested and receive guidance opportunities in order to be directed towards the type of education best for them and for the country.[8]

In addition some isolated efforts are being made by individual counsellors or clinics and centres who devote part of their time and effort to offering guidance services. In spite of the great need for this service, it is not yet known and appreciated. Those who seek and utilize it are still very few. In other words, there is not enough public awareness and sophistication with regard to vocational guidance in Iran.[9]

Prospects

Tests and examinations in Iran are becoming important tools for dealing with large numbers of applicants passing through educational channels and rushing to job opportunities in the government as well as the private sector of employment. There are hopes and plans for universal application of counselling and guidance, and for making such a service available

[7] *Progress*, Quarterly Bulletin of the Institute for Educational Research and Studies, Vols. I to III.

[8] Iraj Ayman, Evaluation and Guidance of Aptitudes in Iranian Schools. *Educational Planning and its Principles* (Tehran: Ministry of Education, 1963.) pp 113–123.

[9] Iraj Ayman, 'Educational Testing in Iran'. Paper read at the International Workshop of Educational Testing Problems, Berlin, June 1967; to be published in the Proceedings.

to every student in Iran so that there will be a more balanced distribution of students and trainees in various fields and different types of schools. There is also a need for the proper selection of candidates for higher education. In 1967 colleges and universities in Iran received over 100,000 applications for a total capacity of about 15,000 vacancies. Since the number of applicants is increasing all the time and it is impossible to increase the number of places at the universities and institutes of higher education, the question of examination and selection of the best candidates for each vacancy as well as proper guidance of those who remain outside these institutes necessitates a complete revision of the system of education and introduction of proper vocational guidance.

As far as career development is concerned, governmental and non-governmental organizations are being faced with an increasing number of applicants. It is becoming impossible for them to screen all of these applicants by traditional techniques. They would like to get the best but they do not know how to do so, and therefore they are looking for opportunities for more objective and better systems of evaluation. In large organizations the question of guidance and placement is specially important in order to keep everybody happy and productive for as long as possible. Therefore, they look upon guidance and counselling as an important internal activity in the orientation of the adult population.

Last, but not least, parents are feeling the need of evaluation and guidance in order to make decisions for their children. It is impossible for an ordinary parent to know all about various educational opportunities and it is also impossible for most of them to help their children with their educational and psychological problems. Therefore, they are looking for better evaluation and guidance facilities to come to their help and support. All this sets the goals in the near future for educational authorities in Iran to do their best to reform the system of examinations, to introduce vocational guidance and to spread these services all over the country. What they need is trained specialists as well as the development of certain instruments and techniques. We are at the very beginning of this effort. In 1967 the first training programmes for the training of specialists were started in a number of colleges and universities and certain centres have been requested to go ahead and produce instruments and techniques needed for guidance and counselling. Through all these measures it is hoped that, in the future, the way examinations are organized and carried out will be changed and more purposes will be served by more objective examinations and better guidance and counselling. Such a change would have a profound effect on the pace and intensity of socio-economic development of Iran. Perhaps in one way, this is the final solution to problems of how the desired development could best be realized!

35

Selection and Social Mobility in Indonesia

I. P. Simandjuntak
Professor in Education Theories, Faculty of Pedagogics and Head of Research Department for Education, Institute for Teacher Training and Pedagogics, Djarkarta

Summarizing the educational situation in Indonesia during the period immediately preceding World War II, one could say that education and consequently selection and examinations were not directed toward 'opening' the social structure by enabling the young to participate in social mobility on a full scale, but rather to ensure the stability of the social class structure with little chance for the lower groups to climb up the social ladder. As far as horizontal mobility was concerned, education and its selective tool (examination) had been promoting it in a way that could be accepted as the beginning of the formation of the Indonesian people into one nation: the best students from the higher social classes in the other islands were sent to Java to attend secondary schools there, together with the youth of the higher classes of Java. Clerical and other administrative personnel who had passed certain civil service examinations were also recruited from all over Indonesia and promoted, thereby ensuring horizontal mobility among the Indonesian people.

Such was the general situation when, during World War II, Indonesia was occupied by the Japanese army. During the occupation external examinations for entrance and for graduation from the secondary school, which were largely organized centrally, were replaced by a locally organized examination (sometimes by the schools themselves, separately from one another). The rigidity of used norms and the toughness of examinations were of almost the same standard as before the occupation, and only examinations in Dutch and other foreign Western languages were replaced by examinations in the Indonesian and Japanese languages.

Selection in the Educational System after Independence

The main target of the Indonesian Government after independence was to provide education for all children at the elementary school level. Therefore it was necessary for the government to form a committee charged with solving the problem of how to put into practice a selection among the graduates.

Before the war, education as such, was, in the eyes of the people, only a means to a white-collar job which enabled one to get away from village life and work in the rice field. For the people of the higher classes, such a job meant a preservation of social status, which was often measured in terms of closeness with the ruling class. Since independence in the early days meant getting rid of the Dutch in every way of life, being educated signified one's ability to step into the jobs left by the Dutch. And the numbers of jobs to be filled after independence increased not by the hundreds, but by the thousands. The creation of ministries which did not exist during the colonial period, for instance the Ministries for Foreign Affairs, for Social Affairs, for Religion, for Trade and Industries necessitated (and still does) a huge increase in trained personnel. Private enterprise in trade, industry, and agriculture also demanded more personnel to replace the former Dutch staff. So the need for more educated officials, together with the general attitude of the people towards education, made them see the government's attempt to provide (elementary) education for all as a way to get a (white-collar) job. Consequently, the demand for more education must be seen in the light of this preoccupation with the aim of obtaining a white-collar job. The following table illustrates the increase in the numbers of students, schools, and teachers:

TABLE I

INCREASE IN NUMBERS OF STUDENTS, SCHOOLS, AND TEACHERS 1945–1965*

Year	Number and type of school			Number of Students			Number of teachers		
	elem sch.	junior high	senior high	elem.sch.	junior high sch.	senior high sch.	elem.sch	junior high	senior high
1945	15,069	49	no fig	2,523,410	19,185	n.a.	36,287	676	n.a.
1950	23,801	679	89	4,926,370	64,029	19,654	83,850	2,517	1,420
1960	37,673	4,628	731	8,955,098	448,343	106,797	230,838	25,792	8,950
1965	53,431	4,239	1,032	11,587,387	800,798	198,687	281,825	38,173	16,417

* These figures have been obtained from the Division for General Education in the Ministry of Education and Culture, Indonesia, 1966.
n.a. = not available

According to the latest statistics, the number of students from all over Indonesia who took part in the entrance examinations for the Junior High School for 1967 was 2,313,000, while the number doing final examinations for the Junior High School, (qualifying them for entrance to the Senior High School) was only 448,550. These results raise the crucial question of the purpose and method of selection, especially in view of the rapid rate of educational development which has left social-economic growth and development lagging far behind. And when the figures concerning candidates seeking entrance to the junior business high school and senior business high school are compared with the number of candidates for the junior high school and the senior high school – 40,050 against 2,313,000 and 40,050 against 448,550 respectively – then the assumption made above that schooling is seen only as a way to get a white-collar job, is justified. Again if the numbers of students taking technical education are compared with the numbers taking business education, the following figures for West Java are significant: 40,000 against 140,000; for Central Java 70,000 against 190,000 and for East Java 70,000 against 220,000. These figures clearly show that the only road seen for progress and development is through the secondary school for general education and after that to the university. In an article in a recent students' weekly magazine (November 1967) comparative figures were given showing the relation between elementary schools and universities in several countries; the ratio for Indonesia was *one* institute for higher learning to *forty-nine* elementary schools.

The trend of development in the field of education can be traced from the middle 1950s, especially since the aim of the government at that time was to provide (elementary) education for all people, as was stated in the Bill of Education of 1954. The method of selection for admission from one stage of education to a higher one was no longer considered satisfactory, as it was based on the examination pattern of the colonial period. Officials in the field of education since the early 1950s made it very clear that a uniform curriculum for the whole territory of Indonesia could not be maintained because of the diversity in the cultural and sociological pattern of living in the many communities in the islands of Indonesia. If democracy in education meant 'giving equal opportunity with full regard to the differences among individuals', then the curriculum would have to be reconstructed accordingly and the method of selection should not be confused with the content of selecting material. It would not be fair, for example, for the ability of children of coastal plains and mountain regions to be measured by a description of rice planting in an essay designed to assess the mastery of language, when the coastal children have never even seen people working in the rice fields. Conversely, almost everything in connexion with fishery would not be familiar to children in the mountain regions.

It was therefore decided by the Ministry of Education in 1958 to set up a State Commission to study problems concerning examinations, since the example put forward in the preceding paragraph was only one of many related difficulties.

The inability of the existing government educational establishments to meet the demand for more education – the figures given previously were total figures combining numbers of children studying at government, privately subsidized and unsubsidized schools – required the establishment of new institutions although the full requirements set by the government were not always met by private school boards. Therefore it sometimes happened that only partially qualified teachers were taking up teaching jobs, either full time or part time. Even government sponsored schools had to be content with secondary school teachers who had just passed their examinations after a three-year course at university; sometimes in the 1950s, even second-year students were appointed to teach, so as to meet the shortage in teachers. It was quite understandable that ministry officials became anxious about what might happen if measures were not taken in time to prevent an eventual collapse of educational standards.

Another, no less important factor to be studied by the State Commission was how to select children according to their ability; should it be done through the old methods of measuring mental abilities by requiring essays, measuring the power of memory and solving classic arithmetic problems? And should one decide upon a person's future after letting him take a two- to three-hour written examination or a thirty-minute oral one? Or should results of careful observations of the child's development during the whole length of his educational course be taken into consideration, when a definite evaluation of his ability has to be given? In other words: should examinations be external ones, either centrally or locally organized, or should they be abandoned to make place for so-called internal examinations?

The most important recommendations delivered to the Minister of Education in 1958 were:

(1) as soon as possible examinations, which should be based on the assumption that differences of locality had to be considered as well as minimum knowledge of facts which must be mastered by all students regardless of their geographical position, should be held.

(2) external examinations should be abandoned in the near future, but before they could be abolished, an upgrading of the teaching staff, especially in the testing and evaluation of the pupil, should take place on a nation-wide scale;

(3) a central board of examination should be established, whose duties would be to control and give advice to local examination boards in connexion with selection of material for examinations, organization and management of examinations, so as to prevent a downward trend in educational standards.

Those recommendations were put into practice, taking into consideration the capability and experience of educational authorities in the different areas. For the junior high school entrance examinations, for example, there was to be a step-by-step decentralization of the examination organization:

(1) up to 1964 material for examinations would be decided on by provincial officials, based on directives given by the central office – these materials had to be approved by the head of the division for elementary education;

(2) in 1965 the approval mentioned above would no longer be essential – the head of the division involved would only have to investigate and ensure that the directives had been followed;

(3) in 1966 the material for examinations would be composed by country educational officials, based on the directives issued by the central authorities as in 1964, but approval by the head of the division would no longer be necessary (see 2);

(4) in 1967 material for examinations would be composed by district officials together with country officials;

(5) in 1968 the district officials would be given the same rights as those given to the country officials in 1966 (see 3);

(6) in 1969 district officials would have to compose examination material from material proposed by school principals, based on directives from the Department of Education; and

(7) by 1970 every school principal and his teaching staff would have to compose school examination material.[1]

The next step taken by the Department of Education, in considering the policy of the government to provide education for the whole nation on a democratic basis (thereby creating an educational system to give equal opportunity to everyone, without discrimination based on social status, creed or economic status) was to define norms and basic specifications of examination material for entering the junior high school. In the directive issued in March 1967 by the Division of Basic Education, the following general specifications which the examination material must fulfil were given:[2]

(1) the material should not be incompatible with the development of the individual toward becoming a democratic citizen, abiding by the *Pantjasila* and the Constitution of 1945; furthermore, it should not consist of anything that does not 'develop the individual toward seeking the truth, fighting imperialism, colonialism, neo-colonialism and feudalism';

(2) the material should mirror the capacity of the elementary school graduate, bearing in mind the local conditions;

---

[1] Translated and summarized from the decentralization plan of the Department of Education in the Ministry of Education and Culture, Indonesia.

[2] Summarized from the above mentioned directive.

(3) the material should consider the harmonious development of the child toward a complete personality;

(4) the material should direct the child toward logical and critical thinking and furthermore it should have a practical function.

It is clear that this directive contains a strong indication of how the curriculum was to be developed. A scrutiny of the material presented to the candidates in 1966 readily assures the reader of the good intentions of the Department of Education to select the best developed individual for an opportunity to climb higher up on the social ladder. No longer is there a tough selection based only on intellectual capacities, for a few positions in a higher social stratum, and designed to prevent a vertical social mobility, to enable the ruling class to maintain its superiority and impose its will on the ruled part of society.

According to the 1961 census, the number of students attending the junior high school in the city of Djakarta was about 30 per cent of the children of high school age. This is an indication that the selection results for upward mobility in the society were parallel with the assumed general capability of individuals to attend instruction on that level.

In a previous paragraph it was mentioned how impossible it was for the government to cope fully with the demand for more education and school instruction for the newly independent Indonesian society and how many schools were therefore established by private school boards, which did not always select their teachers carefully enough. And therefore, that it was one of the concerns of the government to find a means of maintaining adequate educational standards, which were dangerously threatened by unsatisfactorily qualified teachers. That this concern was justified is obvious from the statistical results of junior high school examinations. Tables IIA and B show the percentages of successful candidates and the numbers of students involved at the final examination of the junior high school.

If, to these figures, are added for those three selected academic years, the numbers of candidates who sought a junior high school diploma without

TABLE II A

PERCENTAGES OF SUCCESSFUL CANDIDATES AT JUNIOR HIGH SCHOOL FINAL EXAMINATIONS

Year	Gov. school	Fully subsid.	Partly subsid.	Entirely private
	%	%	%	%
1953/1954	70·5	70·4	26·3	17·4
1958/1959	69·0	74·7	38·7	23·8
1964/1965	75·6	65·6	57·3	48·8

TABLE II B

NUMBERS OF STUDENTS WHO WERE CANDIDATES AT JUNIOR HIGH SCHOOL
FINAL EXAMINATIONS

Year	Govern. school		Fully subsid.		Partly subsid.		Entirely private	
	(a)	(b)	(a)	(b)	(a)	(b)	(a)	(b)
1953/1954	19,130	13,489	6,126	4,317	7,797	2,051	32,322	5,648
1958/1959	40,155	27,723	8,393	6,274	13,471	5,219	68,932	16,406
1964/1965	95,693	72,312	21,372	14,033	21,675	12,419	79,506	38,791

(a) Total number taking part in the examinations; (b) Number of those who passed.

any regular schooling (the so-called extranea) 12·3 per cent (17,675/2,189), 24 per cent (23,917/5,741)and 45·2 per cent (27,323/12,348 respectively – then the role of examinations in preserving a certain educational standard becomes very clear.

The important role of education and its selection methods in the field of social mobility is made even more clear, if the spread of the junior high school throughout Indonesia is kept in mind at the same time. In 1966 there were some provinces with almost the same numbers of government schools as there were private schools (fully, partly or not subsidized at all) as in North Sumatra (143 government schools compared with 22, 51, and 174 private schools of the respective types), while there were some provinces without any private fully- or partly-subsidized schools at all as in Atjeh, Riau, Nusatenggara-Barat (West Lesser Sunda Islands) and Sulawesi Tenggara (South East Celebes). On the other hand, the provinces with very large populations – for example, Djakarta (the national capital has a provincial status), West, Central, and East Java – gave figures of the junior high school population which are by no means proportionate to the size of the population when compared with such provinces as North Sumatra and South Celebes (73,087 and 45,392 junior high school students among an estimated population of respectively 4 and 3 million and 70,236, 106,639, 149,023, and 121,109 in the four provinces of Java with an estimated total population of about 70 million). These figures show that there are areas in Indonesia with a rapid social mobility through education and examinations which should play an important part in selecting those who are enabled to go upwards in society by getting a better education.

How strong this mobility has been is illustrated by the following figures, giving the percentages of number of students at elementary, junior, and senior high levels of education:

In 1950 1·3 per cent of the elementary school students enrolled in the junior high schools and 0·4 per cent of this figure at the senior high

schools (30·7 per cent of the number attending junior high schools).
In 1955 these figures respectively became 2·6 per cent and 0·9 per cent
(33·5 per cent of the junior high school figures).
In 1960 these figures were 5 per cent and 1·2 per cent (23·8 per cent of
the junior high school figure).
In 1964 (the last available figures) the proportions were 7 per cent and
1·7 per cent (24·8 per cent of the junior high school students).

The selective role of examinations becomes even more convincing in
the light of the figures of the final examinations of the senior high schools
in 1963, which never exceeded 62·2 per cent of sucessful students on the
basis of the old curriculum. But when the curriculum was changed in 1961
and the first group of students took their final examinations in 1964, there
was a big improvement. In 1964, 85 per cent of the candidates passed and
for 1965 this figure was 70 per cent. Whether this was due to a better
curriculum and improved teaching or because of a loosening of the rigid
grip of the former method of examinations, has still to be analysed. But
one thing is sure: in 1957 (one year before the Ministerial Commission on
Examinations delivered the recommendations mentioned earlier) Mr. A.
Overas, Unesco Expert in Secondary Education, who was attached to the
Unesco Technical Assistance Mission to Indonesia, recommended in
Chapter V of his report (unpublished) to the Indonesian Government,
that '. . . the present examination system in the Indonesian Secondary
School should be discontinued as soon as circumstances permit and be
replaced by an internal examination with some form of external control
and assessment. This new system must by no means be a *pro forma* procedure. Both firm control and more freedom are necessary in the Indonesian school today . . .' The recommended 'new system' was first
initiated as an experiment at one school in Djakarta in 1961 and the results
were disseminated to chosen schools year by year and this could be the
reason for the better results since 1964.

Due to the rapid large-scale expansion of the school system, including
the senior high schools, the Ministry of Education in 1958 instructed the
institutions for higher learning to take steps towards a more uniform rule
of admission to university. Since officially a holder of a senior high school
certificate is entitled to admission to a university, the Ministry decided
that selection of candidates should be made on the basis of marks attained
at the final examinations and the marks on the report card of a high school
student. The candidate's knowledge of certain subjects may be tested too.
And should the capacity of the university make it impossible to accomo-
date and give admission to all applicants, there must be a general test
designed to select the best qualified of all applicants. This measure has been
in practice for the Medical Faculty of the University of Indonesia since
1955 (where the number of applicants was occasionally twenty times the

number of places available) and for the whole university since 1960. This has been due to the fact that the former practice of liberal studies (as is the practice in many continental European universities) had to make room for a more guided study pattern, as is usual in the Anglo-Saxon countries. But another reason for the rush for entrance to the University of Indonesia was the fame of that institution throughout the country, only matched by the Technological Institute of Bandung, which also inaugurated admission tests in the late 1950s.

The 'jump' since 1964, in the percentage of senior high school students who have passed their final examinations has apparently made university officials hesitant about how to qualify those graduates, and thus, since 1964, almost every major government institution for higher learning has held an entrance examination.

To conclude this short essay on selection as a means of social mobility – especially upward mobility – it can be said that Indonesia is an example of a nation which is seeking to expand its educational opportunities for all solely according to ability. It also wishes to prevent exclusion from any type of vertical mobility resulting from traditional methods of selection, and therefore is attempting to improve its selection system every year both organizationally and in connexion with the content of knowledge tested.

The growing and developing Indonesian society does not yet 'dictate' to the schools on how to select their students for an appropriate job; but the universities are making a beginning with a rigorous selection amongst applicants for entrance to the universities, because of the view held by the university authorities that the quality of intellectual abilities of the senior high school graduate is diminishing. Indonesia has not reached a final consensus on how to make selection amongst school graduates, since modernization of the curriculum and of the methods used in teaching are still under review. It has, however, made a beginning by judging its school graduates not only on their intellectual abilities, but also on the basis of personality trends, which could be developed through education but the quality of which is difficult to evaluate.

If this experiment is to be successful, social mobility – either horizontal or vertical – must take place in a democratic way, taking into account the total personality trends of the individuals concerned; but whether this experiment can ever be successful, only the future will show.

36

The Dimensions of Vocational Preference and Prestige in an African Elite Group

S. H. Irvine
School of Education, University of Ontario

As African students progress through the educational system they be-come, through the attrition of selection examinations, an *élite* in terms of their age group. By the time they complete four years of secondary school, they represent, in Rhodesia, an estimated (see pp. 279–90) 1 per cent of all those who were born in the same year. What they will do when they leave school they do not know for certain, but, like all of the school leavers on the continent of Africa, they have certain vocational preferences. The possi-bility that the aspirations and preferences of African students will be realized is influenced by economic and political factors beyond their immediate control. Their future in a country where many different kinds of occupations are open to them through the replacement of expatriate labour is quite different from that in other countries where job restrictions may be practised and the incidence of expatriate labour is high. On the other hand an expatriate exodus gives only a limited field of opportunity if the economy is not diversified enough to offer job variety. Rhodesia is at present an African country where job opportunities for *élite* African school leavers are narrowed both because of restrictive practices, particu-larly among white trade unions, and because of a low rate of economic growth associated with Commonwealth attempts at sanctions. In this context, a survey of student aspirations was conducted in 1966 in all schools offering Cambridge School Certificate examinations in the fourth year of secondary education in Mashonaland. This was part of a much larger longitudinal study of secondary school progress (Irvine, 1968). The rather special circumstances surrounding the African secondary school leaver in Rhodesia in 1966 make the study of the dimensionality of indi-vidual aspirations at this point in time of some sociological significance. They were leaving school one year after the unilateral declaration of independence; sanctions had been operating with growing severity; and there was increasing evidence that the *de facto* Rhodesian government was pursuing a course of separate development for the ethnic groups within the country.

Previous studies of occupational prestige in neighbouring Zambia, before and after independence (Mitchell and Epstein, 1959; Mitchell and Irvine, 1966; Hicks, 1966, 1967), and in Rhodesia (Mitchell and Irvine, 1962), showed that the prestige rankings of jobs showed only very slight differences between ethnic groups, and between social classes within ethnic groups. From this it is possible to hypothesize an underlying multi-dimensional system of *individual* as distinct from *group* evaluation that operates across ethnic groups: and across socio-economic status within ethnic groups. By corollary it is possible to argue that the job preferences of African students will be influenced by the same hypothetical system of evaluation but will be focused on known avenues for opportunity, or foreseen opportunities. The aim of this study is to map, by means of factorial analysis, the dimensions of evaluation latent in the preferences of an *élite* group of African school leavers. This factorial approach can be replicated elsewhere with other samples in Africa so that the stability of the dimensions may be further investigated.

SAMPLE, INVENTORY AND METHODS

The sample consisted of 266 male and 62 female students, 328 in all, completing the fourth year of secondary education in the Mashonaland area of Rhodesia in 1966. Because of the way in which Mashonaland schools consistently represent the national norms of educational achievement, and because the area itself contains all the necessary variation in urban-rural conditions that characterize Rhodesia as a whole (Irvine, 1968), the sample is taken to be representative, except for tribal origin of the population of Form 4 school leavers for that year, being approximately one-third of the total secondary school output.

The modal age was nineteen years, 262 of the pupils falling in the age-range eighteen-twenty; 260 spoke a form of the Shona language, 52 Nyanja, 12 Sindebele and the remainder other African languages at home. Father's occupation was recorded and 139 fell into the category of semi-skilled workers; 104 were in the unskilled, retired, out of work or no-response categories; 37 were listed in white-collar, 43 in sub-professional and 5 in professional occupations. The sample indicated that 151 fathers had obtained a minimum of seven or eight years of primary education, and of these 26 had gone to secondary school and 7 were stated to have a B.A. or equivalent. As for the mothers, 112 had attained at least seven or eight years of education, of whom 9 had gone to secondary school and 1 had a first degree. One may conclude that this sample came from parents whose educational and occupational background was superior to that of the population as a whole. On the average, there were 4 or 5 children, in addition to the students, in each family. Religious affiliations were given as 116 Roman Catholic, 110 Presbyterian and Methodist, 57

Anglican, 36 other Christian and 9 no response. All students were fully literate in English, the medium of school instruction.

The information relevant to the study was collected as part of a survey of abilities and aspirations that completed a five-year study of selection systems in African Schools in Rhodesia. The writer introduced all the tests and the questionnaires personally and the students had met him on at least one occasion previously. The inventory of questions about job conditions and preferences was devised from a questionnaire generously provided by Professor Alec Rodger of Birkbeck College, University of London. This questionnaire had been used in vocational guidance by Rodger and his colleagues at Birkbeck for many years and its items had even found their way into similar questionnaires used by youth employment officers in Britain. Although the questions in the African inventory owed much to Rodger's original, they were modified to suit local conditions. To conserve space these have been listed below in their rank order of frequency of endorsement by the sample on a forced-choice yes-no response. They were given in random order in the actual inventory.

Job Conditions

These are ranked in response to the hypothetical question 'Would you like a job in which you . . .'

**1 lived in a town (303)
**2 spent a lot of time helping people (301)
3 worked in an office (277)
4 had to study very hard (266)
5 worked on your own (265)
6 lived in another country (250)
7 did a lot of sums (231)
8 looked after young people (203)
9 ran your own business (192)
10 worked in a factory (161)
11 worked long hours (148)
12 often got rather dirty (130)
13 had to be good at drawing (113)
14 learned to boss people (90)
15 worked your own farm (87)
16 worked out of doors (86)
17 did not make a great deal of money (74)
18 lived in a reserve or purchase area (69)
*19 worked in a store selling things (32)

In order to investigate the dimensions of aspirations the results from these questions were intercorrelated, using tetrachoric correlations, omitting all the questions that had fewer than 10 per cent of respondents in any one Yes or No category. This satisfied the minimum statistical conditions for computing tetrachoric correlations, although at the

---

** Fewer than 10 per cent in No category.
* Fewer than 10 per cent in Yes category.
The figures in parentheses indicate the number of respondents endorsing the Yes category.

sacrifice of some data; but it did indicate which conditions and jobs were likely to have significant and reliable association with each other. The variables omitted because of the 10 per cent criterion are marked with asterisks.

Jobs Liked

These are ranked in response to the instruction 'Ring around Yes if this is a job you might like to do; ring around No if it is a job you would *not* like.'

1 Doctor (270)	14 Union Leader (121)
2 Research Worker (268)	15 Primary Teacher (75)
3 Secondary School Teacher (255)	16 Grocer (45)
4 University Lecturer (250)	*17 Policeman (28)
5 TV, Radio Announcer (243)	*18 Hairdresser (26)
6 Clerk (230)	*19 Painter (21)
7 Telephone Operator (227)	*20 Builder (19)
8 Nurse (193)	*21 Carpenter (19)
9 Lawyer (190)	*22 Bus Driver (18)
10 Post Office Worker (181)	*23 Domestic Servant (18)
11 Typist (179)	*24 Tailor (14)
12 Cashier (158)	*25 Cook (9)
13 Politician (141)	*26 Head Waiter (4)

This yielded a 32 × 32 matrix of conditions and job preferences to which was added the sex of the respondent. After preliminary analysis with these and other dichotomies, one variable, *good at drawing*, was omitted because it contributed nothing to the total variance extracted, and the responses to the question 'Are you a scout or guide?' were included since they seemed to be indicative of a personality tendency. This left a final 33 × 33 matrix of intercorrelations. This matrix was factored with the highest correlation in each column as a first estimate of communality. The communalities were not iterated and an optimal solution of 8 factors was subjected to Varimax and Promax rotation of axes. This solution exceeded the communality trace provided by the highest correlation in each column by 4 per cent.

The rank orders of job conditions and job preferences have already been given and provide the final set of results.

GROUP RESULTS

Job Conditions

The results fall conveniently into three sections: job conditions endorsed by two-thirds or more of the total (1 to 9); those endorsed by one-third or more (10 to 13), and those endorsed by less than one-third (14 to 19).

Examination of these indicate that work indoors in an urban area would appeal to most (1, 3); that such work should be essentially cognitive in nature, with an element of social service (4, 7, 2, 8); that it should not be too closely supervised (5, 9). Also, a surprising number of students favoured a job in another country (6). This probably reflects hopes for overseas study or could also be an oblique indication that they foresaw only a limited future for their hopes under the present Constitution.

The next set of conditions indicate partial acceptance of work of a manual and practical nature involving conditions of physical hardship.

The last set indicate job conditions of low popularity. Farming and its attendant conditions of non-urban residence (15, 16, 18) was not favoured, nor was contact with the public in a low-grade service capacity (19); low financial gain seems correlated with all of these conditions.

As learning to take up positions of authority (14) appears as an adverse condition of employment, one must here make the distinction between relative independence of action as favourable characteristics in the first group (5, 9) and responsibility for the actions of others (14) as being much less desirable. This particular role may place Africans in intercalary positions between European directors and African workers (cf. the low preference for policemen in this study, also Mitchell and Irvine, 1966) and result in considerable lowering of status, or increased hardship of working conditions, or both.

Job Preferences and Prestige

Turning now to interpretation of the rank order of occupational preferences established by the present sample, one observes that jobs 1–14 are all white-collar, sub-professional and professional occupations – and these are all that are endorsed by more than one-third of the sample. Thereafter there is a sharp drop to *Primary Teacher*, and a further drop to occupations of a relatively unskilled kind, such as normally occupy the bottom end of a prestige scale. The position of the *Primary Teacher* seems extremely serious, since it is clearly thought to be a low-preference occupation among secondary school leavers, many of whom, if they were leaving school in western societies would be contemplating this as a field of employment. In fact, one can see ahead, in developing countries, to the point where Form 4 education will be a necessary condition for entry into primary school teacher training: and it is a goal towards which many countries will strive in the next twenty years.

The low ranking of the *Policeman* is consistent with the results of other prestige studies in pre-independent Zambia, while the poorly-paid service occupations of *Domestic Servant*, *Tailor*, *Cook*, and *Head Waiter* are at the bottom of the list. The *Head Waiter* is a relatively unexpected last choice, since it is a well-paid job in comparison with the others in this group, and enjoys considerable side-benefits. Hence, some other factor must account for its universal unpopularity. It seems to involve continuous and sub-servient contact with Europeans, and responsibility for the acts of other Africans (learning to boss people). Like the *Policeman*, the *Head Waiter* is in the intercalary position that tends to strain peer-relations. Significantly, too, only the *Tailor*, among the four least endorsed occupations, can avoid face-to-face communication, for a large part of a usually long working day, with Europeans whose demands for service he is expected to fulfil.

The ranking of jobs preferred by an *élite* group such as this is not necessarily related to the prestige of occupations, and the relationship was not experimentally sought. That there should be such a relationship, however, seems a legitimate hypothesis. To test this, rank order corre-lations were compared between 16 identical jobs used in the Mitchell and Irvine (1962) Rhodesia occupational prestige study among primary school and secondary school Mashonaland students, and 18 identified in the Hicks (1967) study of Zambian African and European secondary school students. These selected occupations spanned the total range of those presented to the *élite* group that formed the sample.

The correlations between the rank orders of common occupations given by the present sample and the three other groups compared were 0·92 for the Rhodesian 1962 study ($N = 16$ $p < 0·01$), 0·91 for the Zambian African 1967 study and 0·82 for the Zambian European study (both $N = 18$ $p < 0·01$). As Hicks himself reports a 0·80 rank order correla-tion between European and African groups for all the occupations ranked, two conclusions can be drawn: (*a*) the present group's preferences are very closely associated with the prestige of occupations as they exist among other African respondents in central Africa; (*b*) there is considerable evidence to substantiate the view that a common set of evaluative dimen-sions operates across ethnic groups as well as within ethnic groups. Hence the results of the intercorrelations of job preference and conditions should give a hypothetical frame for dimensions of individual differences for one African group with possible extension to other groups.

To conclude, the results show significant associations with prestige ratings of occupations and there is evidence for more than one operational dimension in the evaluation of occupations by the individuals in the groups.

INDIVIDUAL DIFFERENCES

The Dimensionality of Evaluations

Hicks (1966) summarizes much of the theory behind the prestige ratings of occupations (Rossi and Inkeles, 1957; Tiryakian, 1958; Reiss, 1961;

D'Souza, 1962; Thomas, 1962; Mitchell and Irvine, 1966). His own study shows very high rank correlations between the group means of a range of occupations ranked separately on six categories. These were job responsibility, service value, monetary reward, working conditions, education and intelligence required and personal relationships in the job. The rank orders were summed over all and then correlated with a separate prestige ranking. Although the number of jobs listed by Hicks was small, the correlations between the separate prestige ranking and the combined group rankings on the other six rated attributes approached unity. Nevertheless the intercorrelations of the separate attributes were substantial, suggesting that they could be compressed into fewer dimensions. Finally, there was no opportunity to measure individual differences in the evaluation of occupation within the group sampled.

The next part of this study concentrates on mapping dimensions that may contribute to group ratings of prestige and the discussion attempts to bring together the sociological and psychological implications of the findings. The results of the eight factor solutions are presented in abbreviated form and discussed in relation to the theory outlined, in so far as it is possible to present individual differences in grading occupations. Loadings are presented for the Varimax solution, although the eight first order factors were subjected to second order analysis after Promax rotation.

It should be noted that, through eliminating data to satisfy the conditions for statistical analysis, the results are confined to a restricted range of occupations and conditions of service, and to the responses of an *élite* group.

Factor 1. Indoors: Office/Clerical

Clerk	0·81	Post Office Worker	0·69
Typist	0·76	Grocer	0·51
Work in Office	0·75	Cashier	0·47
Telephone Operator	0·70	TV Radio Announcer	0·39

This factor accounted for a large share of the total variance and is clearly one that relates occupations concerned with clerical tasks. One might predict that people who consistently endorsed this array of items would accept clerical employment.

Factor 2. Political Power

Politician	0·85	University Lecturer	0·46
Union Leader	0·78	Learn to boss people	0·28
Lawyer	0·63	Run your own business	0·23
		Male preference	0·21

The linking of a clear political cluster of jobs with minor loadings on job conditions and maleness is probably indicative of certain personality characteristics associated with preference for political roles. The presence of *Lawyer* and *University Lecturer* shows that this group probably sees people with a capacity for highly analytical thinking taking a leading role in African political systems. In Rhodesia, particularly, university lecturers and lawyers from various ethnic groups have provided such leadership, often aligning themselves with African interests. Hence it appears that aspirations towards an extremely high level of education seems to be strongly associated with readiness to consider participation in politics and a willingness to accept responsibility for the actions of others.

Factor 3. Adverse Environment: Physical

Often got rather dirty	0·74	Worked in an office	−0·35
Worked out of doors	0·60	Research Worker	0·33
Worked in a factory	0·54	Cashier	0·34
Male preference	0·36	Live in reserve or purchase area	0·29

People who endorse this cluster of conditions and jobs, mostly males, seem to support the view that adverse physical conditions *by themselves* do not necessarily constitute a reason for refusing a job. The loadings on *Research Worker* and *Cashier* are perhaps indicative that other factors, such as monetary reward, might have to be compensatory since people who say they accept physical adversity are also endorsing the upper end of the white-collar job scale in terms of wages.

Factor 4. Teaching Preference

Secondary School Teacher	0·80	Looking after young people	0·21
Primary School Teacher	0·72	Doctor	0·26
University Lecturer	0·32	Nurse	0·21
		TV Radio Announcer	0·25

This is essentially a doublet that loads on the two teaching occupations and it is perhaps unwise to lay too much stress on the minor loadings. However, social service, liking for young people, interest in communications media all appear to be predictable, supportive dimensions to the factor.

Factor 5. Determination to Succeed

Study very hard	0·57	Look after young people	0·48
Make little money	0·53	Being a Scout or Guide	0·36
Work long hours	0·54		

These loadings, which are also accompanied by small loadings on *Nurse*, *Primary Teacher*, and *Grocer*, seem to represent an ideal image of the hard-working student with a spirit of social service. On the other hand, they could be acquiescence to a number of socially desirable characteristics reinforced by education in denominational schools. However, second order analysis, which is given below, shows this to be a complex factor that is pervasive in the second order analysis; and it is interpreted as a dimension of individual differences in willingness to strive for a distant goal.

Factor 6. Female Preference

Female Preference	0·70	Typist	0·32
Nurse	0·66	Primary Teacher	0·28
Doctor	0·45		

This factor shows that girls are more likely to endorse the above occupations favourably. Nursing and teaching have been traditionally open to them.

Factor 7. Liking for Cognitive Tasks

Doctor	0·52	Doing a lot of sums	0·45
Research Worker	0·47	University Lecturer	0·38
Another Country	0·47	Living in a reserve or purchase area	−0·34
		Cashier	0·26
		Working alone	0·24

Here are a number of jobs requiring high cognitive capacity, probably involving travel to another country for study purposes. Those who endorse such items like doing calculations: and the *Cashiers'* job is predictably associated with this preference. It is noteworthy that the negative loading on living in a reserve or purchase area is consistent with a desire to travel outside the country. For students, such travel is usually in search of a higher qualification.

Factor 8. Entrepreneurship

Running one's own business	0·58	Learning to boss people	0·37
Working alone most of the time	0·52	Grocer	0·24
Working one's own farm	0·49	Working outdoors	0·23
Living in a reserve or purchase area	0·35	Being a Scout	0·23

The cluster of items identified in this factor seems to point to students who would prefer to chart their own destinies and who prize independence of action. The loadings are consistent with the notion of the self-made man and the smaller loadings suggest that adverse physical conditions would be tolerated for success in one's own business.

The primary factor loadings, unlike group average prestige ratings, indicate possible dimensions of individual differences. They are, to the psychologist, the main avenues of how people, as distinct from groups, may vary. The eight primary dimensions show occupations and employment conditions to be related in certain ways, and it is possible that a study ongoing at the moment will show cognitive and environmental variables related to these dimensions, provided that the individual differences in students among the eight primary factors are based on self-knowledge of one's level in skills that are related to success in a preferred career. This argument does not contradict Hicks' (1966) model, but limits the sense in which he uses 'factors' to account for group prestige ratings. This use of 'factor' is different from the multi-dimensional individual difference model which is proposed here.

An attempt could be made to combine the work on prestige with the individual differences model by studying carefully the occupation of *University Lecturer*. It has high group prestige ratings, but one could expect individuals from the sample, in assigning a prestige rating, to differ in their evaluation of this occupation on at least three of the dimensions indicated here – political, teaching preference, and liking for cognitive tasks. As these factors also appear correlated with the determination to succeed dimension, in the second order analysis, prestige would depend, for an individual, on which one of these he most clearly associated the occupation with and whether he identified, in himself, the qualities he associated with success in the occupation. If he perceived the other dimensions as appropriate, the sample process could be repeated until dimensions were evaluated. Hence there seem to be two cognitive/affective processes in a prestige rating, making aligning of the occupation with a number of individually perceived social roles, and defining a personal standpoint in relation to job preference. In this, sex differences, individual differences in skills and motivation will play a part, so that the single social prestige rating seems an extremely complex concept.

Second Order Analysis

Just as it is possible to look for latent dimensions in a group of inter-correlations of tests on items in an inventory, it is possible to look for latent dimensions in a number of primary factors, such as the eight identified here. Such dimensions are second order factors and they may be interpreted in a hierarchical system. Table I shows the results of a second order analysis of the eight primary factors illustrated above. Two factors were extracted account for 91 per cent of the common variance. Loadings below 0·2 have been omitted for clarity.

TABLE I

SECOND ORDER ANALYSIS
OF PRIMARY FACTORS

	I	II
1 Clerical	24	—
2 Political	43	29
3 Adverse Physical	—	49
4 Teaching	71	—
5 Determination	44	48
6 Female Preference	—	—
7 Cognitive Tasks	58	—
8 Entrepreneur	—	59

Female preference was a specific factor in this analysis, emerging in the third principal axis and the rest of the variance in the analysis showed the clerical factor to be specific also.

Second Order Factors, Discussion

Factor 1 is a preference for occupations involving a great deal of education and indicates a possible high aspiration dimension. Factor 2 with loadings on adverse physical, determination to succeed and entrepreneurship suggests equally high aspirations towards self-sufficiency and independence of action even in the face of severe working conditions. The centrality of the determination to succeed first order factor, represented in Table I, with high loadings on two extremely different dimensions of aspiration, suggests that this is a personality construct measured indirectly. It largely accounts for the correlation of 0·31 between the two factors.[1] It is suggested that females are not nearly so highly motivated as males in Shona society towards success in cognitive or practical tasks, while clerical jobs essentially signify the end of educational hopes and acceptance of this situation. Hence the clerical and female preference factors are taken to be orthogonal to the two main second order factors that account for all but 9 per cent of the common variance.

RELATING INDIVIDUALS AND GROUPS – A RATIONALE

The results presented above shed light on two main issues. The first is what this *élite* group hopes to do in a situation of apparently limited

---

[1] The psychologist who favours hierarchical structure might be tempted to rotate the two second order axes through 45 degrees, interpreting the first factor as general determination to succeed and the second as a bi-polar separating cognitive and practical occupations.

opportunity. The second is the relation of individual differences in the perception of occupations to group prestige ratings.

The results show clearly that the students vary individually in their aspirations for the future, although a great many of them hope that the future will include higher education leading to the professions. Failing this they hope for employment in clerical jobs. The determinants of their choices appear to be complex but the various factors that have been uncovered indicate evaluation of jobs according to whether they (a) include cognitive tasks; (b) have adverse or favourable physical environments; (c) offer avenues of eventual political involvement; (d) offer the opportunity for independence of action on the job, and in the domain of personality; (e) demand high or low individual motivation to succeed.

These dimensions must be, in turn, related to the contention by sociologists that groups use frames of reference like those specified above with which to balance out good and bad qualities of jobs.

Although further studies are necessary to find out how individuals differ in the weightings they give to the dimensions specified, one might now venture a model that combines both the approach of the psychologist and the sociologist. It would be that each occupation may be evaluated in terms of current value systems that are related to the individual's position within a group. In this case one would expect differences in social structure to be reflected in the order of importance of any choice dimension (cf. Mitchell and Irvine, 1966). For example, money may be very important to some classes of people but not to others whose expectations of making a great deal more money by changing jobs does not increase. This may account for some social class differences in the order of importance of Hicks' (1966) dimensions of prestige, and the relatively low correlation between financial gain, for his group of railway workers, and the overall prestige rating. Here we have argued, however, that even within groups that are exactly homogeneous in terms of one social class variable – educational achievement – that individual differences in the perception of relatively well-defined dimensions and the effect of personality differences in their evaluation will exercise considerable influence. Hence, some of the 'factors' elucidated by Hicks may be regarded, as far as the individuals within a group are concerned, as input variables that are processed differentially, and hence correlated differentially. Similarly, all of the dimensions of evaluation are subject to influence by the affective organization of man's perceptions, and positive and negative affect can operate with considerable force. Some of these variables may therefore be regarded as potential moderator variables for some groups of people who perceive them differently from others in the population. In this group, for example, one might predict that those who showed high motivation to succeed would view the prestige of occupations and the interrelations of the underlying dimensions of evaluation differently from those who did not. Similarly one would expect those who preferred cognitive tasks to practical tasks, yet were equal in level of aspiration to succeed, to place different emphasis on jobs that seemed to offer different opportunities in these two dimensions. These are areas for further study; another such area is the relationship of individual differences in cognitive tasks to the factors hypothesized.

Summary and Conclusions

This material represents a departure from the usual studies of aspirations because it focuses on the individual within the group as well as on the group itself. Individual differences, even in extremely homogeneous groups of students, are often the main concern of both the teacher and the vocational guidance advisor who want to place school leavers effectively. The debilitating shortage of high-level manpower in Africa demands that maximum use be made of the manpower available. Studies such as these are important because they show (*a*) what *élites* may expect to do after completing four years of secondary schooling and (*b*) how individuals vary within the frame of these expectations as defined by the group.

Particularly important in this study is the sense of dichotomy rather than of gradation between acceptable and unacceptable jobs and conditions. Aspirations and expectations in this sample are high. On the other hand, the factor analyses clearly indicate the strong sense of motivation that pervades the roles of practical, independent and self-made men and of those who favour intellectual and cognitive tasks. Without high aspirations the probability of success in the private or public sections of the economy seems small.

Finally, while sociological studies are important in illustrating how social structure may influence individual decisions, the role of the individual himself as a decision maker must receive more attention than we have been able to give to it in the past. For example, the supervisory role in African commerce and industry needs understanding both from the viewpoint of social structure and the conditions that individuals will stipulate before undertaking it. Whereas the supervisor may expect social pressures of a fairly predictable kind, his reactions to them must be assessed so that he can be helped, if necessary, to continue to function as a supervisor. Psychologists can now predict individual differences in intellectual performance with reasonable accuracy in many African countries. The whole area of personality organization, however, is relatively uncharted. This paper indicates ways in which surveys can be used to mark certain routes for future investigation. That they must be investigated is clear from the viewpoint of economic investment in human potential, and from fundamental humanitarian concern for the students who emerge from any system of education.

BIBLIOGRAPHY

V. S. D'Souza, 'Social Grading of Occupations in India'. (*The Sociological Review*, 1962,) **10**, 145–149.

R. E. Hicks, 'Occupational Prestige and its Factors'. (*African Social Research*, 1966), **1**, 41–58.

R. E. Hicks, 'Similarities and Differences in Occupational Prestige Ratings'. (*African Social Research*, 1967), **3**, 206–227.

S. H. Irvine, 'A Five-year Follow-up of Secondary School Selection Procedures in Central Africa, 1962–67'. (*British Journal of Educational Psychology*, 1968), **38**, (in press).

J. C. Mitchell and A. L. Epstein, 'Occupational prestige and Social Status among Africans in Northern Rhodesia'. (*Africa*, 1959), **29**, 22–40.

J. C. Mitchell and S. H. Irvine, *Occupational Prestige and Aspirations in some Southern Rhodesian African Schools.* (Mimeographed Report, African Studies Department, University College, Salisbury, Rhodesia, 1962.)

J. C. Mitchell and S. H. Irvine, 'Social position and the Grading of Occupations'. (*Rhodes-Livingstone Journal*, 1966), **38**, 42–54.

A. J. Reiss, *Occupations and Social Status.* (Glencoe, Illinois: Free Press, 1961.)

P. H. Rossi and A. Inkeles, 'National Comparison of Occupational Prestige'. (*American Journal of Sociology*, 1956), **61**, 329–339.

R. M. Thomas, 'Reinspecting a Structural Position on Occupational Prestige'. (*American Journal of Sociology*, 1962), **67**, 561–565.

E. A. Tiryakian, 'The Prestige Evaluation of Occupations in an Underdeveloped Country: the Philippines'. (*American Journal of Sociology*, 1958), **63**, 390–399.

Effects of Examinations on Education, Teachers, Pupils

Brian Holmes
Reader in Comparative Education in the University of London

In the previous section some of the socio-economic consequences of educational policy are assessed. In earlier sections the educational effects of examinations are referred to constantly. Frequently, in describing reform authors emphasize the defects of examinations and tests and by implication at least, stress the baleful influence of traditional systems of examinations on the school system as a whole. In this section attention is directed much more explicitly to these relationships – to do so requires detailed analysis.

In the first place, it should be recognized that examination techniques have changed in a way that has vastly increased the range of things to be tested. F. Bowles surveys the wide variety of forms modern examinations take and shows how they reach today into 'learning behaviour, motivations, aspirations and social attitudes' (p. 336). Consequently, in assessing the effects of examinations, due note should be taken of these developments. The effects of written tests may be different from those which flow from oral examinations. Objective-type testing may have a different import from that of essay type examinations. It is also necessary, however, to note that an educational system itself can be broken down into many constituent institutions. An analysis of structure involves recognition of levels or stages of education – first, second and third – and the types of school within each of these levels. Functional relationships exist between levels and school types. The curriculum includes not only the range of subjects taught and activities encouraged, but also the content of each subject. Methods of teaching are institutionalized and utilize aids ranging from the blackboard and chalk through textbooks to sophisticated programmed learning machines. Rituals also form part of the internal organization of any school. The breakdown into component parts could go on. Certainly it would be unwise to imagine that the effect on any one of the institutions mentioned was the same whatever type of examination is considered. The hope of many educationists is that objective-type tests will have a less harmful influence than traditional examinations on these many institutions. The hope needs to be tested in research inquiries.

R. W. Tyler, in an important review of effects in the U.S.A., shows how research inquiries (the Regents' Inquiry, 1936, the Eight-Year Study, 1934–42), threw light on the possibilities of reconciling conflicting objectives in education (p. 342).

People are involved too. How does each of the types of examination or test affect administrators? Are these influences the same as or similar to those affecting teachers? How does this or that kind of examination affect children? But children are individuals and each may be affected in a somewhat different way. Considered as members of a group the distinction should perhaps be drawn between children of different ages and certainly between those groups whose members have succeeded and those groups whose members have, in effect, failed.

Again, how do examinations influence aims? Important points in the analysis by F. Hotyat are that since a great deal of time is devoted to examinations in European countries, care should be taken to ensure that 'examinations must be devised in accordance with the syllabus and the method of instruction' if stated educational objectives are to be achieved (p. 356).

A final word of caution is needed. The socio-economic context in which examinations function within an educational system will also have some bearing on the kind of relationships which exist between the various parts. Examinations which function well in the United States may have different effects in, let us say, African or European countries. The assumption that examinations are closely related to most features of the educational system in most countries is probably justified. The hypothesis that traditional modes of examining are harmful needs close examination in context before it can be confirmed or refuted. What is evident from the careful studies presented in this section is that the process of analysis is well under way, and that many testable hypotheses, quite limited in range and scope, are thrown up for subsequent detailed investigation.

Dr Bowles takes the view that tests are both complex and indispensable with the result that 'the examination specialist and the classroom teacher have no common language for communication . . .' (p. 336). One conclusion of Professor Tibble's review of examinations in England and Wales is that teachers in training, at least, assessed by course work, work no less hard or 'achieve lower standards than students assessed solely by examination papers'. (p. 354). Dr Langeveld argues that the effect on children of examinations rightly biased may be wonderful, but wrongly biased they may frustrate what a good education tries to further. Dean Ruth Wong analyses some aspects of the situation, taking examples from Malaysia, Vietnam and Pakistan.

The problems in formal systems of education are similar at whatever stage of development they happen to be. Unique features of these problems will be found not only in this section but throughout the volume.

37

Educational Effects of Examinations

Frank Bowles

Adviser to the President on International Education, Ford Foundation, and former President, College Entrance Examination Board

The most important change in education over the past twenty years has not been physical but conceptual. The acceptance of the idea that education is an instrument of development and that national growth rests upon educational growth has resulted in a liberalization and expansion of opportunity which has become visible as a vast physical extension of school systems. With the extension, the ritual of guarding the privilege of education in order that it might be limited to suitable persons is disappearing. In its place we now accept the need to so extend education that each person in a society may be educated as his needs and competencies require.

It is significant that examinations play the key role in either view of education. In traditional systems they are the tool of elimination and selection through which access to middle-class education is controlled. In such a role, the examination is a powerful but limited instrument. Its power rests on its use to set an absolute standard and its limitation comes from the fact that its controlling use forecloses all need for other uses. Hence its possible variations in form and its values for other educational uses are never explored since there is no application for them in a system which lives by a single and rigid standard.

In contemporary education, examinations play a different role. Since the purpose of contemporary education must be to maximize the use of educational potential, it is necessary to determine where the potential is and how it may best be developed. Such an undertaking may begin with an inquiry into the pre-school environment of an individual child, or the analysis of the social environment of a city block, or a study of cultural stratification in a city. Other and less specialized tests may be used to examine the development of potential in formal schooling, and special instruments may be added in a search for explanation of deviant educational behaviour.

Tests, in short, become an indispensable part of the contemporary educational process, simply because the process itself has reached so far into contemporary society that we must now develop techniques of objective and reliable measurement in order to understand the problems with which we are dealing and evaluate the results.

The question of what techniques must be used in examination of educational results is, in the context of contemporary education, unimportant. Significantly, this is not the case in traditional education. Traditional examinations are almost inevitably, in oral or written form, cumbersome, fearsome, and unreliable. Yet, despite the known statistical evidence of their unreliability and unfairness to candidates, they are revered for their form and defended for the very characteristic that produces their unreliability – the direct (though temporary) one-to-one relationship between pupil and examiner which they symbolize.

Contemporary examinations may take a wide variety of forms. They range from the micro-sample opinion polls to standardized classroom tests, and from the laboratory mazes which are as old as Knossos to their modern verbal analogue of the self-scoring test. A demographic study is as surely a form of group examination as a national examination to determine teacher qualifications. A performance test, whether administered to an aspiring surgeon or an agonizing television repairman, is still an examination within the context of contemporary education.

It is worth repeating that the process of examination has long since overpassed the question of whether a student can conjugate a Latin verb, or even describe the reactions of nuclear fission. It reaches today into learning behaviour, motivations, aspirations and social attitudes. It can be applied to evaluation of teaching methods, of curricula, and of learning materials. It is still primarily concerned with the pupil and what he learns, but it now recognizes that variables which exert strong influence on learning must be sought and evaluated by a variety of methods.

As the process of examination has enlarged its scope, it has passed the boundaries of pedagogy and applied psychology and entered such fields as anthropology, biology and sociology. Inevitably, in the process of enlargement, it has developed its own subject matter and its own vocabulary, which, in its higher reaches is probably the most impenetrable dialect of pedagese yet developed. From this development comes one of today's unhappy circumstances – that the examination specialist and the classroom teacher have no common language for communication despite the fact that they share a concern for the measurement of the results of the educational process.

It is this problem of communication to which this indispensable volume is dedicated, in an undertaking of great importance for educational development.

38

Examinations, Education and the Developing Child

Martin J. Langeveld

Professor of Education and Clinical Child Psychology, University of Utrecht

(1) Everyday upbringing and education – which I will take together from now on in this chapter under the latter heading – is not really based on prediction but on expectation and by what implicitly is taken for a self-evident guideline either for the future or in the present situation. Children are born from parents – not from functionaries in an institution such as a school, a foster home, a reformatory. Parents take it for granted that children grow up, boys as boys and girls as girls. The expectations are: adulthood, earning their own living, social responsibility, etc. If parents are interested at all in such predictions as tests often hope to offer, they will be concerned mainly with a prediction for their specific child and for as long a period ahead of the present moment as schooling may last. Whether such predictions can be made with sufficient certainty, exactly where they are needed most – that is, where uncertain factors are most obvious – is another question.

Authorities have little interest in the individual case. They are planning in the macrostructure of the tasks to be fulfilled in society. Will the supply be enough? Will it be trained according to the needs of the market?

To a certain extent the different views on the coming generation are incompatible and to that extent personal decisions, a system open to widely divergent procedures, mutual consultation between parents and authorities with opportunities to give someone the benefit of the doubt, should be built-in escapes from the tyranny of what often is referred to as objectivity. In this objectivity, however, a number of presuppositions are taken for granted. More often than not the test is based on the middle class, its hope for economic stability as a minimum hope but with some belief in continuous prosperity, with its idea of social progress and the rise in the social scale. It also presupposes a continued stability and an omnipresent equality in the educational (home *and* school!) conditions. It takes little heed of what happened in the period before the test was applied – to the baby's environment, a young child's opportunity to acquire and learn in a particular setting. And if it does, are the educational tools available in school and home to create an improvement! As Bettye M. Caldwell has said 'There is much justifiable concern these days with discovering the range of experiences for infants and young children that would be conducive to optimal cognitive development'.[1] 'Optimal cognitive development': 'optimal' according to whose considerations? To the super-schoolmaster or to an idea of maturity of man of a wider scope?

It is nice to *have* opportunities and to develop according to the standards of those who set exams, tests and who interview you. Yet, did the Lord make the shoes or the children?

(2) For a child to pass a 'test' means to stand the test of growing – of growing mastery of a skill or a field of knowledge. It is the test of growing adulthood, of growing independence, of growing acceptability. Failing the test, then, is more than just having failed to get sufficient marks. It means rejection by the standards of a society whose measuring rod is emotionally important; it means failure to obtain recognition. To help a child to become a successful candidate for an examination has, consequently, something to do with helping him to pass the 'tests of life'. Wise people at a writing desk or in a contemplative armchair may consider examinations – and one of their means, now technically called a 'test' – as businesslike matters which should not be overestimated. This, however, is adults' wisdom and not sense common enough to embrace the child's own actual experience as well.

The more traditionally organized the examination system and its contents are, the more the 'socially well adjusted' and the conformist will find it the ideal way to success. A good examination, like a good test, must therefore leave ample opportunity for the child to demonstrate his own interests, his own inventivity or creativity. It is, however, questionable whether the situation of the examination and the scope of the action required in tests or exams encourages the manifestation of such qualities. Nevertheless, exams *may* stimulate more than just conformist or passive learning. Exams may make a pupil's work purposeful. Exams may help a teacher to fill his own yearly programme with a number of indisputable tasks 'to go by' and to keep the pupils in working discipline. Exams provide a goal, or they may open a new period of devotion to a job.

Part of all this may be superstition helpful to adults and, particularly, to teachers and those who run a school system. As we have said already, this means that in the exam the world of the child and adult society are meeting one another – sometimes in a clash, sometimes in an invigorating contest needed by both parties; by the one to prove its case, by the other to see the case proved, by both *to establish a growing participation*. For the main aim of education is to help young people to take over: to take over the full

---

[1] *Annals of the New York Academy of Sciences.* Vol. 118, art. 21, p. 783–866. May 25, 1965.— Editor: Harold E. Whipple, the articles by Robert L. Frantz, Peter H. Wolff, Nahman H. Greenberg and Bettye M. Caldwell.

responsibility for their own acts and negligence; to take over the full responsibility for the social and cultural process, the responsibility for the young, the old, the invalid, the weak; to take over the full responsibility for development towards a future which increasingly makes life worth while.

(3) Educationally speaking then, the planning, the construction of exams and the preparation for them as well as taking them, are of importance and may be of positive value for the individual as well as for his parents (who want to see the progress in their part of the task checked up) and for society. Damage can be done and actually has been done and is being done to all concerned. But encouragement, steadiness on the road to certain aspects of maturity or at least to social independence, well-planned action and a justified gauge of the potential of the coming generation, may be mentioned as some of the positive aspects.

Exams have been rightly criticized for their stifling effect on the learning – and for that matter on the teaching as well – of the pupil. The stereotype may prevail, 'facts' may shrink to what can be crammed into the reproduction machinery of examination. Preference for what is taught best because it can be tested best may bring back into the new approach what it had hoped to overcome. And this brings us back to what might better be called an idolatry of objectivity than real objectivity – however invaluable objectivity may be in itself. The old style examination had strong opinions about the 'intelligence' of the pupils failing or succeeding. The test nowadays suffers, in practice, from much the same mistake. Both do little to clarify their suppositions or to correct their standards accordingly, adding the necessary provisions for the prevention and the rectification of unfavourable causes.

We analyse school success all too often on the basis of school success. We take those who come through the exams as the standard for those who are to be selected for that confrontation, in this way eternalizing the present school, or too much of it at least. In our tests used for prediction, too little has found its origin in a precise analysis of school failure as such, too little of the impact of actual teaching procedures and teacher attitudes is ever applied in the construction of any test. So what the old system took for innate ability plus good teaching and 'putting the boy well into shape', fell back on other presuppositions: the score on the test was supposed to indicate intelligence, this intelligence was by definition successful, teaching had to meet it, logical analysis of subject material is identified with the ideal psychological order of learning, and the psychological order would, of course, be educationally ideal!

We need not concern ourselves too much with those who fall into clearcut categories; our primary concern should be with those on the borderline between success and failure (those whose achievements are almost good enough, but not quite . . .). Will they respond to good teaching, a change in personal approach on the part of the teacher or in his method? How is their performance affected by events at home or the social environment? Today, testing is not confined to 'cognitive development' only; instead of being a formal examination, it has to be a source of information about a child's whole personality – his potential in terms of 'good marks' as well as his ability to profit from the opportunities for personal development offered by a good school.

And what if such schools are too rare? The test would still be objective if it could really break through its limitations set by its idea of 'intelligence'. And that would be fine and helpful for the responsible party in the matter but neither for the parents as such nor for the pupils of that moment. Tests used nowadays for school purposes are mostly limited to sorting and grading on the basis of the existing system and its social presuppositions. They are, in this way, a vast circular argument and thus, in many cases, a *circulus vitiosus*. To be coached for them is a simple act of restoring justice.

And so objectivity is exactly what we need. But not the one guaranteed only by a simplification of the set of variables conditioning the case. Secondly, not the one which rushes ahead of prerequisite steps such as the improvement of teacher training, subject analysis, teaching methods, compensation for inadequate home conditions, the correction of poor school teaching in lower grades, etc. There 'objectivity' would really be needed. What is to be said against the objectivity of 'tests', etc., is not that they should be subjective but that their alleged objectivity may be proclaimed too early and then turn into its opposite which is not 'subjectivity' but supposition.

(4) So exams are or may be of a positive educational value and exams can only be sufficiently objective if the opportunities have been taken earlier to create fair conditions. We also have predictive tools which function as an examination or as a part of it. Of them we have spoken also with critical reservation. But we can neither do without the one nor without the other. We have to be modest and humble, however, in our pretence of selection and prediction. We have to realize where the examination and the test go basically wrong and we have to ask ourselves two questions first of all: What can we do to prevent or repair the harm done? What can we do to improve the instruments we are using?

These questions cannot and should not be discussed in this chapter. They are both essentially educational in purpose though the instruments may in one case also presuppose sociological, in another psychological research.

Education so often has to bring such heteronomous approaches together for one object and purpose. For that reason a watchful human person, responsible for what is going on and aware of what is to come is an essential part of education; the parent, the teacher – generally speaking

– the educator. This is all the more important, as human life consists of a number of heteronomous sets of determinants. To harmonize this heteronomy is a life task for the person who grows up and lives his life himself. It is a primary task for the educator to start this complex dialectic problem and to help the child to sort *himself* out, consequently predictions must not be too pretentious and exams must be based on a form of reasonable control *and* exchange between the examiner and the child.

There is a strong tendency to 'leave things to their natural development'. Within strict limits there is something in this idea. Yet, human nature is of a complex kind and, as has been said before, does consist of a number of heteronomous fields, whilst it has to develop under still more complex and heterogeneous conditions. No test can predict the events of life, no exam eliminate their harmful consequences. Education should respect 'nature' and at the same time guide and influence it.

The 'natural development' theory of Montessori and a number of present-day psychologists encounters opposition from those who stress the importance of environmental conditioning – those who stress a guided process of teaching and education and who do not believe that the child's optimum can be reached naturally without a decisive interference with choice and direction, and, consequently, prevention and correction. Emotional cluttering leads to the idea that the last point of view must be authoritarian, whereas the first should be democratic.

That education may have its optimal periods to acquire a certain cognitive or emotional gain makes it the more serious a task to arrive with the educational means in time. But that in our present world cognitive and emotional maturity and the necessary productivity and creativity can be left to a kindly sequential procedure only is, I fear, sheer romanticism. A number of things have to be learned because they fit in well from points of view which have little to do with nature and another number of things have to be learned simply because, for reasons of programming a human being's youth, they have to be placed *somewhere*.

To be 'examinable' may mean to be able to stand the test of questioning, to be responsible for what one thinks and does and to show one's best personal capacities. If examinations could follow this bias, their educational effect might be wonderful. If they do not find an adequate form of this kind they will tend to frustrate in a number of cases what a good education tries hard to further, what a mediocre education considers as all it can do.

39

Educational Effects of Examinations in the United States

Ralph W. Tyler
Director Emeritus and Member, Board of Trustees – Center for Advanced Study in the Behavioral Sciences

From the standpoint of teachers and school principals, examinations are commonly viewed as essential parts of the educational system. They furnish concrete examples of the educational aims formulated by those who constructed the examinations, and in this way they provide both teachers and pupils with standards external to their own classrooms toward which their efforts can be directed. In the United States, The Regents' Inquiry into the Character and Cost of Public Education begun in 1936 provided objective evidence regarding the influence of examinations on teachers as well as pupils. An intensive study was made of sixty-one school districts within the State of New York, reviewing their curriculum guides and testing their secondary school students for several of the objectives specified in the curriculum guides. It was found that the educational achievement of the students paralleled more closely the objectives tested by the state examinations than the objectives given main emphasis in the local curricula. Interviews with a sample of teachers in these communities revealed the fact that most of them knew what objectives were being appraised by the state examinations and sought to emphasize these kinds of learning in their classes rather than to follow the aims recommended in the local curriculum guides.

My own experience in the Eight-Year study, an investigation of new secondary school programmes that were developed and tried out in thirty U.S. school systems in the period 1934–42, corroborated the findings of the Regents' Inquiry. When new ideas regarding the secondary school curriculum were advanced, teachers usually raised the question of the relationship of these new proposals to the achievements which were being appraised by the College Entrance Examination Board Tests. Only through the arrangement worked out with colleges which permitted high school graduates to be considered for college admission on the basis of scholastic aptitude examinations and test data submitted by the schools participating in the investigation, were we able to get thoughtful consideration of new curriculum proposals by the teachers. They were then able to shift from their previous practice of planning their teaching to correspond to their view of what would be required of their students on college entrance examinations to planning based on judgements of the educational value of various kinds of learning.

A third illustration of the influence of examinations on the educational efforts of students and teachers is the experience of the various 'International Schools'. A major purpose of these schools is to bring young people from different nations into the same institution where by studying and working together on common subjects, broader perspective and more realistic understanding of persons from other nations can be developed. However, the students plan to enrol in various European universities where the entrance examinations are quite idiosyncratic. To prepare students to perform successfully on these examinations the schools have had to provide, during the last year or two of secondary education, different courses for the different universities in literature, history, and even in mathematics and science so that the students spend much of their time during these years in separated classes rather than benefiting from common learning experiences.

A fourth illustration of the educational influence of examinations is the prevalence of coaching for them. Some schools turn to coaching rather than teaching several weeks before important examinations are to be given. Other schools do not modify the teaching in the regular classes but arrange for special coaching for those students planning to take the examinations. In some American communities where no provisions for coaching are made in the schools, some parents arrange for special coaching classes, or for tutoring, in the belief that this will aid their children to make a better showing on the examinations. A quick survey of book stores and advertisements in America also provides an indication of demand for coaching. Books and pamphlets purporting to help students to pass important examinations are widely sold.

It is a fair summary of the current situation throughout the world to say that examinations have profound educational effects on many students and teachers. For pupils who have some confidence in their ability to perform on the examinations, the knowledge that they are to be given serves as a strong stimulation to study, and the later report of the marks given to their performance provides a powerful reinforcement mechanism of reward or punishment that helps to maintain the motivation for learning. Not only does examining afford forceful motivation but it also directs the efforts of many students and teachers toward learning activities which they believe are most relevant to what they think the examination will call for. In many cases, this may focus the attention on goals different from those purportedly emphasized by the school, and in some cases this results in coaching rather than long-term systematic instruction. Furthermore, examinations can be a source of anxiety to some pupils and parents and can become, for some, the ends of education rather than a device for appraisal of learning. Examinations are powerful instruments with potentialities for both good and bad effects on education.

When faced with this generalization, those who are concerned with the improvement of education and the effectiveness of learning must consider how to achieve the maximum good potential in examinations and how to minimize or eliminate the bad. This requires an analysis of the present and potential examinations and their uses.

The first stage of the analysis involves the identification of purposes and uses, since each different function requires some differences in the examinations themselves, in the way in which they are administered, and in the uses made of results. To identify students prepared to profit from current university education, the examinations need to contain exercises that require verbal facility, quantitive logic, and skills and understanding of major concepts used in the several disciplines to treat the phenomena with which they deal. Such an examination, if well constructed, encourages the development in schools of reading and writing skills, of fundamental mathematics and an understanding of subject matter rather than detailed or rote memorization. It need not restrict the specific illustrations through which ideas are learned and applied nor need it foster a particular method or approach to teaching. The use of examinations focused on these general intellectual skills and understanding was first tried experimentally in the Eight-Year study mentioned above. In this experiment, the students admitted to the 'prestige' colleges in the United States, on the basis of the general educational examinations, made better academic records in their first two years of college than did the students admitted on the basis of passing examinations based on syllabuses outlined for specific required courses in the secondary school. The mean grade-point average of the first group was 2·8 and of the second group 2·3, that is, half the difference between a grade of B and of C. Later, the College Entrance Examination Board adopted a programme of examinations using tests of verbal and quantitative skills plus subject tests that seek to emphasize understanding of basic concepts.

To maximize the value of entrance examinations of this sort, it is necessary to involve teachers from schools and colleges in outlining the specifications for the examinations and in developing exercises that meet the specifications. Their work should be widely reported so that all teachers and students will know that the examinations are not tests requiring memory of specific items of information, but are opportunities for students to demonstrate some basic intellectual skills and to show that they understand major concepts of several subjects.

Another widely used function of examinations is to aid the leadership of a school system in monitoring and guiding its educational programme. This requires examinations for all the important fields of instruction and for all the major objectives of these fields. The traditional preoccupation of examiners has been with written exercises requiring memory of information. These are not satisfactory for appraising such subjects as music, art, vocational education and the like, nor are they valid tests of such objectives as oral language skills, interest in reading, appreciation of works of art, ability to carry on independent inquiry. If an examination programme used to monitor the work of the school covers only some of the subjects and a part of the objectives, it will have a serious distorting effect on the efforts of students and teachers. They will give more attention and devote more of their efforts to those subjects and those objectives which they believe will be included in the examinations and neglect the others.

The development of an adequate examining system for this purpose requires the use of a variety of devices, since, for an examination to be appropriate for a given educational objective, it must evoke from the student the kind of behaviour which is implied by the objective and it must also deal with the content which the objective implies. Thus, if one of the objectives of physics in the school is to develop the ability of the students to apply basic principles of physics in explaining common physical phenomena and predicting the probable consequences of particular physical forces in action, then an appropriate examination for this objective will require the student to explain various common physical phenomena using basic principles of physics in the explanation, and it will also include exercises in which the student is expected to predict on the basis of his understanding of these basic principles what the probable consequences will be in various situations involving physical forces. If every major objective of the school is appraised by examinations which are appropriate to evoke the desired behaviour in connection with the specified content, then the examinations not only provide evidence of the results being attained in the school's educational programme, but they also reinforce the efforts of students and teachers to attain these goals rather than distorting them.

Participating in the construction of an examination programme of this sort is a valuable experience for teachers, supervisors, and inspectors. The first step is to identify and define clearly the objectives that are actually sought in each school subject. This step is really essential for intelligent planning of the curriculum and the conduct of teaching but it is commonly done in a vague or inadequate way. In many cases, the objectives published have listed the topics to be covered, but gave no indication about what the student should learn to do with the content of these topics. In other cases the behaviour has been stated in very vague terms, such as 'to think quantitatively', or 'to know about something'. In order to build a valid examination, the behaviour to be learned and the content involved must be identified, and both of these must be defined clearly enough to select and build exercises requiring the student to employ this behaviour with the appropriate content. This clarification of objectives and the development of relevant exercises are very helpful to teachers in planning and carrying on their classroom work.

Another function of examinations is to furnish information to the teacher about pupil performance and progress which will aid in the conduct of teaching. This requires several kinds of examinations, designed closely in harmony with the curriculum, the teaching approach, and the materials employed. Some of the examinations should be built to indicate which students at a given time mastered the basic concepts and skills for this unit of instruction and are ready to move to the next. Some examinations are needed to help diagnose the kinds of difficulties students are encountering, so that teaching efforts can be more efficiently directed. Other examinations should furnish data concerning both the long-term retention of learning and its transfer to the variety of situations to which the learning can be properly applied. As examinations of these types are developed and used by teachers and pupils, their effects are likely to be positive because both the instructor and the student will perceive them as tools of teaching and learning rather than ends in themselves.

Examinations are here to stay and their uses will increase. They can be an obstacle to an effective educational programme, distracting attention from the school's basic purposes, and arousing undue excitement and fear. On the other hand, because examinations can increase motivation and provide an additional source of reinforcement to learning and because they can help to clarify the objectives of the school and focus effort on them, examinations should be used as a positive factor in the educational programme. To do so requires first, the distinction among the different purposes or uses for the examination, namely, to guide or select students for further education, to monitor the educational programme of a school system and to aid the work of teaching and learning. Then, for each major kind of purpose or use, examinations should be designed which maximize their value and minimize their bad effects on education. This can be done.

40

The Educational Effects of Examinations in England and Wales

J. W. Tibble

Emeritus Professor, University of Leicester; Academic Secretary, Universities Council for the Education of Teachers

For the purposes of this chapter, I accept the definition of examinations put forward by Dr Brereton (page 34) and his distinction between examinations and tests. The latter, he says, are 'designed to provide an accurate standardized measurement of certain abilities or skills without influencing teacher or student and without creating any tension in the student'; the former are 'a dynamic part of the whole educational process, involved with motivation and with defining the character of the education in which the student is involved – a type of happening which incorporates many of the characteristics of human life itself – competition and rivalry, purposeful activity directed towards a goal, the planning of a course of work and maintenance of standards.'

Examinations, in this sense, came into being in the second half of the nineteenth century to meet problems raised by the expansion of education-al facilities and opportunities. With the removal of various restrictions on entry to universities, the Civil Service, the Royal Military Academy, some devices were needed to decide who should be chosen. Similarly, with the removal of restrictions on the curriculum and the gradual acceptance of many new subjects, schools felt the need of guidance about what to teach, how to teach it, and what standards to aim at. By 1860, the Universities of Oxford, Cambridge, London and Durham were providing systems of local examinations for schools; examinations were also provided by the College of Preceptors, the Society of Arts, and, later, the City and Guilds of London Institute. As early as 1868, the proliferation of examinations was seen as creating a problem for schools (*Report of the Schools Inquiry Commission*), and by 1911 the problem had become acute. The *Report of the Consultative Committee on Examinations in Secondary Schools* referred to the dangers of the 'existing multiplicity of external examinations' and stressed the need for concerted action. This led in 1917 to some reduction of the multiplicity with the recognition of two levels of examination, School Certificate for pupils aged sixteen and Higher School Certificate for those about two years older. For the between-wars generation the term 'School Cert.' and 'Higher' were almost synonymous with secondary education.

Summary of Good and Bad Effects

As it happens, the 1911 Report gives us a summary of the good and bad effects of examinations on teachers and pupils which cannot be bettered, so I reproduce it here:

(1) The good effects of the examination on the pupil are (a) that they make him work up to time by requiring him to reach a stated degree of knowledge by a fixed date ; (b) that they incite him to get his knowledge into reproducible form and to lessen the risk of vagueness; (c) that they make him work at parts of a study which, though important, may be uninteresting or repugnant to him personally; (d) that they train the power of getting up a subject for a definite purpose, even though it may not appear necessary to remember it afterwards – a training which is useful for parts of the professional duty of the lawyer, the administrator, the journalist, and the man in business; (e) that in some cases they encourage a certain steadiness of work over a long period of time; and (f) that they enable the pupil to measure his real attainment (i) by the standards required by outside examiners, (ii) by comparison with the attainments of his contemporaries in other schools.

On the other hand, examinations may have a bad effect upon the pupil's mind (a) by setting a premium on the power of merely reproducing other people's ideas and other people's methods of presentment, thus diverting energy from the creative process; (b) by favouring a somewhat passive type of mind; (c) by rewarding evanescent forms of knowledge; (d) by giving an undue advantage to those who, in answering questions on paper, can cleverly make the best use of, perhaps, slender attainments; (e) by inducing the pupil, in his preparation for an examination, to aim rather at absorbing information imparted to him by the teacher than at forming an independent judgement upon the subjects in which he receives instruction; and (f) by stimulating the competitive (and at its worst, a mercenary) spirit in the acquisition of knowledge.

(2) The good effects of a well-conducted examination upon the teacher are (a) that they induce him to treat his subjects thoroughly; (b) that they make him so arrange his lessons as to cover with intellectual thoroughness a prescribed course of study within appointed limits of time; (c) that they impel him to pay attention not only to his best pupils, but also to the backward and the slower amongst those who are being prepared for the examination; and (d) that they make him acquainted with the standard which other teachers and their pupils are able to reach in the same subject in other places of education.

On the other hand, the effects of examinations on teachers are bad (a) in so far as they constrain him to watch the examiner's foibles and to note his idiosyncracies (or the tradition of the examiner) in order that he may arm his pupils with the kind of knowledge required for dealing successfully with the questions that will probably be put to them; (b) in so far as they limit the freedom of the teacher in choosing the way in which he shall treat his subject; (c) in so far as they encourage him to take upon himself work which had better be left to the largely unaided efforts of his pupils, causing him to impart information to them in too digested a form or to select for them groups of facts or aspects of the subject which each pupil should properly be left to collect or envisage for himself; (d) in so far as they predispose the teacher to overvalue among his pupils that type of mental development which secures success in examinations; (e) in so far as they make it the teacher's interest to excel in the purely examinable side of his professional work and divert his attention from those parts of education which cannot be tested by the process of examination. It will be seen that the dangers of examinations, and especially of external examinations are considerable in their possible effect both on pupil and teacher. We have no hesitation, however, in stating our conviction that external examinations are not only necessary but desirable in Secondary Schools. But we are equally convinced that if the admitted advantages of external examinations are to be secured and the dangers of them minimised, such examinations should be subjected to most stringent regulations as to their number, the age at which they are taken, and their general character.[1]

It seems reasonable to assume that the balance of pros and cons as set out above will vary according to the educational situation in a particular country at a particular time. Thus I can fully accept the validity of the 1911 Report's conviction that on balance the pros outweighed the cons. In a period when 'the silent social revolution', as Lowndes called it, was still in its early stages, when schools had to cope with masses of children unused to the traditional educational disciplines, coming from homes in which many parents were apathetic about or antagonistic to compulsory education, when teachers in general had only minimal training and most graduate teachers none at all, clearly the predominant need was for devices which (a) provided the pupils with some positive motivation for learning and (b) gave the poorly equipped teachers definite guidance about the nature of their task and what goals and standards might be achieved. Certainly, for the secondary schools in the period between the Education Act of 1902 and that of 1944 the various Examination Boards based on universities did provide this motivation for a good many children and this guidance for their teachers. In the elementary schools during the same period the same needs were met by the examination procedures which the L.E.A.s adopted to select children for entry to grammar schools.

But, surely, the educational situation today is in a number of fundamental respects very different from what it was in that earlier period; and it does not follow that the devices most suitable for achieving given ends in the one situation are equally suitable in the other. Among these changes are the following: the higher evaluation of education generally by our society today, and in particular the gradual percolation down the social strata of

---

[1] Report of the Consultative Committee on Examinations in Secondary Schools, 1911, Chapter IV.

upper- and middle-class attitudes to education; the acceleration in the rate of technical and social change which makes necessary not only the continuous revision of what is learned by each younger generation but also the continuation of learning throughout the whole adult life; the fact that the teaching profession has now many years of collective experience behind it, that standards of entry to courses and the length and quality of the courses themselves have all improved markedly in recent years. Consideration of these changes leads me to the conclusion that devices once very appropriate to the conditions at the time of their institution are now much less so; that indeed their continuance acts as a brake on the development of change in the system and creates anomalies and contradictions.

Incentives

To take first the question of motivation, it will surely be agreed that in a rapidly changing society we need to send out from schools, colleges and universities young people who can cope with changing conditions and accept the necessity for continued learning, the obligation to understand and evaluate the new. I suggest that the system of incentives embodied in traditional examinations does not encourage this appreciation of the intrinsic value of learning. On the contrary, the implication is that nobody in his senses applies himself to learning unless there is some extrinsic reward attached to it, a certificate or other qualification. Not content with this, many schools have elaborate systems for awarding marks, giving prizes, determining form orders as if to ensure that no bit of work at any point should be done for the fun of it, because it is interesting or because the pupil sees some intrinsic value in doing it. Indeed pupils who enjoy work have to exercise some ingenuity to avoid being labelled 'swots' and as such incurring opprobrium. It is as if institutions designed for the pursuit of learning do not themselves at bottom have much faith in the value of the product they sell. There is a further implication built into the traditional system and that is that having achieved the ultimate qualification, there is no further need for learning. The O levels, A levels or degrees tend to become either ends in themselves or intermediate stages in the pursuit of a further award. Certainly, these positive incentives are preferable to the negative incentives, the fear of disapproval and punishment, upon which the traditional schoolmaster relied; they do indeed provide some ground for co-operation between those who traditionally were enemies, teacher and pupil working together against a common enemy, the examiner. But is this extrinsic motivation and this limited form of co-operation between teacher and learner the best we can hope to achieve?

The answer to this is that there are indeed large areas of education where examination incentives are not used: infant schools for example; junior schools in areas where the pressures of 11+ selection have been abolished or reduced; and at least three-fifths of the children in secondary schools. As the Newsom Report commented, 'We are convinced that for a substantial number of pupils public examinations would be entirely inappropriate, and for a considerable number of others would be appropriate only over a small part of their school work; in other words, we do not think that external examinations would provide a valid major incentive for many of the pupils with whom we are concerned.' This is indeed a strange situation. Are we to assume that intrinsic motivation works with younger children and with the less able of the older children but for some reason fails to work with older brighter children? Is it not rather that it has not been tried? Sixth-form pupils, it is often said, will not take seriously courses which are not examined. But is this not because they have become so conditioned to the elaborate game, the kind of obstacle race, of the examination system that their sensitiveness to other kinds of motivation is blunted. By a kind of Gresham's Law, lower motivation drives out the higher.

Effects on Teachers

To turn now to the effects on teachers, there are some strange ironies here too. For example, it is often noted that one of the good points about the British system of education is the freedom which teachers and schools enjoy in curricular matters. The content of the curriculum, syllabuses, methods of teaching and assessment are not prescribed by central or local administrative authorities, as is the case in many countries, and as was the case in this country for elementary schools in the period of the 'Revised Code' and 'Payment by Results'. Bitter memories of the frustrations of that period became a tradition in the profession and in the present century both central and local authorities have carefully respected the autonomy of the schools in matters concerning the curriculum. Thus the central authority has preferred to express its ultimate responsibility for these matters not in directions and regulations but in 'suggestions to teachers', in the Reports of Consultative Committees and in the subtle operations of that peculiar English institute, Her Majesty's Inspectorate.

But what happened to this hardly won and jealousy preserved freedom of schools and teachers in those areas of education which accepted working for examination as the main aim? The exceptional teacher may indeed succeed in limiting the bad effects noted in the 1911 Report; but can there be any doubt that the majority of teachers, in this situation with all its blatant pressures, play for safety and go in for question spotting, dictation of notes, emphasis on memorization, holding 'mock' examinations and all the other gambits of the game? As the Spens Report noted in 1938, the

School Certificate examination had come to dominate the work of the schools and to control both the framework and content of the curriculum.

Current Selection Procedure

There are, however, some hopeful signs in the attempts now being made to break out of the stranglehold which traditional systems of examination impose on schools and teachers. In the primary field, the growing volume of discontent, both with the necessary imperfections of the selection procedures, however refined, and with the constricting effects on the work of the schools, has undoubtedly provided the least controversial argument in favour of comprehensive secondary education. And many authorities, while still committed to selection, have adopted devices which mitigate some of the bad effects. Thus the Thorne system, developed in the West Riding, allots a quota of places to each primary school based on past performance and adjusted in the light of information passed from the secondary to the primary schools. The school decides which children are selected for the quota. Other authorities, like London, use an anonymous intelligence test to decide the quotas for each school.

Changes in Secondary Examinations

In the secondary field, discontent with some of the rigidities of the School Certificate (S.C.) system led to the institution in 1950 of the General Certificate of Education (G.C.E.). It was felt that the School Certificate requirement that pupils must pass in a group of subjects restricted the initiative of teachers and that the artificial division between fifth- and sixth-form work hindered the development of a unified secondary school course. The G.C.E. could be passed in a single subject at three levels, Ordinary, Advanced and Scholarship; the pass standard at O level was equated with the credit level of the S.C. examination. Meanwhile one unintended and, at the time, unforeseen consequence of the 1944 Education Act began to be felt. The Act envisaged 'parity of esteem' among the different kinds of secondary schools and one very obvious ground of esteem in the most esteemed schools, both inside and outside the state system, was the examination successes of their pupils. The number of pupils entered for G.C.E. O level examinations from the non-selective secondary schools rose steadily (in 1959, one-third of the candidates came from schools other than grammar schools); but as these examinations were designed to meet the needs of the top 20 per cent in the ability range, the demand for examinations for those in the 20 per cent below this grew also. A multiplicity of examinations, run by a variety of national, regional and local bodies, came into being to meet this need. For some years, the Ministry of Education opposed this trend (see Circulars 289, 1955, and 326, 1957), but eventually accepted the recommendations of a Sub-

Committee of the Secondary Schools Examinations Council (the Beloe Report, 1960) and a new examination, the Certificate of Secondary Education (C.S.E.) was instituted.

The C.S.E., however, differs from the G.C.E. in a number of fundamental respects. It ensures teacher representation and participation at all levels. As Examination Bulletin No. 1 put it, 'Effective teacher control of syllabus content, examination papers and examining techniques is the rock on which the C.S.E. system will stand.' Three modes of examining are provided, expressing different degrees of teacher involvement. In Mode 1 an examination external to the school is based on syllabuses provided by regional subject panels of teachers. In Mode 2 the examination is external but the syllabuses are provided by the school or a group of schools and approved by the subject panel. In Mode 3 the examinations are set and marked internally with moderation by the regional panel. A hopeful sign is the growth in the number of schools choosing Mode 3; for example, in the area of the South-Western Examination Board, the number of subject entries in Mode 3 increased nearly threefold between 1965 and 1967, against a doubling of the total entry. Another difference is that the G.C.E. operates with a pass/fail classification, the normal failure rate being 40 per cent or more of the candidates; the G.S.E. records 5 grades on the Certificate, Grade 1 being equated with a G.C.E. O level pass, and Grade 4 representing the performance of a sixteen-year-old of average ability. How these equivalences and standards are to be determined is the subject of much inquiry and debate: but clearly most of the pupils properly entered for this examination will have some reward for their effort.

As this is being written, there comes to hand the report (*Sunday Times*, August 25th, 1968) of an experiment in the G.C.E. O level English Examination conducted by the Oxford and Cambridge Schools Examinations Board. This involved the use of three ingredients: the assessment of a candidate's work, during one term; the writing of a mini-thesis of 1,500–2,000 words on a topic related to the syllabus studied in the term's work; and a conventional $1\frac{1}{2}$ hour paper. The report says, 'The argument against reforming the conventional A or O levels has always been based on the difficulties of marking any other system and of getting comparable standards between schools. The new system, using internal and external assessors, suggests that these problems can be solved without using more examiners or money.'

Finally, it is worth noting that in the crucial field of teacher education, some institutes of education have encouraged their colleges for many years now to experiment with course-work assessment, and the writing of special studies in place of or in addition to the conventional examination papers. There is no evidence that students so assessed work less hard or achieve lower standards than students assessed solely by examination papers.

BIBLIOGRAPHY

Board of Education: Reports of Consultative Committees on *Examinations in Secondary Schools*, 1911; *The Education of the Adolescent* (Hadow), 1926; *Secondary Education* (Spens), 1938; *Curriculum and Examinations in Secondary Schools* (Norwood).

Ministry of Education Reports: *Examinations in Secondary Schools*, 1947; *Pamphlet No. 9*, 1947; *Circular 205*, 1949; *Circular 256*, 1952; *Early Leaving*, 1954; *Circular 289*, 1955; *Education 15-18* (Crowther); *Secondary School Examinations other than G.C.E.* (Beloe), 1960; *The C.S.E.: Fourth Report of S.S.E.C.*, 1961; *Fifth Report of the S.S.E.C.*, 1962; *Half Our Future* (Newsom), 1963; *Seventh Report of the S.S.E.C.*, 1963; *S.S.E.C. Bulletins*, 1–14, 1963–6

41

Examinations and Educational Objectives

F. Hotyat
Président de l'Institut de Pédagogie, Centre Universitaire de l'Etat, Mons

As with all human undertakings in which the best results are sought, the process of education must be supervised, more especially because the issues of teaching depend not only on the qualities of the teachers, but even more on the basic intelligence of the children, which may be developed or transferred by their 'affective tone', their motivations and their actuating interests.

Of course such supervision can be carried out from day to day in school life, but many teachers consider that periodic examinations are also necessary and justify them by three main arguments:

1. At the end of an important section of a course in which the ideas have been treated in detail over a series of separate lessons, the examination system seems to encourage the coherent organization of material, so that the initial items already learned are synthesized.

2. The facts taught are not all equally important: some are essential, and over-emphasis and regular repetition help to ensure their retention. The bulk of factual information is only of value in later schemes of association. The volume is of greater interest than the detail, and it is useful, periodically, to try to distinguish between these two forms of knowledge.

3. The school exercises a certain amount of influence, particularly over the direction and the pattern of psychological development: the pupil's confidence in the exercise of his mental powers is strengthened if the challenges to his new abilities result in more successes than failures, and if these failures can be finally overcome.

But even accepting that these aims are valid, do not examinations take up too much time? Already in many European countries, it is clear that too long a period is devoted to preparing for exams, and it appears that even more time is likely to be given in future. For example, in Belgian secondary schools, more than six weeks of the two sessions is taken up in preparation for examinations, taking examinations and relaxation after examinations. But even more serious than the time devoted to examinations is the fact that many teachers tend to over-rate their value.

Satisfactory Educational Objective

In order to achieve the above-mentioned educational objectives satisfactorily, the examinations must be devised in accordance with the syllabus and the method of instruction. However, it often happens that competitive tests have a negative effect, thus defeating the object of those who plan the course of study, as is demonstrated by a piece of research carried out by Yates and Pidgeon.[1] A thousand English schoolchildren took the entrance examinations for secondary education when they were eleven years of age. For administrative reasons some of these pupils remained in primary schools, while the rest went on to secondary modern schools. The same exams were administered again to both groups one year later. The table below, showing the results of the second test in terms of average losses and gains, is sufficiently striking to need no comment.

Test	*Primary group* (*266 pupils*)	*Secondary modern group* (*749 pupils*)
Arithmetic	+ 3·63	− 5·14
English	+ 2·10	− 1·47
Mental Intelligence	+ 2·55	− 2·79

Very often, examinations have a restrictive effect on the extent of educational instruction: they do not measure, for example, the progress of such valuable mental qualities as creativity, the spirit of initiative, the feeling of teamwork etc. and they ignore the analytical descriptions of intellectual skills such as those given as evidence in the classic diagrams of Guildford. Such retroaction is particularly serious when the course is conducted in accordance with a syllabus or manual, and even more so when there is an official examination paper upon which the examiners can draw. From the beginning of the school year, the basic work of the pupils is reduced to mere cramming. They seem to concentrate on conformity to a blueprint instead of trying to develop an inquiring mind, to see things in depth, or to improve their practical ability.

Many teachers really believe that their examinations 'measure' the progress of knowledge and the ability of their pupils, and the confidence gained from the accuracy of these tests seems to reinforce this belief. In reality, however, this belief is an illusion. An examination can only be a partial guide to knowledge, for it is almost impossible to include all the

---

[1] A. Yates and D. A. Pidgeon, *The Use of Tests in Educational Development*. Fifth Paper on Experimental Teaching (University of Caen, 1957).

material covered in a year, or even in a term. In other words, these examinations can only provide results of a limited validity. If we increase the items, for example, in multiple-choice tests, we condense and improvise the material taught, for we are directing the candidate's thoughts. If, on the other hand, we restrict the examination to several questions requiring a combination of intellectual skills so that new ideas are blended with the knowledge and ability previously acquired, we weaken the reliability of the marks. In addition we limit the scope of the material to be taught, by means of the selection we impose.

Teacher Attitudes

It is a very widespread attitude among teachers to attribute absolute value to the verdict of examinations. In reality they lead to errors of the same type as those which we make when we pass judgement on people after only a few seconds. Whether it is a matter of physical or psychological development or educational progress, all the longitudinal studies[2] have clearly shown that as far as general development is concerned individual variations are extremely common. Of ten pupils who have reached the same level on a scale of results at a point in time, only a minority stay approximately in the same place, but others reach it by improving their relative performances and then going on to improve further, or, conversely, by getting even lower marks.

This state of affairs is proof of the complexity of the problem of educational assessment – a problem resulting from a number of factors, all of which are dynamic, interdependent and complementary, and which the examination alone is incapable of revealing. But such a situation should not necessarily make us pessimistic: if it is wrong to condemn a child because of indications of failure in an exam, the comforting lesson to be drawn is that one must never despair of a pupil's lack of results.

If the place held by examinations is abused, especially because of their negative effect, how, then, can we provide the necessary functions of control in the best educational conditions?

Possible Changes

It is possible to limit the use of examinations to critical moments in the school careers of pupils and in between times to verify, by means of questions and exercises, to what degree they have mastered the control of each important section of the course. Such a change cannot be just quantitative; the very spirit of the system of control must be transformed – but how?

---

[2] See, for example, W. Olson, *Les Fondements Psychologiques des Programmes Scolaires* (Unesco, 1958).

(1) Teachers and examiners must constantly bear in mind that the stages of an educational problem fall into logical sequence.

(a) In the teaching of a certain subject, what standard is it reasonable to envisage at a given level?

(b) After that, what programmes should be developed and what methods put into practice?

(c) In carrying out these objectives, what means of evaluation will best control the anticipation of these results and the correction of the weaknesses?

One way of solving the problem is as follows: the project of the questions for examination in a two-way table: the contents in the rows and the intellectual objectives in the columns, the number of items in each square being chosen according to its estimated importance.[3] This method of working allows the examiner to dispense with superfluous material so that the students can concentrate on the essentials.

(2) Supervision, like other scholastic activities, has a role to play in education. In particular, it is important to train pupils to evaluate for themselves. This practice is one of the foundation stones of a progressive educational system. The scholar who tries to set himself these objectives in the light of his intentions and consequently appreciates the degree to which he attains his goal, is aware of his successes and failures, takes note of his methods, moves more rapidly towards a sense of reality, and develops more surely toward self-knowledge and maturity.

In the same way, parents and teachers must break themselves of the common habit of beginning by critizing the pupil's shortcomings. In order to encourage the child, progress, even if it is slight, should be valued from the very beginning. Criticism can then follow later, in an atmosphere that is more encouraging than discouraging. The destruction of self-confidence in a pupil can only result in paralysis of incentive.

(3) One of the essential functions of supervision is the correction of mistakes. Research on learning has established that the maximum psychological effect is obtained if correction is carried out immediately. If this is to become regular practice, without imposing excess work it is advisable that schools allocate material to be re-learned in such a way that weaknesses are helped rather than emphasized.

(4) Consecutive results are registered in the individual files in such a way that they provide a descriptive, rather than normative, picture of the pupil. The information gathered is especially valuable at the critical times in the school career of a child or adolescent, particularly when there are problems of orientation, or when he is about to leave school. This system has already been applied in certain technical schools where the final

---

[3] Cf. Husen et al., *International Study of Achievement in Mathematics* (Stockholm, Almquist and Wicksell, 1967).

diploma has been replaced by a detailed report describing the practical work carried out at the school, so that a prospective employer can readily ascertain from the report what kind of work he can expect from the candidate.

Conclusion

In conclusion, the suggestions outlined above, when considered as a whole, appear to provide a means of true evaluation which will ensure the best possible returns from educational effort in the future.

Educational Effects of Examinations on Pupils, Teachers and Society

Ruth H. K. Wong
Dean and Professor of Education, University of Malaya

On the human plane, the examination involves three parties – the pupil, the teacher, and the community or society which accepts its purpose. Thus in a discussion of the educational effects of examinations, the interaction between the examination and all three severally must be taken into account.

The Examination and Society

The attempt to gauge the individual for what he is worth to his group or society has its mainspring in man's desire for survival. The odds in favour of survival have always been higher through co-operative effort. For this reason, the individual has been tested and scrutinized against the expectations of his group and thereby accepted or rejected. The test or examination – and here the reference does not exclude forms of assessment besides the written – was first used to set the seal on acceptability, but did not thereby cramp the development of individual style. The novice at the task in the primitive society began his training by apprenticeship; close observation and constant practice improved imitative effort to the point where it became individual art. In the attempt, the individual held fully the responsibility of proof – proof of his perseverance, his endurance, and the quality of his aspirations.

The test, applied at first to practical skills, was later also used to assess mental skills. Proficiency tests in writing and arithmetic were added to those for music, archery and horsemanship as early as the eleventh century B.C. in China.[1] Later, the practice of holding civil service examinations, first introduced in China, gained currency also in European countries. Thus the public examination came very much into evidence, to dominate society it is true, yet also to help it achieve qualitative ends. To quote:

Westerners seem to have been particularly impressed with the fact that com-

---

[1] P. H. DuBois, 'A Test-dominated society: China 1115 B.C. – 1905 A.D.', *Testing Problems in Perspective* (A. Anastasi, Ed.) (Washington, D.C.: A.C.E., 1966) p. 30.

petition was open, that distinction came from merit, that a highly literate and urbane group of public officials resulted from the examination system.[2]

That the examination system dominates society today is not, therefore, a new phenomenon. What has changed is the functional nature of its character. It has become an end in itself rather than a means to the end. The reasons for this are to be found in social change, not in the examination *per se*. Preparation by society for function in society is no longer an isomorphic process, even though the examination remains the link between the earlier stage of skill acquisition and the later stage of vocational effectiveness. In earlier societies, skills were more easily classifiable as practical or mental according to occupational goal. The hunter had only to prove prowess by sending his arrows home with the minimum number of shots. The civil servant was expected to be an erudite scholar; that he was also a good hunter and a rider added to his distinction. But erudition remained the main objective associated with his task: so he spent a lifetime acquiring it.

Technological advance in contemporary society has brought about a proliferation of complex and diverse tasks which are increasingly difficult to define in terms of preparatory skills. At the simplest level, the man in the assembly plant who may only be fitting one little cog into a machine may still do well to know why even a slight misalignment is inadmissible. The same mass-production system which robs him of his identity requires that he should appreciate the impact of his efforts on the whole process. So, apart from having mastered a manual skill, he is expected to reason and to anticipate in the abstract to a much greater degree than a worker in an earlier society.

Not only have tasks become more difficult but educational goals have developed increasingly global characteristics which defy analysis in concrete terms of what services and functions a formal system of education may assume to achieve the specified objectives in the end-product.[3] In

---

[2] DuBois, op. cit., p. 34.

[3] The following is a random selection of statements of goals which illustrate the point above.

(a) 'Higher education in Vietnam has the definite object of training sufficient cadres and technicians for all branches of national development.' Nguyen Dinh Hoa, *Higher Education in the Republic of Vietnam*, (Saigon: Directorate of Cultural Affairs, 1963), 30 pp.

(b) 'It must be the foremost aim of our education policy to train the children in our schools so that they can become useful citizens who can adapt themselves to the construction work of re-orienting our economic policy and so form the vanguard in laying down the basis for a future socialist society.'
   N. L. Yong, 'Spring source of our nation', *The Tasks Ahead*, Pt. II, (Singapore Petir, May 1959), 35 pp.

(c) 'At a time when the Revolutionary Council is drawing up economic plans for sufficiency of food, clothing, and shelter and social security of all the people as a whole, it is

the absence of definitive elements in goals and tasks, the set of criteria for gauging individual suitability for society's tasks – criteria which give legitimacy to the examination – become equally vague. Under the circumstances, merely to cry 'Abolish examinations!' is to evade the issue unless a better yardstick for human behaviour is already available. Two courses only remain open to society with regard to the examination: either to accept the traditional form while denying the power thereof, or seek to reappraise the value of the appraisal instrument and redefine its status. Resort is generally made to the first course, which is less demanding.

The situation being so, the educational preparation of individuals for society against vague goals and an obsolete or inadequate interpretation[4] of desirable human behaviour and endeavour either becomes haphazard or, at its best, anchors itself to the form and content of the examination as giving the best approximation to behaviour and goals required. It is therefore clear that heavy reliance on the traditional examination cannot be justified at least on two counts. First, a single examination is made to measure the suitability of individuals for too many different and complex vocational goals. This has the effect of bringing about a standardization of expectation and effort based on a minimal overlap of content. The second objection is a derivative of the first – the predictive value of such an examination can hardly be accepted with equanimity. True, satisfactory correlations have been obtained between the results of the examination and school ratings. But they may merely affirm that the schools have developed an acumen for examination analysis and that the examiners are in agreement with what the schools have accomplished. More desirable would be sustained studies on the predictability of a school, college, or university leaving examination for vocational success in order that more information may be gathered as to the weight that should be placed on such an examination. For in many societies the examination has taken on a withholding rather than an assessment role. To have failed one examination is to retain a stigma for life, and it is not

necessary to draw up an educational system which will help in the implementation of the economic plans.'
  Col. Hla Han, Burmese Minister of Education, *Inaugural Address to the Seminar on Higher Education in Rangoon*, April, 1964.
'Cadres and technicians for *all branches of national development*', '*useful* citizens *who can adapt themselves*', 'educational system which will *help in the implementation* of the economic plans' – these, and educational slogans such as 'educate for *change*', 'educate for *creativity*', 'give opportunity for development of *independent thinking*' all beg skilled analysis. I have underscored those terms and phrases for which a wide range of interpretations is possible, depending on who undertakes to give meaning to them.
  4 The examination as it is used in many countries is largely a measure of likely success at a university. Thus all school pupils are prepared for a strictly narrow, academic-type programme, highly content-oriented.

clear whether many among those who have not succeeded at an examination have not been wasted because of the process.[5]

Thus, surely and almost inevitably[6] the examination dictates the activities in school. Syllabuses, mere catalogues of topics, are issued by examination syndicates and central authorities. These are adhered to strictly by the average school where progress in the classroom is measured by the number of topics covered. Interpretation of the syllabus is carried out chiefly by reference to past examination papers, which unfortunately not only sample a very limited area of the curriculum but also tend to carry questions similar in type and content year after year. In certain countries where school-leaving and pre-university examinations are still external and conducted in English, the high sale annually of the 'Ten Years Series' booklets[7] points to the untiring efforts of pupils and teachers to divine the mind of the examiner. Teaching and learning on such a basis sets a premium on a happy combination of guesswork and memorization. It prevails where public examinations almost exclusively determine the individual's upward mobility in society against a context of limited vocational opportunity.

The Examination and the Pupil

The fewer vocational opportunities there are for distribution, the stronger is the pressure on the testee to succeed. The misplaced confidence in the examination as an accurate quantification instrument generates a fear on the part of the testee, who feels himself exposed once the yardstick is applied. He works hard for examinations, be they school-conducted or

---

[5] Failure rates for examinations in some countries can be extremely high. I give as examples the pass rates in university examinations in Vietnam and Pakistan from 1956 to 1961. Note in terms of actual numbers, the large numbers in the latter country who fail to achieve satisfactorily in the examinations.

Year	Vietnam			Pakistan		
	No. presented	No. of passes	% pass	No. presented	No. of passes	% pass
1956–57	1057	603	57·0	39,869	17,318	43·4
1957–58	1758	851	48·4	31,015	12,347	40·0
1958–59	2867	957	33·4	70,783	27,752	39·2
1959–60	3483	1179	39·9	75,310	30,303	40·2
1960–61	4831	1590	32·9	101,497	40,941	40·3

NOTE: These statistics have been extracted from the Yearbooks of Statistics (1963) of the respective countries.

[6] I use this word deliberately because I think that circumstances conspire to promote this.

[7] These are published annually for each subject area by examinations syndicates responsible for the examinations and they contain copies of all the question papers set in the preceding ten years.

externally administered. All his school life he studies the teacher's predilections in areas of knowledge, and the 'good' teacher, as far as he is concerned, reflects best the requirements of the final scholastic hurdle. For him examinations not only dominate and dictate: they provide him with the only motivation for school work. Because he studies only for examinations, his scholastic efforts are spasmodic, the strongest spurts being made nearest examination time. Malayan school pupils afford a good case study in this respect.

In 1964, the Malaysian Secondary Selection Entrance Examination was abolished, opening the way to a place in a secondary school for three years for any pupil who wished to pursue his studies beyond the primary school. Almost immediately, there came a general complaint from primary school teachers that pupils would not 'work' because the examination had been removed. Presumably the *laissez faire* attitude, which came to be associated with automatic promotion, discounted the need to read or study until the next examination came into sight at the end of the ninth year. Presumably, too, the teachers had become so used to being praised and blamed on the results of an examination that they could not proceed without the examination incentive. As a result, the public examination at primary level was reinstated for 1967. Instead of being held at the end of six years, it now helps to assess pupils in the fifth year of school. To emphasize the fact that it is not a withholding examination, it has been named the Standard Five Assessment Examination. The ostensible objective is to enable teachers and principals to assess the progress of individuals and groups of pupils in their schools against national norms. However, in the debate for and against examinations, the quality of teaching and learning seldom entered as a consideration: only the intensity of effort was judged.

The Examination and the Teacher

In the normal school routine the teacher assumes the role of tester until the public examination takes place. It seems difficult for him to deviate from what he thinks the examination expects of him.[8] Even if he is committed to sound educational aims, both his superiors and his pupils, the consumers, jointly conspire against these aims. Since a school is still rated according to the number and quality of passes its pupils have made in the public examinations, though the payment by results practice whereby schools obtained grants only if examination results are satisfactory has been discontinued, school heads may consider desirable certain activities such as note-giving, writing out sample answers to

---

[8] Read D. J. Isaac, 'Teachers and Examinations', *New Era*, 45 (May 1964), pp. 132–6. The points made in this article are generally true of teachers in an examination-dominated system today.

typical questions culled from past examination papers, intensive practice at manipulative skills in subjects with quantitative content, and so on. The consumer in turn comes to expect an intensely directed chalk-talk, note-rote, and grill-drill programme. For the teacher, coaching for examinations has become a social responsibility thrust upon him. As a teacher, he has lost out on the meaning of his professional task; as a tester, he understands but vaguely the goals of testing or the reliability and validity of his tests.

What has been discussed so far suggests that the rather unfortunate predicament into which classroom teaching and learning has fallen because of examination pressure, requires a solution which appreciates the psychological impact the examination has on all three parties of society, pupil and teacher. To direct exhortation and reform at any one party is to compound the problem and to confound the issues. The solution advocated consists of the following measures:

1 *Lines of communication should be opened between groups in society interested in the useful deployment of individuals*

Committees, composed of educators, representatives of government and other employment agencies, should be set up to discuss aims, goals, and job specifications in order that those concerned with educational policy-making may determine to what extent these may be met by preparation at each school level. Laymen and educators do not always agree on methods of goal attainment because of differences in the philosophical bases for interpretation. The former are more prone to over-emphasize the importance of immediacy and therefore tend to favour quantitative and obvious measures; the latter prefer a perspective that entertains the developmental goals of the individual and often forget current needs. These stances are not irreconcilable provided efforts are made towards more precise articulation of goals, ways and means. Specificity will also help to reduce the predictive burden on the examination.

2 *Change may be necessary in the examination structure*

Arising out of an analysis of aims and objectives, consideration may well be given to the replacement of the comprehensive, single examination by both 'linear' and 'branching' sequences of examinations. Each examination in a sequence must point to a set of well-defined and achievable goals. 'To what extent should preparation be similar?' if answered, will help determine the number of steps in the linear sequence. On the other hand, the answers to how goals and tasks differ may necessitate the establishment of different sets of branch examination sequences.

The sort of action advocated here aims rather at gauging levels of competency, at mastery of prerequisite skills in the preparation, rather than at prediction for success in a future not yet certain. Thus most of the branch hierarchy of examinations may have to be taken in the course of a career within the job sphere in which the individual finds his niche.

3   *Improvements in the content of the examination and the construction and use of educational tests have already been given much attention*[9]

It may be observed that much of the effort for improvement accepts the predictive role of the test. Changes in marking procedures and in the format of questions, attempts to improve reliability and validity of test papers and examinations, use of relevant information besides those of school examinations made possible by the development of multiple-regression analysis are all highly necessary, but they do not ensure the removal of negative educational effects which examinations have on the denizens of our schools. It is therefore necessary to advocate the next measure:

4   *Introduce measures which will remove the threat element in the examination*

First, the question may be asked whether all subjects taken in school have a legitimate place in a common examination. Take the study of literature, for example. The knowledge of language is enriched through a proper study of literature; so it should remain on the curriculum. But the study of texts prescribed for an examination purpose, memorized from cover to cover and studied with a singular neglect of appreciation of the relationship of language and literature to social mores, kills interest in the subject. Thus, while language should be an examination subject, literature should not.

The argument that teachers will not teach except for examinations is often advanced. In this connexion, some thought may be given to substitute incentives. For example, mass media such as television could be used for frequent, regularly-scheduled discussions between groups of students from different schools on problems and topics related to non-examinable subjects. To ensure that teachers pay due attention to all pupils, stipulation could be made for random selection of participating groups, invited without forewarning.

One would go so far as to say that any subject with an *affective* content should not be examinable. Ethics, history, religion, literature – these are

---

[9] Read *Testing Problems in Perspective* (A. Anastasi, Ed.), A.C.E., op. cit. – example of the type of thinking brought to bear on problems in a society where testing has reached a high level of sophistication.

Also refer *Report on Examination Reform*, (New Delhi: 1962), New Age Press, a report which delineates the problems which obtain commonly in developing societies.

some. More important should it be that pupils understand man's struggles, his ideals, his ambitions, and his accomplishments and what meaning these have for us today.

Elsewhere[10] other measures adopted have been described. One is the introduction of 'personalized' testing into classroom work. This enables the individual to assess his own efforts. Briefly, the teacher has available a series of tests related to a sequential set of concepts and skills in a subject. To these the pupil helps himself as he feels himself to be ready. He reports the results of his tests graphically as they are obtained. In this manner he gains immediate feedback, not only on the exercise at the given point of time, but also on his general progress.

Another measure attempted has been the introduction of an occasional exchange of tester and testee roles. Pupils or students are allowed to rate the teacher in the disciplines for which they themselves have been rated, that is, the students sometimes provide the questions which the teacher answers. All then participate in critically analysing and discussing the answers. Students introduced to such a programme[11] have become more critical of their own methods of learning. Psychologically the teacher and pupil co-operate far better in the educational effort.

Conclusion

This paper suggests that the negative effects of examinations cannot be dealt with solely by improvement of examinations. Remedy should aim at an analysis of goals and aims, and at changing the attitudes of teacher, pupil, and society. There has been no mention of improved methods in teaching as helping to overcome the bad effects, for these can be both earnestly advocated and promoted with greater success only when the attitudes which militate against them have been improved.

---

[10] R. H. K. Wong. *A study of student progress through grouping associated with a programme of sequenced instruction in elementary mathematics*, unpublished doctoral thesis, Harvard University, (June 1962).

Also, *Some problems of a society in transition: educational testing for evaluation and improvement*, paper delivered at the Berlin Workshop on Educational Testing (June, 1967).

[11] Wong, op. cit.

Trends and Future Prospects

Brian Holmes
Reader in Comparative Education in the University of London

In this short final section R. La Porta and N. N. Atiyeh assess trends and future prospects for examinations.

The former concludes that the Council of Europe's Council for Cultural Co-operation has achieved much by helping to reveal the inadequacies of various national systems of education when 'confronted with the evolution of educational needs' (p. 374). Co-ordinated European co-operation may well offer the best hope for solutions to what are common problems of comparability and the maintenances of standards in education. Agreement was reached at a conference held in Brussels in 1966 that examinations should be an instrument not of selection but of guidance. A view later stressed by European Ministers of Education was that an 'overall review based on the synthetic evaluation of a long-term assessment' could profitably be developed as a type of European-level examination. Success in terms of acceptable comparison will depend on some unification of curricula towards which the analysis of the Oxford University/Council of Europe investigation will make an important contribution.

N. N. Atiyeh reviews the case for examinations, and suggests that there appears to be no evidence of a decline in their importance – indeed, the trend is towards greater emphasis on them. Such a trend will involve increased activity to improve techniques and train qualified examiners. He considers the relative merits of external and internal examinations. Two schools of thought exist: one stresses the frustrating, circumscribing effects of external examinations – the other, the justice and fairness of such examinations compared with more subjective internal assessments. Atiyeh concludes that the 'strongest dynamics in the development of modern exams is the need for a suitable compromise between external and internal control' (p. 379). He points out that admission to elementary schools is based only on the criterion of age; that internal evaluation tends to determine promotion from class to class and is increasingly in the hands of the teacher or on a series of examination grades given during the year; that the maintenance of external exams at the end of the primary or elementary stages of education is closely related to the accessibility of secondary schooling. Secondary school-leaving examinations vary: at one extreme are U.S.A. policies, at the other, Atiyeh suggests, is the *bachot* system of France. In the U.S.A. there is a tendency to use externally standardized tests; in France to consult school records as correctives to internal and external assessments respectively.

In short, the move is to make the best use of all available kinds and types of examinations and tests. In so doing a better profile of an individual student may be obtained for use in guiding him into, rather than selecting him for, further education or work.

43

The Council of Europe's Programme in the Field of School Examinations[1]

Roberto La Porta
Administrateur, Division des Affaires Culturelles, Conseil de l'Europe, Strasbourg

Considering that the equivalence of school and university qualifications at a European level would considerably increase exchanges of young people willing to follow up their studies in other Continental countries and, consequently, would contribute to the building up of a European spirit and a European unity, the Council of Europe started dealing with the matter as early as 1952. From that date until 1962, the educational policy of the Council of Europe was entrusted to the Committee of Cultural Experts. Then, in 1962, the extension of the programme in this field gave birth to the Council for Cultural Co-operation (C.C.C.)[2] and its three permanent committees: the Committee for Higher Education and Research, the Committee for General and Technical Education, and the Committee for Out-of-School Education. The two bodies had a different approach to the difficult problems of the equivalence of examinations. The Committee of Cultural Experts dealt with the legal aspect of equivalence and the C.C.C. has been concerned with actual equivalence. In both cases we shall deal mainly with what has been achieved in the field of upper secondary school examinations.

I. *Legal Equivalence*

The Committee of Cultural Experts drafted three important Conventions,[3] one of which is entitled *The European Convention on the Equivalence of Diplomas Leading to Admission to Universities* (December 11th, 1953).

It provides that 'Each Contracting Party shall recognize for the purpose of admission to the universities situated in its territory, admission to which is subject to State control, the equivalence of those diplomas

---

[1] The author wishes to emphasize that the views expressed in this chapter are his own and in no way represent those of the Council of Europe.

[2] The member countries of the C.C.C. are Austria, Belgium, Cyprus, Denmark, France, Greece, Holy See, Iceland, Ireland, Italy, Luxembourg, Malta, Netherlands, Norway, Spain, Sweden, Switzerland, Turkey and the United Kingdom.

[3] The two other Conventions are: 'The European Convention on the Equivalence of Periods of University Study' (December 15th, 1956) and 'The European Convention on the Academic Recognition of University Qualifications' (December 14th, 1959).

awarded in the territory of each other Contracting Party which constitute a requisite qualification for admission to similar institutions in the country in which these diplomas were awarded.' But the second paragraph implies a restriction: 'Admission to any university shall be subject to the availability of places'. The application of this Convention, which still awaits signature by three countries (Cyprus, Malta and Switzerland) causes difficulties resulting from political obstacles as well as from differences of standard between comparable examinations.

It was felt therefore that legal equivalence would remain an empty frame if it did not apply to a concrete basis. Hence when the C.C.C. came into being, the work undertaken on equivalence was given a new bias. Equivalence is not considered any more as the first hurdle to be faced, but as a long-term ideal which can be reached after the achievement of the successive steps leading to the harmonization of the educational systems, methods and programmes. These are the three important elements which determine the structure and the aim of examinations. Thus legal equivalence had to be based on actual equivalence.

II. *Actual Equivalence*

This new bias fulfils the European Ministers' recommendation[4] to the Council of Europe, 'to continue its work on the maintenance of educational standards including modern ways of guaranteeing the quality and comparability of the results of pupils' studies.'

The activities promoted by the C.C.C.[5] to face the problems involved in the implementation of this recommendation can be roughly classified in two categories, those concerned mainly with structures and methods of testing and those dealing with syllabus analysis.

(1) *Structures and Methods of Testing*—Harmonization in this field implies first the analysis of the various national systems of examination in order to see what are the differences and the common points. This analysis, entrusted to Dr. E. Egger,[6] a member of the Committee for General and Technical Education, is entitled 'Comparative Study on the Present Situation of Terminal Examinations',[7] and aims at describing the present situation; that is: the purpose of examinations, the conditions for setting them, the authorities which set the papers and choose the questions for them, the various examining boards (external, internal, mixed), examination subjects (written, oral and practical examinations, compulsory and optional questions), the marking of papers, the conduct and

---

[4] Cf. Resolution 3 of the European Ministers of Education (5th Conference, Vienna, October, 1965).

[5] These are carried out by the Committee for General and Technical Education.

[6] Director of the Educational Information Centre, Geneva.

[7] Dr. E. Egger's study will be published in the C.C.C. series *Education in Europe* in the course of 1969.

length of tests, the weight attaching to a child's school record, etc. The study is intended to reveal any discrepancy between the aim pursued and the means used in individual countries, and to show how far the national systems differ or are alike.

The description of the various national systems would be of a very relative usefulness if it were not accompanied by studies on the assessment of their educational value. This is why, at the same time, the Committee for General and Technical Education asked one of its eminent experts, Professor A. Agazzi,[8] to deal with the 'value of examinations'[9]. The purpose of this study is to see, in the light of the rapid changes of our world and the new needs of the individual, to what extent the various types of examinations existing in Europe help to realize the ideal aim of education: the fulfilment of the child's personality. Examinations, far from being considered as a separate entity, are analysed in the context of their links with the syllabus, methods of teaching, and the pupil's psychological and social background.

A short summary of the conclusions of the two studies was made by the authors themselves in a course organized by the Belgian Government in Brussels in October 1966 under the sponsorship of the C.C.C. on the theme: 'Upper Secondary School-leaving Examinations and Access to higher education'. Both experts showed how unsatisfactory the present situation was. They set a background for the course which aimed at establishing the criteria of the desired situation (cf. Document EGT (67) Stage XXI, 4).

The following basic questions were debated: Are examinations necessary? In the case of a positive answer (as was the participants') – What should be their aim? What methods of testing and marking could be suggested in accordance with this aim? How should the teachers be trained to be competent examiners?

All the participants agreed on the aim of examinations; instead of being selective they should be an instrument of pupil guidance, that is to say, they should reveal, apart from the pupil's knowledge, his aptitudes and character. Precise recommendations were made on the teacher's training in the various techniques of assessment and tests.

It was difficult to reach definite conclusions on the types of examination which could be promoted at a European level. The participants took note of the interesting suggestions which were made during the meeting. As an example, let us quote M. Capelle's[10] suggestion which was later

---

[8] Prof. Aldo Agazzi: Ordinario di Pedagogia all' Universita Cattolica di Milano–Bergamo.

[9] Prof. A. Agazzi's study was published in Italian, and in English and French in 1968 in the C.C.C. series *Education in Europe*.

[10] M. Jean Capelle – Recteur, Université de Nancy.

stressed by the European Ministers of Education at their *ad hoc* Conference in Strasbourg (September 1967)[11]: the 'over-all review based on the synthetic evaluation of a long-term assessment'. The participants acknowledged the necessity of promoting numerous experiments and research before making any choice.

All the activities just reviewed belong to one section of the Committee for General and Technical Education's action in the field of examinations. They converge on the following theme: for what purpose and in what way are the pupils to be tested at the end of upper secondary school? But the eventual establishment of common systems of evaluation would not be sufficient to guarantee the comparability of pupils' results. The systems must, moreover, examine a core of knowledge unanimously considered essential by European educational authorities and, therefore, the investigation on examination syllabuses constitutes the second section of the C.C.C.'s over-all programme on examinations.

(2) *Curricula Analysis*—Long-term investigation has been conducted for and on behalf of the Council of Europe by experts from the Department of Education of Oxford University, in conjunction with subject experts from the participating member countries of the C.C.C. This is entitled 'The Oxford University/Council of Europe Study on Curricula, Scientific Evaluation of Results and Examination in Upper Secondary School'. For each subject under study it is hoped to draw a 'profile' of achievement for each country, showing the degree of competence required not only in the subject as a whole, but in each branch of it.

The method of this inquiry consists of:

(a) defining, in the light of comparison of national curricula, a common nucleus of knowledge on which examinations might be set; this shows the degree of 'overlap' existing between the syllabuses of the various countries;

(b) drawing up a list of common educational objectives for each subject;

(c) defining the type of European experimental examination and the subject matter to be set for samples of pupils chosen by the educational authorities of the participating countries;

(d) the administration of tests established according to criteria agreed upon by the participating countries.

In 1967 the subjects chosen were Latin, Mathematics, and Physics. The results of the Mathematics inquiry were published in 1968, and the Latin and Physics results will appear in 1969. The inquiry dealt with Modern Languages, Chemistry and Biology in 1968 and will cover Economics in 1969.

---

[11] The report was published in 1968.

Conclusion

The work which has been achieved so far by the Council for Cultural Co-operation of the Council of Europe has been fruitful because it has helped to give a realistic and comprehensive idea of the inadequacy characterizing the various national systems of examination when confronted with the evolution of educational needs. It has thrown the common problems into a vivid light and it has made it more obvious that the best solution can be contrived through well co-ordinated European co-operation. This is illustrated by Resolution No. 4 adopted by the European Ministers at their last *ad hoc* Conference (Strasbourg, September 1967). This Resolution endorses most of the recommendations made by the Belgian Minister, Mr. Toussaint, in his introductory report, the content of which takes into account the various suggestions made at the above-mentioned Brussels course. Hence the latter, which in a way summarizes the C.C.C.'s activities on examinations, can be considered as a platform for the new perspective defined by one of the Ministers' recommendations (see Resolution No. 4); 'to promote research and experiments with a view to gradually replacing traditional examinations by other forms of assessment.' In this new look the important part of co-ordinator is assigned to the Council of Europe which has been invited by the European Ministers 'to support all research on examinations undertaken in member countries of the C.C.C. and to arrange for such research to be disseminated and studied by organizing courses or study days,' and 'to assist national institutes which undertake extensive inquiries into the question of examinations.'

Thus, following these lines, the Council of Europe hopes, in the long run, to make of each national degree a European cultural passport.

44

Examinations: Trends and Prospects

Naim N. Atiyeh
Unesco Expert in Jordan

Examinations have had a long history of close association with school work. However, less than a half century ago, reference to them in educational literature was spotty and unsustained. Far from being surprising, this may perhaps reflect hidden belief in an inorganic view of education which once considered exams, however close to school work, as a separate activity falling outside education proper. There are indications, in fact, that while confrontations among various national school systems have encouraged ample borrowing between nations, and thus accelerated the pace towards greater convergence in curricular requirements and methods of instruction throughout the world, exams seem to have remained relatively untouched by such developments, and, until recently, to have continued to exist without close ties with educational theory. No wonder that at present, in spite of relatively greater homogeneity in educational views, there still exists a wide variety of examination practices in the world.

However, a new wave of reform which cuts across national boundaries now seems to have swept the field of exams. Hopefully, new practices will emerge, which will, to a greater degree, carry the stamp of views and experiences being shared internationally, and thus contribute to greater homogeneity in examinations.

The Case for Examinations

Naturally, a first question now arises which concerns the very case for examinations: will they survive? Traditional exams indeed, for nearly a century, have been the object of close scrutiny and controversy which tended to cast much doubt on their value as selection devices. The French Carnegie inquiry, the Hartog and Rhodes inquiry, researches by such famous educational psychologists as Burt, Thomson, Pieron and others, in spite of certain differences in their findings, have all aptly succeeded in disclosing the undependability of exams in their various forms, written, oral and practical. Factors denounced as sources of error included: variations in scoring standards among examiners, fluctuations in markings by the same examiner, fluctuations in levels of difficulty from year to year and inadequate sampling of subject matter and/or of the range of abilities and skills implied in educational objectives.

Others rested their case against exams on psychological grounds, and charged them with failure to produce a suitable climate for healthy personality development. They were the source of shattering strain and anxiety, it was thought.

A third source of grumbling came from administrators and teachers alike. The former voiced dissatisfaction with the machinery needed for the set-up of exams in an age of universal education; it was becoming too cumbersome, they thought. The latter complained that, with crowded classes, exams and scoring took too much time and thus interfered with teaching. Still worse, final exams were accused of cutting the school year too short.

In spite of all this, there is no indication, however, of a decline in the importance of exams in modern times. Quite the contrary, there is now what appears to be the beginning of an era when focus on examinations will be at a maximum.

Quantitatively, in many countries, a good student during a career of twelve years normally sits for approximately 16 formal examinations, each covering a variety of subjects. Administratively, new offices to advise on examination policy and technique are being established in various parts of the world: to name only a few – India, Pakistan, West African countries, and most Arab countries, especially Jordan, Iraq, Egypt, Syria and Morocco. Quite revealing in this respect is the creation by Unesco of the post of Expert in Tests and Measurements.

In many countries, East or West, new plans are being formulated and tried out for the reform of examinations. In England, there is the plan (now in operation) for a new Certificate of Secondary Education (C.S.E.); in India a plan for a new approach to school tests, undertaken by the National Council for Educational Research and Training in New Delhi – this without overlooking the continuing pioneering work of the Educational Testing Service at Princeton in the U.S.A.; the Unesco Institute for Education at Hamburg, Germany; the National Foundation for Educational Research in England and Wales; the various national institutes for orientation and research in France, and university research centres all over the world. Furthermore, to the best of my knowledge, in recent years no country is reported to have abolished or to be thinking of abolishing examinations, except, surprisingly, China who in ancient times had the most elaborate system of exams.

Thus it appears that as the demand for education in the world increases, there is a parallel increase not only in the volume of administrative machinery, but, more significantly, in the importance ascribed to exams.

The underlying motive may, in part, have stemmed from the new but rapidly growing idea that education is a rich soil for investment in capital and human resources. Control over school achievement for better planing thus becomes a necessity. Certainly increase in the dimensions of the need for equivalence of standards should not be underestimated. But perhaps one of the strongest motives now stems from educational theory itself and related research. In view of the rapid expansion of mass education, it is becoming all too clear that with regular classroom procedures, individualized instruction or anything close to it is quite impossible, let alone methods of active learning. Exams or methods of instruction with built-in evaluation such as may be found in programmed teaching become the only practical substitutes for individualized attention and concern with student activity. In an exam, or an exam-like situation, every student is given a chance (it is really an obligation) for full participation and active performance, thereby being compensated for his relative inactivity in a teaching regime based mostly on telling, or at best on demonstration techniques.

Thus the odds seem to be against abolition; the trend is rather towards greater emphasis on examinations. However in response to the recommendations of educational psychology and to the pressures created by heavy school enrolments, examinations everywhere seem to be undergoing a basic metamorphosis which mostly touches the question of their control and that of their nature. It is thus expected that in the next decades, we shall witness added activity towards the improvement of exams and the training of qualified examiners.

This will certainly reinforce appreciation for the professional character of the job of examiner, and thus probably increase the prospect for the creation of technical divisions to work in an advisory capacity either in an examination bureau or in a research centre, and for further expansion of autonomous institutes for research and orientation.

Control of Examinations

In the early period of European Renaissance, private initiative was still the rule in educational leadership. Examinations were then held within schools, with little or no interference from outside. There was even a tendency towards a tutorial system similar to that which was also found in the Arab world under Ottoman rule, when the weight of a diploma entirely depended on the weight of the tutor who signed it.

When learning began to appeal to the masses and thus had to seek financial support, internal autonomy of schools, as is well known, gradually gave way to a system of control exercised by subsidizing agencies, whether it be the state, the church or philanthropic groups. External examination was one such form of control.

The clearest expression of this type of exam may be best illustrated in the French *baccalauréat*. Underlying its policy there are three ideas: selectivity, equal opportunity and external central control. In fact, as the French educational system at first could cater only to the few, there was need for selection of the fittest, fitness then being associated in French thought with intellectual superiority. Quite naturally, it was soon realized that to be democratic and fair, selection should take effect with such impartiality that it would truly reflect the principle of equal opportunity. This was thought to require a public examination system with centralized control, which could ensure uniformity in conditions of examining. Differences in achievement would then, indeed, it was thought, mirror differences in talent and personal effort. The underlying motive, to be sure, was the bid for a democracy of merit, where the right to excel is open to all.

In most countries of Europe, if not in all, and in countries which fell under European influence in the nineteenth and twentieth centuries, some form or other of external exam took root, regardless of the type of exam adopted. But, in reaction, another trend gradually crept in, which reflected the ideas of so-called modern progressive education, and whose influence was at first limited to the elementary level.

One basic assumption underlying that trend was the charge against traditional external exams that they were the cause of artificial barriers between ends and means, between goals and practices. As a result, a new reaction set in, which advocated a more organic view of exams. In theory, at least, in a progressive school which uses student-centred activity methods, there should be no need for formal exams. Evaluation of success and failure is an integral part of the learning process, and reinforcement being the operational equivalent of external evaluation, is an integral part of the teaching process. Obviously, in such a system, the emphasis will be not on vicarious experience through hearing about or imagining, and much less on partial intellectual activity such as listening and memorizing, but on the entire range of actual changes in behaviour which should take place in students.

In systems which have followed this theory, particularly in the U.S.A., partly in the Soviet Union and East Europe, and in the experimental schools of West Europe, especially in England, France and Germany, there took root the idea of attendance, of participation, of credit units representing educational segments, of internal assessment of daily progress, and, finally, of the school record as a whole, as opposed to the traditional view that exams are the sanctioning by an external authority of standards attained.

Thus to the concept of excellence in attainment in view of an educated *élite* there was proposed the concept of reinforced behavioural change in all individuals for the benefit of society as a whole. Subsequently, the concept of democracy of merit was to give way to the more democratic concept of social justice, which apportions prizes not according to competitive merit, but according to merit in proportion to one's ability. This was certainly at the basis of decreasing emphasis on competition in exams in favour of greater emphasis on individual progress.

Evidently, activity theory with its implications for regular school attendance and accumulation of credits has in turn been accused of being too restrictive – even tyrannical, and especially, that it continually requires full participation and involvement, not allowing for the right to maintain one's privacy, or simply to hold one's own. Above all, because of its emphasis on behavioural performance, it was also accused of placing serious limitations on the scope of teaching. Subsequently, there soon was a strong case put up for a system of teaching which recognized the shortcomings of an exaggerated emphasis on overt action, and encouraged instead the exercise of higher mental processes. Other voices pleaded for enough freedom and flexibility not to alienate creative students who are often non-conforming and resentful of the drudgery of school routine, to accommodate the self-made student who had not been lucky enough to accumulate course credits, and certainly to sustain the interest of fast-learners who are ill at ease with the slow-motion of teaching methods based on performance and reinforcement. Besides, the idea of the school record itself was not without flaws. It has for instance encouraged, even in the face of new evidence to the contrary, the habit of denying a person with certain dark spots on his record, a true opportunity for redemption.

To restore balance, this has called for the creation of a non-credit system of teaching, relatively free from regular curricular and attendance requirements, which accepted the principle of promotion on the basis of examinations. Robert Hutchins, formerly Chancellor of the University of Chicago, was known to have supported a similar view.

It thus appears that one of the strongest dynamics in the development of modern exams is the need for a suitable compromise between external and internal control. On one hand the astonishing increase in student population has caused public external exams to be cumbersome, time-consuming, and certainly to continue to have a bad influence on teaching. On the other, demand for equivalence of standards, risks involved in relying on local school teachers (especially in developing countries), and need for relative freedom from curricular pressures, all tend to weaken the case for internal exams. Naturally, the likely prospect is to seek to combine the advantages of both kinds of control, internal and external.

Trends of Control in Elementary Schools

No public elementary school system is known to have admission requirements other than that of age. Hence no selective exams are used. Also, in private schools where admission may at times be selective, there is hardly any mention of examinations.

For promotion from class to class, two features seem to prevail. First, there is the tendency to depend on internal evaluation, with greater responsibility being placed in the hands of teachers themselves. Second, wherever formal exams are used, assignment of grades is based not on one final exam, but on all exams given during the year. Spain, Italy, Lebanon, Bulgaria, France, are among countries which fall in this category.

However, with growing aspiration to universal compulsory education, there is a greater tendency at the elementary level to drop exams altogether, and substitute for them automatic promotion. In emulation of other countries, a number of Arab states, Egypt, Syria, Jordan, are now experimenting with this system. But at first, automatic promotion was wrongly interpreted to mean the absence of all evaluation, which threatened to lead to an educational catastrophe. At present two criteria are stressed: cumulative achievement and attendance. There is also a tendency, mostly in Egypt, to group the elementary cycle into units of two grades each. While easy mobility within the unit is encouraged, transition to a new one is made, in theory, to depend on aptitude. In higher classes (4th, 5th, 6th), further control is exercised through internal exams, held on a semester basis, under the supervision of Regional Education Boards. The results are not to be used for fail/pass decisions, but simply to be entered on the school record for educational purposes and for future reference. Dismissal of students is not encouraged, though not forbidden. The tendency is to keep them in attendance throughout the elementary cycle, whereupon a school-leaving 'statement', signed by the local school inspector, may be delivered on request.

In more advanced countries, special provisions are made for weaker students who are not to be 'failed' in the usual meaning of the word, but to be placed for remedial work in special sections. In the Soviet Union, private lessons are given free of charge. In the United States and the United Kingdom, special grouping methods are applied.

Elementary School-leaving Exams

At the end of the elementary stage, the policy towards examinations seems largely to depend on the accessibility of admission to secondary education. In countries with restrictive admission, the holding of an elementary school certificate is a guarantee of social security. The granting of such certificates is usually based on a formal examination, either internal or external. Lebanon, France, Russia, Spain, Libya, Bulgaria, rural schools in the U.S.A., are among systems which fall in this category. Naturally, selection for secondary education is then made on the basis of a special examination with supplementary evidence from the school record.

In countries where school-leaving age is fifteen or more, two trends may be noted. In one group of countries, students are examined for orientation purposes. In some parts of England, for instance, which stands as the best illustration of this policy, students are still required to sit for the 11 + examination, which includes a test of intelligence, a test of proficiency in English, and a test of arithmetic. Results are used in combination with the cumulative school record. Then, upon consultation with parents and teachers, decisions are reached for selection and orientation into various educational streams.

In other countries, where elementary and lower secondary school ladders run into each other, there are no special criteria for admission to secondary classes. This is mostly the case in the U.S.A., except perhaps in some rural school systems. Also, of all Arab States, Jordan was the first to have abolished restrictions at the 11 + or 12 + level, and to raise school-leaving age to 15. Admission to post-elementary schools thus simply follows the rules of ordinary promotion.

Secondary School-leaving Exams

If we now turn to secondary school-leaving exams, here, again, practices in various parts of the world are far from being homogeneous. In fact, a variety of systems may be found, with different kinds of internal or external control.

At one extreme there is the system followed in the U.S.A. (except for the State of New York) where graduation from high school is entirely in the hands of internal school authorities and the faculty. Evaluation is based there on a cumulative school record which contains a summary of student achievements over the years. In addition to assessment of personality variables, entries cover daily assignments, classroom tests, individual projects such as research papers, laboratory work, field work and the like.

This arrangement, naturally, makes it possible to adapt teaching to the infinity of student needs and demands. However, secondary education is not merely a terminal course. It is also preparation for higher learning. Thus to overcome diversity in standards and ensure compliance with university requirements, there is, it is true, the tendency to the educational measure of introducing the system of required courses. However, universities go one step further whereby they impose their own standards. In fact, university admission is gradually becoming more conditional on success in entrance exams, which usually include a battery of standardized tests, such as those produced by the College Entrance Examination Board and other similar boards.

At the other extreme, there is the *baccalauréat* system as applied in

France and other countries which once were under French influence, where graduation almost entirely depends on success in a final examination held by the state. Papers are set and corrected centrally. For greater impartiality, examination booklets are kept anonymous, and in principle, though not in fact, are to receive double evaluation. For greater precaution, borderline students are decided on after examination of their school record and deliberation with the jury. In addition, a supplementary examination is held a few months later, just before the new academic year, for students who have been unlucky. It is of interest to note here that while the French seem to raise no question about the validity or the reliability of the results of successful students, they spare no argument, in the case of borderline students, to defend the right to a 'second chance', that is, to call for further evidence either through the school record, or by reference to make-up exams. Another characteristic of note in the *baccalauréat* exam is that it is organized under the supervision of the university. It thus opens the way directly to higher education.

Although in the U.S.A., there is a tendency to use externally standardized tests as a corrective of internal evaluation, and in France a tendency to consult school records as a corrective of external evaluation, the two systems do not yet seem to be going in the same direction. Other countries however seem to stand mid-way between the two, and to be heading for a suitable compromise.

In India, for instance, where an examination reform project is actively under way, there is no thought of undermining the traditional system. Their policy is rather to correct overemphasis on external exams. This they intend to do, not by weakening external control, but by strengthening internal assessment.

In Russia, East Germany and Bulgaria, among others, exams are subject to a joint control system. That is, formal final exams are conducted by local school staffs (who also set the standards) under the supervision of an Examination Commission for each school, which ensures the application of instructions laid down by the Central Authorities. This certainly allows amply for joint control. What is more, the final exam does not cover all subjects. In Russia, for instance, it covers mathematics, sciences, foreign languages, history of the Soviet Union, and Russian literature, and although exam questions in these subjects are prepared by the Ministry of Education, or by the Regional Institutes of Education, other subjects are evaluated entirely on the basis of the school record. This latter also serves a specially useful function in deciding on students who are borderline in the final exam.

In Sweden, the system adopted presents several points of interest. First, it seeks to ensure equivalence of standards by assigning to a central office the responsibility for setting questions. Second, to involve local interest and safeguard the right of a school to participate in evaluation, scoring is done locally by class teachers. Third, as a further guarantee for equivalence of standards, scoring is moderated through the central office; that is, a sample of schools are first selected and asked to score their papers according to preliminary instructions sent down from the central office. As soon as scoring is done, results are rushed over to the central office, for analysis and determination of standards to be used in final scoring. Once this is over, final instructions are sent down to all schools, who then can get started, and thus establish their own results.

In England, written external exams have been used for over a century. One example is the General Certificate Education (G.C.E.), organized in 1951 by the Secondary School Examinations Council, an independent body which consists of school and university teachers. There are, of course, other types of external examinations in England. Their creation was motivated by the need to maintain a reasonable equivalence of standards. However, public opinion, private and official, soon deplored their adverse effect on school work. That is, because of the prestige of external exams, school work was gradually compelled to limit itself to what was to be examined.

For this reason, and certainly to meet the needs of a growing student body with a wide range of ability, the Council recently adopted a new type of exam, the Certificate of Secondary Education (C.S.E.), which goes to great trouble to establish a new relationship between external control and freedom within the school. The motive is clearly to free teaching from the obsession of examination requirements, without jeopardizing the institution of control by an independent external body. A leading and perhaps promising idea in the new system is the proposal to get away from the pass/fail concept, and to think of exams as 'a source of information about some of the qualities of the candidates, which users must evaluate according to their own requirements.'[1]

General Characteristics

In the countries we have just surveyed, no commonly accepted system seems to emerge. However, there is a clear trend towards a balance between internal and external control of exams, with the accompanying trend towards a balance between formal exams and school records based on daily work. What is more, from a comparison of trends in elementary and secondary schools, we observe that probably within the stage considered as compulsory or terminal, there is decrease in emphasis on external exams. It thus seems that eventually, when the ideal of democratic universal education becomes a reality, exams within schools are likely to

---

[1] For a fuller discussion of G.C.E. and C.S.E., see pp. 110–19.

become the common practice. Formal external exams will have become indeed too cumbersome to be useful.

However, whether evaluation within schools will do away with formal examinations is still difficult to tell. In British Columbia, Iraq, Bulgaria, among others, and many school systems in the U.S.A., high achievers in regular school work are now recommended for exemption from formal exams. This may become a model for other countries. Another equally promising model is the British Certificate of Secondary Education (C.S.E.) which emphasizes the idea of an exam as being principally a source of information about students. In both cases, the cumulative school record stands as a central practice, though to a lesser degree in the British C.S.E.

From analysis of present practice in the U.S.A., England, and France, it appears also that the university will gradually come to play a greater role in the conduct of secondary education and in the setting of standards, mainly through college entrance exams, or even through actual participation in the control of final examinations. In countries with centralized systems, this is indeed a guarantee against school curricula growing stale and rigid; and in countries with greater margin for local school initiative, it is a guarantee against mediocrity and relaxation in standards.

But in general the interest of the university in school exams is certainly conditioned by its concern for better quality in its future clientele. Control exercised by the state or other external agencies may also be explained on the basis of concern for higher standards of education, but also, and perhaps above all, by concern with equivalance of standards for greater justice in the determination of merit for the prizes of life.

It is not difficult to realize here that, with respect to school exams, both the university and other external agencies are mostly concerned with placing the emphasis on the measurement of aptitude, while modern education is perhaps pressing for greater emphasis on achievement. Thus one may venture to state that to the extent that education, merely and simply, will become a right with no prospect for immediate privileges other than that of education itself, school-leaving exams will become mostly a school concern; but to the extent that aptitude for some new type of work or the right to a privilege are involved, there will be greater public pressure for control by an external agency.

Kinds of Examinations

Concern with the control of examinations, undoubtedly, is intimately linked with concern about their quality, that is, to what extent can we say that exams truly reflect desired educational outcomes, and how reliable are they in doing so? Certainly, the advocacy of either internal or external control, or even of a combination of both hides a subterranean quarrel over the validity and reliability of examination results.

For illustration, let us again choose the French *baccalauréat*. This typically traditional examination had been conceived as a device to measure, not the acquisition of knowledge, but certain qualities of the mind consonant with the ideal of humanistic education, such as independence of thought, method in reasoning, depth in outlook, and *une certaine finesse de l'esprit*. For instance, early in the nineteenth century, the *baccalauréat* exam consisted of an oral session of 40 to 45 minutes, which dwelt on the critical analysis of a new reading. As recently as March 10th, 1944, a French minister of education, on the eve of the *baccalauréat* exam, declared that: 'The *baccalauréat* certificate is not to be awarded in recognition of a candidate's mastery of all contents of a course, but of his ability, when confronted with a new problem which he had not covered directly at school, to demonstrate intelligence and a sense of method.' Thus in both cases, the French examiner is concerned with the ability to apply past learning in a new situation not reminiscent of classroom teaching, which logically calls for an outside authority, not directly involved in curricular requirements, to run and control the examination.

What is of greater relevance to us here, is that the examination is bound to be of the subjective type where the student is provided with ample opportunity for self-expression, whether oral or written. For this reason, essays or 'dissertations' became a typical practice in written exams, and oral reporting and discussing (*soutenance orale*) in verbal exams. Both forms are still characteristic of French examinations.

In most countries of Europe and in countries influenced by them, there is also a strong tradition of subjective examining. The form of the exam may, however, differ from one country to another. For instance, in England, India, Egypt, Jordan, Iraq and perhaps other countries which were under British rule, the trend is for written examinations. In Germany, East and West, in Russia, and East European republics, the emphasis is on orals. In the Soviet Union, for instance, apart from a written examination in literature, language and mathematics all subjects covered in the final examination are examined orally. In Lebanon, in Arab countries of North Africa, in Senegal, both written and oral exams are used, with certainly slightly greater emphasis on the written. It may be surprising here that oral exams have not fallen into disrepute. In fact, they are still widely used, not only in languages, but also in a variety of subjects.

A third form of subjective examination in common use is the practical exam, usually run as an individual project that may last for quite some time during the year, such as may be found in the *abitur* examination in East Germany; or as a series of problems covering basic skills, in line with what is now being done in the British C.S.E. The general trend now, though, is to leave the responsibility for practical exams within the school. But for countries with central control, this has created a problem of equivalence of degrees. That is, vocational school-leaving certificates are not recognized in status as equal to academic certificates. And there is no clear prospect as to the way in which this will be approached. So long as central control remains, it appears that the likely solution is for some kind of a basic skills examination to be set centrally, and used in combination with individual projects done at school, with varying weights for each.

To meet objections raised against traditional exams, there have been two trends, one seeking to improve traditional exams without essentially altering them, the other to introduce a new form known as objective examination.

In line with the first trend, new essay-type exams have been tried, such as short essays which it was thought could provide better sampling of subject matter, open-book exam, take-home exam etc. Exams based on short essays are becoming very popular in countries with external exams, where the impact of modern theory of examining has been felt.

As research continued to pile up evidence against the unreliability of essay exams even in their new form, with focus on their inadequate sampling of subject-matter, there was greater readiness, in many school systems in the world, to experiment with new type objective testing methods. Almost everywhere, however, these new methods are being treated with caution. Apart from the United States of America, their use in most countries, was, in the beginning, restricted to elementary experimental classes, to technical school exams, and to admission exams which focus on aptitude rather than achievement. In many places, the prospect of applying objective tests beyond elementary schools is still met with exclamatory surprise.

However, at almost all levels of education, and in countries with vast cultural or political differences, objective methods are now being used more widely and quite systematically, principally as a source of supplementary evidence. The U.S.A., Canada, Russia, East European countries, England, France are among those leading in this trend. But for certification purposes, their use is perhaps limited to the U.S.A. and Canada. There are signs, however, of a world-wide attempt to adopt them, at least in part, for official examinations. This is true of a number of African countries, of India, Pakistan, England in the C.S.E., and of a number of Arab countries, especially Jordan, Iraq and Syria. In these latter countries, and perhaps elsewhere too, the whole thing is approached with caution, however, or one may rightly say, with scientific spirit.

We should note, here, that caution towards the open use of objective methods was not without a rational basis. It was first rightly recognized that they yielded objective scores, and that they provided more adequate sampling of subject matter. But, also, it was soon realized that emphasis on objectivity could be carried too far. That is, to avoid bias in scoring, objective test items concentrated on factual knowledge over which there could be no disagreement. Consequently, coverage of subject matter was based, simply and merely, on a sampling of the content of textbooks, which tended to encourage pure memorization. Like essay exams, objective tests were, in turn, open to the charge of being unfit to measure the true ends of education.

The need was for a new outlook. Owing to the efforts of Ralph Tyler (and his co-workers), at the University of Chicago it was made clear that what provided the basis for examination validity was not textbook content, but the way in which that content was to be utilized in teaching. An examination thus ought to be validated against the philosophy of education.

A new trend thus gradually emerged, which led to extensive research on aims of education and their specific operational equivalents in teaching. To be sure, research then readily entered the field of testing with a new outlook: how to adapt objective methods to the evaluation of each and every behavioural outcome implied in the statement of educational objectives. Coverage in testing now came to mean two things: adequate sampling of subject matter, and more emphatically, adequate sampling of expected behaviours, whether mental, emotional or motor-sensory.

Consequently, this led to two emphases; one is that validity comes first as a characteristic of good testing, even though this may at times entail losses in reliability and objectivity; second, that validity should mean a match between exams and educational objectives, not between exams and the curriculum. A suitable label for this new approach may be: objectives-centred examinations. Naturally, this development calls for an open mind as it clearly appears that there is no royal road to educational evaluation. Methods and instruments should be varied and flexible, for they should suit the nature of the behaviours being examined and the purpose of the examination. Exams may thus, in turn, assume a variety of forms, written, oral, practical; closed objective type or essay type. The first guide in preferring one form to another or a certain combination of them is suitability for a given educational objective.

However, it was also strongly felt that gains in objectivity, reliability and economy already achieved through traditional objective exams, should not go to waste. New enthusiasm was generated henceforth for examinations which could reasonably combine validity, reliability, objectivity and economy. Testing research centres such as the Educational Testing Service in the U.S.A., and other centres mentioned earlier are now actively committed in this respect. Their concern is with the possibilities inherent in objective methods for the evaluation of educational objectives which go beyond memory, namely, reasoning and creativity. Of all objective test types, in this respect, the multiple-choice seems to be gaining more favour in the eyes of specialists, and to stand out as being especially suited for thought questions.

Assuming that multiple-choice questions will be made to suit certain types of higher mental behaviour, to what extent will they suit behaviours which involve synthesis, for example, the ability to produce a continuous writing, such as a literary essay or philosophical 'dissertation', or to plan a project or an experiment or an art design? In this respect, there are attempts to identify correlates of such creative abilities, which may be evaluated objectively. Language, for instance, is evaluated through vocabulary, correct usage, comprehension of texts and such other language arts as can be broken down into measurable bits. For measurement purposes, this substitution may quite possibly prove to be useful; but on educational grounds, it will not be received with favour. Educators will fear its bad influence on teaching, as schools might be tempted to overlook the original activity, and hang on to those skills which were substituted for it in the examination. The issue involved here is reminiscent of an earlier issue about the relative merit, in practical exams, of emphasis on basic skills correlated with success in a job, as opposed to emphasis on the realistic performance of the job itself. In all cases, the trend is for examinations which lead to the best type of teaching, that is, for examinations which contribute to the quality of what is to be examined. For that purpose, tasks to be included in an examination should closely match those required in teaching.

Whether or not multiple-choice tests will solve the problem is perhaps immaterial at this point. What matters is that, as a result of revival in testing reform, there is growing awareness of the existence of a wide range of skills, abilities and personality traits which call for evaluation; and that therefore there can be no one approach which, by itself, could meet the demands of modern evaluation. Consequently, a new idea is now gaining currency, which advocates that examinations can be best studied from within the context of education as a whole. The fortunate outcome is that, in many parts of the world, concern with better examinations has stimulated new interest in philosophy of education. More than anything else, the deepening of philosophical thinking with reference to the role of exams in education has brought into clearer focus the complex nature of educational objectives with all their interrelationships.

As a result, what now faces education is a multiple challenge. First, how to ensure that examinations will encourage the best type of teaching? Second, how to achieve economy, reliability and objectivity without damage to the organic unity of learning? Third, how to find types of questions which would not only reflect stated educational objectives, but also provoke in teachers a critical attitude towards their own methods and open up new horizons before them?

Conclusions

For all practical purposes, we may assume that as a result of this challenge, significant efforts in the field of education will perhaps be directed along the following lines:

Firstly, pressure will be exerted for greater co-ordination between examination practices and educational theory. In many countries, examinations are still conceived as a relatively independent activity and have a theory of their own which reflects only partially the complete picture of education. In some instances, it was examination practices that conditioned the entire system of teaching. The tide now is towards subordinating examinations to educational objectives and integrating them, like any other educational practice, to the context of education as a whole.

Secondly, to ensure that the impact of examinations on teaching will be wholesome, much concern will be shown towards the reformulation of the relationship between external examining bodies and local school authorities and teachers, and the re-definition of their respective roles in the conduct of evaluation programmes.

Thirdly, regardless of what kind of control is to be applied over exams, great concern will be shown for a deeper understanding of the technical nature of examinations and of the role which they ought to play in education. This development being unthinkable without a reform in methods and programmes of teacher training, teaching colleges will have to integrate into special methods courses an important segment on evaluation, with emphasis on applied training in test construction and scoring of exam papers. In-service training also will have to include special intensive sessions for the training of teachers in special methods of examining.

Fourthly, an inevitable corollary will be more extensive research into the improvement of oral and practical examinations. Basic-skills type examinations will receive special attention, as opposed to real productive and situational tests which could provide quite a satisfactory answer to educational needs, if it were not for their complicated and difficult application in mass teaching.

Fifthly, non-cognitive aspects of learning, such as character, emotional development, social maturity, etc., will also receive greater attention than ever before. But there is no indication as to whether they are to become subject to grading and thus to be included with cognitive achievement for pass/fail decisions.

Sixthly, finally, and perhaps most importantly, developing countries will gradually come to realize how important it is for the system of public education to place itself under the supervision of universities and centres of higher learning. In spite of trends pressing for a secondary school based on general unspecialized education, there will be greater pressure in the coming decades to involve university faculties in the supervision of standards and curricula, most particularly through examinations.

BIBLIOGRAPHY

'A Brief Report of the Sixth All-India Conference of Boards of Secondary Education', in *Journal of Teacher Education*, Vol. IX, No. 3, January, 1963 (Directorate of Extension Programmes for Secondary Education, 7, Lancers Road, Timarpur, Delhi-6, India).

N. Aspanasewicz and S. Rosen, *Final Examinations in the Russian Ten-Year School*. Washington, D.C. United States Government Printing Office, 1966.

Naim N. Atiyeh, 'Educational Evaluation', in *Educational Evaluation and Planning in the Arab World*, edited by the Department of Education at the American University, Beirut, Lebanon, 1962 (in Arabic).

B. Bloom, *et al*. *Taxonomy of Educational Objectives* (New York: Longmans Green & Co., 1956).

J. Lloyd Brereton, *Exams! Where Next?* Pacific Northwest Humanist Publications, 305 Windermere Place, Victoria, B.C., Canada.

R. L. Ebel, *Measuring Educational Achievement* (Engelwood Cliffs, New Jersey: Prentice Hall Inc., 1965).

F. S. Freeman, *Psychological Testing*, 3rd ed. (New York: Holt, Rinehart and Winston, 1962).

Will French, *et al. Behavioral Goals of General Education in High School*. (New York: Russell Sage Foundation, 1958).

M. Kh. Harby, 'Examinations in Elementary Cycle', in *Sixth Arab Cultural Conference* (Arab League, Cairo, 1964 (in Arabic)).

Zaynab M. Muhriz, 'Examination Systems in the Arab World' in *Sixth Arab Cultural Conference*.

H. Pieron, *Examens et Docimologie*, Paris: Presses Universtaires de France, 1963.

The Certificate of Secondary Education, Examinations Bulletin No. 1 (London: H.M.S.O., 1963).

J. B. Piobetta, *Examens et Concours*. Paris: P.U.F., 1943.

R. W. Tyler, *Basic Principles of Curriculum and Instruction* (Chicago: University of Chicago Press, 1950).

R. W. Tyler, 'Evaluative Aspects of Learning', in: *The Learning Process*, edited by T. Harris and W. Schwahn (New York, 1961).

University Entrance and School Examinations Council, Annual Report (1965–66, London: University of London).

P. Vernon, *An Introduction to Objective-type Examinations*, Secondary School Examinations Council, Bulletin No. 4 (London: H.M.S.O., 1964).

P. Vernon, *Intelligence and Attainment Tests* (London: University of London Press, 1960).

W. D. Wall, 'The Organization of Educational Research in the U.S.S.R.': in M. Young, *Innovation and Research in Education*, London: Routledge, 1965.

S. Wiseman, *Examinations and English Education* (University of Manchester Press, 1961).

List of Contributors

List of Tables, Figures and Charts

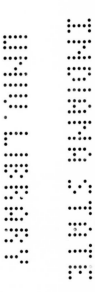

Index